OXFORD ENGLISH MONOGRAPHS

General Editors
SANTANU DAS   PAULINA KEWES
MATTHEW REYNOLDS
FIONA STAFFORD   MARION TURNER

English Humanism and the Reception of Virgil *c.* 1400–1550

MATTHEW DAY

OXFORD
UNIVERSITY PRESS

OXFORD
UNIVERSITY PRESS

Great Clarendon Street, Oxford, OX2 6DP,
United Kingdom

Oxford University Press is a department of the University of Oxford.
It furthers the University's objective of excellence in research, scholarship,
and education by publishing worldwide. Oxford is a registered trade mark of
Oxford University Press in the UK and in certain other countries

© Matthew Day 2023

The moral rights of the author have been asserted

First Edition published in 2023

Impression: 1

All rights reserved. No part of this publication may be reproduced, stored in
a retrieval system, or transmitted, in any form or by any means, without the
prior permission in writing of Oxford University Press, or as expressly permitted
by law, by licence or under terms agreed with the appropriate reprographics
rights organization. Enquiries concerning reproduction outside the scope of the
above should be sent to the Rights Department, Oxford University Press, at the
address above

You must not circulate this work in any other form
and you must impose this same condition on any acquirer

Published in the United States of America by Oxford University Press
198 Madison Avenue, New York, NY 10016, United States of America

British Library Cataloguing in Publication Data

Data available

Library of Congress Control Number: 2022947303

ISBN 978-0-19-287113-8

DOI: 10.1093/oso/9780192871138.001.0001

Printed and bound in the UK by
TJ Books Limited

Links to third party websites are provided by Oxford in good faith and
for information only. Oxford disclaims any responsibility for the materials
contained in any third party website referenced in this work.

Acknowledgements

This book originated as a doctoral thesis, submitted at the University of Oxford in 2019. I was fortunate to be supervised by Daniel Wakelin and Kantik Ghosh. I owe them tremendous gratitude for their mentoring and guidance over the course of the project. I could not have asked for better supervisors. In addition, my work greatly benefitted from the discerning feedback of my two examiners, Vincent Gillespie and Rita Copeland. Their advice was extremely valuable when I was reworking the thesis as a book. Special thanks must also go to the two anonymous readers at Oxford University Press, whose insightful and constructive comments on the initial draft of the book helped me to make substantial improvements for the final version.

Many other individuals have contributed significantly to my research. In particular, I would like to thank: Mishtooni Bose and Jane Griffiths, for their perceptive comments on earlier drafts of chapters of my thesis; David Rundle, for his advice on early English humanist manuscripts; and Sally Mapstone, for fostering my interest in Older Scots poetry during my Master's degree. I am also greatly indebted to the editorial staff at Oxford University Press for their brilliant work in overseeing the various stages of this book's production.

I would not have been able to undertake this project without financial support from a number of institutions. My doctoral research was generously funded by an Oxford-Clayton Graduate Scholarship at Merton College, Oxford. A Jeremy Griffiths Memorial Studentship at St Hilda's College, Oxford enabled me to study for a Master's degree in medieval English literature, helping me to develop my enthusiasm for book history. I am also extremely grateful for research grants from the Huntington Library and Princeton University Library, which gave me the opportunity to carry out research at these libraries in summer 2018. Finally, it is a pleasure to thank my friends and family for their unwavering help and encouragement throughout the project.

Contents

Conventions   ix
Abbreviations   xi

   Introduction   1

1. Manuscripts   14
2. Printed Editions   45
3. Wynkyn de Worde and the *Bucolics*   70
4. Caxton's *Eneydos*   100
5. Douglas's *Eneados*   135
6. Surrey's *Aeneid*   167

   Conclusion   191

Appendix A: List of Manuscripts   195
Appendix B: List of Printed Copies   197
Bibliography   201
Index   219

Conventions

Quotations of Virgil
In Chapters 1–3, quotations of Virgil's Latin are from the fifteenth- and sixteenth-century manuscripts or printed copies under discussion. In Chapter 5, quotations of Virgil's Latin are from Ascensius's 1500–1 edition of Virgil's *Opera* (cited in Abbreviations list). This was the main edition used by Gavin Douglas.

In Chapters 4 and 6, quotations of Virgil's Latin are from the modern Latin-English edition edited by H.R. Fairclough (cited in Abbreviations list). It is not known which texts of Virgil were used for Caxton's and Surrey's translations.

For ease of reference, quotations from fifteenth- and sixteenth-century sources also have line numbers from Fairclough's modern edition.

Quotations of Servius
Unless otherwise stated, quotations of Servius's commentary are from *Servii grammatici qui feruntur in Vergilii carmina commentarii*, ed. G. Thilo and H. Hagen, 3 vols (Lepizig: Teubner, 1878–1902).

Chapters 1–3 and 5 refer to early manuscripts and editions containing Servius's commentary. In these case studies, I quote Servius from the primary sources under discussion.

Transcriptions
Transcriptions from fifteenth- and sixteenth-century manuscripts and printed editions retain original spelling and punctuation. I expand abbreviations in italics, and text added by me to clarify the sense of a quotation is written in square brackets ([]).

I use strokes for virgules (/), and a vertical line to signal line breaks in verse (|). I transcribe *punctus elevati* as a full stop and single inverted comma (.').

Translations
Unless otherwise stated, translations of Virgil are from the modern Latin-English edition edited and translated by H.R. Fairclough (mentioned above).

I give my own translations when my argument requires a more literal rendering of the Latin.

Unless otherwise stated, translations of all other texts are my own.

Citations of Early Printed Editions

Fifteenth-century editions are identified by citation numbers from the *Incunabula Short Title Catalogue* (*ISTC*). For books printed in England, I also include citation numbers from *A Short-Title Catalogue of Books Printed in England, Scotland, & Ireland and of English Books Printed Abroad 1473–1640* (*STC*).

If a volume has neither an *ISTC* nor *STC* citation (i.e. if it was printed outside England and Scotland after 1501), I provide a citation from the *Universal Short Title Catalogue* (*USTC*).

Citations of Specific Printed Copies

Appendix B is a list of specific copies of fifteenth- and sixteenth-century Virgil editions. Each of these copies has English provenance before 1550, and their owners and annotations are discussed in Chapters 2 and 3.

For ease of reference, I have assigned a reference code to each copy in Appendix B. These codes are given in bold, for example '**O.1492.2**'. The code refers to the content of the edition (O=*Opera*, B=*Bucolica*, G=*Georgica*, Op=*Opuscula*, i.e. *Appendix Virgiliana*), and the year of publication (in this case, 1492). The last number distinguishes between different copies from the same year.

Abbreviations

BL	London, British Library
BodL	Oxford, Bodleian Library
BRUC	A.B. Emden, *A Biographical Register of the University of Cambridge to A.D. 1500*, 2 vols (Cambridge: CUP, 1963)
BRUO	A.B. Emden, *A Biographical Register of the University of Oxford to A.D. 1500*, 3 vols (Oxford: Clarendon Press, 1957–9)
BRUO: 1501–1540	A.B. Emden, *A Biographical Register of the University of Oxford, A.D. 1500-1540* (Oxford: Clarendon Press, 1974)
CCC	Oxford, Corpus Christi College Library
Coates	Alan Coates, *A Catalogue of Books Printed in the Fifteenth Century Now in the Bodleian Library*, 6 vols (Oxford: OUP, 2005)
CHBB:III	*The Cambridge History of the Book in Britain: Volume III, 1400–1557*, ed. Lotte Hellinga and J.B. Trapp (Cambridge: CUP, 1998)
CUL	Cambridge, University Library
CUP	Cambridge University Press
DMLBS	*Dictionary of Medieval Latin from British Sources*, ed. R.E. Latham, D.R. Howlett, and R.K. Ashdowne, 3 vols (Oxford: OUP, 2018)
DOST	*A Dictionary of the Older Scottish Tongue from the Twelfth Century to the End of the Seventeenth*, ed. W.A. Craigie, A.J. Aiken, J.A.C. Stevenson and M.G. Dareau, 12 vols (Chicago: University of Chicago Press; London: Humphrey Milford; Oxford: OUP, 1937–2002), online at <https://dsl.ac.uk> (Accessed 9 Feb. 2019)
Fairclough	*Virgil*, ed. and trans. H.R. Fairclough, rev. G.P. Goold, 2 vols (London; Cambridge, MA: Harvard University Press, 1999, repr. 2006)
HEHL	San Marino, CA, Henry E. Huntington Library
ISTC	British Library and Consortium of European Research Libraries, *Incunabula Short Title Catalogue* (London: British Library and Consortium of European Research Libraries, 2016), online at <https://data.cerl.org/istc/> (Accessed 9 Feb. 2019)

JRL	Manchester, John Rylands Library
LPL	London, Lambeth Palace Library
MLGB3	*Medieval Libraries of Great Britain*, ed. Richard Sharpe and James Willoughby (Oxford: Bodleian Libraries, 2015), accessed online at <http://mlgb3.bodleian.ox.ac.uk> (Accessed 29 June 2019)
NLS	Edinburgh, National Library of Scotland
OED	*The Oxford English Dictionary*, ed. John Simpson et al. (Oxford: OUP, 2019), online at <http://www.oed.com/> (Accessed 1 Feb. 2019)
OHCREL: I	*The Oxford History of Classical Reception in English Literature: Volume I: 800-1558*, ed. Rita Copeland (Oxford: OUP, 2016)
Opera (1500–1)	*Opera* [*Bucolica* and *Georgica* (comm. Servius, Beroaldus, and Ascensius), *Aeneis* (comm. Servius, Donatus, Beroaldus, Ascensius), *Supplementum* (comm. Ascensius), *Opuscula* (comm. Calderinus, Ascensius)], ed. Badius Ascensius, 3 vols (Paris: Thielman Kerver, for Jean Petit and Johannes de Coblenz, 1500–1; *ISTC* iv00196000)
OUP	Oxford University Press
PUL	Princeton, NJ, Princeton University Library
SJC	Cambridge, St John's College Library
STC	Alfred W. Pollard and G.R. Redgrave, *A Short-Title Catalogue of Books Printed in England, Scotland, & Ireland and of English Books Printed Abroad 1473–1640*, 2nd edn, rev. William A. Jackson, F. S. Ferguson and Katharine F. Pantzer, 3 vols (London: Bibliographical Society, 1976–91)
TCC	Cambridge, Trinity College Library
USTC	*Universal Short Title Catalogue*, ed. Andrew Pettegree and Graeme Kemp (St Andrews: University of St Andrews, 2017), online at <https://www.ustc.ac.uk> (Accessed 4 Feb. 2019)

Introduction

The aim of this study is to assess the impact of Renaissance humanism on Virgil's reception in fifteenth and early sixteenth century England. The years 1400–1550, straddling the end of the English Middle Ages and the beginning of the Renaissance, were a formative stage in the reading and translation of classical authors. From the early 1400s onwards, humanist ideas began to diffuse from continental Europe to England. In the latter half of the century, the circulation of classical and humanist texts was abetted by the invention of the printing press.[1] Although Virgil had been read throughout the Middle Ages, the spread of humanism further consolidated his preeminent canonical status among Latin poets. By the mid-sixteenth century, his works had become a pervasive feature of school curricula, admired both for their eloquence in the Latin language and their moral value to readers. Fifteenth- and sixteenth-century English reading of Virgil, both in and out of the schoolroom, is attested in the considerable numbers of surviving manuscripts and early printed editions of his poetry. The years 1400–1550 also saw the earliest extant English translations of Virgil's *Aeneid*, by William Caxton (1490), Gavin Douglas (1513), and the Earl of Surrey (c. 1543). These translations have long been implicated in debates about the early impact of humanism on English literature, and are often presented as exemplars of the differences between 'medieval' and 'humanist' translation practice.

Despite this wealth of material, Virgil's reception in the fifteenth and early sixteenth centuries has not received synoptic study. As is common among reception studies of classical authors, research on Virgil tends to focus either

---

[1] For a survey of early humanism in England, see Roberto Weiss, *Humanism in England During the Fifteenth Century*, 3rd edn (1941; Oxford: Blackwell, 1967), consulted in 4th edn, ed. David Rundle and Anthony John Lappin (Oxford, 2010), accessible online at <https://aevum.space/OS4>. For recent revision of Weiss, see David Rundle, 'Of Republics and Tyrants: aspects of quattrocento humanist writings and their reception in England, c. 1400–c. 1460' (unpublished DPhil thesis, University of Oxford, 1997); David Rundle, *The Renaissance Reform of the Book and Britain: The English Quattrocento* (Cambridge: CUP, 2019); Daniel Wakelin, *Humanism, Reading, and English Literature, 1430–1530* (Oxford: OUP, 2007); Daniel Wakelin, 'Early Humanism in England', in *OHCREL: I*, pp. 487–513.

on 'Virgil in the Middle Ages' or 'Virgil in the Renaissance' rather than the changes and continuities between these two periods.[2] In Virgil's English reception, this lacuna is reflected in the lack of writing on the fifteenth century. Christopher Baswell's masterful *Virgil in Medieval England* (1995), despite looking ahead to the 1400s and 1500s, focuses primarily on the twelfth to fourteenth centuries up to the age of Chaucer.[3] Studies of Virgil in the Renaissance, for example by David Scott Wilson-Okamura, Margaret Tudeau-Clayton and Andrew Wallace, tend to discuss England primarily for the literary efflorescence in the Elizabethan and Jacobean eras.[4] Complementing these previous works, the present monograph aims to fill the 150-year gap in the history of reading and translating Virgil in England. It runs from the earliest influence of humanism in the early 1400s through to the Earl of Surrey's *Aeneid* translation in the 1540s, often regarded as a pinnacle of English humanist translation. First, through a study of Virgilian exegesis, then a study of early Virgil translations, it links accounts of Virgil's medieval and Renaissance reception.

While the modern separation of medieval and Renaissance studies has often led scholars to focus on one period or the other, the reception of Virgil across the Middle Ages and Renaissance is characterized more by continuity than by change. Across humanities disciplines, recent critiques of this traditional periodization have sought to destabilize steady distinctions

---

[2] While recent studies of Virgil in the Middle Ages and Renaissance will be discussed below, the two foundational examples are: Domenico Comparetti, *Vergil in the Middle Ages*, trans. E.F.M. Benecke, with introduction by Jan M. Ziolkowski (Princeton: Princeton University Press, 1997); Vladimiro Zabughin, *Vergilio nel Rinascimento Italiano da Dante a Torquato Tasso*, 2 vols (Bologna: N. Zanichelli, 1921–1923). The exceptions to this periodization are surveys of Virgil's reception over 500 years or more, e.g. Craig Kallendorf, *The Protean Virgil: Material Form and the Reception of the Classics* (Oxford: OUP, 2015); Jan M. Ziolkowski, 'Virgil', in *OHCREL:I*, pp. 165–85; *The Virgilian Tradition: the First Fifteen Hundred Years*, ed. Jan M. Ziolkowski and Michael C.J. Putnam (New Haven: Yale University Press, 2008).

[3] Christopher Baswell, *Virgil in Medieval England: Figuring the Aeneid from the Twelfth Century to Chaucer* (Cambridge: CUP, 1995). Also concluding in the late fourteenth century, see *Lectures Médiévales de Virgile: Actes du Colloque Organisé par l'École Française de Rome: Rome, 25–8 Octobre 1982*, ed. Jean-Yves Tilliette (Rome: École de Française de Rome, 1985).

[4] David Scott Wilson-Okamura, *Virgil in the Renaissance* (Cambridge: CUP, 2010); Margaret Tudeau-Clayton, *Jonson, Shakespeare and the Early-Modern Virgil* (Cambridge: CUP, 1998); Andrew Wallace, *Virgil's Schoolboys: The Poetics of Pedagogy in Renaissance England* (Oxford: OUP, 2010). Wilson-Okamura briefly mentions Douglas (pp. 176–7, 239), while Surrey does not appear at all; Wallace discusses Surrey on pp. 182–5. Likewise, 'Virgil in the Renaissance' essay-collections have no discussion of England before the Elizabethans, for example: *The Early Renaissance: Virgil and the Classical Tradition*, ed. A.L. Pellegrini (Binghamton: State University of New York at Binghamton, The Center for Medieval and Early Renaissance Studies, 1984); *Virgil and Renaissance Culture*, ed. L.B.T. Houghton and Marco Sgarbi (Turnhout: Brepols, 2018).

between medieval and Renaissance culture.[5] Building on this work, the present study of Virgil's reception will emphasize the consistency between humanist approaches and preceding traditions of classical study. Even as humanist scholars developed new branches of lexicographic and textual scholarship, the humanist study of classical literature, and certainly of Virgil, continued to draw many of its aims, methods and conventions from late antique and medieval learning. Both the exegesis and translation of Virgil were shaped by the medieval inheritance, and developments were often gradual and piecemeal. Rather than treating Virgil's medieval and Renaissance reception separately, the present study will argue that a more holistic periodization better represents the intellectual continuities of the two periods, the very gradual pace of humanist development and the continuous influence of medieval learning on the *studia humanitatis*.

Studies of the Renaissance have long emphasized that humanism was part of broader trends in western culture. Paul Oskar Kristeller, in his foundational definition, presented humanism as a constellation of interests in grammar, rhetoric, poetry, history and moral philosophy, based in the study of classical Latin and Greek authors and named the *studia humanitatis*. While this new name implied a 'new claim and new program' of learning, humanist studies 'covered a content that had existed long before and that had been designated by the more modest names of grammar, rhetoric, and poetry'.[6] In classical antiquity, the discipline of grammar taught mastery of the Latin language, while rhetoric taught the arts of oratorical composition. Poets such as Virgil were taught within grammar, honing students' language skills before they proceeded to rhetorical training. The classical inheritance of grammar and rhetoric underpinned the teaching in medieval schools as well as the *trivium* at medieval universities. While

---

[5] In the field of English literary history, see for example the following essay collections: *Cultural Reformations: Medieval and Renaissance in Literary History*, ed. James Simpson and Brian Cummings (Oxford: OUP, 2010); *Medieval/Renaissance: After Periodization*, ed. Jennifer Summit and David Wallace, Special Issue, *Journal of Medieval and Early Modern Studies* 37 (2007); *Medieval Into Renaissance: Essays for Helen Cooper*, ed. Andrew King and Matthew Woodcock (Rochester: D.S. Brewer, 2016). For an informed assertion of the medieval/Renaissance periodization, see James Simpson, *Reform and Cultural Revolution: The Oxford English Literary History: Volume 2: 1350–1547* (Oxford: OUP, 2002).

[6] For Kristeller's foundational definition of humanism, see Paul Oskar Kristeller, 'Humanism and Scholasticism in the Italian Renaissance', in *Renaissance Thought and Its Sources*, ed. Michael Mooney (New York: Columbia University Press, 1979), pp. 85–105 (quotation at p. 98). On Kristeller's definition, see also John Monfasani, 'Toward the Genesis of the Kristeller thesis of Renaissance humanism: Four Bibliographical Notes', *Renaissance Quarterly* 53 (2000), 1156–73.

medieval pedagogy did not concentrate exclusively on classical texts, the methods of learning evolved from classical principles.[7] In the Kristellerian view, the humanist movement developed in Italy when medieval traditions of grammatical and particularly rhetorical study intersected with renewed interests in classical literature.[8] Crucially, humanists reasserted the foundational importance of classical Latin authors as models of the Latin language. Emphasizing that eloquence was to be achieved through the imitation of classical literature, humanism reoriented the study of grammar and rhetoric towards classical Latin philology and style.[9] This revival of ancient literature and language was seen as part of a broader moral and cultural revival of Italian civilization.[10]

These broader historical contexts of humanism underlie the major recent studies on its Italian origins and diffusion across Europe. Ronald Witt, in his wide-reaching analyses of thirteenth- and fourteenth-century Italian intellectual culture, has vastly extended and refined current understanding on the evolution of humanism, particularly the development of classical ideals of style in late medieval Italy and the influence of the rhetorical tradition of the *ars dictaminis*.[11] In the field of education, meanwhile, Robert Black has emphasized the continuities between medieval and humanist pedagogy, presenting humanist grammatical and rhetorical education as an evolution of longstanding traditions of classroom study.[12] As humanist ideas diffused

---

[7] For Kristeller's surveys of rhetoric from Antiquity to the Renaissance, see 'Part Five: Philosophy and Rhetoric from Antiquity to the Renaissance', in *Renaissance Thought and Its Sources*, ed. Mooney, pp. 211–59; 'Rhetoric in Medieval and Renaissance Culture', in his *Renaissance Thought and the Arts: Collected Essays* (Princeton: Princeton University Press, 1981), pp. 228–46. For a more recent survey of the development of grammar and rhetoric in this timeframe, see *Medieval Grammar and Rhetoric: Language Arts and Literary Theory, AD 300-1475*, ed. Rita Copeland and Ineke Sluiter (Oxford: OUP, 2010).

[8] Kristeller, 'The Humanist Movement', in *Renaissance Thought and Its Sources*, ed. Mooney, pp. 21–32 (pp. 23–4); Kristeller, 'Humanism and Scholasticism in the Italian Renaissance', pp. 91–8.

[9] On the humanist introduction of classicist tastes, see esp. Kristeller, 'Humanism and Scholasticism in the Italian Renaissance', pp. 91–8.

[10] On the wider cultural and ethical aims of humanism, see recently James Hankins, *Virtue Politics: Soulcraft and Statecraft in Renaissance Italy* (Cambridge, MA: Harvard University Press, 2019), Ch. 1. For humanists' conceptions of the aims of their movement, see Patrick Baker, *Italian Renaissance Humanism in the Mirror* (Cambridge: CUP, 2015).

[11] Ronald G. Witt, *'In the Footsteps of the Ancients': The Origins of Humanism from Lovato to Bruni* (Leiden: Brill, 2000); Ronald G. Witt, *The Two Latin Cultures and the Foundation of Renaissance Humanism in Medieval Italy* (Cambridge: CUP, 2012).

[12] Robert Black, *Humanism and Education in Medieval and Renaissance Italy: Tradition and Innovation in Latin Schools from the Twelfth to the Fifteenth Century* (Cambridge: CUP, 2001). For earlier arguments on the gradual evolution from medieval to humanist education, see for example W. Keith Percival, 'Renaissance Grammar', in *Renaissance Humanism: Foundations, Forms, and Legacy*, ed. Albert Rabil, 3 vols (Philadelphia: University of Pennsylvania Press, 1988), III, pp. 67–84.

across Italy and later Europe, their impact was often gradual, piecemeal, and subject to regional variations.[13] Recent research on fifteenth-century English humanism, particularly by David Rundle and Daniel Wakelin, has emphasized the syncretistic interactions between humanist influences and medieval English political, intellectual and literary traditions.[14] Just as humanism evolved from the specific intellectual conditions of late medieval Italy, its impact across Europe was marked by diverse interchange with pre-existing cultural trends in the various geographical regions.

While previous studies of Virgilian reception have tended to focus either on the Middle Ages or the Renaissance, they have provided valuable insights into the continuities between the two periods. Baswell's *Virgil in Medieval England* focuses on the twelfth to fourteenth centuries, but also glances forward to Virgil's reception after 1400. Through meticulous study of the ownership and use of medieval Virgil manuscripts, Baswell delineates three dominant approaches to reading the *Aeneid* in the Middle Ages: the pedagogic approach, deriving from the schoolroom; the allegorical approach, interpreting the text as a source of moral wisdom; and the romance approach, in which vernacular writers adapted Virgil's epic into romances such as the twelfth-century *Roman d'Eneas*.[15] As Baswell explains, the most common and long-lasting approach was the pedagogic. In the majority of extant Virgil manuscripts, readers' glossing is structured by the pedagogic disciplines of grammar and rhetoric. Through a brief comparison with the glosses of early Italian humanists, Baswell notes that the medieval traditions of pedagogic exegesis were not abandoned in the Renaissance, but remained the 'basis' for Virgilian study even as humanist scholars pioneered new approaches.[16] Having introduced the pedagogic, allegorical and romance approaches, Baswell shows how these three strands of Virgilian reception shaped Chaucer's use of Virgil in *The Legend of Good Women* and *House of Fame*. Baswell's epilogue, titled 'Envoi – to the Renaissance', then indicates how medieval approaches to Virgil went on to influence late fifteenth- and sixteenth-century English vernacular literature, including the Virgilian translators Caxton, Douglas and Surrey as well as the poet Edmund Spenser. In

---

[13] For a survey of regional variations, see essays in *Humanism in Fifteenth-Century Europe*, ed. David Rundle (Oxford: Society for the Study of Medieval Languages and Literature, 2012).
[14] For instance, see Rundle, *The Renaissance Reform of the Book and Britain*, esp. Ch. 2; Daniel Wakelin, 'England: Humanism Beyond Weiss', in *Humanism in Fifteenth-Century Europe*, ed. Rundle, pp. 265–306; Daniel Wakelin, 'Early Humanism in England', in *OHCREL: I*, pp. 487–513.
[15] Baswell, *Virgil in Medieval England*, pp. 9–14, which sets out the structure of the book.
[16] Baswell, *Virgil in Medieval England*, pp. 41, 80–3.

closing, Baswell gestures towards the 'continuities in English Virgilianism' between the Middle Ages and Renaissance.[17]

Just as Baswell's *Virgil in Medieval England* alludes to the rich legacy of medieval traditions, so too do recent histories of Virgil's Renaissance reception. David Scott Wilson-Okamura, in his 'panoramic' European survey of *Virgil in the Renaissance* (2010), frames the period as a combination of both continuity and novelty. Just as Baswell emphasizes the pervading influence of classical commentaries on the twelfth- to fourteenth-century reception of Virgil, Wilson-Okamura notes the continuity 'of classical, medieval and Renaissance scholarship'.[18] In interpretations of particular episodes and characters in Virgil's poetry, he discusses the enduring influence of classical and medieval commentaries, for example the influence of the twelfth-century allegorical commentary of Bernard Silvestris on subsequent fifteenth- and sixteenth-century allegories of the *Aeneid*.[19] Juxtaposed with these areas of consistency, he charts new advances in, for example, Virgilian textual criticism by humanist scholars Piero Valeriano and Angelo Poliziano.[20] Through analysing these diverse strands of Renaissance Virgilianism, Wilson-Okamura assembles a mosaic of continuities and new developments.

Alongside Baswell's analysis of medieval Virgil manuscripts, the most thorough bibliographic research on Virgil's Renaissance reception is the monumental contributions of Craig Kallendorf. Kallendorf's work in cataloguing Virgilian printed editions and manuscripts has dramatically enhanced modern understanding of the extant bibliographic evidence.[21] His recent *Printing Virgil* provides a comprehensive account of how printing shaped Virgil's reception, with particular emphasis on commentaries and translations. Just as Baswell's work has examined glosses in Virgil manuscripts, Kallendorf's *Virgil and the Myth of Venice* is a meticulous study of glosses in Virgil print editions, primarily those owned by sixteenth-century Venetians.[22] His body of work has emphasized the crucial influence of rhetorical traditions in humanist readings of Virgil. Building on the inheritance of classical and medieval poetic theory, humanists understood epic

---

[17] Baswell, *Virgil in Medieval England*, pp. 270–84.
[18] Wilson-Okamura, *Virgil in the Renaissance*, p. 8.
[19] Wilson-Okamura, *Virgil in the Renaissance*, p. 157–63.
[20] Wilson-Okamura, *Virgil in the Renaissance*, p. 15–20, 37–44.
[21] Most significantly, Craig Kallendorf, *A Bibliography of the Early Printed Editions of Virgil, 1469–1850* (New Castle, Delaware: Oak Knoll Press, 2012).
[22] Craig Kallendorf, *Virgil and the Myth of Venice: Books and Readers in the Italian Renaissance* (Oxford: Clarendon, 1999); *Printing Virgil: The Transformation of the Classics in the Renaissance* (Leiden: Brill, 2019).

poetry as a genre of epideictic rhetoric which inspires readers to virtue by praising the good morals of its heroes. As Kallendorf has shown, humanist conceptions both of the *Aeneid* and poetry in general expanded on this longstanding intellectual tradition.[23] Humanist theories on the moral purpose of poetry also underpin Kallendorf's work on the Renaissance schoolroom, in which he emphasizes that pedagogic expositions of classical authors were suffused with moral didacticism. Schoolroom commentaries simultaneously aimed both to teach the Latin grammar and rhetoric and also to improve the morals of students.[24] Like Baswell and Wilson-Okamura, therefore, Kallendorf draws attention to the long-term medieval trends influencing Virgil in the Renaissance.

Building on these appraisals of continuity, the present study will explicitly interrogate how far there was a qualitative difference between medieval and humanist practices of reading and translating Virgil in England. While histories of classical reception have often referred to 'medieval' and 'humanist' reading and 'medieval' and 'humanist' commentary,[25] this terminology obscures the fact that the majority of readers from the twelfth to sixteenth centuries approached the classical poets through a common methodological framework and with a common set of glossing procedures. Moreover, histories of English vernacular translation have posited even sharper differences between 'medieval' and 'humanist' translation practice.[26] As discussed in detail below, such distinctions often reflect modern assumptions about fifteenth- and sixteenth-century translations rather than the complexity of the surviving sources. In emphasizing continuity as much as change, the present monograph identifies more precisely the key areas of humanist innovation, thereby arriving at a revised definition of how humanism did and (just as importantly) did not influence Virgil's reception. Although this study focuses only on a single author, the significant continuities in Virgilian reception are also witnessed in the reading of other canonical classical poets, for example Ovid or Horace. As this book will indicate, the case of Virgil is representative of the wider study of classical poetry throughout this period.

---

[23] Craig Kallendorf, *In Praise of Aeneas: Virgil and Epideictic Rhetoric in the Early Italian Renaissance* (Hanover: University Press of New England, 1989).
[24] Primarily, see Kallendorf, *Virgil and the Myth of Venice*, Ch. 2.
[25] On perceived differences of medieval and Renaissance commentaries, see Marjorie Curry Woods, 'What are the Real Differences between Medieval and Renaissance Commentaries?', in *The Classics in the Medieval and Renaissance Classroom: The Role of Ancient Texts in the Arts Curriculum as Revealed by Surviving Manuscripts and Early Printed Books*, ed. Juanita Feros Ruys, John O. Ward, and Melanie Heywood (Turnhout: Brepols, 2013), pp. 329–41.
[26] See below pp. 10–11.

As if to connect the bibliographic work of Baswell and Kallendorf, the present study encompasses both manuscripts and print editions. There are 25 surviving manuscripts of Virgil containing signs of fifteenth- or sixteenth-century English or Scottish provenance (listed in Appendix A). Some of them were produced as early as the twelfth century, but contain later repairs, ownership inscriptions, and annotations. As Baswell has emphasized, manuscripts of Virgil remained in use for many hundreds of years, accreting layer after layer of new glossing.[27] To analyse Virgil's reception in print, meanwhile, the project focuses on a sample of 48 printed copies of Virgil's works with an English provenance from before 1550 (listed in Appendix B). Whereas the majority of manuscripts were produced in England, readers of print editions overwhelmingly used imported copies from the continent.[28] Prior to the Elizabethan era, there were only five English editions of Virgil: Wynkyn de Worde's four editions of the *Bucolics* (1512, 1514, 1522, 1529), and Richard Pynson's one edition of the *Opera* (c. 1515).[29] Rather than competing with the import market, English presses generally chose not to print classical Latin authors except in English translations or in parallel Latin-English editions.[30] For this reason, the print sample has been composed almost entirely by identifying English inscriptions and annotations in continental printed copies. Most of these copies have not previously been studied and their English provenances are largely unrecognized.

Through close analysis of these manuscripts and early printed materials, the first half of the book demonstrates the intellectual continuities in the study of Virgil's texts throughout the long fifteenth century. While the combined influence of humanism and printing dramatically increased the circulation and readership of Virgil, the New Learning did not change the prevailing *methods* of reading Virgil's texts. This conclusion is grounded in the close analysis of fifteenth- and sixteenth-century readers' annotations in their copies of Virgil. In its intellectual content, their glossing is consistent

---

[27] On the manuscripts, see Chapter 1, p. 15. For Baswell's comments, see *Virgil in Medieval England*, pp. 5–7.

[28] Recent surveys include Alan Coates, 'The Latin Trade in England and Abroad', *A Companion to the Early Printed Book in Britain, 1476–1558*, ed. Vincent Gillespie and Susan Powell (Cambridge: D.S. Brewer, 2014), pp. 45–58; M. Lane Ford, 'Importation of Printed Books into England and Scotland', in *CHBB:III*, pp. 179–201; Martin Lowry, 'The Arrival and Use of Continental Printed Books in Yorkist England', in *Le Livre dans L'Europe de la Renaissance*, ed. P. Aquilon and H.-J. Martin (Paris: Promodis-Ed. du Cercle de la Librairie, 1988), pp. 449–59.

[29] De Worde: STC 24813, 24,814, 24814.5, 24,815. Pynson: STC 24787. These editions are studied in detail for the first time in Chapters 2 and 3.

[30] Daniel Wakelin, 'Possibilities for Reading: Classical Translations in Parallel Texts ca. 1520–1558', *Studies in Philology* 105 (2008), 463–86 (465).

with previous Virgilian glossing traditions. Since Late Antiquity, the practices of Virgilian exegesis had been structured by the pedagogic disciplinary framework of grammar and rhetoric, and this well-established framework continued to structure the humanist study of Virgil. Throughout the fifteenth and sixteenth centuries, the overwhelming majority of readers, at all levels of study, continued to read Virgil much like their ancestors had in previous generations. In their thousands of annotations, they followed age-old processes of correcting scribal errors, glossing obscure and ambiguous passages, marking rhetorical figures and noting moral *sententiae* and *exempla*. From the evidence of readers' glosses, the methods of reading Virgil 'in the Middle Ages' are virtually indistinguishable from reading Virgil 'in the Renaissance'.

Although humanism was slower to penetrate England than many parts of continental Europe, the lack of change in Virgilian exegesis cannot be attributed purely to this geographical issue. As discussed above, recent scholarship on early English humanism, in particular by David Rundle and Daniel Wakelin, has emphasized the rich diffusion and influence of humanist ideas in England during the fifteenth century.[31] From this perspective, the continuities in English Virgilian exegesis do not primarily reflect English backwardness or geographical variations in the adoption of humanism. Rather, they reveal broader continuities between humanist and medieval study of the classics. While humanism had wide-reaching impacts on certain fields of classical study, such as textual criticism, and on the reception of certain authors, most prominently Cicero,[32] common practices in reading classical poetry remained consistent with earlier traditions.

Such observations call for reassessing the dissemination and impact of humanist scholarship. How and to what extent did humanist advances in classical studies influence the majority of Virgil's readers? Although leading humanist intellectuals, such as Lorenzo Valla or Angelo Poliziano, made their radical innovations in philology and textual criticism, their work had only gradual effect on the reading of Virgil outside scholarly circles. New methods of philological and textual scholarship took time to permeate Virgil's wider reception. Throughout the early sixteenth century, for example, readers continued to use the well-established dictionaries and textbooks of twelfth- and thirteenth-century grammarians. Only gradually did they adopt new

---

[31] See above, p. 1, fn. 1.
[32] On changes in the reception of Cicero, see John O. Ward, 'The Medieval and Early Renaissance Study of Cicero's *de Inventione* and the *Rhetorica ad Herennium*: Commentaries and Contexts', in *The Rhetoric of Cicero in its Medieval and Early Renaissance Commentary Tradition*, ed. Virginia Cox and John O. Ward (Leiden: Brill, 2006), pp. 1–75.

humanist dictionaries and commentaries. Likewise, humanist emendations to Virgil's texts and humanist standards of orthography took decades to become standard across print editions. Although humanism ultimately had major effects on the quality of editions and the understanding of classical Latin, its influence should be seen in the context of broader exegetic continuities. In the exegesis of classical poets, humanist developments supplemented, but did not replace or overshadow, the continuous methodological influence of well-established grammatical and rhetorical interpretative traditions. While late fifteenth- and early sixteenth-century English readers gradually began to use new humanist dictionaries and explore textual critical issues, these added interests did not alter the fundamental aims, methods or conventions of the *enarratio poetarum*.

While the first half of the monograph demonstrates the continuities in practices of Virgilian study, the second half makes an analogous argument for practices of Latin-to-English translation.[33] These chapters analyse the earliest extant translations of the *Aeneid* into English: William Caxton's *Eneydos* (1490), Gavin Douglas's *Eneados* (1513), and the Earl of Surrey's translations of *Aeneid* II and IV (c. 1543). Scholars of English translation, most recently James Simpson, have often taken this trio of texts as representatives of a putative progression from 'medieval' adaptations of the classics to 'humanist' translations.[34] Whereas 'medieval' adapters reworked the ancient text for a contemporary readership, 'humanist' translators sought to make a closer reproduction of the original Latin, imitating its style and form.[35]

---

[33] Humanism affected different fields of translation in different ways. While this monograph's discussion concerns English vernacular translation of Latin classics, humanism occasioned different changes in, for example, Latin translation of Greek texts. For example, see Paul Botley, *Latin Translation in the Renaissance: The Theory and Practice of Leonardo Bruni, Giannozzo Manetti, and Desiderius Erasmus* (Cambridge: CUP, 2004).

[34] For example, see Colin Burrow, 'Virgil in English Translation', *The Cambridge Companion to Virgil*, ed. Charles Martindale (Cambridge: CUP, 1997), pp. 21–37 (pp. 22–4); James Simpson, 'The Aeneid Translations of Henry Howard, Earl of Surrey: The Exiled Reader's Presence', in *OHCREL:I*, pp. 601–23. There is also a tendency to incorporate Chaucer's *House of Fame* and 'Legend of Dido' in these comparisons, as if their brief retellings of the *Aeneid* are directly comparable to full-length translations or adaptations. For example, Burrow writes (p. 22), 'the 'Medieval' free paraphrase of Chaucer is superseded by a 'Renaissance' concern with the accurate understanding of ancient literatures and *mores*.' Simpson makes similar comments in 'The Aeneid Translations of Henry Howard', pp. 603–4.

[35] Features of the comparison vary. Simpson, in 'The Aeneid Translations of Henry Howard', pp. 602–7, also points out that 'medieval' Caxton and Douglas insert translators' asides in Virgil, whereas the 'humanist' Surrey does not. Thomas Greene, in *The Light in Troy: Imitation and Discovery in Renaissance Poetry* (New Haven: Yale University Press, 1982), pp. 242–4, compares anachronisms in Caxton, Douglas, and later Thomas Wyatt and the Earl of Surrey to chart the development of a 'humanist' historical consciousness.

Modern scholars have frequently criticized Caxton's work, since he translated a French prose version rather than the Latin *Aeneid*. According to English literary scholars, neither he nor the French writer made any effort to reproduce Virgil's original text. Gavin Douglas famously shared this derogatory perspective, lambasting Caxton for using a French intermediary. Finished in 1513, Douglas's *Eneados* is the earliest full translation of the *Aeneid* into the Scots language and indeed any language related to English. Explicitly contrasting Douglas with Caxton, modern scholars have commended his higher standard of textual fidelity, regarding it as a humanist quality.[36] The Earl of Surrey's translations, meanwhile, are famously one of the first examples of English blank verse. Compared with Douglas, Surrey not only translated with greater textual precision, but he also experimented with his new verse-form to imitate the formal effects of Virgil's unrhymed Latin hexameters. As Simpson puts it, 'We recognize the Virgilian effect in Surrey...but not in Douglas'.[37]

By contrast, this book suggests that an idealized progression of 'medieval' to 'humanist' misses the continuities between these three translations, and more broadly in fifteenth- and sixteenth-century English vernacular translation practice. Although close translations of classical authors became more common after 1500, the humanists did not initiate this approach. Just as the New Learning popularized the reading of Virgil in Latin, the initial effect of humanism was primarily to increase the number of Virgil translations. As Jacques Monfrin has observed of French literature, earlier translators of ancient texts had generally (but not exclusively) selected practical, historical or philosophical works in prose, such as Vegetius's *De Re Militari* or Boethius's *De Consolatione Philosophiae*.[38] Only in the mid- and later fifteenth century did translators turn to major classical poets, the first being the English translation of Claudian's *De Consulatu Stilichionis* (1445), while the next was Douglas's *Eneados* in 1513.[39] Rather than 'medieval adaptations', Caxton's *Eneydos* and its French source, the *Livre des Eneydes*, are important early stages in this humanistic trend. The French text

---

[36] See Chapter 5, p. 136.
[37] Simpson, 'The Aeneid Translations of Henry Howard', p. 611.
[38] Jacques Monfrin, 'Humanisme et traductions au moyen âge', *Journal des savants* 148 (1963), 161–90 (183). For a survey of English translations of the classics up to 1500, see Daniel Wakelin, 'Classical and Humanist Translations', in *A Companion to Fifteenth-Century English Poetry*, ed. Julia Boffey and A.S.G. Edwards (Cambridge: D.S. Brewer, 2013), pp. 171–85.
[39] In French literature, the same progression is marked by Octavien de St-Gelais's translations of Ovid's *Heroides* (c. 1496) and Virgil's *Aeneid* (c. 1500).

had an unusual production history, and (as Chapter 4 explains in detail) approximately half of the volume is in fact a direct translation of *Aeneid* IV. This is the earliest translation of Virgil into French, and Caxton's rendering is the earliest into English. As much as Douglas's, their translations of Virgil reflect the rising popularity of reading classical poets.

Even as vernacular translators took greater interest in classical poetry, the three Virgil translations of Caxton, Douglas and Surrey do not evince a clear progression in methods of translation. Most importantly, none of the three translations is straightforwardly representative of broader historical trends. Although Caxton's *Eneydos*, for example, significantly amplifies the source, not all fifteenth-century vernacular translators shared this free approach to the text. Even by fifteenth-century standards, Caxton's *Eneydos* is an extreme example of textual reworking. Just as Caxton's *Eneydos* does not represent all 'medieval' translations, neither does Surrey's *Aeneid* stand for 'humanist' practice. His formal experiments were not widely adopted by his immediate contemporaries. In his blank verse and scrupulous concision, Surrey represents only a modern ideal of English 'humanist' translation, unrepresentative of broader sixteenth-century practice. What is more, Caxton, Douglas and Surrey show many areas of continuity in their methods of translation. Fifteenth-century practices of vernacular translation, for instance, pervasively influenced Douglas approach to Virgil's text in the *Eneados*. For this reason, there are significant, and surprising, parallels between Douglas's *Eneados* and Caxton's *Eneydos*, stemming from shared stylistic conventions and the common influence of Virgil glossing and commentaries. Far from a straightforward progression from 'medieval' to 'humanist', the translations of Caxton, Douglas and Surrey, when properly contextualized, evince a more complex blend of continuity and change.

Together, both halves of the monograph argue that an emphasis on humanist development obscures the continuities in Virgilian exegesis and translation across the fifteenth and early sixteenth centuries. To distinguish too rigorously between 'medieval' and 'humanist' intellectual and literary culture understates the very gradual pace of humanist development and the continuous influence of medieval learning on the *studia humanitatis*. In making this broader argument, the monograph draws on fine-grained readings of original manuscripts, printed editions and translations. Just as the first half discusses linguistic glosses and textual emendations, the analysis of translations draws its evidence from numerous small amplifications and omissions, often numbering only one or two words at a time. By collecting this granular evidence, the monograph looks beyond broad period divisions between the Middle Ages and Renaissance, and focuses on the detail of how readers and translators engaged with Virgil's text. Complementing modern accounts of humanist innovations and discoveries, the accumulation of this fine-grained evidence reveals the less studied, yet far more numerous examples of consistency and traditionalism.

1
Manuscripts

From Antiquity to the sixteenth century, the study of Virgil was shaped by the pedagogic discipline of grammar. Largely unchanged through the centuries, the exegesis of the poets (*enarratio poetarum*) was a core part of the grammatical curriculum. Originating in the expositions of ancient grammarians, the methods of the *enarratio poetarum* had a pervasive influence both inside and outside the schoolroom. Certainly by the fifteenth and sixteenth centuries, the methods of reading the poets in schools structured the reading of the poets in general, both within *and* outside pedagogic contexts. The wide reach of pedagogic reading procedures is attested in the glossing of Virgil manuscripts. Annotators of Virgil, in and out of the schools, consistently used similar glossing procedures. Following the procedures of the *enarratio poetarum*, they parsed the literal construction of the text, elaborated on difficult points of grammar, lexis and etymology, identified rhetorical figures, and explained allusions to ancient history and myth. Humanist studies of the authors, both within and outside the schoolroom, continued to use these traditional glossing procedures. While humanists cultivated a more classical Latin idiom, this new development is not reflected in a distinct change of glossing methods, at least not in the Virgilian tradition. The classicizing focus of the *studia humanitatis* manifested itself in the greater popularity of studying Virgil rather than in a different glossing practice. Were it not for changes of script, the annotations of fifteenth- and sixteenth-century bishops would be indistinguishable from the glosses of twelfth-century schoolmasters.

Although the major histories of reading classical authors frequently discuss this consistency of glossing practices, their separate disciplinary aims and period boundaries obscure its degree. Studies of glossing classical manuscripts often focus on a particular historical period, such as the Middle Ages or Renaissance, or a particular reading context, for example the schoolroom. In *Virgil in Medieval England*, for example, Christopher Baswell observes that pedagogic glossing practices have 'links (through similarity of aim and direct verbal dependence) back to the late antique commentary of Servius, and forward to the school commentaries of the

English Humanism and the Reception of Virgil c. 1400–1550. Matthew Day, Oxford University Press.
© Matthew Day 2023. DOI: 10.1093/oso/9780192871138.003.0002

earlier Italian humanists', although his main analysis focuses on manuscripts between the years 1100 and 1400.[1] Robert Black, in his magisterial study of Italian educational practices from the twelfth century to 1500, concludes 'that methods of reading and using school authors hardly changed over this long period'.[2] Likewise focusing on the history of education, Suzanne Reynolds's *Medieval Reading* and Ralph Hexter's *Ovid in Medieval Schooling* have compared glossing practices in school manuscripts of the eleventh, twelfth, and thirteenth centuries.[3] Meanwhile, historians of the Renaissance reading of classical authors, for example Craig Kallendorf, have tended to focus on annotations in sixteenth-century printed copies.[4] While these studies of reading classical authors each have differing aims, evidence and emphases, they collectively attest to a broader continuity of approach across different historical periods and in a broad range of reading contexts. Building on their collective insights, the present chapter will foreground the consistency of Virgilian glossing practices from Middle Ages to Renaissance, from schoolroom to adulthood.

Survey of Virgil's Readers

All the extant English Virgil manuscripts, with only a handful of exceptions, were books for study. They often have annotations in several different hands, and their pages bear traces of frequent reading. Even with the advent of print, English manuscripts of Virgil remained in continuous use at least until the mid-sixteenth century. Twenty-five extant Virgilian manuscripts have a fifteenth- or sixteenth-century English or Scottish provenance (Appendix A). Eleven were produced from the twelfth to fourteenth centuries, and their margins had accumulated many layers of glosses even before 1400. Fourteen more were produced in the fifteenth century, nine in England and five imported from the continent. The latest two manuscripts both date from around the turn of the century. Some of these manuscripts were owned by monastic libraries, others by schools and

---

[1] Baswell, *Virgil in Medieval England*, pp. 41, 80–3.
[2] Black, *Humanism and Education*, pp. 275–330 (quotation on p. 275).
[3] R.J. Hexter, *Ovid and Medieval Schooling: Studies in Medieval School Commentaries on Ovid's Ars Amatoria, Epistulae ex Ponto, and Epistulae Heroidum* (München: Arbeo-Gesellschaft, 1986); Suzanne Reynolds, *Medieval Reading: Grammar, Rhetoric and the Classical Text* (Cambridge: CUP, 1996).
[4] For example, see Kallendorf, *Virgil and the Myth of Venice*.

universities, and clergymen had copies in their private collections. Readers of Virgil, as the following survey will detail, ranged from students and schoolmasters to monks, bishops, and university fellows. Although there are differences between individual annotators, these differences do not amount to broader, collective trends. Neither the subject-matter nor complexity of glossing necessarily correlates with a given historical period or reading context. The same pedagogic procedures, as this overview will show, recur throughout Virgil's readerships.

Many of the glosses were written by scribes involved in the original production of the manuscripts. Of the nine English manuscripts produced after 1400, six have scribal glossing.[5] While some copies were intended for pedagogic use, scribes applied this glossing framework even to manuscripts never used in teaching. Although originating in the schoolroom, the content of the *enarratio poetarum* became a standard textual apparatus in manuscripts of Virgil. Conventions of spoken pedagogic exposition informed the conventions of scribal production and manuscript design.[6] In Virgil copies, the most common types of scribal annotation are interlinear lexical glosses, and glosses marking rhetorical figures (especially 'comparatio' beside epic similes).[7] Some scribes might have composed the glosses themselves, but they might also have been copied from the scribes' exemplars. Although a convention of book-design, these scribal annotations also facilitated future comprehension and study of the text. Given the difficulty of Virgil's poetic language, glosses would have helped both students and capable Latinists to understand the more obscure passages. Moreover, scribal glosses would have assisted in grammatical and rhetorical learning. In marking rhetorical figures and difficult points of language, scribal glossing provided a rudimentary framework for readers wishing to study Virgil's text more closely. When readers made annotations of their own, their additions embellished and expanded this original scribal apparatus. Just as scribes prepared manuscripts for grammatical and rhetorical reading, the cumulative layers of later glossing show that readers followed a similar approach.

---

[5] BodL, MS Ashmole 54; TCC, MS R.1.40; BL, Add. MS 11959; BodL, MS Auct. F.2.7; Peterhouse, MS 159; London, Society of Antiquaries, MS 44. One of the five imported manuscripts, definitely not used in schooling, also has scribal glosses: Oxford, New College, MS 271.

[6] For similar observations on glossed manuscripts of Scripture, see for example Lesley Smith, *The Glossa Ordinaria: The Making of a Medieval Bible Commentary* (Leiden: Brill, 2009), pp. 91–3.

[7] For example, TCC, MS R.1.40 (discussed below); BodL, MS Ashmole 54 (e.g. fols 56r, 72r, 74r).

Among these readers were monks. Monastic collections of the classical authors, many dating back to the twelfth century and before, were originally established for pedagogic use.[8] Although the teaching of pagan authors waned in succeeding centuries, there are signs of revived interest from the later 1300s onwards. James Clark, most importantly, has traced a 'literary turn' in the fifteenth-century monastic curriculum up to the Reformation. The growing study of rhetoric and poetry is chiefly seen in Benedictine houses such as St Albans, and in their colleges at Oxford University.[9] This trend in monastic studies developed before the works of the humanists received wide circulation. While the monks, as Clark has discussed, knew the works of Boccaccio and later of Valla and Bruni, Italian influence nourished rather than initiated these classicising studies.[10] Among the classical authors, the main interest seems to have been Ovid's *Metamorphoses* and its commentaries, but Virgilian study has left a few traces.[11] Three surviving copies of Virgil have a definite fifteenth-century monastic provenance, one at St Augustine's, Canterbury, two at Bury St Edmunds.[12] Surviving library catalogues of the period, however, suggest that overall holdings of Virgil were larger. The Benedictines at St Augustine's, Canterbury, had no less than eight copies in their fifteenth-century catalogue, and there were three among the Austin canons at Leicester. At least one institution, the wealthy Syon Abbey, acquired a print copy. The early sixteenth-century catalogue lists an *Opera* 'cum triplici commento', one of the printed commentary-editions described in Chapter 2.[13]

---

[8] Baswell, *Virgil in Medieval England*, pp. 41–7.
[9] On this literary turn, see James Clark, 'Humanism and Reform in Pre-Reformation English Monasteries', *Transactions of the Royal Historical Society* 19 (2009), pp. 57–93 (esp. pp. 71–82). On the Benedictines and their rhetorical studies at Oxford, see Martin Camargo, 'Rhetoricians in Black: Benedictine Monks and Rhetorical Revival in Medieval Oxford', in *New Chapters in the History of Rhetoric*, ed. L. Pernot (Leiden: Brill, 2009), pp. 375–84; 'The Late-Fourteenth-Century Renaissance of Anglo-Latin Rhetoric', *Philosophy and Rhetoric* 45 (2012), 107–33. On the study of Virgil in universities, see below, pp. 28–30.
[10] On the circulation of humanist works in English monasteries, see Clark, 'Humanism and Reform', esp. pp. 73–6.
[11] On the extensive evidence for reading Ovid, see James Clark, 'Ovid in the Monasteries', *Ovid in the Middle Ages*, ed. J.G. Clark, F.T. Coulson, K.L. McKinley (Cambridge: CUP, 2011), pp. 177–96.
[12] BL, Royal MS 15.B.VI; TCC, MS R.3.50; BL, MS Add. 16,166, described in Baswell, *Virgil in Medieval England*, pp. 300, 295, 302.
[13] St Augustine's, Canterbury: *MLGB3*, BA1.*1476, BA1.1471–2, BA1.1474–5, BA1.1477, BA1.1473, BA1.1479h-i. As listed in *MLGB3*, the Austin Canons at Leicester; A20.1673, A20.1040–1. Premonstratensians, Tichfield (1400 catalogue): P6.174, P6.104. The *c.* 1500–*c.* 1524 Syon Abbey *Opera* is SS1.¶62. Also at Syon: SS2.1, SS2.7d-e, SS2.19b, SS1.895h.

As was common in many copies of Virgil, the annotations in the extant monastic manuscripts suggest a close attention to language. The one surviving Canterbury manuscript, for instance, was produced in the thirteenth century, but was glossed in several hands right up to the fifteenth.[14] Irrespective of the annotator and the date, the principal types of annotation are textual corrections, and interlinear glossing of basic lexis and grammar. The fifteenth-century hand glosses unclear referents, cases, tenses, and words used in secondary senses. For example, he marks the historic infinitive 'exurere' (*Aeneid* III.141) with the gloss 'bat' (since it translates as the past tense 'burned up'), and 'ancipiti' (*Aeneid* III.47, literally meaning 'with two heads') is glossed in the sense 'dubitanti' ('doubting').[15] Although the manuscript might have been used in a pedagogic context, its annotators were more likely independent, adult readers. Considering that they annotate inconsistently and infrequently, they had the linguistic competence to read Virgil, and glossed only to elucidate the more obscure words and phrases. Rather than skim over these ambiguities, they took the time to parse the language. Recalling their schoolroom training, they deployed traditional pedagogic procedures on the difficult passages, glossing word-by-word. At the very least, the evidence shows that monks of St Augustine's were reading Virgil, and the same textual approach characterizes each layer of glosses from the twelfth to the fifteenth centuries.

Not only is the reading of Virgil attested in surviving monastic manuscripts, but Virgilian references also appear in the works of two well-known St Alban's monks, Thomas of Walsingham (c. 1340–c. 1422) and John Whethamstede (c. 1392–1465).[16] Walsingham included Virgil in his *Prohemia Poetarum*, a collection of *accessus* and *argumenta* to the poets. The Virgil section consists of Servius's prefaces to the *Bucolics*, *Georgics*, and *Aeneid*, verse arguments to each book of the *Aeneid*, and the Ovidian tetradistich arguments to the *Georgics*. The rest of the volume discusses classical poets, such as Seneca and Terence, and classicizing twelfth-century writers, such as Alan of Lille. By compiling these *accessus*, Walsingham created a primer of information about the poets and their works.[17] Whethamstede,

---

[14] BL, Royal MS 15.B.VI, fol. 4r; *MLGB3*, BA1.*1476.

[15] BL, Royal MS 15.B.VI, fols 25v, 24v.

[16] On their classicizing works, see James Clark, *A Monastic Renaissance at St. Albans: Thomas Walsingham and his Circle, c. 1350–1440* (Oxford: Clarendon Press, 2004), pp. 163–208, 234–7.

[17] The *Prohemia Poetarum* is extant in one manuscript, BL, MS Harley 2693, fols 131r-202v, with Virgil sections at fols 131r-141v. For an overview of the *Prohemia*, see Clark, *Monastic Renaissance*, pp. 164–5, 170, 181–3, 195–200, 208.

likewise, used Virgil as a source in his verse *Pabularium Poetarum*. It is an encyclopaedic reference-work on characters and places from classical myth, and each entry (like a *florilegium*) consists of verse excerpts from classical or twelfth-century poets. For example, the 'harpies' entry quotes Virgil's description of the harpies from *Aeneid* III.209-18.[18] Providing information on mythological topics, easily memorizable in verse, Whethamstede made 'a readers' companion to the fables of the poets', helping monks at St Albans understand the poets' more obscure cultural references.[19] Both Whethamstede and Walsingham, in this light, intended their projects to facilitate wider monastic study of the authors. Not only did they read widely in Virgil and the other classical authors, but they also sought to encourage and assist the studies of their fellow monks.

The earliest signs of humanist influence are the imports of five continental manuscripts during the mid-fifteenth century. Their humanist script and rich illumination distinguish them from almost every other manuscript owned in England at the time. In these imports, the *studia humanitatis* is more a palaeographic and decorative phenomenon than a programme of study.[20] Three of the five manuscripts were made in Italy, one in France, and the last in Flanders. Two of the manuscripts were written in textura script, the remaining four in humanist minuscule or italic.[21] Continental book producers, particularly in Italy, produced these illuminated manuscripts of the authors throughout the fifteenth century. The humanists promoted the pagan poets as objects of prestige, and there was a market for expensive copies among wealthy laypersons and clerics. The illumination registers the changing status of and demand for classical poetry across continental Europe.[22] In fifteenth-century England, by contrast, humanist influence was not yet as pervasive as in France and Italy. For an Englishman to

[18] BL, MS Egerton 646, with the harpies on fol. 3r. On Whethamstede's other encyclopaedic works, see Alfred Hiatt, 'The Reference Work in the Fifteenth Century: John Whethamstede's *Granarium*', in *Makers and Users of Medieval Books: Essays in Honour of A.S.G. Edwards*, ed. C.M. Meale and D. Pearsall (Cambridge: D.S. Brewer, 2014), pp. 13–33. On his well-known interest in classical and humanist writings, see Rundle, 'Of Republics and Tyrants', pp. 86–100; and Weiss, *Humanism in England*, pp. 50–62.

[19] Clark, *Monastic Renaissance*, p. 236.

[20] Other than these five, the only other illuminated Virgil manuscript owned in England was the twelfth-century LPL, MS 471. See Baswell, *Virgil in Medieval England*, pp. 296–7.

[21] The Italian manuscripts are: Oxford, New College, MS 271; Oxford, Balliol College, MS 140; and SJC, MS C.4. The French manuscript is Edinburgh, Edinburgh University Library, MS 195, and the Flemish manuscript is SJC, MS H.2. See Baswell, *Virgil in Medieval England*, pp. 303–7.

[22] Christopher de Hamel, *A History of Illuminated Manuscripts*, 2nd edn (London: Phaidon Press, 1994), pp. 232–56.

own illuminated copies of Virgil is an indicator of continental travel and exposure to continental attitudes.

The names of the owners are all familiar to scholars for their interests in the *studia humanitatis* and large libraries of humanist books. For example, the earliest of the Italian manuscripts, produced in Florence around 1400, has the inscriptions of William Brygon (d. 1469), canon of Salisbury, and John Russell (d. 1494), Bishop of Lincoln and Chancellor of Oxford University.[23] The manuscript was originally brought to England by a lesser-known clergyman, Thomas Candour (d. 1477), who travelled widely in Italy and had several positions at the Curia in the mid-fifteenth century. Candour was one of the first Englishmen to learn humanist minuscule, and was Poggio Bracciolini's earliest English copyist.[24] Once he was back in England, Candour extended the manuscript with the 'thirteenth book' of the *Aeneid* by Italian poet Maphaeus Vegius, which circulated widely in Italy during this period. A second English scribe added *De Morte Astyanactis*, another of Vegius's narrative poems.[25] Just as the Italian portion of the manuscript had elaborate decoration, the scribes decorated their extensions with vine-stem initials, imitating a common Italian decorative style.[26] English imitations of vine-stem initials are found in several manuscripts connected with Candour, Russell and Brygon. The scribes, using the humanist minuscule and the vine-stem decoration, were recreating a humanist *mise-en-page*.[27]

Despite their rich style of decoration, these illuminated manuscripts were still annotated with a pedagogic, linguistic focus. Three of the five manuscripts have annotations, all of them conforming to longstanding pedagogic

---

[23] Oxford, New College, MS 271. For descriptions of the manuscript, see A.C. de la Mare and R. Hunt, *Duke Humfrey and English Humanism in the Fifteenth Century* (Oxford: Bodleian Library, 1970), pp. 34–5; David Rundle, 'The Scribe Thomas Candour and the Making of Poggio Bracciolini's English Reputation', *English Manuscript Studies* 12 (2005), 1–25 (16–17); Baswell, *Virgil in Medieval England*, p. 303. On Russell, see also *BRUO*, pp. 1609–11.

[24] On Candour, see *BRUO*, pp. 2158–9; Hunt and De la Mare, *Duke Humfrey and English Humanism*, pp. 32–5; David Rundle, *The Renaissance Reform of the Book and Britain: The English Quattrocento* (Cambridge: CUP, 2019), pp. 100–5; Rundle, 'The Scribe Thomas Candour'.

[25] Oxford, New College, MS 271, fols 157r-72v. On Vegius, see briefly Wilson-Okamura, *Virgil in the Renaissance*, pp. 239–51.

[26] Rundle, in *The Renaissance Reform of the Book and Britain*, p. 249, identifies the hand in *De Morte Astyanactis* as a young Robert Sherborne, later bishop of Chichester. On Sherborne's books, see *BRUO*, pp. 1685–7.

[27] For other English manuscripts with vine-stem initials, see Rundle, 'The Scribe Thomas Candour', pp. 16–17.

procedures.[28] Although bishop Russell's manuscript evidently was not produced for schooling, its Italian scribe nonetheless adorned the *Aeneid* text with neat rows of interlinear glosses, sometimes on virtually every consecutive line. In other word, this richly-illuminated copy had the conventional scribal apparatus of the time, densely glossing the language.[29] Bishop Russell later added to their annotations, his hand appearing throughout *Aeneid* I-IX and Vegius's *Supplementum*. He wrote corrections to the text, further interlinear glosses, and marks of *Nota* beside certain passages.[30] These *Nota* marks evince a combination of moral and rhetorical interests, some of them pertaining to moral *sententiae*, others to figures and tropes. One of the marked lines, for example, is 'Tante molis erat romana*m* co*n*tere gente*m*', which annotators often marked as an example of *epiphomena*.[31] In the opening lines of Book I, other marked lines include the description of Aeolus's storm, and the famous 'seditio' simile. Russell writes only cursory *Nota* marks, but other *Aeneid* copies have longer headings such as 'descriptio' and 'comparatio'.[32] Russell's reading, then, was grounded in linguistic procedures, from the interlinear glossing of lexis to the annotation of rhetorical figures. Although bishop of Lincoln, Chancellor of Oxford University, and Lord Chancellor of England, he glossed Virgil through a pedagogic lens.

The most elaborate of the decorated manuscripts, now in Edinburgh University Library, is the only extant Virgil manuscript to have a Scottish provenance during the Middle Ages. It was produced in Paris probably in the late 1440s, and bears the arms of the Scottish royal family. The scribe, who was Italian, writes in a textura book-hand with humanist influences.[33]

---

[28] New College, MS 271; SJC, MSS C.4 and H.2.

[29] For the scribe's glossing, see especially fols 3r (dense marginalia on first page of *Aeneid* I) and 100r-33r (consistent interlinear glossing and occasional marginal glossing throughout *Aeneid* IX.1-XI.410). The scribe also makes occasional glosses in books VI-VIII and XII. As well as the scribe and John Russell, several other hands (I have counted eight) each make a couple of scattered annotations in the volume.

[30] For Russell's lexical glosses (most interlinear, a few marginal), examples in *Aeneid* I are at fols 3v, 4v, 5r, and 6v-7v (with construe marks). While he tends to mark figurative passages only with *Nota*, he writes one gloss of 'hysteron proteron' at fol. 6r.

[31] Fol. 3v, meaning 'So vast was the effort to found the Roman race' (Fairclough). MS 271 has '*contere*' for '*condere*'. For a note of 'epiphomena', see the annotations possibly by John Gunthorpe in Cambridge, St John's College, MS C.4, fol. 55v.

[32] In Russell's copy, these passages are marked on fols 4v, 5v.

[33] Edinburgh, University Library, MS 195, esp. fol. 65r (coat-of-arms), described at Baswell, *Virgil in Medieval England*, p. 307. On the date, scribe and decoration, see Charles P. Finlayson, 'A Glamis Virgil?', *Scottish Historical Review* 32 (1953), 99-100; 'Florius Infortunatus', *Scriptorium* 16.2 (1962), 378-80; 'Florius Infortunatus, Scribe and Author', *Scriptorium* 19 (1965), 108-9. The manuscript is commonly mentioned in discussions of early Scottish

Whereas the other decorated manuscripts only have decorated initials and borders, the Edinburgh Virgil also has four full-page illustrations. This elaborate production was possibly commissioned for Eleanor, daughter of James I of Scotland. She lived at the French court from 1445 until her marriage to Sigismund of Austria in 1449. Eleanor is known for her education and literary pursuits, and she possibly knew Latin herself.[34] During this period, humanist tastes were increasingly prevalent at the courts of France and in the Low Countries. Her ownership of this elaborate manuscript reflects her life in this cultural milieu. Although she was neither a cleric nor a friend of Poggio, it suggests that she had a similar regard for the pagan authors as Candour, Russell, or Brygon.[35]

The owners of other illuminated manuscripts studied in Italy, and maintained their classical interests through the rest of their lives. Two of the Italian manuscripts were owned by William Grey (c. 1414–1478), Bishop of Ely, and Robert Flemmyng (1416–1483), Dean of Lincoln.[36] During the 1440s and 1450s, they and several other Englishmen attended the lectures of the famous humanist Guarino da Verona (1374–1460).[37] In his teaching, Guarino professed to train his students to read and write classical Latin, attracting students from across Europe. To cultivate their Latin style, he lectured widely on the classical authors, including Virgil.[38] Although humanist works had a growing readership in England, dedicated lecturing

---

humanism, for example: Thomas Rutledge, 'Humanism in Late-Fifteenth-Century Scotland', in *Humanism in Fifteenth-Century Europe*, ed. David Rundle (Oxford: Society for the Study of Medieval Languages and Literature, 2012), pp. 237–63 (p. 255).

[34] Eleanor's possible ownership is discussed in all the above articles on the manuscript. For another short biography, see also Priscilla Bawcutt, '"My bright buke": Women and their Books in Medieval and Renaissance Scotland', *Medieval Women: Texts and Contexts in Late Medieval Britain: Essays for Felicity Riddy*, ed. Jocelyn Wogan-Browne (Turnhout: Brepols, 2000), pp. 17–34 (p. 30).

[35] One cannot say for certain whether Eleanor or anyone else actually read the manuscript. The manuscript has occasional textual corrections, at least some of them by the scribe. There is only one other annotation, a line in the margin to mark *Georgics* I.268–72 (fol. 24v).

[36] Grey's manuscript is Oxford, Balliol College, MS 140; Flemmyng's is SJC, MS C.4. Since Grey's manuscript is not listed in Baswell, see R.A.B. Mynors, *Catalogue of the Manuscripts of Balliol College Oxford* (Oxford: Clarendon Press, 1963), no. 140. On Grey, Flemmyng and their manuscripts, see biographies in *BRUO*, pp. 809–14, 699–700; Weiss, *Humanism in England*, pp. 86–96, 150–62.

[37] On Guarino's English students, see Weiss, *Humanism in England*, pp. 84–127. For a revisionist account, see David Rundle, 'Beyond the classroom: international interest in the *studia humanitatis* in the university towns of Quattrocento Italy', *Renaissance Studies* 27 (2013), 533–48.

[38] On the diffusion of humanist Latin style in England, see David Rundle, 'Humanist Eloquence among the Barbarians in fifteenth-century England', in *Britannia Latina: Latin in the Culture of Great Britain from the Middle Ages to the Twentieth Century*, ed. Charles Burnett and Nicholas Mann (London: Warburg Institute, 2005), pp. 68–85.

on the classical authors was not yet common in English schools and universities. Grey and Flemmying might have read Virgil, but likely had not received formal teaching before Guarino. Familiarity with classical Latin, moreover, had practical, vocational value. The ability to compose formal letters and diplomatic orations in the right style opened careers in the Church, law, and bureaucracy. Both Flemmyng and Grey rose to high-ranking positions in the Curia, their classical eloquence being an important qualification.[39] They both assembled large collections of Italian manuscripts during their time in Italy. Grey's manuscript was copied in Florence, while Flemmyng acquired his illuminated Virgil in Rome.[40] Flemmyng, densely annotating his manuscript with passages of Servius, continued studying classical poetry from Guarino's lecture-hall to the Curia in later life.

Guarino's lectures on Virgil are preserved in the 'notebook' of Bristol-born humanist John Free (1430–1464/5).[41] A clergyman educated at Oxford, he studied at the schools of northern Italy from 1456 until his death, including two years under Guarino (1456–1458). Besides various letters and orations, his papers include lecture-notes (*recollectae*) from Guarino's expositions of Terence, Horace and Virgil.[42] The content of the lectures exemplifies the continuity of Virgilian exegesis from Antiquity to the Renaissance. Working through the text line-by-line, Guarino follows the conventional procedures of the *enarratio poetarum*. Frequently quoting and paraphrasing Servius, he expounds points of grammar, lexicography and etymology, explains mythological and historical allusions, and analyses rhetorical figures. Although Guarino was innovative to lecture so widely on the classical authors, his overall approach was consistent with established exegetical procedures.[43] Guarino's teaching, from his grammar-books to his

---

[39] Weiss, *Humanism in England*, p. 152.

[40] The scribe of Flemmyng's manuscript, Johannes Hornsen of Münster, was active in Rome in the 1450s and 1460s, coinciding with Flemmyng's time at the Curia. See J. Ruysschaert, *Miniaturistes 'Romaines' Sous Pie II* (Siena: Accademia Senese degli Intronati, 1968), p. 253, no. 44. On Grey's manuscript, see Weiss, *Humanism in England*, p. 141 (Weiss's addendum printed in 4th edition).

[41] On Free, see Weiss, *Humanism in England*, pp. 106–12; *BRUO*, pp. 724–5.

[42] BodL, MS Bodley 587, 'Free's Notebook', contains lecture-notes on several authors, but they are incomplete, unlabelled, and bound out of order. The notes are: *Georgics*, I.43–99 (fols 137r-v); Terence, *Adelphoe*, 209–601 (138r-v); *Aeneid*, VI.373–473 (139r-v), 199–382 (140r-1v), 38–193 (142r-3v); Horace, *Epistulae*, I.1.1–5.31 (147r-8v, 146r), I.7.1–40 (146v); Horace, *Sermones*, II.2.53–4.88 (149r-52v, 155r), II.5.53–6.55 (153v), II.8.42–95 (154v); *Aeneid* X.215-XII.946 (179r-190r). For a description of the manuscript's other content, see De la Mare and Hunt, *Duke Humfrey and English Humanism*, no. 2.

[43] While the Virgil teaching is grounded in Servius, this consistency is not observed in his lectures on every author. Marijke Crab and Jeroen De Keyser, in 'Il commento di Guarino

lectures on the authors, has been a *locus* for debates on the novelty and efficacy of humanist pedagogy. Lisa Jardine and Anthony Grafton, for example, quoted John Free's notes in their major evaluation of Guarino.[44] Commenting on the 'gruelling detail' of the exposition, they use Guarino's teaching-methods to critique idealized views of the humanist classroom. Rather than a 'deep knowledge of any one subject or subjects', they dismiss his lectures as a mass of 'disconnected facts', as he worked through points of lexicography, mythological references and etymologies. 'Poor John Free's notes', they observe, 'are peppered with grammatical errors as he struggles to keep up.'[45]

Much as Grafton and Jardine criticize Guarino's schoolroom, the lectures themselves follow conventional grammarians' teaching of the poets, a tradition dating back to Antiquity. Even if Free had not heard Virgil lectures before coming to Italy, he would have been familiar with the method of the exposition. After taking his lecture notes, he subsequently made notes in a twelfth-century English manuscript of the *Aeneid*. This manuscript had been annotated only in the twelfth and thirteenth centuries, so Free's humanist minuscule is visually striking on the page. He must have taken the manuscript on his travels to Italy, since he never returned to England.[46] Compared with earlier annotations of Virgil, the main difference is Free's use of Greek. Guarino encouraged his students to learn the language, and Greek words occasionally appear in Free's manuscript and his lecture notes. Until the later fifteenth century, knowledge of Greek remained rare among Englishmen.[47] Free's books are the earliest English Virgil manuscripts to contain Greek annotations, and the language appears more frequently in annotations to printed books.[48] In Virgilian glossing, therefore, early signs of humanist influence are more prominent in visual features than intellectual approach. Free uses Greek letters and humanist script, but his

---

Guarini a Valerio Massimo', *Aevum* 87 (2013), 667–684, observe that Guarino's lecturing on Valerius Maximus is relatively unoriginal. By contrast, John Ward identifies innovations in his exposition of *Rhetorica ad Herennium*, for example in teaching the topics. See 'The Lectures of Guarino da Verona on the *Rhetorica ad Herennium*: A Preliminary Discussion', in *Rhetoric and Pedagogy: Its History, Philosophy, and Practice: Essays in Honor of James J. Murphy*, ed. Winifred Bryan Homer, Michael Leff, et al. (Hillsdale, NJ: Erlbaum, 1995), pp. 97–127.

[44] Anthony Grafton and Lisa Jardine, *From Humanism to the Humanities: Education and the Liberal Arts in Fifteenth- and Sixteenth-Century Europe* (Cambridge, MA: Harvard University Press, 1986), pp. 1–28.

[45] Grafton and Jardine, *From Humanism to the Humanities*, pp. 15, 20.

[46] Cambridge, Jesus College, MS 33. Baswell describes the manuscript in *Virgil in Medieval England*, pp. 294–5; and refers to it at pp. 47, 315–16.

[47] Micha Lazarus, 'Greek Literacy in Sixteenth-Century England', *Renaissance Studies* 29 (2015), 433–58 (discusses Guarino's pupils at 437–8).

[48] For example, see O.1480, O.1491.

glossing otherwise conforms to traditional procedures of grammatical and rhetorical study.

While Italian educators were making pagan authors the centrepiece of their curricula, contemporary English pedagogy was as yet unaffected by these distant, Italian trends. The popularity of classical authors had declined since the twelfth and thirteenth centuries, and they were no longer a prominent feature of English schooling. Since the fourteenth century, schoolmasters more commonly taught post-classical, moral texts, the most popular being the *Auctores Octo*. Ranging in date from the third to twelfth centuries, the texts included Cato's *Disticha*, Theodulus's tenth-century *Ecloga*, Alan of Lille's *Liber Parabolarum*, and Gualterus Anglicus's twelfth-century version of Aesop's fables. Although this collection was never a fixed curriculum, at least one or two of the texts appear in most English school manuscripts.[49] Over the course of the century, Italian pedagogues eliminated the *Auctores Octo* from their curricula, but English masters continued using them for several decades into the 1500s.[50] Only a handful of fifteenth-century masters taught classical texts with any consistency. One example is the London schoolmaster John Seward (1364/5–1435/6), known for writing poetry and metrical textbooks from *c.* 1400 onwards. He advocated the wider use of classical authors in grammatical pedagogy, particularly in the teaching of metre.[51] Throughout his metrical works, he draws his examples from classical authors, including Virgil, and from twelfth-century classicizing works. Seward's stance, nonetheless, was exceptional, and he fell into disputes with less classicizing contemporaries.[52]

To judge from surviving schoolbooks, Virgil was not a common curricular choice. Only two English Virgil manuscripts were definitely used in fifteenth-century education. Two of them are compilations of grammars, the *Auctores Octo*, and other school texts. One thirteenth-century collection contains Virgil's *Bucolics*; another, dating from the late fourteenth or early fifteenth centuries, includes texts of the *Opuscula*. Both of these compilations

---

[49] On the content and development of the collection, see Vincent Gillespie, 'The Study of Classical Authors from the Twelfth Century to c. 1450', in *Cambridge History of Literary Criticism, Volume 2, The Middle Ages*, ed. A.J. Minnis and I. Johnson (Cambridge: CUP, 2005), pp. 145–235 (pp. 150–60). On their use in England, see Nicholas Orme, 'Schools and School-books', in *CHBB: III*, pp. 449–69 (p. 456); and his *English Schools in the Middle Ages* (London: Methuen, 1973), pp. 102–6. On the circulation of such collections, see also Christopher Cannon, *From Literacy to Literature: England, 1300–1400* (Oxford: OUP, 2016), pp. 41–4.
[50] On Italian use of *Auctores Octo*, see Black, *Humanism and Education*, pp. 218–22, 225–36.
[51] On Seward, see Clark, *Monastic Renaissance*, pp. 218–26.
[52] For his disputes on metrical topics, see his *Invectivae* in Edinburgh University Library, MS 136, fols 189v–203v, 206r–12r, 217r–20r, including citations of Virgil at fols 190r, 196r.

have fifteenth-century extensions, indicating their continued use. Their only annotations were written by the scribes, covering the conventional array of linguistic topics. The scribes write interlinear glosses to lexis, and their marginalia explain points of grammar and historical allusions.[53] Other Virgil manuscripts might have been used in schools, but there is no material evidence to prove it definitively. Besides these surviving manuscripts, Virgil leaves only a few other traces of educational use. For example, the 1405 inventory of books at Winchester College lists a copy of Virgil, no longer extant.[54] A notebook from the school, dating from the late fifteenth century, contains a series of verse arguments to the *Aeneid*.[55] This scattered evidence indicates that Virgil was indeed studied in the fifteenth century, although not widely. To study Virgil was the choice of particular institutions and individual schoolmasters. Only with the influence of humanist curricula did it become a standard practice across the country.

The earliest evidence of humanist teaching in English schools dates from the last quarter of the fifteenth century, the leading centre being Magdalen College School, Oxford. William Waynflete, bishop of Winchester, founded the school in 1480 to advance the *studia humanitatis*. The early headmasters, John Anwykyll (d. 1487) and John Stanbridge (1463–1510), famously wrote the earliest English humanist grammars. Influenced by grammarians Niccolò Perotti and Lorenzo Valla, they illustrated grammatical rules with examples from the classical authors, including Terence, Cicero and Virgil.[56] Although Virgil is not among the school's known books, the masters at Magdalen College School almost certainly taught his works. A surviving manuscript, probably written by one of the masters around 1512–1527, contains a set of grammar exercises, one of which reads:

Auspicaberis-ne tu illum librum Maronis quem ceteri ex condiscipulis auspicaturi sunt videris mihi minime maturus ei audiendo. Primo enim grammatices rudimenta non-dum intelligis, quibus ignoratis nec in hoc nec in vllo poetarum opere proficere possis.[57]

---

[53] BL, MS Harley 4967; BodL, MS Digby 100. For discussion, see Chapter 3, pp. 88–9.
[54] *MLGB3*, SC330.90d.   [55] BodL, MS Bodley 487, fols 48v-50v.
[56] For surveys of early humanist education in England, see James P. Carley and Ágnes Juhász-Ormsby, 'Survey of Henrician Humanism', in *OHCREL: I*, pp. 515–40 (pp. 517–24); Orme, *English Schools*, pp. 106–15; Orme, 'Schools and Schoolbooks', pp. 449–69 (pp. 458–69).
[57] BL, Royal MS 12.B.xx, fol. 49v. For a full text of the exercises, see Nicholas Orme, *English School Exercises, 1420–1530* (Toronto: Pontifical Institute of Mediaeval Studies, 2013), pp. 378–414. The Latin quote is from p. 414, and Orme's translation reads: 'Are you ready to begin the book of Maro which the rest of your school-fellows are ready to begin? You seem to

As in previous decades, the uptake of classical teaching probably remained scattered. Even as late as the 1510s, it would have been dependent on the preferences of particular masters, rather than standard across the whole country. Besides the growing influx of print editions, one of the surviving Virgil manuscripts was likely used in schools of the period. Written around 1500, it contains Virgil's *Bucolics* with another common school text, Aesop's *Fabulae*.[58]

The beginnings of humanist teaching in Scotland probably came at around the same time, but understanding of Scottish education prior to 1500 is hampered by lack of evidence.[59] The earliest reference to teaching the *Aeneid* appears in a dedication-poem at the end of Gavin Douglas's *Eneados* (1513). Douglas suggests that his translation might be of use to schoolmasters:

> Ane othir profit of our buke I mark,
> That it salbe reput a neidfull wark
> To thame wald Virgill to childryn expone;
> For quha lyst note my versys, one by one,
> Sall fynd tharin hys sentens euery deill,
> And al maste word by word, that wait I weill.
> Thank me tharfor, masteris of grammar sculys,
> Quhar 3e syt techand on 3our benkis and stulys.
>   ('Direction', ll. 41–8)[60]

It is difficult to say whether Douglas himself would have studied Virgil at grammar school. He would have attended school in the 1480s, the same time as historians traditionally date the early beginnings of English humanist pedagogy. The evidence of the *Eneados*, nonetheless, suggests that Douglas knew grammar schools teaching the *Aeneid* by 1513. For the previous decade, he had been provost of St Giles Church at the centre of

---

me not at all ready to hear it. First of all, you do not yet understand the rudiments of grammar, being ignorant of which you will not be able to make progress either in this or in any work of the poets.'
    [58] Shrewsbury College, MS IV, described in Baswell, *Virgil in Medieval England*, p. 308. Evidence for the scattered, gradual increase in teaching classical texts will be given in Chapter 3.
    [59] John Durkan, 'Education in the Century of the Reformation', *Innes Review* 10 (1959), 67–90, begins at *c.* 1500. More recent is his *Scottish Schools and Schoolmasters, 1560–1633*, ed. and rev. J. Reid-Baxter, Scottish Historical Society (Woodbridge: Boydell, 2013).
    [60] For the edition, see Chapter 5, fn. 1.

Edinburgh, and this urban setting might have been one of the earlier sites of the New Learning in Scotland.

The first extant curricula of English schools date from the early sixteenth century, and widely include Virgil. Two of the early curricula appear in John Colet's founding statutes for St Paul's School (1509), and Thomas Wolsey's for Ipswich Grammar School (1523).[61] Further curricula were written at the re-founding of Cuckfield School, Sussex (1528), and by the masters of Eton (c. 1529–1531) and Winchester (c. 1529–1531).[62] Colet's statutes are the only curricula not to have Virgil. They exclude all pagan poetry, and instead prescribe the Christian Latin authors Sedulius and Prudentius. Virgil appears only through the *Cento* of Proba, in which his poetry is thoroughly accommodated to Christian morals.[63] The subsequent curricula, however, all name Virgil among the set-texts, usually as one of the more advanced authors. In the Eton curriculum, for instance, students first read Virgil's *Bucolics* in the fourth form, in tandem with Terence. By that time, they had already learned basic grammar, and had read Aesop, Cato and hymns. The *Aeneid*, meanwhile, was reserved for the fifth, sixth and seventh forms. These older students had started to learn rhetoric, and were also studying Horace, Sallust and Cicero. Much like Magdalen College School, no Eton student was ripe to hear Virgil until he had mastered the rudiments of grammar.

As well as an increase in Virgilian schooling, the fifteenth century saw the more widespread study of the authors in English universities. The earliest reference to Virgil in the statutes of the University of Oxford occurs in the well-known 1431 statutes for the Faculty of Arts. Unlike the earlier statutes of 1268 and 1409,[64] the statutes of 1431 detail the lecture-texts for each of

---

[61] For St Paul's, see Nicholas Carlisle, *A Concise Description of the Endowed Grammar Schools in England and Wales*, 6 vols (London: Baldwin, Craddock and Joy, 1818), II, pp. 71–81 (esp. pp. 76–7). For Ipswich, T. W. Baldwin, *William Shakespere's Small Latine & Lesse Greeke*, 2 vols (Urbana: University of Illinois Press, 1944), pp. 123–5.

[62] On Cuckfield, see Carlisle, *Endowed Grammar Schools*, II, pp. 594–7. For Winchester and Eton, see Baldwin, *Small Latine*, pp. 135–43. A 1541 curriculum survives from Canterbury Grammar School, but does not explicitly mention Virgil. See Baldwin, *Small Latine*, pp. 164–8. In Scotland, the 1553 statutes of Aberdeen Grammar School mention Virgil, Terence and Cicero, but do not detail a full curriculum. See *Records and Reminiscenses of Aberdeen Grammar School*, ed. H.F.M. Simpson (Aberdeen: D. Wyllie and Son, 1906), p. 98.

[63] By the mid-century, however, the teaching at St Pauls was in line with the other extant school curricula. In the 1558 curriculum, Virgil's *Bucolics* are read in the sixth form, *Aeneid* in the seventh. See Michael McDonnell, *The Annals of St. Paul's School* (Cambridge: Privately printed for the Governors, 1959), p. 75–7.

[64] For the 1268 and 1409 statutes, see *Statuta Antiqua Universitatis Oxoniensis*, ed. Strickland Gibson (Oxford: Clarendon Press, 1931), pp. 25–7, 199–204. The lists of texts are on pp. 25–6 and p. 200.

the seven Arts. Virgil is one of five possible lecture-texts for the rhetoric component: 'videlicet *Rethoricam* Aristotelis, seu quartum *Topicorum* Boecii, aut Tullum in noua Rethorica, vel Ouidium *Methamorphoseos* siue poetriam Virgilii'.[65] Although possibly a sign of early humanist influence, this statute does not attest to widespread teaching of Virgil, especially since Virgil is only one of five potential options.[66] The teaching of poets, moreover, is uncharacteristic of fifteenth- and sixteenth-century Arts courses, considering that Virgil is not mentioned in comparable statutes at other British universities. Rhetoric was generally taught from a dedicated rhetorical textbook, not from reading poetry.[67] Lists of lecture-texts in later Oxford statutes, for example in 1549 and 1564/5, mention neither the poetry of Virgil nor Ovid, only the rhetorics of Aristotle, Cicero, Quintilian and Hermogenes.[68] In this light, J.M. Fletcher has suggested that the 1431 Arts statutes were an attempt to appease an illustrious benefactor, Humphrey, Duke of Gloucester. Known for his patronage of humanist studies, he had written to the university asking for reforms, and would make large donations of books in the 1430s.[69] Lectures on Terence and Virgil are recorded in the Oxford University registers (for example, in 1508 and 1510), but classical poets were not regular lecture-texts during this period.[70]

Even so, students still had access to written copies of Virgil. Manuscript holdings in universities, probably reflecting the interests of donors more

---

[65] The full 1431 statutes are in *Statuta Antiqua Universitatis Oxoniensis*, pp. 233–8. This quotation, which covers the *trivium* only, is from p. 234.

[66] For a summary of scholarly discussion of this statute, see J.O Ward, 'Rhetoric in the Faculty of Arts at the Universities of Paris and Oxford in the Middle Ages: A Summary of the Evidence', *Archivum Latinitatis Medii Aevi* (Union Académique Internationale: Bulletin Du Cange) 54 (1996), 159–231 (183–8).

[67] For lecture-texts at Cambridge, see *Statuta academiæ Cantabrigiensis* (Cambridge: J. Archdeacon, 1785), pp. 137–8, 179, 227–8 (all sixteenth-century, none with Virgil). At St Andrews, see *Acta Facultatis Artium Universitatis Sanctiandree, 1413-1588*, ed. Annie I. Dunlop, 2 vols (Edinburgh: T. & A. Constable, Printers to the University of Edinburgh, for the Scottish History Society, 1964). Although there are no systematic lists of lecture-texts, the only texts mentioned at St Andrews are Aristotle and Cicero (e.g. I, p. 15 (1419), 40 (1435)).

[68] *Statuta Antiqua Universitatis Oxoniensis*, pp. 343–4, 378. A second list of lecture-texts from 1564/5, pp. 389–90, lists Virgil under grammar rather than rhetoric.

[69] J.M. Fletcher, 'Developments in the Faculty of Arts 1370-1520', in *The History of the University of Oxford: Volume II: Late Medieval Oxford*, ed. J. I. Catto and T. A. R. Evans (Oxford: OUP, 1992), pp. 315–45 (pp. 323–5).

[70] *Register of Congregations, 1505-1517*, ed. W.T. Mitchell, 2 vols (Oxford: Oxford Historical Society,1998), II, pp. 1, 122; Fletcher, 'Developments in the Faculty of Arts', p. 343. Outside the Arts Faculty, there might have been Virgil lectures in certain college halls. For example, see *The Foundation Statutes of Bishop Fox for Corpus Christi College, in the University of Oxford, A.D. 1517: Now First Translated into English, With a Life of the Founder*, trans. G.R.M. Ward (London: Longman, Brown, Green, and Longmans, 1843), p. 100.

than the needs of the faculty, gradually increased throughout the period. As Baswell has observed, it was common for high medieval Virgil manuscripts to end up in university college libraries in the fifteenth and sixteenth centuries.[71] One extant Virgil manuscript was in Cambridge by 1418, and a further five were donated to Oxford and Cambridge by 1550. The donations included the manuscripts of several early English humanists: Grey, Flemmyng, and Russell.[72] One surviving manuscript of the *Opera*, now in Peterhouse, Cambridge, was most likely produced in the city itself. A single scribe, working in the late fifteenth or early sixteenth century, wrote the entire text with extensive glossing. He was probably a scholar or student at the university, and made the book for his personal use. He also glossed an incunabular copy of Juvenal and Persius, and a contemporary Cambridge binder then bound both volumes together.[73] As typical of other Virgil manuscripts, the scribe's exegesis has a grammatical and rhetorical focus, both in the Virgil sections and the satires. It consists of dense interlinear glosses, notes on rhetorical figures, and excerpts from Servius's commentary. His glossing, though likely produced for university-level study, thus followed the conventional pedagogic procedures of the *enarratio poetarum*.[74]

This stability, as this broad survey has shown, is witnessed across all extant Virgil manuscripts. Glossing procedures remained consistent throughout the long fifteenth century and in a range of reading-contexts. Although there are differences between individual annotators, these differences do not amount to persistent trends. They do not evince historical changes in the study of Virgil, nor do they correlate with different groups of readers. Glosses on basic grammar and lexis, for instance, are as common

---

[71] Baswell, *Virgil in Medieval England*, p. 47.

[72] Peterhouse, MS 158 is in the 1418 college catalogue as *MLGB3*, UC48.*231 (Baswell, *Virgil in Medieval England*, pp. 292–4). The five donated manuscripts are: Oxford, All Souls College, MS 82 (donated in 1438); Cambridge, Pembroke College, MS 260 (donated in mid-fifteenth century); Oxford, New College, MS 271 (Russell); SJC, MS 54 (Flemmyng); Oxford, Balliol College, MS 140 (Grey). Flemmyng's manuscript appears in the Lincoln College, Oxford inventory of 1474 (*MLGB3*, UO25.¶71). Cambridge, Jesus College, MS 33 (John Free's manuscript) was donated to Jesus College in the later sixteenth century, probably 1570s (Baswell, *Virgil in Medieval England*, p. 294–5). In *MLGB3*, five more Virgils appear in lists of university donations 1400–1550: S30.¶1 (St Andrew's, 1496); UC165.10 (Cambridge, 1503); UO24.¶4 (CCC, Oxford, early s.xvi); UO25.¶71 (CCC, Oxford, 1520); UC22.¶30 (CCC, Cambridge, 1525). The later copies are probably printed books, UO24.¶4 almost certainly. Four further copies, possibly MS or print, appear in inventories: UO6.*171 (All Souls, c. 1443); UC29.163 (King's, c. 1457); UO15.¶84 (All Souls, early s.xvi); UO43.¶28 (Lincoln, 1543).

[73] Cambridge, Peterhouse, MS 159. On the binding, see Baswell, *Virgil in Medieval England*, p. 308.

[74] The next chapter will discuss corroborating evidence in print editions.

among learned clergymen as in schoolroom manuscripts. University and school students often marked rhetorical figures, but this apparatus was also a standard feature of scribal layout. In the vast majority of cases, the intellectual content of Virgil glosses does not provide reliable evidence of their date or context of use. Although there are differences of script, the glosses' subject-matter would not allow us to distinguish different strata of annotations through the centuries.

Types of Annotations

Virgilian glossing was particularly consistent due to the pervasive influence of Servius. A grammarian by profession, Servius wrote his commentary as an aid to his teaching, and it became the foundation for the subsequent study of Virgil's texts. Servius was not only a source for interpretations of particular lines, but also a general model for pedagogic exposition of the poets. Up to the sixteenth century, his practice of commentary was a template for the *enarratio poetarum*. The influence of humanism, with its specific focus on classical Latin, only increased his importance. Owing to his early date, the humanists considered Servius a principal source of classical grammar and lexicography as well as a model of classical exegetic practice. From the early Middle Ages to the humanists, grammatical exegesis of Virgil largely consisted of excerpting, supplementing, and imitating this foundational commentary.[75]

Servius's influence is witnessed throughout fifteenth-century manuscripts of the *Aeneid*, and many glosses are verbatim excerpts of the commentary. One example now resides in the library of Trinity College, Cambridge.[76] A single scribe, probably of the mid-fifteenth century, wrote the *Aeneid* text in several stints with a neat cursive hand. The first folio bears two ownership signatures, 'Iohannes Walsynghames' and 'John Raynoldes'. The latter, Baswell suggests, might be the same 'John Raynolds' who was a sixteenth-century Oxford graduate and Dominican friar (fl. 1513–1549).[77] Several fifteenth-century hands make annotations, and a sixteenth-century reader added a few

---

[75] On Servius's pervasive influence on manuscript glossing, see Baswell, *Virgil in Medieval England*, pp. 47–53.
[76] TCC, MS R.1.40, described at Baswell, *Virgil in Medieval England*, p. 305.
[77] BRUO 1501–1540, p. 477.

scattered glosses, possibly Rainoldes.[78] The earliest, most comprehensive annotation, however, is in the hand of the original scribe. Considering that the annotations contain an unusually high number of syntactic glosses, the scribe might have intended the manuscript for a more basic learner, but this is only speculation. The majority of annotations are concentrated in the first six books of the *Aeneid*, and this focus is typical of both manuscripts and print editions. Possibly the scribe copied the annotations from an earlier manuscript, or possibly he composed some of the glosses independently. Whichever is the case, they show pervasive reference to Servius's commentary.

Interlinear glosses, elucidating the letter of the text, are the most common type of annotation in Virgil manuscripts. Most annotated manuscripts have at least a few interlinear glosses. In the Trinity manuscript, for example, the scribe provided an initial layer of glossing, and several other hands supplemented it over the fifteenth and sixteenth centuries. The scribe's glosses on the opening lines read:

ego virgili*us*
.i. bella .i. eneam   .i. canto   .s. eneas   .i. finibus
Arma viru*m* q*ue* cano troie qui pri*mus* ab oris

ad .i. p*er* fatu*m*   .i. p*er*   accessit
Italiam fato p*ro*fugus lauina q*ue* venit

.i. fatigat*us*   .i. p*ro*fundo mare
Littora. multu*m* ille *et* terris iactat*us* et alto

.i. deor*um*   .i. memorata*m*   propter
Vi sup*erum*. seue memore*m* iunonis ob iram.

(*Aeneid*, I.1–4)[79]

Some of the glosses are excerpts of Servius, while others were produced independently. Servius, for instance, interprets 'arma' ('arms') as a metonymy for 'bella' ('wars'), and identifies 'virum' as Aeneas. As with here, these two interpretations are typically the first glosses in *Aeneid* manuscripts.[80]

---

[78] The sixteenth-century glosses are on fols 2r, 10r, etc. The same hand adds the last few lines of *Aeneid* XII on 203v.

[79] TCC, MS R.1.40, fol. 2r. Because of limited space, I have omitted several non-scribal glosses: 'cano'/'et describo', 'profugus'/'exul', 'alto'/'per', 'Vi'/'violencia', 'seve'/'.i. magne'.

[80] On 'arma' and 'virum', Servius writes 'per "arma" autem bellum significat, et est tropus metonymia', and 'quem non dicit, sed circumstantiis ostendit Aeneam'. 'Arma virumque' was also interpreted as a hendiadys for 'armatum virum', for example in the twelfth-century commentary ascribed to Anselm of Laon (cited below). On the 'Anselm' commentary, see

'Cano', Servius goes on, is a polysemous term with three meanings, 'laudo', 'divino' or 'canto' ('praise', 'prophesy', 'sing'). He prioritizes the third of these meanings, and the Trinity scribe copies it in his gloss.[81] In the fourth line, Servius also helped the glossator elucidate the obscure phrase 'memorem iram'. Although it literally means 'mindful anger' or 'remembering anger', the transferred epithet 'memorem' properly applies to Juno, harbouring her long grudge against the Trojans. As Servius puts it, Virgil does not mean 'the anger which had remembered', but 'the anger which was in her memory'.[82] The glossator condenses this explanation into the pithy gloss 'memoratam iram', 'the anger which had been remembered'. Servius thus helps the annotator to clarify Virgil's figurative, often ambiguous diction.

Where Servius does not provide an explanation, the scribe improvises glosses of his own. Servius, after all, does not explain every detail of the literal sense, and his exposition clusters around the more complex points of language. Manuscript annotators, however, often parsed the grammar in greater detail. The scribe of the Trinity manuscript is particularly thorough, making glosses to almost every line. Besides figurative and poetic expressions, his glosses cover even the slightest grammatical ambiguities, diligently elucidating the literal sense. For instance, he commonly specifies unclear referents, and supplies elided terms. He clarifies that 'ego Virgilius' is the subject of 'cano', and that 'virum' and 'qui' refer to Aeneas. A little later, he adds the prepositions 'ad' for the locative 'Italiam', and 'per' for 'lauina littora'. The gloss 'per fatum' ('through fate'), likewise, specifies the meaning of 'fato', distinguishing a particular use of the ablative case. As typical of glossators, he uses synonyms to expound items of vocabulary. When the lemma is a general or polyvalent term, the gloss will specify a particular meaning, as when glossing the more general 'venit' ('came') with 'accessit' ('reached'). For the more obscure vocabulary, meanwhile, the expositor opts for a simpler, generalized option, such as 'deorum' for 'superum'. While none of these glosses are controversial, the scribe clearly took time to clarify even simple ambiguities in the grammar and lexis.

Baswell, *Virgil in Medieval England*, pp. 63–8; and his 'Master Anselm', in *The Virgilian Tradition*, ed. Putnam and Ziolkowski, pp. 717–21. My quotations are from the text in BL, MS Add. 16,380 (Rochester, s.xii).

[81] Servius: 'cano polysemus sermo est. tria enim significat: aliquando laudo...aliquando divino...aliquando canto, ut in hoc loco'. A later annotator of the Trinity manuscript supplemented the scribe's 'canto' with another gloss of 'describo'. This gloss is found in the Anselm commentary ('cano .i. metrice describo', BL, MS Add. 16,380, fol. 2r), and was widespread in glossed Virgil manuscripts. Gavin Douglas uses it for the first line of the *Eneados*.

[82] Servius: 'non quae meminerat, sed quae in memoria erat.'

Subsequent annotators, both in the fifteenth and sixteenth centuries, added to the work of the main scribe. Much like the scribal glossing, the content of their annotations shows the same combination of Servian excerption and independent improvisation. For example, one later annotator glossed 'vi superum' with Servius's 'vio*le*ncia deorum'. Likewise, 'seve Iunonis' ('of cruel Juno') is glossed 'magnae' ('great'), because (Servius says) 'the ancients used to say "saevus" as "magnus"'.[83] Improvising on Servius, this later annotator went on to gloss 'alto' (metonymically, 'the deep sea') with '*per*' ('through', 'across'). Similar to 'fato', his explanation suggests a locational use of the adverb, since Aeneas was tossed *across* the seas. As with the main scribe, it is difficult to distinguish whether all the non-Servian glosses are the annotator's own. Rather than composing them himself, he might have copied his annotations from another glossed manuscript. Whichever is the case, the very activity of interlinear glossing would have facilitated a close attention to the grammar and lexis. The production of the glosses forced the later annotator to analyse the construction of the text with greater precision. Even if he merely copied the glosses from another source, the process focused his reading on the word-for-word interpretation of the language, from the ablative in 'alto' to the semantic range of 'saevus'.

Interlinear glossing, with close reference to Servius, was common to readers at all levels of study. Neither the frequency nor the complexity of the glosses necessarily correlates with an annotator's linguistic ability. Well-educated readers sometimes made hundreds of such interlinear glosses even to the most basic words.[84] The early English humanists, as already discussed, furnished their manuscripts of classical authors with hundreds of interlinear glosses. Bishops such as John Russell still conducted this pedagogic process despite already being proficient in Latin. Interlinear glossing, while learnt in the schoolroom, was a habitual practice in their reading. The glossed manuscript above, likewise, circulated in clerical circles, probably among friars. Although they might have used the manuscript in teaching, their glosses could equally derive from private study of the text. No intellectual aspect of the glossing precludes either conclusion. After all, Virgil's compressed, ambiguous language presented challenges even to advanced readers. The practice of glossing was a useful tool to structure the reading process, and to focus the reader on Virgil's exact grammatical meaning.

---

[83] Servius: 'quod saevam dicebant veteres magnam'.
[84] Further examples are in Chapter 2.

Longer explanations, both among scribes and later annotators, are written as marginal glosses. Their topics include summaries and paraphrases of the plot, points of grammar and lexicography, and references to ancient customs, geography, history, and mythology. As with the interlinear glosses, Servius remains the principal source. The producers of these glosses must have been reading Virgil and Servius side-by-side, since they directly copy passages into the manuscript. For example, when Virgil mentions the mythical king Rhesus (*Aeneid* I.469), the scribe copies Servius's short biography, describing his divine lineage and death at Troy.[85] It clarifies why the lesser-known Rhesus is mentioned in the context of Achilles and Diomede. While the Rhesus exposition is a verbatim copy from the commentary, most of the other glosses are excerpts or paraphrases, significantly shorter than Servius's original. For instance, when Virgil alludes to the myth of Penthesilea (*Aeneid* I.491), the scribe excerpts one sentence of Servius's exposition, describing why she is described as 'furens'.[86] This activity of excerpting and paraphrasing is typical of Virgil annotators, and most sets of marginal glosses shows this selective use of Servius.[87] It is sometimes possible to discern interests in particular subject matter. Baswell, for example, has discussed a fourteenth-century annotator who copies Servius's explanations of references to ancient religion.[88] As with the interlinear glosses, the use of Servius was not slavish copying, but involved selection and discrimination.

A prominent, and often understated, theme is grammar, lexicography, and etymology. Whereas Baswell, for example, concentrates on historical and mythological annotations, linguistic topics were equally prominent, such as the usage of 'impleor' or the definition of 'fores'.[89] The Trinity scribe, like many others, commonly copies *differentiae verborum*, definitions distinguishing two synonymous terms. Servius's commentary contains many examples, and he distils them into pithy, memorizable maxims. They are often marked in manuscripts of the commentary, and copied in the margins of Virgil manuscripts. For example, the Trinity annotator excerpts:

---

[85] TCC, MS R.1.40, fol. 12v.
[86] TCC, MS R.1.40, fol. 13r. Copied from Servius, the scribe's gloss reads: '<u>Penthesilea</u> d*icitur* furens. q*uod* s*ororem* sua*m* in venac*i*one confixit simulans se cervam ferire'.
[87] Baswell, *Virgil in Medieval England*, pp. 47–63, describes this process of excerpting and paraphrasing Servius. Besides the Trinity manuscript, good fifteenth-century examples include: SAL, MS 44 (scribe's interlinear and marginal glosses to the *Georgics*); and Peterhouse, MS 159 (scribe's glosses throughout).
[88] Oxford, All Souls College, MS 82. Baswell, *Virgil in Medieval England*, pp. 68–83.
[89] In TCC, R.1.40, these glosses are to *Aeneid* I.215 and I.449 (fols 6r, 12r), and both are copied from Servius.

Pollicem*ur* sponte.
Pr*o*mittim*us* rogati.

(Gloss to *Aeneid* I.237)[90]

Servius originally composed his memorizable *differentiae* for grammar students, but his lexicographic insights ultimately had broader appeal. As Chapter 2 will show in more detail, the distinctions of 'pollicemur' and 'promittimus' were copied by adult clergymen and university scholars as well as schoolboys. Not only did these insights elucidate the meaning of the text, but they also provided practical guidance in speaking and writing Latin. Given the widespread use of Latin in the Church, law and government, the reading of a classical author was a means to practise one's skills. The influence of humanism, promoting the use of classical idiom, only increased the utility of such reading.

Just as the interlinear glosses improvise outside of Servius's commentary, so too do the marginal glosses. The scribe, like many contemporaries, supplements Servius's expositions with other sources. For example, his marginal gloss on 'ardet' is copied from John of Garland's *Aequivoca*, a verse vocabulary written in the twelfth century. It was a common school text in England up to the beginning of the 1500s, probably chanted by the pupils.[91] Every line of the poem introduces a polyvalent term, listing its multiple senses. For 'ardeo', Garland includes its proper meaning of 'burn', and then its common figurative usages 'hurry' and 'desire'. After quoting the line, the scribe then selects an appropriate option for his interlinear gloss:

versus / Ardeo festino. cupio. cremo. splen*d*eo. demo. /

.i. festinat
Pentesilea furens. mediis qu*e* in milib*us* ardet

(*Aeneid* I.491)[92]

---

[90] The gloss is on TCC, MS R.1.40, fol. 6v, and is copied verbatim from Servius's commentary on I.237. It translates 'We promise [pollicemur] of our own accord; we promise [promittimus] when asked'. In the Trinity manuscript, further examples copied from Servius include: 'Dissimulam*us* nota. | Simulam*us* ignota.' (fol. 13v; on *Aeneid* I.516); 'Angues s*unt* aquar*um*. serpen | tes t*er*rarum. dracones te*m*plorum.' (fol. 24v; on *Aeneid* II.204).
[91] On his grammatical works, see G.L. Bursill-Hall, 'Johannes de Garlandia—Forgotten Grammarian and the Manuscript Tradition', *Historiographia Linguistica* 3 (1976), 155–77.
[92] TCC, MS R.1.40, fol. 13r. The manuscript also has an interlinear gloss '.i. regina' for 'Pentesilea'. Fairclough translates the Virgil as, 'Penthesilea in fury leads the crescent-shielded ranks of the Amazons and blazes amid her thousands', and the gloss reads, 'Verse: I burn; I hurry; I desire; I burn; I shine; I remove'.

Much like Servius's pollicemur/promittimus *differentia*, Garland intended his verse vocabulary to be memorizable, and this Virgilian example demonstrates its usefulness in reading the authors. When the student encountered a difficult word in Virgil, he needed only recall the relevant line of *Aequivoca*, and Garland's definition supplied him with several potential meanings. The use of *Aequivoca*, in this case, might derive from the scribe's memory from his school days. Alternatively, he might have been preparing the manuscript for school use, showing his pupils how to deploy their knowledge of Garland.

While annotations of grammar and lexicography are common in Virgil manuscripts, the Trinity scribe is unusual for his frequent discussions of syntax. To assist readers' comprehension of difficult passages, commentators and glossators demonstrated how the 'artificial' word-order of the poets (*ordo artificialis*) could be rearranged into more natural syntax (*ordo naturalis*).[93] In manuscripts, the most common device for clarifying these difficult lines are construe marks. The annotator shows the natural order by writing numbers above the Latin words, for example:

 2   5   6   1   2   3   6   4
Vna dolo diuum si fe*mi*na victa duoru*m* est.

(*Aeneid*, IV.95)[94]

Besides construe marks, the Trinity scribe also makes marginal glosses on Virgil's syntax. The Trinity copy contains more of these glosses than any other extant Virgil manuscript from England. For example:

**Vina bon*us* que dein*de* cadis onerarat accestes
Litore t*ri*nacrio / dederatq*ue* abeuntib*us* heros
Dividit.**

Sic ordi*na*. dein*de* diu*i*di*t* vina
q*ue* bonus heros acestes
onerarat cadis litore
trinacrio *et* dederat abeu*n*tib*us*.

(*Aeneid* I.195–7)[95]

---

[93] On syntactic annotations, see Reynolds, *Medieval Reading*, pp. 97–120.
[94] TCC, MS R.1.40, fol. 55v. Fairclough translates: 'If one woman is subdued by the guile of two gods'.
[95] TCC, MS R.1.40, fol. 6r. The Trinity scribe originally had 'onerauerat' for I.195, but a later annotator corrected it to 'onerarat'. Fairclough translates: 'Next he shares the wine, which good Acestes had stowed in jars on the Trinacrian shore, and hero-like had given at parting.'

These glosses, beginning with the imperative 'ordina', perform the same function as construe marks. Rather than using numbers, they rewrite the whole line in the margins. Although several expositions of the 'ordo' appear in Servius's commentary, most of the Trinity examples were composed independently.[96] Given the quantity of syntactic glosses, the scribe possibly intended the manuscript for a readership of basic learners. Should they not have a teacher to explain and answer questions, they would need greater assistance in comprehending Virgil's intricate syntax.

While attending closely to grammatical construction, the Trinity manuscript has no allegorical glosses. The scarcity of allegory is typical of *Aeneid* annotations in general, both in manuscripts and in printed books. This wider aspect of Virgilian exegesis probably reflects the dispositions of Servius's commentary. Servius (as noted above) directs the majority of his exposition at expounding lexicography, grammar, and allusions to history and myth. While allegorical exegesis falls within his remit as a grammarian, his allegories are few in number and limited in scope. They pertain exclusively to particular lines and passages, and do not encompass the *Aeneid* as a whole.[97] Most of the later commentaries on Virgil follow these Servian precedents, and have only scattered allegorical content. For example, a twelfth-century commentary, commonly attributed to Anselm of Laon, includes short Christianizing allegories, but the majority of the material remains grammatical in focus.[98] Only three English manuscripts of the *Aeneid* contain allegorical glossing, two of which are discussed by Baswell. A fourteenth-century annotator makes short, Christianizing allegories of certain episodes, while two twelfth-century manuscripts have moral and physical allegories of the pagan gods.[99] Although evidently in circulation, allegorical interpretations were not a standard feature of *Aeneid* glossing. If readers chose to pick up their pens, they were concerned with the literal rather than allegorical sense.

---

[96] For example, Servius on *Aeneid* I.109 reads: 'ordo est, quae saxa in mediis fluctibus Itali aras vocant'. The Trinity scribe, however, does not use the 'ordo est' or 'sic ordina' formula for this line, but instead uses construe marks.

[97] For a list of allegorical passages in Servius, see J.W. Jones, 'Allegorical Interpretation in Servius', *The Classical Journal* 56 (1961), 217–26.

[98] On the allegorical content of the 'Anselm' commentary, see Andrew Kraebel, 'Biblical Exegesis and the Twelfth-Century Expansion of Servius', in *Classical Commentary: Explorations in a Scholarly Genre*, ed. Christina Kraus and Christopher Stray (Oxford: OUP, 2016), pp. 419–34.

[99] Respectively, BL, MS Add. 27,304; BL, MS Add. 32319A; Cambridge, Peterhouse, MS 158. See Baswell, *Virgil in Medieval England*, pp. 84–167, 292–4, 295–6, 298.

Although some commentators produced extended, book-length allegories for the first six books of the *Aeneid*, they typically set down these interpretations in dedicated allegorical treatises and commentaries. Well-known examples are Fulgentius's *Expositio Virgilianae continentiae secundum philosophos moralis* (late fifth or early sixth century), the Platonizing commentary attributed to Bernard Silvestris (twelfth century), and the *Disputationes Camuldulenses* by the humanist scholar Cristoforo Landino (c. 1473-4).[100] Only rarely did commentators integrate this extended allegoresis in grammatical-rhetorical commentaries. Thirteen years after the *Disputationes*, for example, Landino produced a line-by-line Virgil commentary for print publication. In his preface, he sharply distinguishes between the philosophical-allegorical mode of interpretation in the *Disputationes* and the rhetorical-grammatical exposition in the 1487 commentary.[101] Although his Platonizing allegorical interpretations appear throughout the line-by-line exposition, he often refers his readers to the longer discussions in his earlier, specialized *Disputationes*. The bulk of the commentary consists of lexicography, rhetoric, history and myth, following the Servian model. For Landino, then, the *Disputationes* and 1487 commentary each served distinct functions. The first provided a systematic allegorical exposition, the latter a more conventional *enarratio*.

The *Bucolics*, meanwhile, have a different allegorical tradition from the *Aeneid* and *Georgics*. Since Antiquity, these poems were interpreted as veiled references to Augustan politics. The allegories feature prominently in Servius's commentary, and subsequent commentators repeated and embellished them into the Renaissance. In *Bucolics* I, for example, Virgil is said to allude to Augustus's confiscations of property in his hometown, Mantua. When Meliboeus bemoans the loss of his fields, he allegorically represents the evicted citizens. According to commentators, the poem was Virgil's attempt to shed light on the plight of his fellow Mantuans.[102] The fourth

---

[100] For an overview of medieval allegorical traditions, see Baswell, *Virgil in Medieval England*, pp. 84–135. Landino, writing in the later fifteenth century, drew on Silvestris and other medieval allegorists. On the sources of Landino's *Disputationes*, see Craig Kallendorf, 'Cristoforo Landino's *Aeneid* and the Humanist Critical Tradition', *Renaissance Quarterly* 36 (1983), 519–46.

[101] First edition is *Opera*, comm. Servius, Donatus and Landinus (Florence: [Printer of Vergilius (C 6061)], 18 Mar. 1487/88; *ISTC* iv00183000). In the *Aeneid* preface, Landino writes: 'Nam quemadmodum in chamaldulensibus philosophi interpretis munus obivimus, sic in his commentariis grammatici rhetorisque vices praestabimus' (recto of second unfoliated leaf at beginning of *Aeneid*). In later chapters, this edition will be cited as '*Opera* (1487/8)'.

[102] Servius's interpretation is widely copied in *Bucolics* manuscripts. For a fifteenth-century example, see BL, MS Add. 11,959, fol. 1r.

Eclogue, as is well known, acquired a Christian interpretation, connecting its prophecy of a new Golden Age with the birth of Christ.[103] Whereas the allegories of the *Aeneid* were an infrequent occurrence, every annotated manuscript of the *Bucolics* (known to me) contains allegorical glosses at least in *Bucolics* I. Even the school manuscripts, used in basic literacy training, have allegoresis in the margins.[104] Unlike the allegories of the *Aeneid*, which could be omitted from expositions of the poem, the allegories of the *Bucolics* were considered integral to their interpretation, even for elementary students. These attitudes, as Helen Cooper discussed, shaped later writing in the bucolic genre. Just as commentators universally allegorized Virgil's *Bucolics*, so Petrarch and Boccaccio wove moral and political allegory into their own bucolic poems.[105] In treating allegory as integral to the poem's interpretation, the *Bucolics* commentary tradition is similar to Aesop's *Fabulae*, Theodulus's *Ecloga*, and Ovid's *Metamorphoses*.

More prominent than allegory were annotations to Virgil's rhetoric. Since Late Antiquity, grammarians commonly used their expositions of the poets to introduce rudimentary rhetorical concepts. In Servius's commentary, his most frequent kind of rhetorical teaching is to identify figures and tropes.[106] This activity was a component of the *enarratio poetarum* down to the sixteenth century, both in and out of the schoolroom. As with interlinear glosses, it is unusual for Virgil manuscripts not to have annotations of figures. In the Trinity manuscript, some of these glosses were produced by the Trinity scribe, others by later fifteenth- and sixteenth-century readers. Like other types of glossing, this activity included copying passages from Servius's commentary and supplementing it with independent observations.[107] Whereas the Trinity scribe writes names of figures in full, some annotators simply use *signes de renvoi*, manicules, underlining, or marks of *Nota*. Unlike the Trinity scribe, their hasty markings were not designed to produce a structural apparatus for later readers. Even so, annotations of both kinds evince the same intellectual

---

[103] On *Bucolics* IV and its allegorical tradition, see *The Virgilian Tradition*, ed. Putnam and Ziolkowski, pp. 487–503, providing sources and bibliography.
[104] BL, MS Add. 11,959; BL, MS Harley 4967.
[105] Helen Cooper, *Pastoral: Mediaeval into Renaissance* (Cambridge: D.S. Brewer, 1977), pp. 36–46.
[106] On grammarians' teaching of rhetorical figures, see survey in Reynolds, *Medieval Reading*, pp. 121–34.
[107] In TCC, MS R.1.40, glosses to figures include the following from Servius: 'sincopam' (fol. 2v; I.26, on 'repostum'); 'pleonasmus' (fol. 6r; I.208); 'eclipsis *est* color' (fol. 4v; I.135, but Servius calls it aposiopoesis). Glosses not from Servius include: 'ypalage' (fol. 4r; I.103); 'Exclamac*io est* color rhet*oricus*' (fol. 4r; I.94); 'c*om*paracio' (fol. 11v; I.430); 'Themesis' (fol. 15v; I.610, referring to 'Que...cumque').

concerns, mainly covering eloquent turns of phrase and a few moral *sententiae*. As with the grammatical glosses, this rhetorical analysis not only aided comprehension of the text, but could also have a practical purpose in honing one's language-skills. While schoolboys needed to use rhetorical figures for schoolroom exercises, so too did adults writing political orations and correspondence. Scribes and annotators, in particular, marked the beginnings of speeches. Not only did annotations such as 'Oratio iunonis' and 'Aeneas loquitur' serve a practical, structural function, but speeches were also a major focus of study. Servius, throughout his commentary, uses speeches to introduce and demonstrate basic rhetorical terminology, such as parts of orations and topics of argument.[108] Servius makes his first speech analysis when Juno petitions Aeolus to send a storm against Aeneas (I.65-75). The Trinity scribe copies most of Servius's comments in his marginal glosses. In the right hand margin, copying almost verbatim from Servius, the annotator details the particular type of speech, a petition. In the left margin, he identifies the parts of the oration and the *captatio benevolentiae*, again based on Servius's discussion.[109] Another example occurs at the start of Book IV, this time independent of Servius. After Dido tells Anna about her love of Aeneas, Anna has a speech persuading her to pursue her passion (IV.31-53).[110] Anna's first reason, that her love of Aeneas will bring 'praemia Veneris' and 'dulces natos', is marked 'bonum delectabile' (IV.33). The next, that the Trojans can aid Dido against enemy tribes in North Africa, is a 'bonum utile' (IV.40). Finally, the annotator notes a 'bonum honestum', that Trojan aid will make her city rise to greatness (IV.47). This analysis follows the terminology of Ciceronian rhetoric, when students are urged to argue cases 'ab honesto' and 'ab utile'.[111]

In Late Antiquity, this analysis of speeches prepared students for the next stage of the curriculum, the formal teaching of rhetoric. The orations of Aeneas were a training-ground, as it were, for those of Cicero. While many of Cicero's speeches were lost between the ninth and late fourteenth

---

[108] On annotations of speeches, see Marjorie Curry Woods, 'Rhetoric, Gender, and the Literary Arts: Classical Speeches in the Schoolroom', *New Medieval Literatures* 11 (2009), 113-32; Black, *Humanism and Education*, pp. 308-11. Focusing on Italian Virgil manuscripts, they discuss similar examples to those in the Trinity manuscript. The same kinds of rhetorical analysis are seen in sixteenth-century teaching of the poets: Peter Mack, *Elizabethan Rhetoric: Theory and Practice* (Cambridge: CUP, 2002), Ch. 1.

[109] TCC, MS R.1.40, fols 2r-3v. Following Servius, the scribe marks the 'Exordi*um*' beginning at I.65, the 'narracio' at I.67, the 'peticio' at I.69, and the 'Remun*er*acio' at I.71.

[110] TCC, MS R.1.40, fols 54v-5r.

[111] Servius gives a topical analysis of this speech, but it does not, in this instance, use the terms 'honestum' or 'delectabile'. For Servius's analysis, see his commentary to *Aeneid* I.31.

centuries, the rhetorical analysis of the poets continued unabated and widespread. Besides Virgil, similar speech analyses have been identified across various classical and non-classical texts, from Statius's epics to Walter de Châtillon's *Alexandreis*.[112] Scholars of medieval rhetoric have suggested that students used Virgil's speeches for practice in declamation. They might also have referred to poets' orations when composing their own compositions, using them as examples for imitation.[113] The techniques of speech analysis, examining parts and topics of orations, continued unchanged into the late sixteenth century and the seventeenth. Over a hundred years after the production of the Trinity manuscript, a similar terminology of rhetorical analysis appears in the commentaries of Melanchthon and Ramus.[114]

While the practices of glossing classical authors remained consistent, the influence of humanism shifted their disciplinary contexts. Although the original conventions of *enarratio* descended from grammarians such as Servius, the impetus of studying the poets increasingly derived from the discipline of rhetoric as well as grammar. The humanists, after all, promoted the classical authors not only as a standard of grammatical correctness, but also more generally as models of written composition and style. By the sixteenth century, the main theoretical guidance for reading the authors came from rhetoricians, such as Erasmus in *De Copia* and *De Ratione Studii*. The commonplace method, promoted by Erasmus, was designed to facilitate this more rigorous compositional focus in reading of the classics. Melanchthon and Ramus, likewise, devised their commentaries on Virgil for a programme of rhetorical rather than grammatical teaching.[115] This theoretical shift, however, is not reflected in bibliographical evidence of Virgil

---

[112] Woods, 'Rhetoric, Gender, and the Literary Arts'; Black at *Humanism and Education*, pp. 308-11.

[113] As Woods suggests in 'Rhetoric, Gender, and the Literary Arts', pp. 125, 131-2. For the use of speeches in classroom performance and composition exercises, see also Marjorie Curry Woods, 'Performing Dido', in *Public Declamations: Essays on Medieval Rhetoric, Education, and Letters in Honour of Martin Camargo*, ed. Georgiana Donavin and Denise Stodola (Turnhout: Brepols, 2015), pp. 253-65; Martin Camargo, 'Medieval Rhetoric Delivers: or, Where Chaucer Learned how to Act', *New Medieval Literatures* 9 (2008, for 2007), 41-62.

[114] Peter Mack, 'Ramus Reading: The Commentaries on Cicero's *Consular Orations* and Vergil's *Eclogues* and *Georgics*', *Journal of the Warburg and Courtauld Institutes* 61 (1998), 111-41; 'Melanchthon's Commentaries on Latin Literature', in *Melanchthon und Europa*, ed. Günter Frank, Treu Martin, and Kees Meerhoff, 2 vols (Stuttgart: Jan Thorbecke, 2001-2), II, pp. 29-52 (pp. 43-9).

[115] For a discussion of the commonplace method with respect to Virgil, see Craig Kallendorf, 'Virgil in the Renaissance Classroom: From Toscanella's *Osservationi... sopra l'opere di Virgilio* to the *Exercitationes rhetoricae*', in *The Classics in the Medieval and Renaissance Classroom*, ed. Ruys, Ward and Heyworth, pp. 309-28; Kallendorf, *Protean Virgil*, pp. 88-106.

annotators, nor in a practical change in glossing technique. Just as the ancient *enarratio* had never confined itself solely to grammar, neither do fifteenth- and sixteenth-century humanist annotations of Virgil focus on rhetorical figures or speech analysis (quite the contrary, as the next chapter will show).[116] Because the exposition of the poets had always been a site of disciplinary overlap, the conventional procedures of glossing already involved rhetorical, compositional analysis. In their theoretical writings, therefore, humanist rhetoricians drew attention to a traditional element of the *enarratio poetarum*.

Conclusion

The evidence of manuscript glossing, therefore, attests to the enduring influence of the disciplines of grammar and rhetoric in shaping the history of reading the classical authors. The procedures of the *enarratio poetarum*, established since Antiquity, consistently structured the glossing of Virgil's text throughout the fifteenth and early sixteenth centuries. After all, 'humanist' readers approached classical poets for the same purposes as their 'medieval' forebears. They mined Virgil for historical and mythological lore, interpreted his moral and allegorical lessons, and, most importantly, developed their skills in the Latin language. Although the *studia humanitatis* gave this training a new stylistic focus, the reading of the classical poets remained fundamentally consistent with established procedures of the *enarratio poetarum*. As this chapter has shown, readers of the later fifteenth and sixteenth centuries sought to cultivate a classical style more by their choice of models than by their reading method. The impact of the New Learning is witnessed in the increasing readership of classical texts rather than the intellectual content of the said reading. Fifteenth- and sixteenth- century glossing is, notwithstanding individual variations, highly consistent with that of earlier generations. The *studia humanitatis*, from the perspective of these readers, did not constitute a new method of study, but a canon of texts. While the New Learning was 'new' in terms of the elevated canonical status of classical

---

[116] For example, see the later sixteenth-century annotator in O.1494, who excerpts most of his annotations from Ramus's *Bucolics* commentary. He makes many interlinear lexical and grammatical glosses and marks rhetorical figures. I cross-referenced with the second edition of the commentary, USTC 152391 (Paris: André Wechel, 1558).

Latin authors, it drew its reading practices from centuries of earlier pedagogic tradition.

For these reasons, the effects of 'humanist' reading, conversely, are best observed in 'humanist' writing. As this chapter has shown, the traditional evidence of the history of reading, namely readers' annotations, implies the overwhelming consistency of reading practices across the centuries. Since the pursuit of the *studia humanitatis* was a matter of models rather than method, readers' attempts to cultivate a classical Latin style did not leave a distinctive mark in the margins of their books. Rather than in annotations and glosses, the effects of their reading are evident primarily in their Latin compositions. As the writing of the later fifteenth and sixteenth centuries attests, some English readers indeed succeeded in cultivating such a style, both in prose and poetry. In combining traditional exegetical methods with a new canon of classical models, the New Learning thus contributed to promoting humanist stylistic idioms throughout fifteenth- and sixteenth-century Latin discourse.

2
Printed Editions

The library of New College, Oxford has the earliest extant printed copy of Virgil imported into England. The *editio princeps* of Virgil's works was printed in Rome in 1469, and the New College edition was produced in Strasbourg the following year. By 1482, it was the property of John Russell (d. 1494), then Bishop of Lincoln.[1] Russell, as seen in Chapter 1, owned a large library of classical and humanist texts, including an illuminated Italian manuscript of Virgil. An avid bibliophile, he is the first Englishman known to have purchased printed books, the earliest being his 1466 edition of Cicero's *De Officiis*.[2] He later obtained a second incunabular copy of Virgil, which bears his coat of arms on the first page.[3] All of Russell's editions were imports from continental presses, and his books mark the beginning of England's large import trade in the classics. For the next hundred years, most English readers would encounter classical texts in imported copies such as these.[4] The arrival of printed books, however, did not lead to a major intellectual change in readers' approaches to Virgil. Although there were differences of design between manuscripts and printed copies, most importantly in the provision of commentaries, these changes were driven instead by technological and commercial factors. While the developing print market initiated new sizes, layouts, and paratexts of classical edition, these books were used in the same intellectual settings as their manuscript forebears. From manuscript to print, readers' glosses were shaped by well-established procedures of *enarratio poetarum*.

Due to the aims and periodization of their respective studies, current histories of printing and reading classical authors have not yet examined this dichotomy of changing design and consistency of use. In the field of classical reception, Craig Kallendorf's *Virgil and the Myth of Venice* and, more recently, his magisterial *Printing Virgil* focus almost exclusively on printed

---

[1] O.1470, a copy of *ISTC* iv00151000 ([Strasbourg: Johann Mentelin, about 1470];). Russell's inscription reads: 'Le Ruscelluy je suis Jo. Linoln. 1482'. On Russell, see Chapter 1, pp. 20–1.
[2] LPL, MS 765 ([Mainz]: Johann Fust and Peter Schoeffer, 4 Feb. 1466; *ISTC* ic00576000).
[3] O.1476.2. [4] See Introduction, p. 8, esp. fn. 28.

sources. While examining the content and use of printed Virgil editions in the Renaissance, these works do not set Virgil's printed reception in the context of his earlier manuscript reception, and therefore do not elaborate on the continuing influence of earlier glossing traditions. Recent histories of printing, meanwhile, have tended to emphasize continuities between manuscript and early print cultures. Reacting to Elizabeth Eisenstein's *The Printing Press as an Agent of Change*, recent historians such as David McKitterick have argued that the effects of print developed gradually over several centuries.[5] Such a long timeframe reflects the consistencies of glossing Virgil, but not the abrupt changes in the design of Virgil editions. The development of new sizes and layouts began within six years of the *editio princeps*.

Similarly to many manuscripts of Virgil, all editions of Virgil's *Opera* contained his three main works, accompanied by Ovid's verse arguments. For a preface, virtually every *Opera* edition had Aelius Donatus's *Vita Virgilii*. At the end of the volume, most printers also included Maphaeus Vegius's 'thirteenth book' of the *Aeneid*, as well as some or all of Virgil's *Opuscula*.[6] The very earliest print editions, much like manuscripts, presented Virgil's texts in a single column with wide margins for annotations. A few were printed in quarto, but most in folio.[7] From 1475, sharply breaking with manuscript traditions, Italian presses began to print Servius's commentary in the margins of the folio editions. Whereas the glosses of Virgil manuscripts (as seen in Chapter 1) comprised only excerpts of Servius, these commentary-editions contained the full Servius text. By the mid-1480s, almost all new editions of Virgil's *Opera* had at least Servius's commentary, if not additional commentaries by contemporary humanists.[8] Not until the turn of the century did printers again start producing uncommented editions in significant numbers, but this time they used the smaller octavo size. One example is Richard Pynson's edition of c. 1515 (discussed below), the only *Opera* edition printed in England before the Elizabethan era. Rather

---

[5] Elizabeth Eisenstein, *The Printing Press as an Agent of Change: Communications and Cultural Transformations in Early Modern Europe*, 2 vols (Cambridge: CUP, 1979); David McKitterick, *Print, Manuscript and the Search for Order* (Cambridge: CUP, 2003).

[6] On the humanist version of the Donatus *Vita*, see discussion and references in Wilson-Okamura, *Virgil in the Renaissance*, pp. 49–56. Seeing as neither text was a standard feature in English *Opera* manuscripts, the widespread circulation of Donatus's *Vita* and Vegius's *Supplementum* in England is another immediate effect of print.

[7] On the relatively few quarto printings of the *Opera*, see Kallendorf, *Protean Virgil*, p. 85.

[8] 41 *Opera* editions were printed without commentary up to 1501, 34 of which were printed before 1485 (*ISTC* iv00149000-iv00164300).

than a commentary, printers would furnish the text with brief printed marginalia, pointing out an 'Oratio' or 'Comparatio'. By the first half of the sixteenth century, therefore, there were two distinct trends of *Opera* editions: either a voluminous folio commentary-edition or a compact octavo.[9]

Despite their different sizes and layouts, these printed copies of the classics were used and annotated in the same contexts as manuscripts. As in previous generations, Servius's commentary remained the foundation of Virgilian reading, further encouraged by its wide circulation in folio editions. At all levels of study, annotators continued to follow well-established modes of grammatical and rhetorical study. Not only teachers and students, but also learned clerics devoted time and energy to glossing the text line by line. Among students, the process of glossing was a necessity for comprehension; among capable Latinists, it was an opportunity to focus on particular points of ambiguity, figurative language, and rare usages. In working through the literal meaning of Virgil's text, readers sought to hone their knowledge of the Latin language, frequently noting Servius's discussions of grammar and lexicography. Although this focus on the letter of the text might seem a humanist enterprise, the activities of parsing, glossing, and correcting are as much a legacy of earlier reading practices as a pursuit of the *studia humanitatis*.

Reading Servius from Manuscript to Print

Commentary-editions of the *Opera* were owned in a wide range of contexts. Although some modern scholars have suggested a narrower, more learned readership, these observations are not supported by the provenances of surviving books.[10] Some copies were owned in grammar schools, others in monasteries and universities, some by high-ranking clerics, and some by gentry.[11] Gavin Douglas used commentary-editions for his famous translation of the *Aeneid*, but so too did schoolboys simply glossing the Latin text. Much like the annotators to Virgil manuscripts, the annotators of

---

[9] This paragraph summarizes the main stages of early Virgilian printing, explained more fully in Kallendorf, *The Protean Virgil*, pp. 80–8.
[10] On this debated issue, see Kallendorf, *Protean Virgil*, pp. 84–8; *Virgil and the Myth of Venice*, pp. 44–50.
[11] For instance, this study includes copies owned by bishops (O.1476.2 (John Russell), O.1476.3, O.1527 (Thomas Cranmer)), a monk (O.1491), a university fellow (O.1487) and a knight (O.1522).

commentary-editions followed similar glossing procedures, clerics and schoolboys alike. As they worked through Virgil's text, they clarified difficult passages with interlinear glosses, corrected printers' errors, and produced finding-aids for the commentary. Through these annotations, they sought to improve the text of the edition, and to expand its paratextual apparatus. Corrections and glosses made Virgil's Latin more comprehensible, while simple strategies of underlining and indexing made voluminous commentaries easier to use. These annotations were motivated by practical problems of parsing Virgil's language, of coping with an imperfect text, and of finding information in Servius's lengthy exegesis. The same procedures of annotation, as we shall see, are also applicable to commentary-editions of other classical authors.

To describe these activities, a useful example is a copy of Antonio Miscomini's 1476 edition of Virgil's *Opera*, now in All Souls College, Oxford.[12] The main annotator wrote in an English cursive hand, likely dating from around the year 1500.[13] His annotations are representative of many fifteenth- and early sixteenth-century copies, but are considerably more numerous. Unlike most annotators, who concentrate mainly on *Bucolics* and *Aeneid* I-VI, the All Souls annotator provides marginal and interlinear glosses throughout all of Virgil's three main works, as well as to the prefatory materials, Vegius's *Supplementum* and the *Opuscula*. Although their frequency declines after *Aeneid* VI, he keeps annotating right to the end of the volume. His annotations also attest an unusually wide range of independent reading, citing Ovid, Augustine, Claudian, John of Salisbury, Johannes Balbus, Lorenzo Valla and Giovanni Tortelli. Although he leaves no signature or inscription, the All Souls annotator was almost certainly an educated man. In this regard, he is typical of the earliest English owners of Virgil editions. At least up to 1500, Virgil was not yet a staple text in English schools and universities, and the main interest came from university-educated individuals.[14] As well as bishop John Russell's two early printed Virgils, another commentary-edition, likewise containing Virgil and Servius,

---

[12] Virgil, *Opera*, comm. Servius (Venice: Antonio di Bartolommeo Miscomini, Oct. '1486' [i.e. 1476]; *ISTC* iv00167000). The copy is **O.1476.1** (Oxford, All Souls, a.1.9). For a more detailed description of the edition, see Coates, VI, pp. 2622-5 (V-088, although neither Bodleian copy was owned in England). On the text of the edition, see Matteo Venier, *Per una storia del testo di Virgilio nella prima età del libro a stampa (1469-1519)* (Udine: Forum, 2001), pp. 74, 101 (siglum C 6044), but Venier agrees with the 1486 date over 1476.

[13] Contains occasional vernacular glosses. At *Aeneid* XII.120 (sig. z5r), for example, the annotator notes the medical properties of the herb *verbena*, writing '...*cum ceruisia et vino confert asmaticis anglice* short | wyndedde.', and 'asmatico. short brethed'.

[14] Eight copies from my sample were printed before 1490. One was owned by the All Souls annotator, two by Russell, one by Haster (introduced below), and the others unknown.

was owned by John Haster, one of the founding fellows at Brasenose College, Oxford in 1509.[15] The All Souls annotator, possibly from Oxford University himself, must have had a similar level of education.

In appearance, the 1476 Miscomini edition is typical of fifteenth- and early sixteenth-century commentary-editions. Virgil's text is encircled on three sides by Servius's commentary, and the commentary, in turn, is surrounded by margins for readers' annotations. This layout was a decisive break from Virgilian manuscript traditions. Besides a few (mostly Carolingian) manuscripts, it was not common to have Servius's complete *catena*-commentary written in the margins of Virgil.[16] Scribes (as detailed in Chapter 1) would instead furnish Virgil's works with excerpts from Servius in the form of marginal and interlinear glosses. Depending on their particular needs and interests, other annotators might add further excerpts to this scribal apparatus, but no English Virgil manuscript contains the full Servius text.[17] For the complete commentary, scribes and readers would have had to consult a separate Servius manuscript. In the printed circulation, by contrast, Servius almost never circulated independently of Virgil. Fifteenth- and sixteenth-century printers produced only five independent editions of Servius's commentary, all in the early 1470s. To judge from these surviving copies, separate printings of Servius ended after printers started including it with Virgil's *Opera* in 1475.[18] Both in print and manuscript, Servius remained a constant presence in the study of Virgil, but printers, unlike earlier scribes, combined these texts in a single book.

The printing of Virgil with rather than without commentary was in large measure a commercial choice. If printers wanted to add value to Virgil editions, one method was to include additional paratexts.[19] The paper was the most expensive part of the book, and uncommented editions, whether

---

[15] O.1487; probably *MLGB* UO23.¶*24 (Inventory of Brasenose College Library, 1556). On Haster, see *BRUO*, p. 846.

[16] On trends in the size and glossing of Virgil codices, see Birger Munk Olsen, 'Virgile et la renaissance du XIIe siècle', in *Lectures Médiévales de Virgile*, ed. Tilliette, pp. 31–48; *L'Étude des Auteurs Classiques Latins aux XIe et XIIe Siècles*, 3 vols (Paris: Éditions du CNRS, 1982–9).

[17] In England, only two Virgil manuscripts contain even a partial copy of Servius in *catena*-format, SJC, MS C.4 and London, Society of Antiquaries, MS 44. In the first, the early English humanist Robert Flemmyng copies Servius's commentary in *catena*-format from *Aeneid* I.606 to the end of *Aeneid* II (fols 65v-78r), but he does not go further. In the second, the scribe copies Servius's commentary in *catena*-format for two pages (fols 72v-3v).

[18] The five editions of Servius without Virgil are *ISTC* is00478000, is00479000, is00480000, is00481000 and is00482000, dated between 1470 and 1475.

[19] Howard Jones, *Printing the Classical Text* (Utrecht: Hes & de Graaf Publishers BV, 2004), pp. 52–3.

folios or quartos, always had wide, blank margins. Printers could justify the expense of the paper by filling this space with commentary.[20] In printing Servius's commentary as opposed to a set of glosses, they probably reasoned that the full commentary of a famous ancient author would be more marketable to buyers than mere excerpts.[21] Despite Servius's voluminous length, it was also easier to print a *catena*-commentary than to reproduce more complex layouts of marginal and interlinear glossing. Unlike scribes of classical manuscripts, who did not even include extra ruling for their glosses, printers would have to type-set the entire page.[22] Commentary-editions, then, provided buyers with Virgil's texts and their most important expositor in a commercially advantageous format. By the end of the century, all the major classical authors were available in commentary-editions.[23] From the late 1480s, Italian presses also began producing Virgil editions with multiple commentaries. As well as Servius, they typically included the *Aeneid* commentary of fifth-century grammarian Tiberius Claudius Donatus, and the *Opera* commentary by humanist scholar Cristoforo Landino (1424–1498).[24] Editions of the sixteenth century could have as many as ten commentaries in the margins. Although it contains only Servius's exegesis, Miscomini's 1476 edition stands at the beginning of a long trend.[25]

While readers now had commentaries printed alongside Virgil's text, this arrangement did not negate the value of adding interlinear lexical glossing. From manuscripts to print editions, interlinear glosses remain the most common type of annotation.[26] Like the Trinity annotators (described in

---

[20] Kallendorf, *Protean Virgil*, pp. 117–18.

[21] Wilson-Okamura, *Virgil in the Renaissance*, pp. 31–5.

[22] No editions of Virgil (that I have seen) contained printed interlinear glossing. To my knowledge, printers confined it to shorter texts (such as Aesop's *Fables*) rather than the *Opera* of major authors. For an exception, see Johann Grüninger's 1496 and 1499 Strasbourg editions of Terence (*ISTC* it00094000, it00101000). He reorganized Guy Jouenneaux's *catena*-commentary on Terence (discussed in next chapter) as an interlinear gloss.

[23] Jones, *Printing the Classical Text*, pp. 52–5, 64–6, 86–8, 99–103.

[24] The first of these editions was *Opera* (1487/8), cited in Chapter 1, p. 39. On the transmission of Donatus, see Peter K. Marshall, 'Tiberius Claudius Donatus in the Fifteenth Century', in *Tria Lustra: Essays and Notes Presented to John Pinsent, Founder and Editor of Liverpool Classical Monthly by Some of its Contributors on the Occasion of the 150th Issue*, ed. H.D. Jocelyn and Helena Hunt (Liverpool: Liverpool Classical Monthly, 1993), pp. 325–9.

[25] For a 'Virgilius cum decem commentis' edition, see O.1527. For the sake of simplicity, I shall not discuss the many new commentaries appearing in continental *Opera* editions from 1500–1550, as Servius and Donatus were printed most frequently. Wilson-Okamura, *Virgil in the Renaissance*, pp. 32, 252–81, compares commentaries by estimated numbers of printings.

[26] In my sample of 48 print copies, 36 have interlinear glosses. Of the 12 without interlinear glosses, five are completely un-annotated (B.1493, Op.1509, O.1507.1, B.1522.3), while seven have other types of annotation (O.1475, O.1476.2, O.1476.3, O.1500.1, O.1522, O.1527, B.1514, and O.1529).

Chapter 1), the All Souls annotator makes hundreds of glosses to Virgil's grammar and lexis, many of them excerpts copied from Servius's commentary. Rather than consulting a separate manuscript of Servius, the All Souls annotator evidently worked from the copy in his print edition, transposing the commentary's lexical and grammatical material into the interlinear spaces.[27] At future readings, this glossing apparatus would have saved him trawling through the commentary to look up every word. In print editions as in manuscripts, glossing ensured that relevant linguistic information was written conveniently between the lines, readily accessible to later use. Moreover, just like the annotators of the Trinity manuscript, the All Souls annotator covers Virgil's text more comprehensively than does the commentary. Although Servius writes at great length, many difficult and ambiguous phrases have no explanation, prompting the All Souls annotator to improvise glosses himself.[28] He also identified rhetorical figures and metrical issues, sometimes copying from Servius's commentary, sometimes making independent observations. As in manuscripts, these notes would have alerted later readers to the presence of synecdoche, hypermetrical lines, and other poetic devices.[29] Compared with the commentary, the resulting glosses are not only more concise and easier to use, but also provide a more thorough explanation of Virgil's literal meaning.

As the All Souls annotator worked through Virgil's text, this glossing would have focused his reading on word-by-word problems of interpretation. To craft a gloss often required him to distil large portions of commentary into one or two words. For example, when Jupiter promises Venus that her son is still destined to found Rome, the god confirms 'manent immota tuorum | Fata tibi' (*Aeneid* I.258, 'your children's fates abide unmoved [for you]'). Servius discusses the meaning of 'tibi':[30]

---

[27] At sigs g1v-2r (beginning of *Aeneid* I), for example, he supplies a 'quam' to I.12 (Servius: 'deest quam'), glosses 'studiisque asperrima belli' with Servius's 'quia ter rebellauit con*tra* roma*nos*' (I.14), glosses present infinitive 'duci' as Servius's future 'ductum iri' (I.19), 'fatis' as '.i. volu*n*tate Iunonis' (I.32), 'molis' as '.i. difficultatis' (I.33), etc.

[28] At sig. g1v, he clarifies that 'Progeniem' refers to '.s. troiana*m*' (I.19), and supplies the subject of 'Audierat' as '.s. Iuno' (I.20). In the next line, he repeats the verb '.s. audierat' to clarify that 'Hinc populum... venturum...' is an indirect statement.

[29] In *Aeneid* I, for example, such annotations appear at sigs h1v ('hypermetru*m*', I.332), h7v ('synodoche', I.579) and h10v ('synodoche', I.713), all from Servius. On the second page of *Aeneid* II (sig. i2v), he marks 'abiete' (II.16) as a 'proceleuaticus' (i.e. proceleumaticus, from Servius), 'armato milite' (II.20) as an instance of 'exallage' (i.e. enallage, not in Servius), and 'petiisse' (II.25) as 'epe*n*thesis' (from Servius).

[30] Fairclough does not translate 'tibi', so I add '[for you]' in square brackets.

Fata tibi non propter te. fati *enim* immobilis ratio *est*. sed aut vacat tibi: ut qui mihi accuba*n*tes i*n* co*n*uiuiis [Cicero, *In Catilinam* II.10].' aut certe tua sunt tibi fata: no*n* tamen propter te.

(Servius on *Aeneid* I.258)[31]

While explaining that 'tibi' cannot mean 'because of Juno', Servius does not supply a clear alternative. In order to elucidate the line, the All Souls annotator glosses 'ad vtilitatem', identifying that the dative here is used to express utility. Whereas Servius simply reads 'the fates remain unmoved for you', the gloss provides a more precise interpretation, 'the fates remain unmoved to your advantage'.[32] As he parsed through Virgil's poetry, the All Souls annotator constantly had to interpret these ambiguities, solecisms and metaphors, and to refine his interpretations into a precise, pithy gloss. Considering that the *Bucolics* and *Aeneid* I–II have glosses on virtually every line, their production must have been a considerable portion of his reading activity.

Glosses such as 'ad vtilitatem', elucidating the finer points of Virgil's meaning, are particularly common among the more capable Latinists rather than students. John Russell and John Haster, contemporaries of the All Souls annotator, target their glosses only at these more difficult passages. Adult readers who used Latin professionally, they tend to gloss only a couple of times per page, focusing almost exclusively on classical epithets, terms used in secondary or figurative senses, and obscure points of syntax.[33] To pick a typical example, when Virgil urges Maecenas to continue reading his *Georgics*, his exhortation 'primi lege littoris oram' (II.44) puns on proper meaning of 'lege' ('read') and the nautical phrase 'lege oram' ('to sail along a coast'). Just as 'ad vtilitatem' identifies a particular use of the dative, Haster glosses 'nauiga' to elucidate the sailing metaphor.[34] Although Haster's

---

[31] O.1476.1, sig. g9v. My translation: '**Fates for you**: not because of you, for the reason of fate is immobile. Either the "for you" ('tibi') is omitted, as in 'qui mihi accubantes in conviviis' ('those who lie about in feasts'), or certainly the fates 'for you' are 'yours', not however because of you.'

[32] This gloss does not appear in the printed commentaries of Landino or Donatus. Ascensius probably comes closest with 'ad tuu*m* co*m*modu*m* aut placitu*m*'. See *Opera* (1500–1), II, fol. 22v.

[33] Compare Russell's glosses in **O.1470**, first fol. of the *Aeneid*. For example, he glosses the epithet 'saturnia' as '.i. Iuno' (I.23), the noun 'regem' as the participle '.i. regentem' (as does Servius, I.21). Russell's parsing of the *Aeneid*, however, is not without fault, such as his incorrect reading of 'Troas: reliquias danaum: atq*ue* inmitis achilli' (I.30). Possibly knowing that classical authors sometimes wrote third declension plurals with 'is', he glosses genitive singular 'inmitis' as accusative plural '.i. tes', incorrectly taking it with 'Troas' ('the Trojans') rather than 'achilli'.

[34] See Haster's copy **O.1487**, sig. d8v. Haster derives his gloss from Servius: 'lege nauticus sermo *est* q*ui* nu*n*c & ad navigandu*m*: & ad lectione*m* pot*est* referri'. All Virgil and Servius quotations in this paragraph are from the original edition. Servius's text, as edited by Thilo and

glossing is highly selective, he still uses techniques commonly associated with 'basic' literacy training. At another passage, 'Virgea præterea cælei uilisque suppellex:' (*Georgics* I.165), he clarifies the hyperbaton ('Virgea' and 'suppellex') with construe marks, a device which he likely learned from the schoolroom.[35] Rather than supporting elementary comprehension, Haster uses these glossing techniques to clarify specific semantic and syntactic ambiguities. Given the difficulties of Virgil's poetry, these tools were just as useful to a capable Latinist as a student. For Haster, Russell and the All Souls annotator, the reading of Virgil involved them in closely parsing the poet's artificial diction.

As well as the selectivity or originality of glosses, their written form also helps to distinguish learned men from other groups of annotators. School editions of Virgil, used by students over several generations, usually have dense lexical glosses scrawled in multiple hands. In this pedagogic glossing, the writing tends to be hurried and untidy, mainly in Latin, but showing frequent recourse to the vernacular.[36] Unlike Haster or the All Souls annotator, who clearly knew Latin to a high level, students would have needed their glosses to help them understand the basic meaning of the text. Line by line, they would look up words in the commentary, copy the definitions into the interlinear spaces, and gradually piece together Virgil's meaning. If they read the text again, they would have relied on their glosses as a crib.[37] In Haster's copy and the All Souls edition, meanwhile, the glosses are neat and well-spaced, suggesting that the annotators took time over their production.[38] Interlinear lexical glossing (as Chapter 1 showed) had been a standard feature of manuscript layout for hundreds of years, prepared as often by scribes as by

---

Hagen, has no 'est', and has 'navigium' instead of 'navigandum'. For similar glosses, compare Russell in O.1470, seventh fol. of *Aeneid*. Following Servius, he glosses 'plurimus' in the sense 'longus' (I.419), and interprets 'ardentes' as a metaphor for 'festinantes' (I.423).

[35] O.1487, sig. d2r, which Fairclough translates as 'the common wicker ware of Celeus'. For Haster's other construe marks in *Georgics*, see sigs c6v, d8v.

[36] Observed in Mark Purcell, 'Master Petypher's Virgil: The Anatomy of a Tudor School Book', *The Book Collector* 50 (2001), 471–92, which discusses a 1493 commentary-edition owned in a school during the Elizabethan period. Based on these observations, four commentary-editions in the sample were possibly used in pedagogic contexts: O.1492.1, O.1492.4, O.1492.5, O.1515.1. One uncommented *Opera* edition, O.1489, might also have been used in this context, as well as the octavo editions discussed below p. 64, fn. 86. Outside of *Opera* editions, similar glossing is seen in G.1498.2, and B.1522.1.

[37] Similar glossing can be observed in commentary-editions of other authors, such as Cicero. For example, Oxford, Magdalen College, Arch.B.III.1.13 once belonged to John Stanbridge (1463–1510), master of Magdalen College School. It is a copy of *Epistolae ad familiares*, comm. Hubertinus clericus (Venice: Baptista de Tortis, 24 May 1485; *ISTC* ic00525000).

[38] See All Souls annotator's glosses to *Aeneid* I, but ignoring the later (and untidier) annotator on sigs g1v-4v, h7r.

readers. In making their annotations, Haster and the All Souls annotator intended to furnish their printed copies with the same textual apparatus. Rather than an aid to immediate comprehension, they saw their annotations as an integral part of the page design, an extension of the book's production. At the same time as his glossing, the All Souls annotator made corrections to the text and punctuation. In print as in manuscript, he is typical of most English Virgil annotators in that he restricts his interventions to grammatical errors.[39] While some are obvious typographical mistakes, he found others by cross-referencing Virgil's text with the lemmata in Servius's commentary.[40] John Haster, a contemporary of the All Souls annotator, was slightly more adventurous, comparing his Virgil edition against another copy. At *Georgics* II.71, for example, he emends 'incanuit' ('become white or grey') to 'incanduit' ('glow white'), another common reading of the line in that period.[41] Some of his corrections were possibly his own conjectures. In *Aeneid* I, for example, Juno complains:

et quisquam numen iunonis adoret:
Præterea aut supplex aris imponit honorem.

(*Aeneid* I.48-9)[42]

Haster corrects the conjunction 'aut' to 'ut', making 'aut supplex' the appositive phrase 'ut supplex' ('as a suppliant'). In this case, his conjecture was misled by the punctuation in his edition. Whereas modern editors

---

[39] On errors in early editions of the classics, see Kallendorf, *Protean Virgil*, pp. 10–6; Jones, *Printing the Classical Text*, Ch. 4. On readers' corrections of early printed books, see overviews in Ann Blair, 'Errata Lists and the Reader as Corrector', in *Agent of Change: Print Culture Studies after Elizabeth L. Einstein*, ed. Sabrina Alcorn Baron, Eric N. Lindquist and Eleanor F. Shevlin (Amherst, MA: University of Massachusetts Press, 2007), pp. 21–41; McKitterick, *Print, Manuscript and the Search for Order*, pp. 97–165.

[40] For example, see O.1476.1, sig. f10r. At *Aeneid* I.6, he adds a second 'r' to 'inferetque', probably having seen Servius's lemma 'Inferretque'. When there is no lemma in Servius, he likely found the correct spelling in a dictionary. At sig. g5r, he corrects 'grandæus' to 'Grandevus a u*m* .i. grandus evi'. If he looked up 'grandæus' in *Catholicon*, for example, he would have seen that Latin has no such word. He would have come across the correct term 'grandevus' on the same page. See *Catholicon* ([Mainz: Printer of the 'Catholicon'], '1460' [not before 1469]; *ISTC* ib00020000), entries arranged alphabetically. Since he frequently used such dictionaries (see discussion below), I do not think that his textual corrections required him to look at another Virgil edition.

[41] O.1487, sig. e1r. Besides correcting minor grammatical and typographical errors, Haster adds a missing line to his edition (*Georgics* I.76, sig. c8r), which must have been copied from a second text.

[42] O.1487, sig. h3r, which Fairclough translates: 'And will any still worship Juno's godhead or humbly lay sacrifice upon her altars?'

punctuate between 'Præterea' and 'aut', some sixteenth-century editors (as in the above quotation) punctuated after 'adoret', thus making it difficult to see 'aut' as a conjunction.[43] With the exception of Haster, however, most early English annotators of Virgil editions do not show rigorous engagement with textual issues. In their corrections, the All Souls annotator and his contemporaries primarily sought to produce a useable, grammatically-correct text of Virgil, not to make critical distinctions between textual variants.

Besides making corrections and interlinear glosses to the text, the All Souls annotator equips Servius's commentary with extra finding-aids. In the fifteenth and early sixteenth centuries, *catena*-commentaries of classical authors were typically printed in long blocks of undifferentiated text. From the 1490s and early 1500s onwards, a few printers began to divide the text into paragraphs and print the lemmata in capitals, but these improvements were by no means universal. Numbering systems, which linked words in the text to relevant passages of commentary, only gradually became a feature of Virgil editions. Most readers would have to search through the whole page of commentary to find any given lemma.[44] To make his edition more useable, the All Souls annotator, as did other readers of commentary-editions, underlines every lemma in Servius, thus helping to distinguish the different sections of the commentary. When Servius refers to lines in other parts of Virgil's text, the annotator adds precise folio references from this edition. At *Aeneid* I.71, for example, Servius refers his readers back to his commentary on *Georgics* IV.336, but simply writes 'in georgicis'. The annotator took the time to search the commentary for this reference, adding in the margin 'In 4° ge*orgicorum* in 6° fo°' (i.e. 'in the fourth [book] of the *Georgics* on the sixth leaf').[45] A few readers also inserted rubricated paraphs before every lemma of the commentary, and added line

---

[43] Similar conjectural emendations have been noted among a few other English annotators of early classical editions. For example, John Shirwood (d. 1493), bishop of Durham and another early English humanist, makes emendations in his Plautus. See Lowry, 'The arrival and use of continental printed books', p. 455.

[44] Although legal texts, for example, had numbering systems from their earliest fifteenth-century editions, classical texts initially did not. To my knowledge, the first Virgil edition to have this apparatus was Sebastian Brant's 1502 commentary-edition, famous for its woodcuts. See Virgil, *Opera*, ed. Sebastian Brant, comm. Servius, Donatus, Landinus, Mancinellus and Calderinus (Strasbourg: Johann Grüninger, 28 Aug. 1502; *USTC* 688629). Some annotators equipped their copies with similar apparatus. An English example is O.1510, but the annotator gave up after the first 21 leaves of *Aeneid* I (fols 122r-143r).

[45] O.1476.1, sig. g3v, referring to a passage on sig. f6r.

numbering to the text.[46] Much like interlinear glossing or corrections, this apparatus would make the edition easier to use in the future.

For the same purpose, the All Souls annotator writes marginal headings beside the lemmata in Servius's commentary. Although some of his contemporaries would simply mark every lemma, he works more selectively, choosing particular points of lexicography, history and myth. At *Aeneid* I.1, when Servius describes the polysemous senses of 'cano', the annotator writes in the margin, 'vide quot modis su*mitur* h*oc u*erbum cano'. Below, he lists the meanings from the commentary: 'dat cano laudare dat scribere vaticinare'.[47] Shortly after, Servius discusses the geographic bounds of Italy, prompting the annotator's heading 'Te*m*pore enee fines italie erat usq*ue* ad rubicone*m*'.[48] Most readers simply copy out lemmata and other keywords from the commentary, but the All Souls annotator often prefers to make his headings more descriptive.[49] He uses 'fabula' and 'historia' when Servius recounts a myth, 'opinio philosophorum' when Servius explains an allusion to ancient philosophy, and 'proverbium' for a moral comment.[50] Manuscripts of Servius and other *catena*-commentaries had been annotated in this manner for hundreds of years. Even if the commentary was not in the same manuscript as Virgil, it still helped to have marginalia to navigate the contents.[51] When printers started publishing commentaries in editions of Virgil, it is no surprise that marginal headings of this kind continued to be the most common type of annotation.[52] Some annotators simply marked

---

[46] Rubrication is uncommon in English-owned Virgil editions, but examples are O.1476.2, O.1476.4, O.1492.3, B.1492, G.1498.1. For line-numbering, see O.1491 (*Bucolics, Aeneid* I.1–200), B.1492, G.1498.1, O.1522.

[47] O.1476.1, sig. f10v. Servius reads: 'Cano: polysemus sermo est Tria enim significat: aliquando laudo: [...] Aliquando diuino: [...] Aliquando canto: ut hoc loco. Nam proprie canto significat: quia cantanda sunt carmina.' In the annotation, 'scribere' is the annotator's addition. He probably remembered that it was a common gloss on Virgil's 'cano'.

[48] O.1476.1, sig. f10v. In his commentary on 'primus' (*Aeneid* I.1), Servius writes: 'Namque illo tempore quo Aeneas ad Italiam uenit finis erat italię usque ad Rubiconem fluuium'.

[49] Haster, for example, copies most of Servius's lemmata in the margins. See O.1487, esp. sigs c6r-e1v (*Georgics*), h1r-4v (*Aeneid* I).

[50] In O.1476.1, examples include 'No*ta* historiam' beside the tale of Romulus and Remus (Servius on *Aeneid* I.273, sig. g10r) or 'Fabula de atreo *et* tieste frat*ri*bus' (Servius on *Aeneid* I.568, sig. h7v). For 'opiniones', see 'Opi*nio* platonis' (Servius on *Aeneid* I.387, sig. h3r); 'Opi*nio* epicureo*rum* de sole' (Servius on *Aeneid* IV.584, sig. m10r); or the 'Optim*a* parabola lucrecii' (Servius on *Aeneid* VI.596, sig. p8v). For 'proverbium', see 'No*ta* prouerbium' (sig. l1r, Servius on III.279); or "Bo*num* d*i*ctum terencii" (sig. h10r, when Servius quotes a line of *Eunuchus* at I.686). The annotator occasionally marks sententious phrases in Virgil's text itself, such as a 'Ve*r*sum de fortunam' (sig. A4v, probably referring to *Aeneid* XII.676–7).

[51] For example, see Oxford, Lincoln College, MS 91, esp. fol. 78v onwards.

[52] Besides Haster and the All Souls annotator, further print examples include O.1480 and O.1476.4, esp. sigs c4r-e6r. Many editions have a few sporadic headings. For example, O.1492.3, e.g. fols 1r-v, 112v-4v; O.1492.1, e.g. fols 70r, 71r, 86r.

passages with underlining or *signes de renvoi*, but marginal headings were evidently preferable, since they made it easier for annotators to locate an item at a later date.[53] Besides the All Souls annotator, Haster too makes hundreds of headings, and the practice is seen in commentary-editions of other classical authors.[54]

Although the All Souls annotator had a range of interests, encompassing history, geography, philosophy, and myth, Latin grammar and lexicography are prominent throughout his annotations. Like the manuscript annotators in Chapter 1, he commonly marks Servius's *differentiae verborum*. Just as the Trinity scribe copies them into his marginal glosses, the All Souls annotator routinely marks them in the printed commentary. For example, when he reaches Servius's 'pollicemur sponte: promittimus rogati' (commentary on *Aeneid* I.237, sig. g8v), the All Souls annotator writes the heading '*Differentia inter* pollicere | *et* promittere'.[55] Particularly in the later books of the *Aeneid*, when his annotations are less frequent, his attention to Servius's lexicography continues unabated, pointing out a 'Bona nota de procul' at *Aeneid* VI.10 and marking Servius's distinction of 'posco' and 'peto' at *Aeneid* IX.194.[56] From the start to the end of the edition, the All Souls annotator also takes note of grammatical rules in the commentary, usually with the headings 'regula' or 'bona regula'. On the line 'Nos contra effusi lachrymis coniunxque creusa' (*Aeneid* II.651),[57] Servius's metrical discussion caught his interest:

Nos contra: prepositiones uel aduerbia in a exeuntia modo producunt ultimam litteram: excepto puta:

(Commentary on *Aeneid* II.651)[58]

For an annotator in the sixteenth century, this rule was not merely a point of philological study, but would have had practical use. Since Latin was still a

---

[53] For an example of underlining and manicules in the commentary, see throughout O.1492.2 and O.1492.4.

[54] On Haster, see above fn. 49. Although I have not found a Virgilian example, the more dedicated annotators of commentary-editions would compile these headings into an index of the commentary. For an example, see Ovid, *Fasti*, ed. and comm. Paulus Marsus (Venice: Antonius Battibovis, 27 Aug. 1485; *ISTC* io00172000; CCC, phi.C.3.3(2)). The annotator is John Claymond (1467/8–1536), first President of Corpus Christi College, Oxford, and he compiled indexes for many of his books.

[55] O.1476.1, sig. g8v. 'Pollicere' should be 'polliceri'.   [56] O.1476.1, sigs o6r, t5v.

[57] Fairclough: 'But we were dissolved in tears—my wife Creusa [, Ascanius, and all our household]'.

[58] O.1476.1, sig. k3r. My translation: '**But we**: Prepositions or adverbs ending in 'a' only lengthen the final letter, with exception of 'puta'.

spoken language, it evidently benefitted to know the correct pronunciation of adverbs and prepositions ending in 'a'. Servius originally intended his linguistic lessons for Roman schoolboys, but they were equally applicable to an educated sixteenth-century adult, eager for his insights into classical Latin.[59]

The All Souls annotator was by no means alone in these linguistic interests. Servius had always been a valuable source for grammarians and lexicographers, particularly for humanists seeking information about classical usages. Guarino Veronese (discussed in Chapter 1) produced a lexicon of Servius, listing all Servius's definitions of Latin terms.[60] Not only did annotators of Virgilian commentary-editions mark these linguistic passages, but so too did annotators in separate manuscripts and editions of the commentary. Approximately fifty years before the All Souls annotator, one of the early English humanists, the clergyman Robert Flemmyng, owned and annotated a manuscript copy of Servius, regularly marking the grammatical rules, *differentiae verborum*, and other lexicographic content.[61] From the 1480s onwards, *Opera* editions of the classical authors increasingly had printed indexes for their commentaries, allowing readers to use them as works of reference. When Robert Estienne published his 1532 commentary-edition of Virgil and Servius, his title page advertised 'An index of those things explained by Servius, so copious that it can be like a dictionary' ('Index eorum quæ à Seruio explicantur, ita copiosus vt vel Dictionarii instar esse possit').[62] One could learn the nuances of classical Latin from reading Lorenzo Valla's *Elegantiae*, but also from reading Servius's commentary.

The All Souls annotator also supplemented Servius's lessons in grammar and usage with other sources. Referring frequently to dictionaries and grammars, he looked up proper names, rare vocabulary, and words used in their secondary senses. As was characteristic of the late fifteenth and early sixteenth centuries, he draws both on humanist and pre-humanist writings. His main sources were well-established works of the twelfth and thirteenth

---

[59] For examples of more 'regula' annotations, see sigs g8v (Servius on *Aeneid* I.232), h2v (on I.374), h7v (on I.587), k1v (on II.554), k8r (on III.91), etc.

[60] The lexicon was later printed, the first edition being Servius, *Vocabula* ([Milan: Uldericus Scinzenzeler, about 1480]; *ISTC* is00485000).

[61] Oxford, Lincoln College, MS 91, fols 82r, 86r-7r, 88v-9r, 92v, 97r, etc. On Flemmyng's annotations and emendations, see Giuseppe Ramires, 'Servio e l'Umanesimo inglese: Robert Flemmyng, allievo di Guarino Veronese', in *Servius et sa réception de l'Antiquité à la Renaissance*, ed. Bruno Méniel, Monique Bouquet and Guiseppe Ramires (Rennes: Presses universitaires de Rennes, 2011), pp. 539–54.

[62] *Opera*, comm. Servius & Valeriano, 2 vols (Paris: Robert Estienne, 16 Jul. 1532 & 24 Nov. 1529; *USTC* 146074, 203,367).

centuries: Hugutio of Pisa's *Derivationes Magnae*, Johannes Balbus's *Catholicon*, Papias's *Vocabularium*, Évrard of Béthune's *Graecismus*, and John of Garland's *Aequivoca*.[63] In three glosses he also cites newer, humanist authors. Lorenzo Valla's *Elegantiae*, a textbook on the finer points of classical usage, provided a gloss on the uses of 'senior' (*Aeneid* V.179).[64] For the plants 'Narcissus' and 'casia' (*Bucolics* II.48-49), he consulted Giovanni Tortelli's *De Orthographia*, a study of Greek loan-words to Latin.[65] While humanist intellectuals sharply distinguished their classicizing lexicography from their barbarous forebears,[66] the All Souls annotator treated all his sources as equally valuable insights into the Latin language. On 'casia', for example, he first marked the definition in Servius's commentary, 'herba suauissimi odoris' ('a plant of a very sweet smell'). Next consulting Papias, his second gloss identifies 'casia' as an 'arbor odori*fera*' ('odoriferous tree').[67] Tortelli, by contrast, makes no mention of the scent, but describes 'casia' as a 'frutex', a shrub or bush.[68] Squeezing another marginal gloss beside Servius and above Papias, the annotator briefly notes '*secundum* tortel*lum* frutex *est*'.[69] When writing his marginal glosses, he accumulates interpretations side-by-side rather than discriminating between them.

---

[63] In **O.1476.1**, the annotator explicitly cites Hugutio at sigs a5r, a6r, a9r, b9r, c4v, g2r, h10v, k5v, k7v, k8v, l4v, m1r, n1r, n2v, n7r, n10r, and 34v; *Graecismus* at sigs a6v, i6v, k4r; *Catholicon* at sigs a7v and l10r; Papias at sigs a9r and c4v; and John of Garland at sig. i6v.

[64] For the relevant passage, see *Lavrentii Vallensis De Linguae Latinae Elegantia: Ad Ioannem Tortellium Aretinum: Per me M. Nicolaum Ienson Venetiis Opus Feliciter Impressum Est. M. CCCC.LXXI*, ed. Santiago López Moreda, 2 vols (Cáceres: Universidad de Extremadura, 1999), I, p. 93. Like so many of Valla's observations, the source is Servius's commentary, this time his exposition of *Aeneid* V.409. For similar citations of humanist lexicography, see **O.1492.1**, fols 8r, 8v, 25r, 77r, in which one of the annotators refers to Valla's *Elegantiae* and Niccolò Perotti's *Cornucopiae*.

[65] **O.1476.1**, sigs p3r, a9r.

[66] To humanists, these authors were quintessential representatives of barbarism. In *Elegantiae*, Book II, Valla contrasts 'Donatus, Servius, Priscianus' with 'Papias, aliique indoctiores: Eberardus, Hugutio, Catholicon, Aymo'. See *Lavrentii Vallensis De Linguae Latinae Elegantia*, I, p. 184. Erasmus similarly criticizes Papias, Evard, Hugutio and *Catholicon* in Epistle 31. See *The Correspondence of Erasmus*, trans. various, 17 vols (Toronto: University of Toronto Press, 1974–Present), I, no. 31 (esp. p. 60).

[67] While the All Souls annotator writes 'arbor', Papias's text in fact describes casia as a 'herba', as does Servius. See *Vocabularium*, ed. Boninus Mombritius (Venice: Andreas de Bonetis, 30 June 1485; *ISTC* ip00078000), sig. d7v. Seeing as the annotator usually copies dictionary definitions verbatim, perhaps he used a manuscript with a slightly different version of Papias's text.

[68] For an edition, I use *Orthographia* (Venice: Nicolaus Jenson, 1471; *ISTC* it00395000). No foliation or quire signatures, but all entries are arranged alphabetically.

[69] The Tortelli reference is in darker ink, and was possibly made by the same annotator at a later date.

As witnessed in the annotator's combination of sources, the adoption of humanist dictionaries was a gradual process. Prior to printing, for instance, only a handful of English readers knew Valla's *Elegantiae*.[70] The twelfth- and thirteenth-century dictionaries, meanwhile, remained in print until the 1520s, and the *Catholicon* was available even in revised humanist editions.[71] Far from anachronisms, these works remained the most comprehensive dictionaries available to late fifteenth- and early sixteenth-century readers. Whereas Valla and Tortelli were specialist works, the one focusing on nuances of classical Latin, the other on Greek loan-words, the *Catholicon* presumed to cover the entire Latin language. Not until the sixteenth century did a humanist produce a new alphabetic dictionary of similar scope.[72] Even if the All Souls annotator attended school in the late 1400s, his education would have been structured by these well-established texts, since only a few institutions were teaching humanist grammars at that time. When he came to read Virgil around 1500, it is unsurprising that Papias, *Catholicon* and *Graecismus* remained his main points of reference. In this light, his use of older dictionaries does not reflect an indifference to humanist studies or classicizing usage, but a gradation of humanist interest. Although humanist intellectuals would have been more scrupulous in their sources, the All Souls annotator was nonetheless using these dictionaries in service of a humanist aim, the reading of a classical text. Balbus and Papias, at least in his eyes, could be auxiliaries to the *studia humanitatis*.

The All Souls annotator, then, followed similar aims, processes, and sources to earlier annotators of manuscripts. While his interests ranged from classical philosophy to myth and history, much of his reading time focused on parsing and glossing Virgil's language. The use of a commentary-edition, already furnished with Servius's expositions, did not make this glossing obsolete. As we have seen, he condenses long passages of commentary into pithy, precise interlinear glosses, elucidating figurative and obscure language, complex syntax and other interpretative difficulties. In his

---

[70] On Valla's limited circulation in fifteenth-century England, see Rundle, 'Humanist Eloquence among the Barbarians in fifteenth-century England', p. 84.

[71] On humanist reception of *Catholicon*, see John Considine, '"Si hoc saeculo natus fuisset": Refurbishing the Catholicon for the 16th Century', *Historiographia Linguistica* 44 (2018), 412–29. All the annotator's dictionaries were printed except Hugutio's *Derivationes*, so he must have consulted a manuscript for this.

[72] John Considine, 'Neo-Latin Lexicography in the Shadow of the *Catholicon*', in *Acta Conventus Neo-Latini Vindobonensis. Proceedings of the Sixteenth International Congress of Neo-Latin Studies (Vienna 2015)*, ed. Astrid Steiner-Weber and Franz Römer (Leiden: Brill, 2018), pp. 206–15.

marginalia, meanwhile, he constructs an apparatus to help locate information in the printed commentary. Not only do his annotations provide useful finding-aids, they also supplement Servius's explanations, sometimes drawn from his independent observations, sometimes from wider reading. While the All Souls annotator referred to recent humanist works including Valla's *Elegantiae* and Tortelli's *Orthographia*, most of his research was grounded in well-established dictionaries, such as Balbus, Hugutio and Papias. In his approach and sources, therefore, the annotator's reading of Virgil was steeped in past tradition.

Reading Virgil in Octavo

While humanist commentaries and dictionaries became more prominent over succeeding decades, the prevailing methods of the *enarratio poetarum* continued to structure processes of annotation. Just as in folio commentary-editions, this continuity is also witnessed in octavos. As noted at the start of the chapter, they were the second common format for printing classical texts during the sixteenth century. Among them is the first English edition of Virgil's *Opera*, printed by Richard Pynson around 1515.[73] The compact, compressed book design saved printers time and expense, since octavos had narrow margins, no commentaries and minimum blank paper. If readers neither wanted nor needed a voluminous commentary-edition, the octavo was the dominant medium for circulating uncommented texts of the classical authors. In their approach to Virgil, however, readers' annotations still consist predominantly of lexical glossing, focusing on the letter of the text and following the traditional procedures of grammatical and rhetorical study.

The printing of the Latin classics in octavo was famously popularized by the Venetian printer, Aldus Manutius (*c.* 1450–1515). He printed a string of classical *Opera* editions in this format, the first being the Aldine Virgil of 1501. His typographer, Francesco Griffo (1450–1518), prepared a new italic

---

[73] STC 24787; USTC 501334. I know of three extant copies: Oxford, Exeter College, Strong Room: 9M 24,787; JRL, 12272; and PUL, VRG 2945.1501.3 (**O.1515.2-4**). The Princeton copy has not previously been identified as Pynson's edition, since it is missing its title page and colophon. All pages are missing before *Georgics* III.229 and after *Aeneid* X.699. For a description, see Craig Kallendorf, *A Catalogue of the Junius Spencer Morgan Collection of Virgil in the Princeton University Library* (New Castle: Oak Knoll Press, 2009), pp. 52–3 (listed at the year 1501).

typeface specifically for this project. Within a matter of years, Aldus's editions had been copied and counterfeited by printers across Europe.[74] By the 1520s, his combination of italic type and octavo format had become a common design for printing classical and humanist texts.[75] While the numbers of editions show the popularity of the octavo, its intended readership is debated. According to Martin Lowry, Aldus intended his editions for educated readers, 'busy men of affairs'. The small size made them portable, and they had no burdensome pedagogic commentaries. Other scholars, led by Craig Kallendorf, argue instead that Aldus made these portable books for a student market.[76] Whichever Aldus might have intended, many sixteenth-century pedagogic editions of classical texts were indeed printed in octavo, both in plain-text and later also with commentaries. To choose a Virgilian example, the *Bucolics* editions of educational reformer Petrus Ramus used italic type and the octavo format similar to the Aldine Virgils.[77] Aldus is rightly famous for shaping the design of classical editions over a hundred years after his death.

Pynson's *Opera*, however, is not related to the well-known Aldine octavos, but to a contemporaneous set of Parisian Virgil editions. The first octavo edition of Virgil was not printed by Aldus in 1501, but in Paris three years earlier by a German printer, Johann Philippi de Cruzenach (1498).[78] Printed in Roman type rather than italic, the text of the *Opera* was based on the 1478 edition of Filippo Beroaldo the Elder, produced during his time at the Sorbonne. This text, along with Donatus's *Vita Virgilii* and Beroaldo's dedicatory epistle, had been printed four times by Paris printers during the last quarter of the century.[79] For the 1498 edition, it

---

[74] On this edition and its type, see Martin Lowry, *The World of Aldus Manutius: Business and Scholarship in Renaissance Venice* (Ithaca, NY: Cornell University Press, 1979), pp. 137–40.

[75] On the connotations of italic, see Harry Carter, *A View of Early Typography up to about 1600* (Oxford: Clarendon Press, 1969), pp. 73–5.

[76] Lowry, *The World of Aldus Manutius*, pp. 142–7; Kallendorf, *Protean Virgil*, pp. 85–6; *Virgil and the Myth of Venice*, pp. 46–8.

[77] Examined in *USTC* 152391 (cited in Chapter 1, p. 43).

[78] The edition is *Opera*, ed. Philippus Beroaldus, rev. Augustinus Caminadus (Paris: Johann Philippi de Cruzenach, 19 Feb. 1498; *ISTC* iv00165400). In this chapter, my quotations of the text and marginalia are from Cruzenach's 1501 reprint in PUL, VRG 2945.1501.2 (not listed in *ISTC* or *USTC*). For a description of the 1501 edition, see Kallendorf, *A Catalogue of the Junius Spencer Morgan Collection*, pp. 51–2.

[79] As listed in the *ISTC*, the four editions are: iv00160800 (Ulrich Gering, Sept. 1478); iv00164200 (Ulrich Gering, July 1484); iv00164800 ([Georg Wolf], 20 Nov. 1489); iv00165000 (Ulrich Gering and Berthold Rembolt, 12 Sept. 1494). The latter two editions used a revised text by Paulus Malleolus Andelocensis (Paul Hemmerlin of Andlau). For copies owned in England, see O.1489, O.1494.2.

was revised by humanist editor Augustine Caminade (Augustinus Caminadus, d. 1511). Modern scholars know Caminade for his friendship with Erasmus, who wrote a poem praising the 1498 Virgil edition.[80] As well as revising Beroaldo's text, Caminade added several works of the *Opuscula*, and wrote a second dedicatory epistle praising the divine Maro. He also furnished Virgil's Latin with an entirely new set of paratexts. To supplement the standard verse arguments of the *Opera*, he included a prose argument for each of the *Bucolics*, and for each book of the *Georgics* and *Aeneid*. Moreover, he wrote a set of marginalia to accompany all the works. As he writes in his title, these 'annotatiunculae' would 'light up Virgil like little stars' ('tanq*uam* stellulis illustratus'), pointing out rhetorical figures, speeches, and other major structural features. He addresses the book to 'adolescentes', evidently with pedagogic purpose.[81] Up to 1520, Caminade's edition of Virgil was printed a total of eight times in Paris, three times in Strasbourg, and once by Pynson in London. At least in these early years, it was reproduced almost as frequently as the Aldine octavo.[82]

Pynson's copy-text was almost certainly one of the reprints rather than the original edition. Like several of the later copies, his octavo does not include Caminade's name, title or dedicatory epistles. He adopted a distinctive new title found in at least two prior editions:[83]

---

[80] On their friendship and quarrels, see Franz Bierlaire, 'Augustinus Vincentius Caminadus', in *Contemporaries of Erasmus: A Biographical Register of the Renaissance and Reformation*, ed. Peter G Bietenholz and homas Brian Deutscher, 3 vols (Toronto: University of Toronto Press, 1985–1987), I, pp. 250–1; and 'Érasme et Augustin Vincent Caminade', *Bibliothèque d'Humanisme et Renaissance* 30 (1968), 357–62. For Erasmus's poem praising Caminade's Virgil edition, see Erasmus, *Poems*, ed. Clarence H. Miller and Harry Vredeveld, 2 vols (Toronto: University of Toronto Press, 1993), no. 116 (I, pp. 334–5; notes at II, pp. 691–3).

[81] The title reads: 'Augustinus Camynadus studiosæ Iuuentuti: S.D. | En adolescentes optimi Vergilius ille omnis doctrinæ | parens denuo p*er* me exactissima cura emaculatus: cu*m* sum | ma ueteris orthographiæ obseruatio*ne*: nouis insup*er* anno | tatiunculis tanq*uam* stellulis illustratus:' (1501 edition, sig. a1r).

[82] After Cruzenach's 1498 and 1501 editions, further Paris reprints were: USTC 182666 (Johann Philippi de Cruzenach, 1505), 182,815 (Jean Seurre for Pierre Baquelier, 30 Dec. 1507), 143,738 (Jean Petit and François Regnault, [1510?]); 183,270 (Thomas Anguelart, 1512). Strasbourg reprints are: 682250 (Johann Prüß, 27 Jul. 1508); 682,079 (Reinhard Beck, 1514); 682,080 (Reinhard Beck, 1518). There were two sextodecimo editions, one being USTC 182028 ([Paris, Frederic d'Egmont Jean Barbier, for Pierre Baquelier, 1520]). For descriptions of Baquelier's 1507 edition, the 1520 edition, and another undated sextodecimo edition, see Philippe Renouard, *Imprimeurs et Libraires Parisiens du XVIe siècle: Ouvrage publié d'après les manuscrits de Philippe Renouard*, 5 vols (Paris: Service des travaux historiques de la Ville de Paris, 1964-Present), III, nos 10, 37–8.

[83] In USTC, this title is catalogued in two reprints of Caminade's octavo, namely 143,738 (Paris: Jean Petit and François Regnault, [1510?]) and 183,270 (Paris: Thomas Anguelart, 1512). However, USTC does not routinely record long titles, and there might be other un-catalogued

Vergiliana poesis que Latinitatis norma est Et propulsatis *et* elimatis mendis omnibus felici gaudet exordio.[84]

Besides making conventional statements of textual correctness, the title advertises Virgil as 'Latinitatis norma', the standard of good Latin. Such a declaration, that Virgil's classical Latin is to be learned and imitated, evidently draws on humanist sensibilities, presenting the Virgil edition as an indispensable tool of language study. Pynson's edition of Virgil, furnished with Caminade's pedagogic marginalia, is one of his broader attempts to capitalize on the growth of humanist learning in England. He started to print humanist grammars from the 1490s onwards, produced an edition of Terence in *c.* 1494–1497, and went on to print Cicero's *Philippics* in 1521. Together with Virgil, these authors were staple features of humanist curricula, models of classical grammar and style.[85] All three surviving copies of Pynson's Virgil have frequent interlinear lexical glosses in Latin and English. In one case, the dense annotations are scrawled in almost every consecutive line. Although, as we have seen, this glossing is not necessarily evidence of a given readership, these editions were likely used by learners, closely parsing Virgil's model Latin.[86]

While the title foregrounds the humanist significance of Virgil's language, the textual apparatus in the edition derives from long-established approaches to the *expositio auctorum*. As with the commentaries and annotations in folio *opera* editions, the content of Caminade's marginalia

---

editions named 'Vergiliana poesis...' I have not examined the 1512 edition, but have compared Pynson with the 1510. If indeed the 1510 edition was indeed Pynson's exemplar, he must have cross-referenced it with at least one other reprint of Caminade's edition. All the reprints of Caminade frequently omit a few of his scholia, but Pynson's edition has more marginalia than does the 1510 edition. For example, at *Bucolics* I.9 (sig. b3v), Pynson has the annotation 'Melibe*us* | Uide du | ctam egri- | tudine*m*', while the 1510 edition does not. Although the texts of Virgil are very similar, Pynson has notable differences of punctuation and a few textual corrections, possibly from his own proofreading, possibly corrected against another edition. For example, at *Bucolics* I.79, Pynson correctly has 'noctē', whereas the 1510 edition has 'nocte' without the abbreviated 'm'. The 1510 edition also has a dedicatory epistle and Antonio Mancinelli's verse arguments to the *Bucolics*, none of which was included by Pynson.

[84] Pynson's edition, sig. a1r. The title is shortened from the 1510 and 1512 Paris editions. As listed in *USTC*, they have: 'Uergiliana poesis (que latinitatis norma est) et p*ro*pulsatis et eliminatis mendis omnib*us* quib*us* antea: vt pard*us* maculis asp*er*sus erat. sereno gaudet celo.'

[85] In *STC*, Pynson's Terence is 23885 and his Cicero is 5311. In *ISTC*, his Terence is listed as seven separate editions from 1494–1497 (it00107100-700), including two editions of *Andria*, while the other five comedies have one edition each. For references to extant curricula, see above Chapter 1, p. 28.

[86] Details of surviving copies are listed above, the Princeton copy having the densest glosses. In my sample of Virgil editions, all the imported octavos have similar glossing, namely O.1520.1, O1520.2, and O.1520.3.

is largely similar to manuscript glosses of Virgil written centuries before. They pertain to similar subjects, and the influence of Servius is evident throughout. By far the largest group of marginalia is structural headings, indicating descriptions, orations, prophecies, and the content of important passages. For example, when Jupiter famously prophesies the rise of Rome and the Emperor Augustus (*Aeneid* I.257-96), Caminade marks 'Vaticinium iovis' and 'Adulatio ad cesarem'.[87] Other printed marginalia aid comprehension of the text by explaining points of history or lexicography. For example, when Juno travels to Aeolia (*Aeneid* I.52), Caminade copies Servius's explanation, 'Eolie insule post Sicilie fretum'. At the line 'Implentur veteris Bacchi' (Aeneas's men 'take their fill of old wine'), he then points out 'Implentur cum genitivo' (*Aeneid* I.215), evidently having read Servius's note on the subject.[88] These types of gloss, clarifying rare words and points of grammar, have already been observed throughout manuscripts and print editions alike. Albeit in a compressed form, Caminade provides his octavo with the same glossing framework, marking the structure of the text and helping comprehension of the more obscure passages.

In comparison with the annotators discussed so far, Caminade gives proportionally more attention to Virgil's poetic licence, guiding his students through the difficult language. For example, he frequently points out instances of syncope and syneresis, including those not mentioned by Servius.[89] Given that he was writing for 'adolescentes', they might have needed help pronouncing 'Oilei' and 'Cytherea'. Likewise, his student-readers might not have recognized irregular, syncopated word forms such as 'compostus' and 'accestis'. In manuscripts, annotators had usually handled these terms in the interlinear glosses 'compositus' or 'accesistis *per* sincopa*m*'.[90] Moreover, it was important that students did not copy these terms in their own Latin compositions. Poetic language, as medievalists have remarked, is not ideal for teaching grammar to schoolchildren, since many rhetorical and poetic effects depend on barbarisms and solecisms.[91] Whereas Pynson's title markets Virgil as the 'norma Latinitatis', Caminade's

---

[87] Quoted from Pynson's edition, sigs m5r-v. For *descriptiones*, see sigs m1v (*Aeneid* I.81 onwards, the tempest), m3r (I.159 onwards, Aeneas's safe harbour).

[88] Quoted from Pynson's edition, sigs m1r, m4r.

[89] Examples of syncope include 'repostu*m*' (*Aeneid* I.26, sig. l9r), 'accestis' (I.201, sig. m3v), 'compostus' (I.249, sig. m5r), etc. Examples of syneresis are 'Oilei' (I.41, sig. l9v), 'Cytherea' (I.257, sig. m5r), etc. Servius identifies all of them except the 'Oilei' example. Caminade could have found it in Landino's *Aeneid* commentary, or he could simply have identified it himself.

[90] TCC, MS 457, fols 7r, 6r.

[91] Zeeman, 'The Schools Give a License to Poets'; Reynolds, *Medieval Reading*, pp. 121-34.

annotations ironically draw attention to the abnormal aspects of Virgil's language rather than demonstrate a paradigm for students to imitate. Because the marginalia fit in the narrow margins of an octavo, their compression occasionally renders their meaning obscure. For example, at the line 'Quippe ferant rapidi secum vertantq*ue* per auras' (*Aeneid* I.59), Caminade follows Servius in indicating an instance of 'Apheresis'.[92] Caminade's gloss gives no direct help for comprehension, but simply alerts the reader that the line contains a poetic word-form. As the full commentary explains, Virgil uses the truncated form 'ferant' to mean 'auferant'. Perhaps Caminade intended his annotations as prompts, so that students would look up fuller explanations in Servius.

Besides aiding comprehension and annotating structural features, Caminade devotes the bulk of his annotations to rhetorical study. As seen in earlier glosses and commentaries, these rhetorical marginalia typically identify parts of orations, topics of argument, and instances of *captatio benevolentiae*.[93] For example, when Juno petitions Aeolus to begin the storm (*Aeneid* I.65-75), Caminade provides almost exactly the same marginalia as the scribe of the Trinity manuscript. Both following Servius's analysis, they identify the speech as a petition and mark its structure. Caminade's marginalia read: 'exordiu*m*', 'Oratio iunonis o*mn*ib*us* petitioni-b*us* absoluta', 'narrat*io*', 'Modus' and 'Rem*une*ratio'.[94] As well as the rhetorical analyses in Servius, Caminade also had a full copy of Tiberius Donatus's *Interpretationes Virgilianae*. When Juno, for example, gives her causes for punishing the Trojans, she cites the example of Pallas, who was allowed to take violent revenge on Ajax (*Aeneid* I.39-45). Following Donatus, Caminade's marginalium identifies it as an argument 'A m*in*ore ad mai*us*'.[95] Given that Pallas, the lesser goddess, burnt Ajax's entire fleet, Juno argues that she, the wife of Jupiter, should be allowed to harm Aeneas.[96] Caminade's other rhetorical annotations pertain to figures, particularly similes ('Comparatio').[97] None of these marginalia would look out

---

[92] Pynson's edition, sig. m1r.
[93] For an example of *captatio benevolentiae*, see sig. n2r (*Aeneid* I.522). This is the start of Ilioneus's speech, and the comment derives from Servius.
[94] Pynson's edition, sigs m1r-v.   [95] Pynson's edition, sig. l9v.
[96] Donatus: 'in ipsa conparatione persistens utitur argumento a minore ad maius. minor enim fuerat Minerva aetate et potestate [...]'. See *Tiberi Claudi Donati ad Tiberium Claudium Maximum Donatianum filium suum Interpretationes Virgilianae: Primum ad vetustissimorum codicum fidem recognitas*, ed. H. Georges, 2 vols (Leipzig: Teubner, 1905-6), I, p. 19.
[97] For 'Comparatio' annotations, see the famous storm simile (*Aeneid* I.148, sig. m2v) and bees simile (I.430, sig. m8v). For other figures, see 'hystero*n* protero*n*' (I.179, sig. m3r) and 'zeugma' (I.120, sig. m2r), both identified in Servius.

of place in fifteenth-century manuscripts, which often have glosses to 'Comparationes' and parts of orations (as discussed in Chapter 1). In furnishing Virgil's text with these 'annotatiunculae', the humanist Caminade and his printer in England, Pynson, provide an apparatus for the same rhetorical analysis.

Whereas the content of the annotations builds on traditional modes of pedagogic exposition, the edition as a whole looks forward to a long history of octavo printing across the sixteenth century. Caminade's 'annotatiunculae' became a major new genre of classical commentary. Just as folios had their voluminous *catena*-commentaries, future octavos were adorned with these sets of short marginalia, usually titled 'adnotamentis', or 'scholiis'. From 1515, a second set of Virgil marginalia began to circulate in Parisian octavo editions, this time written by the printer Jodocus Badius Ascensius (1462-1535). Although better known for writing longer pedagogic commentaries (discussed in Chapter 3), his octavo editions and their marginalia served a similar readership, identifying rhetorical and structural features for students.[98] In 1530, Philip Melanchthon prepared further *adnotamenta*, which became the most widely-printed Virgil marginalia of the sixteenth century. Compared with Caminade, Melanchthon's marginal headings have an even sharper focus on rhetoric and argumentation. Melanchthon, a major author of rhetorical textbooks, prepared his textual apparatus to complement this pedagogic programme.[99]

Although Caminade's edition and the octavo became widely popular, Pynson's own venture does not seem to have been a commercial success. Much like his printings of Terence and Cicero, he produced only one Virgil edition in his career. England's printers of classics (as noted in the Introduction) had to compete with a large trade in continental imports, and most of them chose not to take the risk. There were no further Latin editions of Virgil's *Opera* until Henry Bynneman's octavo of 1570.[100] Whereas Pynson took his octavo from the Paris tradition, Bynneman's edition bears the influence of the Aldine press, both in its typography and its text. By the Elizabethan era, printing in italic was standard for many

---

[98] As listed in *USTC*, Ascensius's octavo is 183591 (1515), but I have not examined a copy. At least one later Paris octavo, *USTC* 184099, contains Ascensius's scholia, and two copies were imported to England: O.1520.2 and O.1520.3.
[99] For the first edition, see *Opera*, ed. Philip Melanchthon (Haguenau: Johann Setzer, 1530; *USTC* 701364). On the wide printing of the marginalia, see Wilson-Okamura, *Virgil in the Renaissance*, p. 268. For analysis, see Mack, 'Melanchthon's Commentaries on Latin Literature', pp. 43–9.
[100] Virgil, *Opera*, ed. Paulo Manuzio ([London]: Henry Bynneman, 1570; *STC* 24788).

classical works, even in England. Bynneman adopted the design and paratexts from a set of *Opera* editions prepared by Aldus's son, Paolo Manuzio (1512-74). From 1558 onwards, Paolo's Virgil editions included a new set of marginalia and prose arguments, all of which Bynneman reprinted.[101] Like Pynson decades before, Bynneman probably intended to supply the pedagogic market.[102] His edition, based on Manuzio, brought about a revival of octavo classical printing in England. Over the next three decades, London presses produced eight editions of Virgil's *Opera*, six in octavo and two sextodecimos. There were also new editions of Ovid, Terence and Horace.[103] Over half a century after Pynson's first venture, the octavo editions of the classics eventually became a standard fixture of English printing.

Conclusion

As this chapter has shown, the reading of early printed editions from the late fifteenth and early sixteenth centuries is characterized by similar intellectual approaches to the reading of Virgil manuscripts. The history of early Virgilian printing, in this light, challenges traditional conceptions about the relative impact of humanism and the printing press. Although recent studies often downplay the impact of printing, technological and commercial factors of the print market in fact caused significant and immediate developments in contents and design, particularly in the sizes of Virgil editions, the layout of the page, and the provision of commentaries. These changes of book design, however, do not reflect a contemporary intellectual change of book use. The printers' paratexts, as in manuscripts, were grounded in the same traditions of grammatical and rhetorical pedagogy. Servius's commentary, the mainstay of Virgilian study since Antiquity, was printed widely in folio editions. Octavo editions, meanwhile, contained brief

---

[101] USTC 862801 (Venice: Paolo Manuzio, 1558). Manuzio printed earlier *Opera* editions in 1553 and 1555, but they did not have marginalia. See USTC 862794, 862,725.

[102] Wallace, *Virgil's Schoolboys*, p. 57 ff.

[103] Virgil octavos were: STC 24788-9 (1570, 1572, 1576, 1580), 24790.7-91 (1593, 1597). The two sextodecimo editions were: 24790-90.3 (1583, 1584). There was also a *Georgics* octavo edition with a prose paraphrase by Nicholas Grimmald. See STC 24822 (London: George Bishop and Ralph Newbery, 1591). During the same period, the STC lists nine octavo editions of Ovid's Latin works: 18926.1-18926.7 (1570, 1572, 1576, 1585), 18,927 (1583), 18,929 (1594), 18947.5 (1574), 18,951 (1584), and 18976.4-6 (1574, 1581). There were also four sextodecimo editions: 18928-8a (1583, 1583) 18951.5-52 (1582, 1589). The Terence and Horace editions are STC 23885.7-888, 13,784-87a.

printed marginalia to elucidate obscure points of language, delineate structural features and mark rhetorical figures. Building on these paratexts, Virgil's annotators show a close attention to the letter of the text, schoolboys and learned clerics alike. While some readers also marked moral *sententiae* or ancient myths, the most common causes of annotation were to correct the text, compile interlinear glosses, and identify rhetorical figures, just as they had been for centuries before.

Despite the increasing diffusion of humanist scholarship in the late fifteenth and early sixteenth centuries, its influence should not be overstated. While the title page of Pynson's edition evinces a humanist attitude in advertising Virgil's exemplary Latin style, Caminade's marginalia would not have been out of place in a manuscript a century earlier. Although the All Souls annotator referred to Valla's *Elegantiae* and Tortelli's *Orthographia*, his reading also involved a wide range of more traditional works, notably Johannes Balbus's *Catholicon*, Papias's *Vocabularium*. The continuous prevalence of the *enarratio poetarum* and, connectedly, the abiding use of well-established grammars and dictionaries indicate an underlying traditionalism in late fifteenth- and early sixteenth-century reading of the classics.

Although the combined effects of humanism and the printing press promoted Virgil to an ever-wider readership, longstanding traditions of medieval learning continued to provide readers' primary tools of interpretation. While this chapter has focused on editions of Virgil's *Opera*, the same continuities are also observed in editions of Virgil's individual works. As the next chapter will demonstrate, well-established traditions of pedagogy and commentary shaped the content and use of fifteenth- and early sixteenth-century editions of the *Bucolics*.

3
Wynkyn de Worde and the *Bucolics*

In the early sixteenth century, the London printer, Wynkyn de Worde, printed four quarto editions of the *Bucolics* (1512, 1514, 1522, 1529).[1] Although rarely studied by modern scholars, they are often and rightly mentioned as one of De Worde's attempts to capitalize on the growing popularity of humanist curricula in England.[2] As discussed in the previous two chapters, English schoolmasters of the late fifteenth and early sixteenth centuries increasingly incorporated classical texts in their teaching. Responding to this new trend, contemporary printers changed their repertoires of schoolbooks. De Worde started his career printing medieval grammars and the *Auctores Octo*, but later introduced humanist curricular texts including Virgil's *Bucolics*. While historians of education, most importantly Nicholas Orme, have produced excellent accounts of this transition, they usually treat the printing of pre-humanist schoolbooks separately from the new humanist programme.[3] As the following case-study will show, however, the early stages of humanist schooling were as much a period of continuity as of change. Well-established schoolbooks, especially the *Auctores Octo*, had a pervasive influence on the content, design, and use of early school editions of the classics.

Like many of his Latin productions, De Worde's *Bucolics* quartos were reprints of a successful continental edition, titled 'Bucolica Virgilii cum commento familiarissimo'. As advertised by the title, the editions contain a 'familiar' or 'easy' commentary, a common commentary genre in the late fifteenth and early sixteenth centuries. These commentaries were designed to assist learners with elementary comprehension of the text. The familiar commentary in De Worde's editions was first printed by a Parisian printer,

---

[1] STC 24813, 24814, 24814.5, 24815.

[2] Among histories of humanism and education, these editions are mentioned in: Nicholas Orme, 'Schools and School-books', in *CHBB: III*, pp. 449–69 (p. 456); Daniel Wakelin, 'Humanism and Printing', in *A Companion to the Early Printed Book in Britain, 1476–1558*, ed. Gillespie and Powell, pp. 227–47 (p. 238); J.B. Trapp, 'The Humanist Book', in *CHBB: III*, pp. 285–315 (p. 311).

[3] Orme, *English Schools in the Middle Ages*, pp. 106–15; 'Schools and School-books', pp. 461–9.

Antoine Caillaut, appearing in his 1492 quarto edition of the *Bucolics* (henceforth, 'Parisian commentary').[4] The same year, he also printed a *Georgics* edition of exactly the same kind. The Parisian commentary to the *Bucolics* was reprinted in at least 23 editions up to 1501, becoming one of the most frequently-printed Virgil commentaries of the period.[5] Even before it was printed by De Worde, many copies had been imported to England. Given that De Worde was involved in the import business, he might have managed the sale of these continental *Bucolics* editions, showing him first-hand their popularity among English buyers.[6]

Despite its success in the late fifteenth and early sixteenth centuries, the Parisian commentary is little-known to modern scholars. When studies discuss familiar commentaries, they usually associate this commentary genre with one of its later practitioners, the Flemish printer, editor and commentator Jodocus Badius Ascensius (also known as Josse Bade, 1462–1535).[7] Originally a schoolmaster in Lyon, Ascensius wrote familiar commentaries for 21 Latin authors, starting with Boethius (1498), Juvenal (1498) and Persius (1499). After moving to Paris in 1500, he produced the first familiar commentary for all Virgil's *Opera* (1500–1), which was reprinted throughout the sixteenth century and was notably used by the

---

[4] The name 'Parisian commentary' is my own. In the *ISTC*, editions containing this anonymous commentary are called simply *Bucolica (cum commento)*. To my knowledge, it has not previously been argued that Caillaut was the first printer of the commentary. According to the *ISTC*, two editions of *Bucolica (cum commento)* were printed in 1492: 1) Deventer: Jacobus de Breda, 31 Oct. 1492 (*ISTC* iv00208700); and 2) Paris: Antoine Caillaut, [about 1492] (*ISTC* iv00208750). The French origin is to be preferred for the following four reasons. First, the Parisian commentary of the *Bucolics* contains French glosses (discussed below). Second, German printers titled their editions 'cum commento familiarissimo Parisius elucrubato' i.e. composed in Paris. For example, see *ISTC* iv00210000 (Cologne: Heinrich Quentell, 6 Apr. 1495;), sig. A2r. Third, the colophon of the 1498 Seville edition reads 'impressa primum parisiis'. See *ISTC* iv00220000 (Seville: Compañeros alemanes (Johann Pegnitzer, Magnus Herbst and Thomas Glockner), for Johannes Laurentius, 3 Oct. 1498;), sig. o4r. Fourth, Caillaut also published the first edition of the *Georgics* 'cum commento familiari' in the same year, namely *ISTC* iv00225000 (Paris: Antoine Caillaut, 7 June 1492).

[5] Up to 1501, the *ISTC* lists 21 *Bucolica (cum commento)* editions and two joint *Bucolica et Georgica (cum commento familiari)* editions. On later editions up to 1559, see below p. 81.

[6] On De Worde's prominent role in the import trade, see C.P. Christianson, 'The Rise of London's Book Trade', in *CHBB: III*, pp. 128–47 (pp. 139–42).

[7] On Ascensius's works, the foundational text remains: P. Renouard, *Bibliographie des impressions et des œuvres de Josse Badius Ascensius: imprimeur et humaniste, 1462–1535*, 3 vols (Paris: E. Paul et fils and Guillemin, 1908). The main studies of his commentary technique are: Paul White, *Jodocus Badius Ascensius: Commentary, Commerce and Print in the Renaissance* (Oxford: OUP, 2013), esp. Chapters 3 and 7; Mark Crane, '"Virtual Classroom"': Josse Bade's Commentaries for the Pious Reader', *The Unfolding of Words: Commentary in the Age of Erasmus*, ed. Judith Rice Henderson (Toronto: University of Toronto Press, 2012), pp. 101–17.

translator Gavin Douglas (discussed in Chapter 5).[8] By Ascensius's time, however, this commentary genre was already well-established among French printers. Over the previous two decades, they had printed many familiar commentaries for the hymns and the *Auctores Octo*.[9] As increasing numbers of young men began to study classical texts, this well-known genre of pedagogic commentary was applied to the *antiqui*. Caillaut's Parisian commentary to the *Bucolics* was an early example of this innovation. When it was first printed in 1492, it was only the second familiar commentary to a classical text, the first being Guy Jouenneaux's (Guido Juvenalis's) edition of Terence's *Comoediae* (1490).[10] Modern studies of familiar commentaries rarely acknowledge that Ascensius was building on these earlier, non-classical models. De Worde's editions—and indeed, the intellectual influences on Ascensius himself—cannot be understood without this wider context.

Far from a purely humanist genre, the history of familiar commentaries reflects the continued use of traditional curricular texts as much as the gradual transition to the classics. De Worde produced thirteen familiar commentary editions of the *Auctores Octo*, and his four Virgil editions are his only extant classical ventures in the genre.[11] Typical of many of his contemporaries, he continued to print the *Auctores Octo* and their commentaries even while he was printing Virgil. Around the turn of the century, these well-established schoolbooks were the main context for the study of the *Bucolics*. Surviving copies from the period are more often bound with the *Auctores Octo* than with classical texts. Only in the later 1510s and 1520s, when the New Learning was more established in England, do *Sammelbände* consist entirely of humanist curricular choices. During the 1520s, De Worde improved the Latin text and design of his *Bucolics* editions, seeking to

---

[8] For lists, see Renouard, *Bibliographie*, I, pp. 140–56; White, *Jodocus Badius Ascensius*, pp. 297–9.

[9] These commentaries are not usually discussed in the context of Ascensius, probably because the hymns and *Auctores Octo* editions were simply titled 'expositio' or 'cum commento' rather than 'cum commento familiari'. In print, the term 'familiaris' originated with commentaries to Terence (cited in next footnote).

[10] *Comoediae*, comm. Aelius Donatus, Guido Juvenalis and Johannes Calphurnius (Lyon: Johannes Fabri, 28 May 1490; *ISTC* it00086700). Ascensius later produced a revised version of Guido's edition, which had several reprints. Ascensius's revised edition is *ISTC* it00091000 (Lyon: Johannes Trechsel, 29 Aug. 1493), hereafter abbreviated 'Terence, *Comoediae* (1493)'.

[11] De Worde also sold imported copies of Ascensius's revised edition of Guido's Terence. See *STC* 23885.3 (Paris: Badius Ascensius, for Wynkyn de Worde, Michael Morini and John Bray in London, 1504). De Worde possibly printed a copy of this Terence edition himself, now extant only in a few leaves and listed as *STC* 23885.5 (London: [Wynkyn de Worde, 1510]).

appeal to this increasingly humanist readership. His changes were driven by commercial needs of supplying these new educational trends and emulating continental competitors.

Content

Before approaching this argument, it is first necessary to describe the generic features of a familiar commentary. Modern studies typically approach this issue by analysing the prefaces of Ascensius.[12] These are among the earliest printed prefaces to contain substantial discussions of the genre and its intended readership. Earlier commentators, such as the *Auctores Octo* commentators and Parisian commentator, launch directly into an *accessus* or *vita auctoris* without pausing to reflect on their chosen type of commentary. Writing several years later, Ascensius provides a necessary, albeit belated, insight into their intentions. He envisages that his familiar commentaries would be used by young learners of Latin, helping them with basic comprehension of Latin texts. He routinely refers to his readers as 'iuuenes' and 'adolescentes'.[13] As Ascensius indicates on several occasions, the aim of the familiar commentary is to facilitate independent study of the authors. According to his Persius preface, his comprehensive exposition of the text will help learners to 'comprehend the abstruse meanings of poets without a teacher'.[14] In his Virgil preface, Ascensius aims to write his *expositio familiaris* 'for those who lack an abundance of teachers', providing them 'an easy way to this author'.[15] Although, Ascensius goes on, his commentary could be read both by school students and even their teachers, his aim as a commentator was, as far as possible, to recreate the teacher's exposition with a written substitute. Ascensius guides the readers through the text as a teacher would his listeners. As Mark Crane has neatly described it, the familiar

---

[12] For example, White, *Jodocus Badius Ascensius*, pp. 61–106.

[13] For example, see Virgil, *Opera* (1500–01), II, sigs 1v-2r. For a discussion of intended readership, see White, *Jodocus Badius Ascensius*, pp. 83–90.

[14] 'Neque enim omnes sine præceptore: vel argutiores commentarios: vel abstrusiuscula Poetarum sensa compræhendere possumus'. See Persius, *Satyrae*, comm. Joannes Britannicus, ed. and comm. Ascensius (Lyons: Nicolaus Wolf, 27 Jan? 1499; *ISTC* ip00359000), sig. a1v.

[15] Ascensius's wording, 'quibus pręceptorum deest copia', was likely influenced by Guido's earlier preface to Terence. Ascensius's preface reads: 'Hunc autem poetam familiariter exponere constitui vt quibus pręceptorum deest copia / habeant ex nobis facilem ad eum viam'. Guido's preface describes the Terence commentary as an: '...adiumento: quibus interpretum facilis copia non est'. See Virgil, *Opera* (1500–1), II, sig. 2r; Terence, *Comoediae* (1493), sig. a2r.

commentary is a 'virtual classroom', simulating the presence of a living schoolmaster.[16]

Although these prefaces, as I shall later discuss, are not straightforward evidence of actual readership and use, the idea of 'replacing' a teacher is a useful starting-point to describe this commentary genre. Familiar commentaries followed the structure and content of a classroom exposition. As discussed in Chapters 1 and 2, teachers would expound literary texts in short passages, first construing the Latin, then explaining particular historical references and grammatical features. In familiar commentaries, the text is likewise divided into passages, and each passage is followed by its commentary. Since most of the *Bucolics* consist of dialogues, the passage-breaks in the Parisian commentary usually correspond with the speeches of Virgil's shepherd-interlocutors. For example, Tityrus's first speech in *Bucolics* I:

O Melibœe deus nobis hæc otia fecit.
Namq*ue* erit ille mihi semper deus: illius aram
Sæpe tener nostris ab ouilib*us* imbuet agnus.
Ille meas errare boues (vt cernis) *et* ipsu*m*
Ludere (quæ vellem) calamo permisit agresti.

¶Co*n*strue sic. O melibee o pastor d*eus* .i. cesar august*us* / fecit .i. dedit / hec otia .i. ista bona vel quiete*m*. Namq*ue* ille .s. cesar / erit mihi .s. virgilio / semp*er* d*eus* .i. in vita *et* post mortem sua*m* ag*n*us .i. ouis tener .i. iuuenis ab ouilib*us* n*o*s*t*ris .i. a pecorib*us* n*o*s*t*ris / imbuet .i. sacrificabit ara*m* .i. sup*er* altare / illi*us* .s. augusti cesaris. Ille .s. cesar permisit boues meas sc*ilicet* vaccas / errare .i. per ca*m*pos esse / vt cernis .i. vt vides / et p*er*misit ipsu*m* .i. me virgiliu*m* / ludere calamo agresti .i. fistula rustica / que velle*m* .i. quecunq*ue* carmina velle*m* ludere. ¶O melibee. resp*on*det tityr*us* .i. virgili*us* ad melibeu*m*. dicens q*uod* [deus] .s. cesar / dedit sibi illa otia .i. facultate*m* viuendi ex prop*r*iis agris sine graui labore. Namq*ue* ille .i. cesar / erit mihi d*eus* in vita sua *et* post morte*m*. Nam alii imperatores reputaba*n*tur inter deos post morte*m* / sed augustus cesar in vita sua meruit deitate*m* *et* habere te*m*plum sicut deus...

(*Bucolics* I.6–10)[17]

---

[16] Crane, '"Virtual Classroom"', p. 102.

[17] All quotations of the Parisian commentary are from De Worde's 1522 edition, hereafter '*Bucolica* (1522)', and this passage is on sig. A2v. In order to make the text more readable, I have expanded abbreviations, written lemmata in bold, and corrected obvious spelling errors. For '*dicens* q*uod* [deus] .s. cesar / dedit', I have supplied '[deus]' from the 1492 De Breda edition (sig. a2v), cited in fn. 4.

Typical of familiar commentaries, the exegesis consists of two parts, sometimes called the 'constructio' ('grammatical construction') and the 'sententia' ('meaning').[18] As would a teacher's exposition, the commentator uses the first part to construe the text ('¶Construe sic... quecumque carmina vellem ludere.'). He rearranges the syntax into *ordo naturalis*, and provides explanatory glosses to every word. The opening imperative, 'Construe', is a common formula in many familiar commentaries, and possibly imitates the speech of contemporary teachers.[19] The second part of the commentary ('¶O melibee. *respo*ndet tytir*us*...') provides a brief summary of the passage and explains references to classical history, mythological allusions, allegories, and points of grammar. In this particular passage, the commentator explains an allegorical reference to Augustus, the emperor's deification, and the niceties of pagan sacrifice. As would a teacher, the familiar commentary leads the reader through the material in ascending order of difficulty, starting with the grammatical construction of the passage, before tackling its finer details.[20]

Most scholarly discussions of the genre focus on print examples, but the main features of the familiar commentary originated in manuscript traditions. The alternating layout, the distinctive 'constructio', and the formulaic imperative 'construe' are all seen in fourteenth and fifteenth-century commentaries to the *Auctores Octo*. Some of these commentaries were eventually printed, and they served as templates for the later commentaries to the classics. For example, the most frequently-printed familiar commentary to Theodulus's *Ecloga* was written in 1406/7 by French grammarian Odo Picardus (Eudes de Fouilloy).[21] While Picardus's work is extant only in continental manuscripts, similar commentaries to Theodulus were also circulating in English copies during the fifteenth century.[22] In contrast

---

[18] Some editions of the Parisian commentary provide marginal headings for the two parts of the commentary. For example, *Bucolica (cum commento)* (Paris: Wolfgang Hopyl, 1 Feb. 1494; ISTC iv00209000). Ascensius's commentaries usually have marginal headings, but he writes 'ordo' instead of 'constructio'. See Virgil, *Opera* (1500-1).

[19] White, *Jodocus Badius Ascensius*, pp. 96-103, has discussed how Ascensius's familiar commentaries evoke spoken interactions of the classroom.

[20] Some of the older familiar commentaries, such as the *Auctores Octo* commentaries, do not adhere rigidly to this order. In Odo Picardus's commentary to Theodulus (discussed below), the *constructio* is printed at the end of each section.

[21] On this commentary, see Betty Nye Quinn, 'ps-Theodulus', in *Catalogus Translationum et Commentariorum: Mediaeval and Renaissance Latin Translations and Commentaries: Annotated Lists and Guides*, ed. P.O. Kristeller, et al., 10 vols (Washington, D.C.: Catholic University of America Press, 1960-Present), II, pp. 386-408 (pp. 405-8).

[22] For example, BL, MS Add. 10089, a compendium of school texts including Aesop's *Fabulae*, Alan of Lille's *Parabola* and John of Garland's *Synonyma*. Theodulus's *Ecloga* and its

with the many *Auctores Octo* commentaries, only one extant English manuscript contains a familiar commentary to Virgil. The manuscript was probably copied in the middle decades of the century, and the commentary covers the *Bucolics* and part of the *Georgics*. Although not identical to the Parisian commentary, it clearly belongs to the same genre, beginning with the characteristic imperative '*Con*strue. o. **tytire tu recubans** .i. iacens **sub tegmine patule fagi**'.[23] When Antoine Caillaut originally printed the Parisian commentary in 1492, he might have taken his text from a similar exemplar.

In comparison with other types of commentary, the familiar commentary had particular advantages for learners. In order to guide independent readers through the difficult Latin, the 'constructio' section provides meticulous help with syntax. Unlike other genres of exegesis, the 'constructio' in the familiar commentary discusses the lemmata in *ordo naturalis* rather than using the original order of the text. As quoted above, the Parisian commentator rearranges 'O Melibœe deus nobis hæc otia fecit' into:

¶ Co*n*strue sic. **O melibee** o pastor d**e***us* .i. cesar augus*tus* / **fecit** .i. dedit / **hec otia** .i. ista bona vel quiete*m*.

As might a teacher in a classroom exposition, the commentator guides the reader through the line in natural word-order. He first glosses the vocative 'O melibee', next the subject, the verb, and finally the object. Since this reordering continues for the whole commentary, the reader receives syntactic assistance for every line of the text, even for simple constructions. By comparison, other annotators and commentators usually restrict their syntactic comments to the more difficult lines. As seen in Chapters 1 and 2, no annotator of a manuscript or print edition writes construe marks for the entire text. Likewise, Servius and other *catena*-commentaries contain only scattered discussions of the 'ordo'.[24] Because of this convention, familiar commentaries can easily be distinguished from other types of basic pedagogic commentary, such as the widely-used commentaries of the humanist

---

commentary are on fols 2r-18r. The incipit of the commentary is: 'Construe: fervida estas torruit, i. cremavit iam, i. illo tempore.' The commentary is listed in Quinn, 'ps-Theodulus', p. 401.

[23] BL, MS Add. 11959. The manuscript contains a short *Vita Virgilii*, the *Bucolics*, and the *Georgics* up to II.13. Not only does it have the familiar commentary alternating with the text, the main scribe also writes marginal and interlinear glosses. In the above quotation from the commentary, the emphasis (my own) indicates lemmata from Virgil's text.

[24] On construe marks and other syntactic glosses, see Chapter 1, pp. 37–8.

Antonio Mancinelli. Although he pitched his *Bucolics* and *Georgics* commentaries for learners, he discusses the lemmata in the original order of the text, and does not construe every line.[25] More than any other feature of the familiar commentary, this insistent reordering of syntax alleviates the pupil's dependence on the schoolmaster. It neutralizes the difficult word-order of Virgil's poetry, explaining all the ellipses, rearranging all the hyperbatons. While the commentary still assumes basic competence in Latin vocabulary and morphology, the aspiring Latinist (at least in theory) can attempt an independent reading of the *Bucolics*.

As well as guiding the reader through basic comprehension, the Parisian commentator also treats Virgil's text as a vehicle for teaching wider points of vocabulary and grammar. Similar to many annotations discussed in Chapters 1 and 2, his commentary includes discussions of rhetorical figures, analysis of metrical features, and extended definitions of rare or important terms. For example, when Virgil uses the imperative 'da' ('give') in the secondary sense 'say', the commentator elaborates on its multiple usages:

O **tytire da** .i. dic mihi quis est ille deus qui dedit tibi ocia *et* ludere que velles. Ubi notandum est q*uod* dare significat tria s*cilicet* dicere / co*n*tribuere / *et* co*n*cedere iuxta illos versus.

(*Bucolics* I.18)[26]

In identifying the multiple meanings of 'dare', the commentator turns his literal explanation of the text into a general teaching-point about the Latin language. Like a schoolmaster speaking to his class, he implores his readers to take note of the definition. As with the imperative 'Construe', the gerundive 'notandum est' ('It is to be noted that...') and the imperative 'nota' ('Note that...') are common formulas throughout this and other familiar commentaries, pointing out the lessons for readers to memorize. The Parisian commentator simulates a schoolmaster not only in explaining Virgil's meaning, but also in his broader educative purpose of teaching Latin.

In these grammatical discussions, the commentator clearly intended his student-readers to recall their schoolroom lessons. With the exception of

---

[25] For the first edition of Mancinelli's commentaries, see *Bucolica et Georgica*, comm. Mancinellus (Rome: Eucharius Silber, 20 Oct. 1490; *ISTC* iv00219500). As discussed in Chapter 2, his commentaries were later reprinted in the 'Opera cum quinque commentariis' editions.

[26] *Bucolica* (1522), sig. A3r. The Virgilian line reads 'Sed tamen iste deus quis sit da Tityre nobis.'

Virgil's works, the most frequently cited text in the Parisian commentary is Alexander de Villa Dei's *Doctrinale*, which had been a core text of the grammar curriculum since the thirteenth century.[27] Although humanist grammarians critiqued, revised, and ultimately replaced *Doctrinale*, Alexander's text continued to be taught widely at least until the 1520s.[28] By linking his expositions of Virgil to this staple curricular text, the Parisian commentator helps his readers to consolidate their schoolroom knowledge of grammatical rules. In one line of *Bucolics* III, he even invokes *Doctrinale* to contradict the interpretation of the ancient commentator Servius. The metre of 'reiice capellas' ('Turn back the goats') yields the following discussion:

Et d*ic*it seruius **reiice capellas** est p*r*oceleumaticus p*r*o dactilo / sed secu*n*-du*m* doctrinale et modernos reiicio refert pro distat producu*n*t re / *et* sic no*n* potest esse p*r*oceleumaticus / sed syneresis / et confluunt due vocales in vnam / et debet proferri rice.

(*Bucolics* III.96)[29]

To resolve the hypermetrical syllable in 'reiice capellas', Servius writes that Virgil uses a four-syllable proceleusmatic foot ('re-ii-ce ca') in place of a three-syllable dactyl.[30] While other fifteenth- and sixteenth-century commentators accept this reading,[31] the Parisian commentator proposes a

---

[27] The citations of *Doctrinale* are at sigs A6v (twice on *Bucolics* II.1), C1r (III.79), C1v (III.96), E5r (VII.53) and F4r (VIII.108).

[28] On the widespread and continuing use of *Doctrinale*, see Philip Ford, 'Alexandre de Villedieu's *Doctrinale puerorum*: A Medieval Bestseller and Its Fortune in the Renaissance', in *Forms of the 'Medieval' in the 'Renaissance': A Multidisciplinary Exploration of a Cultural Continuum*, ed. George Hugo Tucker (Charlottesville, VA: Rookwood Press, 2000), pp. 155–71. Citations will use *Das Doctrinale des Alexander de Villa-Dei: Kritisch-exegetische Ausgabe mit Einleitung: Verzeichniss der Handschriften und Drucke nebst Registern*, ed. Dietrich Reichling (1893; New York: Lenox Hill, 1974).

[29] *Bucolica* (1522), sig. C1v. In fifteenth- and sixteenth-century editions, the compound verb 'reice' ('re' + 'iace') is often spelled 'reiice'. As in 'iace', the first 'i' in '-iice' is consonantal. In the final word of the commentary, De Worde's editions have 'reiice', which repeats the standard spelling rather than offering any new guidance on pronunciation. To convey the syneresis of the first two syllables, I have substituted 'rice' from De Breda's 1492 edition, sig. c3v.

[30] On this line, Servius writes: 'reice capellas "reice ca" proceleumaticus est pro dactylo'. On 'reice', *Doctrinale* says 'reicio, refert distat dant re tibi longam; | corripies aliis, nisi duplex consona subsit' ('Reicio, refert [as is the case in] distat give to you a long "re"; | You will reduce the others [i.e. the length of prefixes on other occasions], unless there is a double consonant', ll. 1617–8).

[31] For example, Torrentinus has: 'Reiicere *est* retrorsum iacere vel repellere. & *est* reiice p*r*oceleumaticus pes q*u*i co*n*stat q*u*attuor breuib*us* sillabis'. See *Bucolica*, comm. Torrentinus (Cologne: Heinrich Quentell, 1506; *USTC* 617336), fol. 15v. For similar comments in Ascensius, see *Opera* (1500–1), I, fol. 28r.

different scansion, taking the opportunity to apply and demonstrate one of Alexander's rules. As pupils would have learnt in the schoolroom, Alexander states that the prefix 're' in 'reiicio' should be pronounced as a long rather than a short syllable. Because this long 're' cannot subsist in a proceleusmatic foot, the commentator proposes a syneresis of 're' and 'iice', turning the four syllables 're-ii-ce ca' into the dactyl 'ri-ce ca' (nowadays the accepted reading of the line). Although some humanist commentators contradicted and revised Servius's readings, they tended to ground their observations in ancient texts rather than modern grammars. The Parisian commentator, by contrast, refers to Alexander's precepts as if they were generally applicable to the *Bucolics*. Only in one line does he identify a difference between Virgil's classical and Alexander's modern diction, but he still cites Alexander to elucidate this contrast.[32] Even when Virgil apparently deviates from Alexander's 'modern practice of versifying', the Parisian commentator continues to use the rules of *Doctrinale* as a touchstone for his *Bucolics* exposition.

The Parisian commentary, then, is grounded in the well-established curricular texts of the late fifteenth-century schoolroom. Although the commentator cites Ovid, Plutarch and other classical authors, Alexander is his main grammatical authority. He also refers to Évrard of Béthune's *Graecismus*, another popular school textbook, and uses Johannes Balbus's *Catholicon* for lexicographical discussions.[33] While humanist commentators of classical texts (as Chapter 2 showed) avoided citing these pre-humanist grammars and dictionaries, the majority of readers and annotators had no such scruples. During the late fifteenth and early sixteenth centuries, humanist texts were only starting to be adopted in Northern Europe, and these older grammatical works remained in widespread use. Among other familiar commentaries, this frame of reference is shared by the expositions of the *Auctores Octo*, all of which were written before the 1480s. The similarities of the Parisian commentary perhaps suggest an early date of

---

[32] On *Bucolics* VIII.108, the Parisian commentator writes '*et* est trocheus in secundo pede versus hexametri / nam "an qui amant" faciunt trocheum faciendo synalimpham non obstante doctrinalis regula. "Sedes nulla datur. et cetera." Quia iste liber factus est multo ante alexandrum qui locutus est secundum vsum metrificandi modernum' (sigs F4r-v; I add inverted commas for quotations of Virgil and Alexander). Whereas Alexander states that trochees can only appear in the sixth foot of a hexameter (*Doctrinale* l. 1577), the Parisian commentator allows Virgil an exception, making a putative distinction of classical and modern versification.

[33] For classical authors, see *Bucolica* (1522), sigs A7r, E4v (Pliny's *Historia*), A8r (Plutarch), C2r, C5v, E2r, F2v (Ovid) and D2v (Horace). For the *Catholicon* references, see sigs A2r and C5r. The *Graecismus* citation is at sig. C5r.

composition, at the latest 1492.[34] Anchored in the established curriculum of the day, this commentary is well-suited for introducing early humanist learners to a classical text. When Caillaut originally printed the *Bucolics* in the 1490s, he might have chosen the Parisian commentary for this reason. Perhaps its popularity, first in France and then in England, reflects its particular relevance to these early stages in the development of humanist education.

By the end of the fifteenth century, the success of the Parisian commentary had inspired competitors. Dutch grammarian Hermannus Torrentinus (Herman van Beek, c. 1450–c. 1520) produced new familiar commentaries both to the *Bucolics* and to the *Georgics*. Richardus Pafraet, a major printer of the Parisian commentary, printed them in Deventer around the year 1496.[35] Torrentinus's work, first of all, was more concise than the Parisian commentary. It might have appealed to cost-conscious printers and to readers intimidated by longer expositions. Second, the structure of his commentary was more accommodating to readers. For every passage of text, he typically begins his exposition with a short summary of the passage's content. Unlike the Parisian commentator, he does not launch straight into the 'constructio', and does not mix his summaries with the later 'sententia' section. Possibly because of his brevity and structural improvements, Torrentinus quickly overtook the Parisian commentary in the Dutch and German markets, and further copies were imported to England. Although their heyday ended in c. 1521, Torrentinus editions continued to be printed in Antwerp until 1556.[36] The success of Torrentinus's *Bucolics* and *Georgics* likely prompted German presses to release similar editions of the *Aeneid* and *Opuscula*.[37] By 1509, all Virgil's works were available in familiar commentary quartos.

---

[34] For example, Odo Picardus's commentary on Theodulus (c. 1406–7) refers to *Catholicon* (sigs A2v, A3r, A8v, etc), *Graecismus* (sigs A3r, B3r, B4r, etc) and *Doctrinale* (sig. B3v). It also cites Papias's eleventh-century *Elementarium Doctrinae Rudimentum* (sigs A3r, A4r, etc). References are from De Worde's 1515 edition (cited above).

[35] *Bucolica*, comm. Torrentinus ([Deventer: Richardus Pafraet, about 1496–1500]; *ISTC* iv00214000); *Georgica*, comm. Torrentinus (Deventer: Richardus Pafraet, 26 Aug. 1496; *ISTC* iv00229000).

[36] According to the *USTC*, there were 28 *Bucolics* and 10 *Georgics* editions up to 1521, then no further editions for a decade. From 1531 to 1556, 11 *Bucolics* editions were printed in Antwerp, the last being *USTC* 409303 (Antwerp: Hans de Laet, 1556).

[37] *Opuscula (cum commento)* (Cologne: Heinrich Quentell, 12 Mar. 1499; *ISTC* iv00231600); *Aeneis (cum familiari expositione)*, ed. Johann Schott (Strasbourg: Johann Knobloch, 28 Mar. 1509; *USTC* 682141).

In France, meanwhile, the development of the genre was dominated by Ascensius. At the turn of the century, he printed a series of *Opera* editions of the classical authors with familiar commentaries, including his major Virgil edition of 1500–1 (mentioned above). He was the first to write a complete familiar commentary to the *Opera*, including the *Opuscula* and Vegius's *Supplementum*. In a sharp break from prior familiar commentaries, Ascensius printed his Virgil edition in folio rather than quarto. Unlike the Parisian commentary and other precedents in the genre, he based the book's design on commentary-editions of the *Opera*, such as those discussed in Chapter 2. Moreover, Ascensius included several other commentaries, including Servius, Donatus, Filippo Beroaldo's *Annotationes contra Servium*, and Domizio Calderini's commentary on the *Opuscula*. As if to evoke this higher level of erudition, his familiar commentary is longer and more detailed than the Parisian commentary. His 'sententia' sections run for pages at a time, often sharing the encyclopaedic tendencies of Servius and Landino. More so than Torrentinus and the Parisian commentator, he emphasizes the role of the text in teaching Latin lexicography and grammar. For every passage of the *Bucolics*, he finishes his commentary with a list of grammatical and rhetorical rules to be memorized by the student. Like any good teacher, Ascensius not only explains the passage, but also summarizes the main teaching-points.[38] While it remains a resource for learners, this familiar commentary imparts a greater volume of information than any of its predecessors.

After 1500, Northern European printers more or less ceased printing the Parisian commentary, instead favouring Ascensius and Torrentinus. Although the Parisian commentary remained in print until the 1550s, the later editions were mainly printed in Italy, not in France, Germany or the Netherlands.[39] The ready supply of the Parisian commentary editions, which had been so widely imported to England, thus ended in the first decade of the sixteenth century. When De Worde first printed the Parisian commentary in 1512, he was possibly trying to exploit this downturn of supply. Although it was not as up-to-date as the more recent familiar commentaries, one might speculate that its former popularity assured De Worde of its commercial potential. As we shall see, he was still printing Alexander's *Doctrinale*, so perhaps he thought the Parisian commentary a suitable

---

[38] On Ascensius's lists of *regulae*, see the more detailed discussions in White, *Jodocus Badius Ascensius*, pp. 211–3, 214–7, 219.

[39] The latest of the Italian editions is *USTC* 862804 (Brescia: Lodovico Britannico, 1559).

companion to his other pedagogic texts. Just as continental supplies were dwindling, De Worde revived this popular classic for the English market.

Use

The Parisian commentary, then, is designed to help learners read the *Bucolics* independently. As if to replace a teacher's exposition, it guides the student through grammatical construction, basic allegory, historical references, and salient points of language. Unlike other familiar commentaries of the classics, its teaching of Latin is grounded in pre-humanist sources, such as *Catholicon* and *Doctrinale*. These intellectual affiliations, which reflect an early stage in the introduction of the New Learning, are witnessed in the wider printing of familiar commentaries and the use of the *Bucolics* editions. For De Worde and most printers of the day, their output in this genre was predominantly non-classical. Early readers, likewise, studied the *Bucolics* alongside the *Auctores Octo* and other established curricular texts. De Worde and his contemporaries would have considered the familiar commentary generally as a pedagogic genre rather than associating it specifically with the *studia humanitatis*.

If the genre was ever turned to humanist ends, it was the doing of Ascensius. As we have seen, most studies on the readership and use of familiar commentaries relate to Ascensius's oeuvre. Since he wrote predominantly on classical texts, scholars tend to present the genre as a means of popularizing the New Learning in northern Europe. Together with his forerunners, Torrentinus and Guido, he explicitly states this aim in his prefaces: to help young men engage in humane studies.[40] In addition to schoolmasters and pupils, recent scholars have also emphasized his intended readerships outside school institutions. Ascensius explicitly criticizes contemporary schooling in the classics, and laments the difficulties of finding good teachers. In Ascensius's hands, the 'virtual classroom' was a potential means to circumvent this perceived shortfall of institutional instruction, and to disseminate reliable teaching of the *studia humanitatis*.[41] To the same end, he also envisaged some of his familiar commentaries being used by

---

[40] As White puts it, 'essentially he was a popularizer and mediator, who made it his business to bring the new Italian learning to Northern Europe'. See *Jodocus Badius Ascensius*, p. 2.

[41] On Ascensius's criticism of contemporary education, see Crane, '"Virtual Classroom"', pp. 101-2.

adults, pursuing their own interests in Italian learning. As Paul White puts it, 'Badius suggests a variety of uses for the familiar commentary, depending on the particular needs of its users. It is clear that the commentary is not only intended for schoolboys and their tutors, but also for adults engaged in private study.'[42] Although this range of reading contexts is relevant to all familiar commentaries, Ascensius's emphasis on humane letters was his own particular vision of the genre. To describe De Worde's and his contemporaries' conception of the familiar commentary, the evidence of surviving printed editions provides a broader perspective than do Ascensius's prefaces.

In De Worde's oeuvre and in Europe as a whole, the most common texts to be printed with familiar commentaries were hymns and sequences. The earliest edition of the *Expositio hymnorum* was printed in 1476, and there were 55 further editions up to 1501.[43] In design, these hymns editions were the direct antecedents to the editions of the *Bucolics*. The editions were printed in quarto, had the commentary alternating with the text, and displayed the distinctive 'constructio'. Beginning in the 1490s, Pynson and De Worde printed a version for the Sarum rite, titled *Expositio hymnorum secundum usum sarum*. In 1502, Ascensius also produced an edition for export to England, and De Worde adopted Ascensius's text in his later printings. Sixteen editions were printed in London, as listed in Table 3.1.[44]

These editions were principally intended for pedagogic use. Hymns (as noted in Chapter 1) were common school texts in England, and the *Expositio Hymnorum* commentaries were written for learning Latin. Ascensius addresses his edition to the youths of Britain, and praises English schools for teaching sacred letters as well as poetry.[45] Like many editions of familiar commentaries, the title pages of De Worde's hymns editions bear woodcuts of a master and pupils holding quarto-sized books.

---

[42] White, *Jodocus Badius Ascensius*, p. 85.

[43] *ISTC* lists 55 editions of *Expositio Hymnorum*, and four English editions of *Expositio hymnorum secundum usum Sarum*. On the medieval development of *Expositio Hymnorum* commentaries, see Tony Hunt, *Teaching and Learning Latin in 13th-Century England*, 3 vols (Cambridge: D.S. Brewer, 1991), I, pp. 38–43.

[44] Pynson's: *STC* 16113/*ISTC* ie00164000 (1498), 16123 (1511), 16121a (1509); 16111/ie00163300 (1496), 16112/ie00163500 (1497), 16117.5 (1506), and 16127 (1515). De Worde: 16123a (1512), 16114/ie00164200 (1500), 16116a (1502), 16120 (1508), 16121 (1509), 16125 (1514), 16126 (1515), and 16128 (1517). Julian: 16117 (1505), 16122 (1510). The first copy of Ascensius's edition is *STC* 16116 (Paris: Andre Bocard, for John Baldwin in London, 1502). De Worde used Ascensius's text from 1509 onwards, and Julian printed it in 1510. Details lifted from *STC*.

[45] For Ascensius's preface to 'Britannie iuuenibus', see *STC* 16116, sig. A1v.

Table 3.1. Familiar commentary editions of the hymns and sequences printed in London

	Pynson	De Worde	Julian the Notary
Hymns	2 (1498, 1511)	–	–
Sequences	1 (1509)	1 (1512)	–
Combined Editions	4 (1496–1515)	7 (1500–1517)	2 (1505, 1510)

One surviving copy also appears in a pedagogic compilation with Virgil's *Bucolics* and several grammars.[46] Outside of institutional pedagogy, the *Expositio Hymnorum* also had an extensive readership among adults. In these cases, the familiar commentary was an aid to private devotion, helping adults to read the hymns independently in the original Latin.[47] This use of the hymns editions was perhaps Ascensius's inspiration in advertising some of his familiar commentaries to adult readers of the classics.

Within years of the first hymns editions, familiar commentaries were printed for the *Auctores Octo*. As discussed in previous chapters, these were staple curricular texts on the continent, and had a relatively wide usage in England. From the early 1480s onwards, printers made familiar commentary editions for the separate authors, the earliest being for Cato, Aesop and Theodulus.[48] In 1487, they started producing collected editions of the *Auctores Octo cum glossa*, in which each author was accompanied with a familiar commentary.[49] As for the *Bucolics* editions, the original centres of printing were Paris and Lyons, later spreading into the Netherlands and Germany. These books were widely imported to England, and several were reprinted in London. De Worde, Pynson and Julian the Notary produced

---

[46] For De Worde's editions containing schoolmaster woodcuts, see Edward Hodnett, *English Woodcuts, 1480–1535* (Oxford, OUP, 1935; repr. 1973), nos 918–923, which include De Worde's editions of hymns, grammars, *Auctores Octo*, and his 1514 *Bucolics*. For the pedagogic compilation, see discussion of **B.1493** below.

[47] For example, BodL, Auct. 1Q 6.35, a copy of *Expositio sequentiarum secundum usum Sarum* ([Cologne: Heinrich Quentell, c.1496]; ISTC is00454000). The owner signs himself 'William Jayne of Bristow marchant' (sig. F1r).

[48] Theodulus, *Ecloga*, comm. Odo Picardus (Eudes de Fouilloy) ([Paris: Ulrich Gering, between 1478 and 1483]; ISTC it00151650); Cato, *Disticha de moribus*, comm. 'Summi deus largitor praemii...' ([Paris: Ulrich Gering, about 1482–83]; ISTC ic00302600); *Aesopus moralisatus*, comm. 'In principio...' ([Toulouse: Henricus Mayer, not before 1484]; ISTC ia00144400). All three commentary editions were later printed by De Worde.

[49] According to the ISTC, the earliest edition was *Auctores Octo cum Glossa*, ed. Johannes Vincentius Metulinus ([Lyons: Printer of Guido, 'Casus longi', about 1487]; ISTC ia01181600). The ISTC lists 23 editions up to 1500.

Table 3.2. Familiar commentary editions of the *Auctores Octo* printed in London

	Pynson	De Worde	Julian the Notary
Theodulus	3 (1497/8–1508)	2 (1509–1515)	1 (1505)
Alanus	–	4 (1508–1525)	1 (1505)
Aesopus	1 (1502)	3 (1503–1516)	–
Cato	–	4 (1508–1515)	–

familiar commentary editions of Theodulus's *Ecloga*, Alan of Lille's *Parabola*, Aesop's *Fabulae* and Cato's *Disticha* (Table 3.2).[50]

Although Pynson was the first to print familiar commentaries in England, De Worde produced no fewer than thirteen editions. Besides one plain-text edition of Cato and one of Aesop,[51] these commentary editions were the only Latin editions of the *Auctores Octo* at English presses during the period. De Worde stopped printing these texts around 1515–6, shortly after his first two *Bucolics* editions (1512, 1514). After these crossover years, he printed only one outlying edition of Alanus's *Parabola* in 1525. By this time, schoolmasters were presumably teaching the *Auctores Octo* less frequently, and demand was shifting to the classics. Although it is possible that copies of later editions simply have not survived, the same decline of the *Auctores Octo* can also be observed among continental printers.[52]

During this period, the design of the *Auctores Octo* and hymns editions was applied to several other pedagogic works and their commentaries. Among them were Alexander's *Doctrinale*, discussed above, and John of Garland's *Synonyma* and *Aequivoca*, two popular verse-vocabularies mentioned in Chapter 1. These schoolbooks were typically printed in quarto, and had elementary commentaries alternating with the text. Whereas students

---

[50] Pynson's Theodulus: *STC* 23939.5/*ISTC* it00153200 (1497 or 1498?), 23940/it00153300 (1503?), 23940.7 (1508?). Julian's and De Worde's Theodulus: 23940.3 (1505), 23941 (1509), 23943 (1515). Julian's and De Worde's Alanus: 252 (1505), 253 (1508), 254 (1510), 254.3 (1513), 254.7 (1525). Pynson's and De Worde's Aesop: 168 (1502), 169 (1503), 169.5 (1514?), 170 (1516). Cato: 4839.4 (1508), 4839.7 (1512), 4841 (1514), 4841.3 (1515). Although De Worde printed further editions of Cato in 1525 and 1532, these have expositions by Erasmus, not a familiar commentary. Details lifted from *STC*.

[51] The Cato was printed by De Worde in 1513 (*STC* 4840), the Aesop by Henry Pepwell in 1520 (*STC* 170.3).

[52] According to the *USTC*, the last edition of Theodulus was printed in Rouen in 1520 (*USTC* 145347). The last Latin edition of *Parabola* was De Worde's in 1525 (listed in *USTC* as 518005). Collected editions of the eight authors also declined during this period, but remained in print until the Limoges editions of 1540 and 1544 (*USTC* 110199, 110182).

Table 3.3. Familiar commentary editions of grammatical texts printed in London

	Pynson	De Worde	Other
Synonyma	4 (1496–1509)	7 (1502–1518)	–
Aequivoca	4 (1496–1514)	7 (1499–1518)	–
Doctrinale	6 (1492–1516)	3 (1503, 1515)	–

used the *Auctores Octo*, the hymns and the *Bucolics* to practise their reading, the works of Alexander and John of Garland were text-books for learning vocabulary and grammatical rules. The *Doctrinale* commentaries occasionally construe Alexander's verses, but their main concern is to paraphrase and explain the content of his lessons. The John of Garland commentaries, meanwhile, were familiar commentaries, construing every verse thoroughly and providing definitions for all the words taught. These three texts and their commentaries were widely printed in London (Table 3.3).[53] Therefore, when De Worde and his readers first saw the Parisian commentary editions to the *Bucolics*, they would have associated its commentary and design with a string of common pedagogic texts. Its main comparisons were the *Auctores Octo*, verse vocabularies and *Doctrinale*, not editions of the classics.

Most importantly for the reception of Virgil, the *Bucolics* was studied alongside these established curricular texts during the late fifteenth and early sixteenth centuries. This grouping of Virgil, John of Garland and the *Auctores Octo* survives in two English *Sammelbände* from the period. The first was compiled probably in the last few years of the fifteenth century, and survives in its original binding. All the editions have familiar commentaries:

1. *Facetus*, comm. anon ([Paris: André Bocard, c. 1491-93]).
2. John of Garland, *Aequivoca*, comm. Galfridus Anglicus (London: Richard Pynson, 1496);

---

[53] Pynson's *Synonyma*: STC 11609/ISTC ig00086500 (1496), 11611/ig00087300 (1500), 11612 (1502), 11615 (1509). Pynson's *Aequivoca*: 11601/ig00074400 (1496), 11604 (1503), 11606 (1508), 11607 (1514). Pynson's *Doctrinale*: 316/ia00435800 (1492), 317/ia00437700 (1498 or 1492), 317.5/ia00437800 (1500? or 1498–1505), 319.3 (1505), 319.5 (1513), and 320 (1516). De Worde's *Synonyma*: 11610/ig00086700 (1500), 11613 (23 Nov. 1502), 11614 (20 Nov. 1505), 11615.5 (1510), 11616 (1514), 11616a (1517), 11617 (1518). De Worde's *Aequivoca*: 11602/ig00074600 (1499), 11603 (1502), 11605 (1505), 11606.5 (1510), 11608 (1514), 11608a (1517), 11608a.3 (1518). De Worde's *Doctrinale*: 319 (1503), 319.7 (1515?), 320.5 (1515). Details taken from *STC*.

3. John of Garland, *Synonyma*, comm. Galfridus Anglicus (London: Richard Pynson, 1496);
4. *Expositio sequentiarum secundum usum Sarum* ([Cologne: Heinrich Quentell, c. 1496]);
5. Virgil, *Bucolica*, with Parisian commentary (Paris: Félix Baligault, [c. 1493-94]).[54]

The second compilation, again in its original binding, is similar in date and composition. The contents are:

1. *Manuale Scholarium* ([Deventer: Richardus Pafraet, between 21 June 1491 and 2 Dec. 1497]);
2. *Facetus*, comm. anon ([Paris: André Bocard, c. 1495-1500]);
3. Theodulus, *Ecloga*, comm. Odo Picardus ([Paris]: Pierre Levet, [about 1497]);
4. Virgil, *Bucolica*, with Parisian commentary (Deventer: Jacobus de Breda, 6 Nov. 1495);
5. *Georgica*, comm. Torrentinus (Deventer: Richardus Pafraet, 26 Aug. 1496).[55]

In both compilations, the combination of texts demonstrates a pedagogic purpose, mixing the classical Virgil with an older, pre-humanist style of curriculum. To learn Latin at the turn of the century would involve a blend of classical and non-classical texts.

These compilations are far from the ideals of later sixteenth-century humanist pedagogy. As seen in Chapter 1, the earliest written curricula in England date from the 1510s, 1520s, and after. They include only classical and Neo-Latin texts, and the *Facetus* and Theodulus's *Ecloga* are nowhere in sight. The teaching of the 1490s and early 1500s, however, more closely resembled the teaching of the thirteenth, fourteenth, and fifteenth centuries. These two *Sammelbände*, combining Virgil with the *Auctores Octo*, are comparable to pre-humanist manuscript compilations of school texts.

---

[54] CUL, Peterborough.Sp.61 (**B.1493**). The copy of the *Facetus* is quires o and p of an *Auctores octo cum glossa* edition printed by Bocard in c. 1491-3. ISTC citations are: ia01182270, ig00074400, ig00086500, is004540000, and iv00208850. STC citations for Pynson's editions are: 11601, 11609.

[55] Oxford, Corpus Christi College, phi.C.1.9 (**B.1495, G.1496**). As before, the copy of the *Facetus* is quires o and p of an *Auctores octo cum glossa* edition, this time printed by Bocard in c. 1495-1500. ISTC citations are: im00226100, ia01183200, it00153700, iv00211000, and iv00229000.

Classical Latin authors were not a prominent feature of these earlier schoolbooks, but a handful of masters chose to teach them alongside the more common *Auctores Octo*. As Christopher Cannon has shown, manuscript schoolbooks display a variety of curricular choices, and teachers were not confined to a fixed curriculum. Classroom literature depended as much on the master's inclinations as curricular convention. Should the master have more classicizing tastes, he might choose to integrate one or two classical texts into his classes.[56] The early effect of humanism was simply to make this choice more common.

Whereas there are many print survivals from the 1490s, only two English manuscript schoolbooks from the preceding centuries contain texts of Virgil (as mentioned in Chapter 1). In a compilation of the thirteenth century, Virgil's *Bucolics* appear with Alan of Lille's *Liber Parabolarum*, an *Expositio Hymnorum*, and the fables of Avianus, all of which were common curricular texts.[57] The other classical components include Persius's *Satires* and the *cento* of Proba, and all the texts have marginal and interlinear glossing. A fourteenth- or fifteenth-century hand later extended the manuscript with John of Garland's *Synonyma*. This combination of classical texts, *Auctores Octo*, and John of Garland evidently resembles the printed compilations centuries later.[58] A second manuscript, this time produced in stages from c. 1350–c. 1450, bears similar curricular affiliations. An early fifteenth-century hand copies five texts of the *Opuscula*: *Copa*, *Est et Non*, *De Institutione Viri Boni*, *De Rosis Nascentibus* and *Moretum*.[59] Although they seem unusual choices, the poems might have been chosen for their rare vocabulary. The same hand also copies two vocabularies of rare words, including Alexander of Hales's *Exoticon* with an alternating commentary, as well as a verse-vocabulary of Greek loan-words into Latin.[60] The glosses to the *Opuscula* poems are concerned with defining unusual words, since the *Moretum* refers to various rare foods and the *Copa* has several Graecisms. The rest of the manuscript comprises a range of pedagogic works on Latin prosody, figures, and verbs. Besides the *Opuscula*, the literary choices include a short

---

[56] Cannon, *From Literacy to Literature*, pp. 60–9.
[57] BL, MS Harley 4967. For a description, see Baswell, *Virgil in Medieval England*, pp. 300–1. The Virgil is at fols 126v-138v.
[58] BL, MS Harley 4967, fols 78r-91v (Hymns), 92r-102v (Alanus), 151r-60v (Avianus), 139r-49r (Persius), 169r-74v (Proba), 186r-93v (*Synonyma*).
[59] BodL, MS Digby 100, fols 137v-42v. For the other contents of the manuscript, see R.W. Hunt and A.G. Watson, *Bodleian Library Quarto Catalogues IX: Digby Manuscripts*, Reproduction of 1883 Catalogue by W.D. Macray (Oxford: Bodleian Library, 1999), no. 100.
[60] BodL, MS Digby 100, fols 129r-37r, 143r-7v.

collection of hymns, Theodulus's *Ecloga*, the *Disticha Catonis*, Book I of Horace's *Epistles*, *Carmen de Poenitentia* (another common pedagogic text of the period), and Aesop's fables (fragments). The Theodulus and Cato have commentaries alternating with the text, while the others have marginal and interlinear glosses.[61] None of these choices would be out of place in a late fifteenth- or early sixteenth-century *Sammelband*. Although by happenstance rather than direct influence, the early humanist schoolmasters have much in common with the more classicising schoolmasters of earlier generations.[62]

The similarities of these manuscript and print compilations suggest that the transition to a humanist curriculum was a gradual process. During the late fifteenth and early sixteenth centuries, more and more schoolmasters were teaching the *Bucolics*, but the spread of the New Learning did not immediately cause an overhaul of former pedagogic practices. If they wanted to teach Virgil, they accommodated the *Bucolics* and *Georgics* within existing curricular structures, as a few masters had done in previous centuries. Rather than adopting the classical curriculum wholesale, they responded to humanist influences in particular textual choices, integrating one or two pagan texts, while retaining the more familiar hymns and *Auctores Octo*. Although some teachers and learners might well have studied the *Bucolics* in a full roster of classical texts, these surviving compilations emphasize a mixed curriculum of classical and non-classical components.

By the time De Worde printed his first edition of the *Bucolics* (1512), the humanist curriculum was becoming more established in England. Since 1500, he and Pynson had been printing increasing numbers of humanist grammars, such as the works of Italian grammarian Giovanni Sulpizio, fl. 1470–90). At the same time, English schoolmasters were writing a host of new grammatical texts, most importantly John Stanbridge (d. 1510), Robert Whittinton (c. 1480–1553?), and Willam Lily (1468?–1522/3). Their works, both in English and Latin, covered every level of grammatical education, and also included verse-vocabularies and collections of *vulgaria*. By the 1510s and 1520s, editions of these new titles were appearing every

---

[61] For the literary texts mentioned, see BodL, MS Digby 100, fols 71r-7v, 100r-102v (Hymns), 75r-100v (Theodulus), 148r-164v (Cato), 155r-68v (Horace), 171r-2v (*Carmen de Poenitentia*), 173r-7v (Fragments of Aesop).

[62] Similar compilations of Virgil and school texts can be identified in the fifteenth-century library catalogues in *MLGB3*. See BA1.1479h-i (St Augustine's, Canterbury, fifteenth-century catalogue), SS2.7d-e, SS2.19b, SS1.895h (c. 1500–c. 1524 Syon Abbey).

year at the presses of Pynson and De Worde.[63] In addition to Virgil's *Bucolics*, this new repertoire included one other text with a familiar commentary. In 1523 and 1526, De Worde printed Ascensius's commentary edition to the *Bucolics* of the Neo-Latin poet Mantuan (Johannes Baptista Spagnolo, 1447–1516). During this period, Mantuan was becoming one of the most popular curricular authors in England and France. Ascensius's familiar commentaries abounded at French presses and in the import market.[64] As these new productions show, De Worde was gradually shifting his roster of curricular authors away from John of Garland and the *Auctores Octo*. He now supplied readers with the grammars of English humanists and the new fashions in schoolroom literature.

Later pedagogic compilations register this shifting context. For example, De Worde's 1514 *Bucolics* edition survives in four copies, and one is bound in a collection of Erasmian school texts and English humanist grammars. The contents are:

1. Desiderius Erasmus, *Familiarium Colloquiorum Formulae* (Louvain: Thierry Martens, 1519);
2. Robert Whittinton, *Lucubrationes* [*Synonima, Epitheta, De Variandi Formulis*] (London: Wynkyn de Worde, [1517?]);
3. Virgil, *Bucolica*, with Parisian commentary (London: Wynkyn de Worde, 1514);
4. William Lily and Desiderius Erasmus, *De Octo Orationis Partium Constructione Libellus* (Paris: Nicolaus de Pratis, 1515[6]);
5. Cato, *Disticha*, comm. Desiderius Erasmus (Strasbourg: Matthias Schürer, 1519).[65]

Unlike the compilations of the previous decade, Virgil now appears among a catalogue of famous humanists. Erasmus's *Colloquies* were common school texts, of which De Worde printed editions in 1519 and 1520.[66] Likewise, Lily's *De Octo Orationis Partium* was a staple in the English curriculum throughout the mid-sixteenth century. For practising vocabulary and composition, John of Garland's *Synonyma* is replaced with Whittinton's

---

[63] On the printing of humanist grammars in England, see Orme 'Schools and Schoolbooks', pp. 458–69.

[64] De Worde's editions are *STC* 22978 (May 1523) and *STC* 22979 (Nov. 1526).

[65] BodL, 4°E 6 Art.Seld (**B.1514**). The *Colloquies* edition is *USTC* 437048 or 403077; Cato, 625049; Lily, 183660 or 183661. The Whittinton edition is *STC* 25527.3.

[66] *STC* 10450.6, 10450.7.

widely-printed *Lucubrationes*, which lists synonyms and epithets to help students vary their diction. Cato, as we have seen, remained in use throughout the sixteenth century, but this compilation uses Erasmus's new edition, first printed in 1514. Similar changes are witnessed in a *Sammelband* of the 1520s, this time containing:

1. Virgil, *Bucolica*, with Parisian commentary (London: Wynkyn de Worde, 1522);
2. Mantuan, *Bucolica*, comm. Ascensius (London: Wynkyn de Worde, Nov. 1526);
3. William Lily, *Rudimenta* ([York: U. Mylner, 1516?]).[67]

Mantuan's works, as discussed above, were popular school texts of the period. The *Rudimenta* is another of Lily's elementary grammars, this time written in English. Far from the *Auctores Octo* and *Doctrinale*, this compilation situates Virgil's *Bucolics* in a curriculum of popular humanist texts.

As well as showing a humanist affiliation, the content of these compilations indicates an early level of schooling. Corroborating the evidence in extant school curricula, they show that the *Bucolics* was read in parallel with basic grammatical textbooks. As seen in Chapter 1, the sixteenth-century Eton curriculum placed the *Bucolics* in the fourth year, when students also learned Lily's *Octo Partes Orationis*. Grammars of Lily, including the *Octo Partes*, are bound in both the above *Sammelbände*, suggesting that the compilations were used at a similar stage of instruction. During the first four years of grammar school, the students would study Lily and other grammarians, while reading Cato's *Distichs*, Aesop, Terence, Erasmus's *Colloquies*, and Virgil's *Bucolics*. Most other classical texts, including the *Aeneid*, were delayed to the fifth, sixth and seventh years, when the students started reading Cicero and learning the arts of rhetoric. Although neither of the above compilations precisely matches any surviving curriculum, they provide material evidence at least that two masters taught the *Bucolics* in the context of grammatical rather than rhetorical pedagogy. These two copies of the *Bucolics* travelled from De Worde's press to the early years of grammar school.

---

[67] BodL, Ox, BodL, 4° Rawl. 206 (**B.1522.1**). *STC* 24814.5; 22979; 15609.3.

Editing

Printing classical texts and humanist grammars, however, was only the first step in supplying the needs of humanist pedagogy. English readers, as we have seen, used continental copies for most classical texts, and De Worde was competing with a large import market. By the 1510s and 1520s, booksellers were not only importing the *Bucolics* with the Parisian commentary, but also the newer familiar commentary editions by Torrentinus and Ascensius. Faced with these commercial pressures, De Worde progressively revised the text and design of his editions to match changing continental standards. For instance, De Worde's efforts to emulate imported editions famously motivated him to acquire an italic fount in 1528. By that time, continental presses commonly used italic for classical texts, and De Worde was the first English printer to follow this trend.[68] Although he never printed Virgil in italic, his four editions of the *Bucolics* trace a series of similar developments, not only in their typography, but also in the quality of text. In each successive printing, De Worde made frequent corrections and emendations to improve the scholarly quality of his product. Foreshadowing his eventual shift to italic, he also started printing Virgil in Roman type after 1520. Although, like many printers of the day, De Worde was restricted by his available resources and limited scholarly expertise, he consistently tried to make his products more competitive in the developing market for classical Latin literature.

In his first two editions, De Worde makes only a few substantive interventions, but clearly shows a concern for the intelligibility and correctness of his text. While early English printers are better known for their editing of vernacular than Latin authors, De Worde evinces similar attention to orthography, punctuation, and *mise-en-page* in this classical work. When De Worde prepared the Parisian commentary for print in 1512, his first intervention was to translate two vernacular French terms into English. At the start of *Bucolics* II, the Parisian commentator explains the etymology of the name 'Corydon' from the bird 'corydalis gallice chardonnereau', and goes on to describe that 'vaccinium est flos herbę que dicitur vaide gallice'. In De Worde's edition, these glosses become 'anglice (gold fynche)' and

---

[68] Pamela Robinson, 'Materials: Paper and Type', in *A Companion to the Early Printed Book in Britain*, ed. Powell and Gillespie, pp. 61–74 (p. 71).

'anglice wadde'.[69] De Worde commonly made cosmetic changes to adapt the texts of French printers for an English readership.[70] When he reprinted the 1512 edition in 1514, De Worde made small revisions to the 1512 copy-text. Besides correcting a few grammatical errors, he eliminated medieval Latin spellings from the text of Virgil, particularly uses of 'michi'. These spellings were common in the 1490s Parisian commentary editions, but would not be found in major sixteenth-century editions, such as those of Ascensius.[71] Although De Worde's changes might seem superficial, they show him improving the text to match humanist standards of orthography, ensuring that his student-readers learned correct spellings.

These humanistic improvements foreshadow the more pervasive revisions in the 1522 edition eight years later. In this third edition of the *Bucolics*, the most visible change was typographic. De Worde printed his first two editions of the *Bucolics* in blackletter (1512, 1514), his third and fourth in Roman (1522, 1529). Italian printers had devised Roman type specifically for classical and humanist learning. By the sixteenth century, it was the norm for continental editions of the *antiqui*.[72] Perhaps because classical texts were only a small part of their output, English printers were relatively late to adopt Roman type, Pynson in 1509, De Worde in 1520.[73] As we have seen, most of De Worde's familiar commentary editions were for the hymns and the *Auctores Octo*. Since their earliest printings in the 1470s and 1480s, these non-classical texts were routinely printed in blackletter types. When the familiar commentary genre was applied to Virgil and other classical authors, continental printers initially used the same type, but shifted to Roman in the mid-1490s. By the 1510s, when De Worde produced his first two *Bucolics* editions, the competing continental editions of the classics were widely printed in Roman type. After acquiring his first Roman fount in 1520, De Worde started using it for many of his humanist pedagogic texts, one of the first being his 1522 Virgil.

Despite this technical innovation, De Worde was unable to imitate continental editions in every respect. Whereas continental printers would

---

[69] The French glosses are quoted from De Breda's 1492 edition, sigs b1r-v, the English glosses from De Worde's 1512 edition, sig. A6v.

[70] For example, see De Worde in his familiar commentary edition of Theodulus. See *STC* 23943 (1515; cited above), sig. A3r.

[71] For example, compare uses of michi/mihi in Quentell's 1495 edition of the *Bucolics* (cited fn. 4, hereafter '*Bucolica* (1495)') with Ascensius's *Opera* (1500-1).

[72] Carter, *A View of Early Typography*, pp. 70-81.

[73] Frank Isaac, *English and Scottish Printing Types 1501-35, 1508-41* (Oxford: Printed for the Bibliographical Society at the Oxford University Press, 1930), pp. 3, 14.

print the entire edition in Roman, he did not have Roman type in a small size suitable for the commentary. As such, the Parisian commentary appears in the same blackletter type as it had in De Worde's previous editions.[74] In approximately the same period, this problem recurs in his printing of humanist grammatical texts, such as Whittinton's grammars. These editions, like the *Bucolics*, contained passages of commentary and interlinear glossing. When De Worde produced his first Roman editions of Whittinton, he used the same combination of types as the 1522 Virgil, printing the main text in Roman, but retaining his blackletter type for the expository material.[75] Throughout the 1520s, this design typifies De Worde's other commentary editions of humanist pedagogic texts, most prominently his 1523 and 1526 editions of Mantuan with Ascensius's familiar commentary, as well as his 1525 edition of Cato's *Disticha* with Erasmus's short expositions.[76] While De Worde clearly faced technical impediments, the combination of types might also have been a deliberate design. In bilingual Latin-English editions of classical texts, Roman and blackletter were often used to distinguish between languages.[77] When De Worde printed Latin commentary editions, the typography was likewise an effective means of distinguishing the text from the expository notes. In a later 1532 reprint of Cato, he does likewise with Roman and italic.[78]

De Worde's use of Roman type was not merely an aesthetic decision, but also allowed practical improvements to the Latin orthography. Unlike his blackletter fount, De Worde's Roman fount included ligatures, thus allowing him to represent the diphthongs in Classical Latin. The 'ae' in 'patriae' or 'praedicere' could be rendered with 'æ', the 'oe' in 'foetus' or 'Meliboee' with 'œ'. Although some blackletter founts had an 'ę' for 'ae', De Worde had to use 'e' in both instances throughout his 1512 and 1514 editions. The differences of these vowel sounds were particularly relevant to sixteenth-century pedagogy, given the emphasis on oral delivery. Not only were students expected to write like the *antiqui*, but an education in Classical

---

[74] On De Worde's available types, see Isaac, *English and Scottish Printing Types*, pp. 2–12.

[75] For example, Robert Whittinton, *Syntaxis* (London: Wynkyn de Worde, 13 Mar. 1520; STC 25547).

[76] The Mantuan editions are cited above. For De Worde's Cato, see *Disticha Catonis*, trans. and comm. Desiderius Erasmus ([London: Wynkyn de Worde, c. 1525?]; STC 4841.5). Another English printer, Peter Treveris, printed Erasmus's edition in 1531 (STC 4841.7). He used the same combination of types for text and commentary.

[77] On the types used in bilingual Latin-English editions, see Wakelin, 'Possibilities for Reading', esp. 485–6.

[78] STC 4842. Reprinting the 1525 Cato, De Worde puts the text in Roman, the commentary in italic.

Latin also included speaking. As discussed in Chapter 1, classical poets were used for practice in declamation. When reading the *Bucolics* aloud, the improved orthography would have helped students with correct pronunciation, particularly for unfamiliar names such as 'Melibœe'. If the student were reading independently without a teacher, he would have relied completely on the text. Just as the familiar commentary guided his comprehension, the orthography would have guided his pronunciation even for basic words. The use of Roman type, therefore, directly impinged on the utility of the edition in humanist pedagogy.

As well as making these orthographic improvements, De Worde revised his *Bucolics* text. De Worde might have completed the task himself, but the corrector was more likely another man in his workshop.[79] In preparation for the 1522 printing, he corrected the text of the 1512 and 1514 editions against another exemplar, probably a recent continental edition. As well as correcting obvious typographic errors,[80] De Worde's 1522 edition has many critical emendations, which must have originated from the second text. For example, *Bucolics* I has the added line:

Sæpe sinistra caua prædixit ab ilice cornix.
(Between *Bucolics* I.17–8)[81]

This line, nowadays considered an interpolation by modern editors, appeared in many fifteenth- and sixteenth-century editions of the *Bucolics*, yet not in the Parisian commentary editions.[82] Other substantial emendations include:

1514:   Sed tamen iste deus <u>quis</u> sit da tytire nobis.
1522:   Sed tamen iste deus <u>qui</u> sit: da Tityre nobis.

1514:   Et sic muneribus certes <u>concedit</u> yolas
1522:   <u>Nec si</u> muneribus certes: <u>concedat</u> Iolas.
(*Bucolics* I.18, II.57)[83]

---

[79] For speculation that De Worde knew Latin, see N.F. Blake, 'Wynkyn de Worde: The Later Years', *Gutenberg Jahrbuch* (1972), 128–38 (137).
[80] Thankfully, he corrects 'Pollio amat nostram...mensam' (1514, sig. B4v) to 'Pollio amat nostram...musam' (1522, sig. C1r).
[81] *Bucolica* (1522), sig. A3r, 'The crow on the left often foretold it from the hollow oak' (my translation).
[82] When the line was not included, annotators often supplied it themselves. For example, see B.1514.
[83] In the 1514 edition, see sigs A2v, A8v. In 1522, see sigs A3r, A8v. For both examples, the commentary has the 1514 reading. Underlining is my own.

Both of these emendations are accepted by modern editors, and were common in other fifteenth- and sixteenth-century editions.[84] Rather than the scholarly excellence of the new exemplar, they reflect deficiencies in De Worde's original 1512 and 1514 copy-text. De Worde thus improved his editions to match the standard of his competitors.

As well as these critical emendations, De Worde's revision of his earlier text included a range of other changes to orthography and punctuation. De Worde or his corrector followed the new exemplar closely, even for minor changes of spelling. For example, the 1522 edition frequently changes instances of 'i' to 'y', probably reflecting the preferences of De Worde's new text.[85] In 1522, De Worde also eliminated the few medieval spellings remaining in his 1514 edition, such as one last instance of 'michi'.[86] Most strikingly, he added more punctuation to the text. In his 1512 and 1514 editions, the only regular punctuation marks were capital letters at the beginnings of lines, and punctus at the ends of the shepherds' speeches. Except for these instances, punctuation was a rare occurrence.[87] Although a few 1490s editions share this deficiency,[88] most of De Worde's competitors punctuated their texts more thoroughly. In his 1522 text, therefore, virtually every clause ends with a punctuation mark, and many of the proper names are capitalized. This punctuation would have been helpful to any reader, but particularly to a student readership. De Worde's improvements ultimately made the text more intelligible, and imitated the common practice of his continental counterparts.

Although De Worde evidently made an effort to improve the quality of his text, many errors from the 1514 and 1512 editions remain unchanged. To choose an example, his 1522 text of *Bucolics* I retains the following:

De Worde: Quamuis multa meis <u>exirent</u> victima ceptis
Correct Version: Quamuis multa meis <u>exiret</u> victima septis

(*Bucolics* I.33)[89]

---

[84] Even editions with Parisian commentary had some or all of these emendations. The 'qui' and 'nec si' emendations, for example, both appear in De Breda's 1492 edition (sigs a2v, b3v). De Breda, however, does not have 'concedat'.

[85] In *Bucolics* I.1–5, for example, the 1514 edition has 'Tytyre', 'Siluestrem' and 'siluas' (sig. A2r), the 1522 'Tityre', 'Syluestrem', 'syluas' (sig. A2r).

[86] *Bucolics* IV.53. The 1514 edition has 'michi' (sig. C4r), the 1522 'mihi' (sig. C4v).

[87] In the 1514 edition, *Bucolics* I has only six other punctuation marks (I.4, 7, 9, 16, 22, 80). See sigs A2r-5v.

[88] Compare the variable punctuation in Quentell's *Bucolica* (1495). In his edition, for example, the Virgil text has little punctuation on sigs a2r, a3r-v and a4v, yet an abundance of punctus on sig. a2v.

[89] *Bucolica* (1522), sig. A3v. For the correct version, I use *Opera* (1500–1), I, fol. 7r. The underlining is my own.

This error, to my knowledge, does not appear in any editions of Virgil except De Worde's. In using the plural verb 'exirent', perhaps De Worde or his corrector believed that 'victima' was a neuter plural noun. Later in the line, De Worde's 'ceptis' should be 'septis' or 'saeptis', meaning 'enclosure'. As already discussed in Chapter 2, such simplistic errors were common in many editions of the time. Often working in haste, correctors did not always show close attention to detail. It is likely that De Worde's corrector was a workman rather than a scholar, and did not have a high standard of Latin. Besides overlooking these grammatical mistakes, he also applied the orthographic changes incorrectly and inconsistently. The corrector was sometimes too enthusiastic in using the new ligatures 'æ' and 'œ', and the capitalization of proper names is sporadic at best.[90] De Worde might have had a shortage of capitals in his Roman fount, or perhaps these inconsistencies were a feature of his 1522 exemplar.[91] Although De Worde made his edition look more continental and humanistic, the editing was often more cosmetic than scholarly. If they were only glancing at the edition, potential buyers might have been attracted by the updated punctuation, classicizing orthography and Roman type, but their eventual use of the text would have been impeded by the inconsistencies in the corrector's work.

When De Worde reprinted the 1522 edition seven years later, he attempted to correct some of these errors and inconsistencies. In this 1529 printing of the *Bucolics*, he capitalized more of the proper names, removed obvious grammatical mistakes, and made further revisions to orthography and punctuation. Although continuing the trends of the 1522 editing, none of these emendations would have required De Worde or his corrector to refer to another exemplar. Probably because the corrector was only skimming over the text, he failed to notice many of the 1522 edition's glaring grammatical errors. Working independently of any exemplar, he also made a few ill-conceived conjectural emendations. In *Bucolics* II, for example, he emended 'Florentem Cytisum sequitur lasciua capella' ('The frisky goat follows the flowering clover') to 'lasciua puella'. Perhaps he was misled by the later 'lasciua puella' at *Bucolics* III.64, referring to Galatea.[92] Because the 1529 edition adds these new errors, the 1522 edition probably has the more

---

[90] For an instance of hypercorrection, see *Bucolics* I.17, when he changes 'quercus' (1514, sig. A2v) to 'quęrcus' (1522, sig. A3r). While sixteenth-century editors would consider this instance incorrect, the 1522 edition also includes other more common hypercorrect spellings, such as 'fœlix' for 'felix', which was common in many editions of the time.

[91] For the inconsistent capitalization, an example in the 1522 edition is 'Et me Phœbus amat: phœbo sua se*m*per apud me' (III.62, sig. B4r).

[92] In both the 1522 and 1529 editions, see sig. A8v.

correct and readable text. Although the corrector attempted to make textual improvements, his very effort to improve the edition unfortunately made it worse.

Even if the editing could be careless in details, De Worde evidently invested time and money in the quality of his works. In his editions of Mantuan, for example, he or his corrector revised the Latin text in the same way as the Virgil. Compared with the 1523 edition, he gave the 1526 edition more punctuation, and introduced minor orthographic changes, such as the increased use of ligatures. Both of these measures, as we have seen, would have made the Latin more useable for young readers.[93] For his 1525 edition of Cato, meanwhile, he selected an entirely new text, much like choosing the new exemplar for his 1522 *Bucolics*. Instead of repeating the text and commentary from his previous four editions, he reproduced a more recent edition by Erasmus. As seen in one of the above *Sammelbände*, copies were already circulating in England by the early 1520s.[94] After acquiring his italic fount, De Worde's first productions were likewise texts edited by famous humanists. He printed Erasmus's edition of Lucian's *Dialogi* in 1528, and reprinted Erasmus's edition of Cato in 1532. Shortly before his death in 1535, he also published a fable collection prepared by Maartan van Dorp. In these cases, the choice of editor was just as important as the work itself.[95]

Conclusion

Seen in this light, the changes across De Worde's four *Bucolics* editions reflect wider developments in his printing of Latin literature. When he first decided to produce an edition of Virgil, his repertoire of school texts included the *Auctores Octo* and centuries-old grammar books. Schoolmasters of the late fifteenth and early sixteenth centuries taught Virgil's *Bucolics* alongside these well-established, pre-humanist curricular texts. Only gradually did they adopt a full roster of classical and Neo-Latin authors. As contemporary tastes shifted to the New Learning, De Worde adjusted his output accordingly, printing familiar commentaries of Mantuan and the works of humanist grammarians. Investing first in Roman and later in italic founts, he redesigned his books to

---

[93] De Worde's Mantuan editions (1523, 1526) are cited above. For the opening five lines, De Worde's 1526 edition adds a set of brackets, two cola and a punctus (sig. A3v in both editions). Soon after, 'preda' in 1523 becomes 'præda' in 1526 (sig. A3v in both), 'tedia' becomes 'tædia' (sig. A4v), etc.

[94] Cited above, the Cato edition STC 4841.5.   [95] STC 16891, 4842, 171.

appeal to current trends in Latin-language printing, emulating his continental competitors. With each successive printing of the *Bucolics*, he emended his Virgilian texts, selecting a new exemplar in 1522 and seeking to improve on his past editions. Albeit with mixed success, he tried to correct the Latin according to humanist standards of orthography, making them more suitable for the humanist schoolroom. Although ligatures and punctuation might seem like nugatory changes, they each affected the utility of the edition to a prospective learner. While, like many printers of his day, De Worde was not a scholar himself, he marshalled his available skills and resources to meet the needs of humanist pedagogy.

As this case study has indicated, the development of De Worde's editions was far from unique. The gradual changes in his repertoire of works, typography, and textual editing are witnessed across European pedagogy and printing. On the continent, as well as in England, schoolmasters and learners continued to use the *Auctores Octo* and *Doctrinale* into the sixteenth century. Printers such as De Worde continued to provide for this market even while they began supplying humanist works. Moreover, these editions of the *Auctores Octo*, in their commentaries and layout, provided the templates for subsequent commentary editions of the classics. The familiar commentary genre, though originating in the Middle Ages, was co-opted by humanist grammarians to advance their classicizing curriculum. While humanism ultimately caused significant change in grammar school education, the initial influence of the New Learning was to begin a phase of tentative experimentation and syncretism. During this period, the piecemeal adoption of humanist texts and approaches was driven primarily by the choices of individual schoolmasters and printers. In the history of their content, production and use, De Worde's four *Bucolics* editions thus reveal how the New Learning gradually developed from earlier tradition.

4
Caxton's *Eneydos*

After dyuerse werkes made / translated and achieued / hauyng noo werke in hande. I sittyng in my studye where as laye many dyuerse paunflettis and bookys. happened that to my hande cam a lytyl booke in frenshe. whiche late was translated oute of latyn by some noble clerke of fraunce whiche booke is named Eneydos / made in latyn by that noble poete *and* grete clerke vyrgyle /

(*Eneydos*, sig. A1r)[1]

The English printer and translator William Caxton (1415x24–1492) began his famous prologue to the *Eneydos* (1490) by introducing his French source-text. Like most of his written oeuvre, Caxton's *Eneydos* is a close English translation of 'a lytyl booke in frenshe', known today as the *Livre des Eneydes*. It survives in a single edition, printed in 1483 at the Lyon press of Guillaume le Roy.[2] There is no evidence that Caxton referred to the *Aeneid* outside of this French intermediary. In saying that the *Livre des Eneydes* was 'translated oute of latyn', he was simply copying the French edition's

---

[1] *Eneydos* ([Westminster]: William Caxton, [after 22 June 1490]); *ISTC* iv00199000, *STC* 24796). The modern edition is *Caxton's Eneydos, 1490: Englisht from the French Liure des Eneydes, 1483*, ed. W.T. Culley and F.J. Furnivall, Early English Text Society, Extra Series 57 (1890; London: OUP, 1962).

[2] *Eneydes* (Lyons: Guillaume Le Roy, 30 Sept. 1483; *ISTC* iv00200000). On the *Livre des Eneydes*, see Jacques Monfrin, 'L'Histoire de Didon et Enée au XVe siécle', *Études littéraires sur le XVe siècle, Actes du Ve colloque international sur le moyen français, Milan 6–8 mai 1985*, ed. Sergio Cigada (Milan: Vita e Pensiero, 1986), pp. 161–97; 'Les *translations* vernaculaires de Virgile au Moyen Âge', in *Lectures Médiévales de Virgile*, ed. Tilliette, pp. 189–249 (pp. 211–20); Eberhard Leube, *Fortuna in Karthago: Die Aeneas-Dido-Mythe Vergils in den romantischen Literaturen vom 14. bis 16. Jahrhundert* (Heidelberg: Carl Winter, 1969), pp. 65–75. On the *Eneydos* and *Livre des Eneydes*, see Louis Brewer Hall, 'Caxton's "Eneydos" and the Redactions of Virgil', *Mediaeval Studies* 22 (1960), 136–47; Marilynn Desmond, *Reading Dido: Gender, Textuality, and the Medieval Aeneid* (Minneapolis: University of Minnesota Press, 1994), pp. 167–76; and Jerome E. Singerman, *Under Clouds of Poesy: Poetry and Truth in French and English Reworkings of the 'Aeneid', 1160–1513* (New York: Garland, 1986), pp. 197–216. In this chapter, quotations from the *Livre des Eneydes* are accompanied by Caxton's translations from the *Eneydos*. When my analysis focuses on specific details of the French, I shall provide literal translations of my own.

prologue, which states 'ce present liure compile par virgille... a este translate de latin' (sig. a2r).[3] Since the French has many deviations from Virgil's text, modern studies normally avoid calling it an *Aeneid* 'translation'. Instead, they use the terms 'retelling', 'paraphrase', 'redaction', 'adaptation' and 'romance'.[4] Although, as we shall see, both the French and English prologues evoke the romance genre, these various descriptions of the *Livre des Eneydes* are misleading in that they over-simplify the content of the text and understate its close dependence on the original Latin. The *Livre des Eneydes* was compiled from an unusual patchwork of sources but approximately half of the text is in fact a direct translation of *Aeneid* IV. It is the earliest translation of Virgil into French, and Caxton's rendering is the earliest into English. Because this fact is rarely mentioned in English studies of the *Eneydos*, English literary scholars under-appreciate how Latin academic traditions influenced the *Livre des Eneydes* and thereby one of Caxton's most famous works.

As a result, the *Eneydos* tends to be classified with adaptations and retellings of Latin texts rather than with translations. In his career, Caxton translated three other French works on classical subjects: *Recuyell of the Historyes of Troye* (c. 1473-4), *The Historie of Jason* (1477), and *Metamorphose* (c. 1480).[5] Likely encouraged by humanist influence, Caxton sought to supply English readers with continental fashions in vernacular classicism, often deriving from Burgundian sources.[6] Although *Recuyell*, *Jason*, *Metamorphose*, and *Eneydos* reflect a common commercial aim, this grouping suppresses their differences of source-material. Whereas the *Livre des Eneydes* is heavily dependent on Virgil, Caxton's sources for *Recuyell* and *Jason* were original French retellings of classical myths by Burgundian clergyman Raoul Lefèvre (completed in 1464 and 1460).[7]

---

[3] Caxton's *Eneydos* includes a translation of the French prologue, reading 'this present booke compyled by virgyle [...] hath be translated oute of latyn' (*Eneydos*, sig. B1r).
[4] Brewer Hall, in 'Caxton's "Eneydos" and the Redactions of Virgil', 136, uses 'adaptation' and 'redaction'; Singerman, in *Under Clouds of Poesy*, p. 198, says 'prose romance'; Desmond, in *Reading Dido*, p. 167, calls it a 'loose paraphrase'.
[5] The *Jason*, *Recuyell* and *Eneydos* are often grouped as Caxton's 'classical romances'. For example, Jennifer R. Goodman, 'Caxton's Continent', in *Caxton's Trace: Studies in the History of English Printing*, ed. William Kuskin (Notre Dame: University of Notre Dame Press, 2006), pp. 101-23 (pp. 105-9, 18-9).
[6] On Burgundian influence, see N.F. Blake, *Caxton and his World* (London: Deutsch, 1969), pp. 67-70. On Caxton's possible humanist influences, see also William Kuskin, *Symbolic Caxton: Literary Culture and Print Capitalism* (Notre Dame, IN: University of Notre Dame Press, 2008), pp. 236-83.
[7] The first editions of Caxton's translations are: Raoul Lefèvre, *Recuyell of the Historyes of Troye*, trans. William Caxton ([Ghent?: David Aubert?, for William Caxton, c. 1473-74]; *ISTC*

Throughout his prologues, Lefèvre explicitly states that his works are not translated or adapted from any classical author, but are new histories of Troy and the Argonauts.[8] Meanwhile, Caxton's source for the *Metamorphose* was a French prose adaptation of Ovid's *Metamorphoses*.[9] Although aptly describing the treatment of the Ovidian text, the term 'adaptation' is anachronistic, since the *Metamorphoses* adaptations were routinely titled 'Metamorphose Translatee de latin en Francoys'.[10] In contrast with modern usage, 'translation' did not necessarily imply a close reproduction of a Latin text, but could encompass these looser rewritings. The *Livre des Eneydes* and *Eneydos*, however, not only have the title of 'translation', but significant portions of these works are indeed direct renderings of Virgil's *Aeneid*. Unlike *Metamorphose*, their content demands comparison with other close translations of classical authors.

Besides understating their dependence on the Latin *Aeneid*, modern evaluations of these texts also depreciate their stylistic and intellectual craft. In the French *Livre des Eneydes*, however, the embedded translation of *Aeneid* IV uses common translation practices of the fifteenth and early sixteenth centuries. Characteristic of the period, the translator (henceforth, Dido-translator) referred frequently to Virgil commentaries, amplifying his source with additional exegetic and rhetorical detail. Whereas scholars of English literature often criticise his prolixity, this quality was admired by fifteenth-century standards. Through his circumlocutions, the Dido-translator cultivated an elaborate prose style to parallel Virgil's epic poetry. Caxton's translation practice is likewise derogated for its uninspired, word-by-word rendering of French, but in the *Eneydos* he shows greater flexibility. Although he probably did not recognize that his French source was a

---

il00117000); *The Historie of Jason*, trans. William Caxton ([Westminster: William Caxton, 1477]; *ISTC* il00112000). On their sources and content, see Goodman, 'Caxton's Continent', pp. 105–9.

[8] Lefèvre uses 'traicter' (i.e. to treat a topic) to indicate this difference. See *Le Recueil des histoires de Troyes* (Lyons: Jacques Maillet, 16 Apr. 1494/95; *ISTC* il00114500), sig. a2r-v.

[9] Namely, the *Ovide Moralisé en Prose II* (1470), one of three fifteenth-century prose versions of the verse *Ovide Moralisé*. For parallel-text editions of the French and Caxton's English, see *The Middle English Text of Caxton's Ovid, Book I*, ed. Diana Rumrich; and *Books II–III*, ed. Wolfgang Mager (Heidelberg: Winter, 2011, 2016).

[10] The quotation is from the title page of *Ovide Moralisé en Prose III*, the most widely printed *Metamorphoses* adaptation. For the first edition, see *ISTC* io00184000 (Bruges: Colard Mansion, May 1484). After Antoine Vérard's revised edition, later copies up to 1531 were styled 'La bible des Poetes de Ouide Methamorphose. Translatee de latin en Francoys'. For Vérard's edition, see *ISTC* io00184200 (Paris: Antoine Vérard, 1 Mar. 1493/4). In the prologue of the *Ovide Moralisé en Prose II*, likewise, the French writer states his intention 'a translate ledit Ouide en langaige Francoys'. See *Caxton's Ovid, Book I*, ed. Rumrich, pp. 54–5.

patchwork of different texts, he was sensitive to the stylistic disparities between its parts. As he translates into English, he makes minor editorial changes, eliminating pleonasms in the Dido-translator's prolix *Aeneid* IV translation, while amplifying the briefer treatment of the other *Aeneid* books. The *Eneydos* was among Caxton's last translations, and it demonstrates a lifetime of practice.

Content of the Livre des Eneydes

Before discussing Caxton's translation practice, it is first necessary to describe the exact sources, contents, and structure of the *Livre des Eneydes*. The text was compiled from a convoluted range of sources, and there are no adequate descriptions in English. It comprises:[11]

1) **Fall of Troy (sigs a2r-5r):** Original composition, not related to Virgil's account of these events in *Aeneid* II.
2) **Aeneas's Burial of Polydorus (sigs a5r-b1r):** Translation of *Aeneid* III.1-68 with amplifications.
3) **Introduction to Boccaccio's and Virgil's different narratives of Dido's death (sig. b1r-v):** Original composition.
4) **Boccaccio's Dido narrative (sigs b1v-8v):** Translation of Dido's biography in Giovanni Boccaccio's *De Casibus Virorum Illustrium*, Book II, Chapters 10-11 (titled 'De Didone', 'In Laudem Didonis').
5) **Virgil's Dido narrative (sigs c2v-h8r):** Translation of *Aeneid* IV with amplifications.
6) **Aeneas's voyage to Italy and wars against Turnus (sigs h8v-m5v):** Verbatim transcription from the Aeneas section of the thirteenth-century *Histoire ancienne jusqu'à César*, which is an abridged version of *Aeneid* V-XII.

Encompassing the fall of Troy, the story of Aeneas and Dido and the conquest of Italy, this patchwork of original composition, translation and abridgement roughly approximates the events of the *Aeneid*. With the

---

[11] The best account of the *Livre des Eneydes* is Monfrin, 'L'Histoire de Didon et Enée au XVe siécle'. Also useful are Monfrin, 'Les *translations* vernaculaires de Virgile au Moyen Âge', pp. 211-20; Leube, *Fortuna in Karthago*, pp. 65-75; Singerman, in *Under Clouds of Poesy*, pp. 197-216.

exception of Boccaccio's *De Casibus*, none of the sources are named in the text, so these internal divisions were not evident to readers. It is not known when or by whom the *Livre des Eneydes* was compiled, although Jacques Monfrin has attributed it to the printer Guillaume le Roy in 1483.[12] Whoever the compiler was, he evidently took short-cuts in producing his vernacular *Aeneid*, transcribing half the narrative from an earlier prose work, the *Histoire ancienne*. Moreover, Monfrin has suggested that the Boccaccio and *Aeneid* IV translations (sections three to five) also originated as a separate text, since the two contrasting Dido-narratives function together as a diptych.[13] Although Monfrin does not discuss it, the Dido-translator probably was also responsible for the *Aeneid* III.1-68 translation, since it uses the same elaborate, amplified style of prose. Perhaps the Dido-translator and the overall compiler were the same person, or more likely all three translated sections pre-date the *Livre des Eneydes* in manuscripts no longer extant. The compilation, therefore, probably has no original material, and was a hasty production in Le Roy's printing-house.

While the compiler called the volume a 'translation' of Virgil, his compilatory approach saved him the labour of translating, adapting or retelling the whole *Aeneid* from scratch. The finished compilation broadly resembles the structure of earlier vernacular adaptations of the *Aeneid*, for example the twelfth-century *Roman d'Eneas*.[14] In his prologue, the compiler frames the *Livre des Eneydes* in terms of chivalric romance, saying 'auquel pourront tous valereux princes et aultres nobles veoir moult de valereux faictz darmes' (sig. a2r).[15] Common to many vernacular adaptations, he recounts the events of the *Aeneid* in chronological order. Rather than beginning with the storm in *Aeneid* I, he opens with the fall of Troy. Moreover, the compiler gives disproportionate space to the story of Aeneas and Dido. Whereas it comprises only one of Virgil's twelve books, the two Dido narratives from Virgil and Boccaccio extend through seven of the volume's thirteen quires. These structural features, however, might not reflect the compiler's coherent design, but simply the assortment of texts at his disposal. He had high-quality translations of *Aeneid* IV and *De Casibus* in a prolix, amplified style,

---

[12] Monfrin, 'Les *translations* vernaculaires de Virgile au Moyen Âge', pp. 216-7, 220; Monfrin, 'L'Histoire de Didon et Enée au XVe siécle', pp. 185-8.
[13] Monfrin, 'L'Histoire de Didon et Enée au XVe siécle', pp. 182-5; 'Les *translations* vernaculaires de Virgile au Moyen Âge', pp. 217-20.
[14] Brewer Hall, 'Caxton's "Eneydos" and the Redactions of Virgil', 137; Singerman, *Under Clouds of Poesy*, pp. 200-1.
[15] Caxton: 'In whiche may alle valyaunt pryncves and other nobles see many valorous fayttes of armes' (*Eneydos*, sig. B1r).

but no comparable source for the remainder of Virgil's epic. Whereas the *Roman d'Eneas* was adapted from Virgil's Latin by a single author, the compiler of the *Livre des Eneydes* might not have composed even a word of his vernacular *Aeneid*.

If the compiler wrote any part of the text, it was most likely the opening account of Troy's fall (sigs a2v-a5r). Unlike the remainder of the *Livre des Eneydes*, this section has no known source, and is probably an original composition. It is notably silent about the specifics of the city's destruction, and bears virtually no resemblance to Virgil's account in *Aeneid* II.[16] Not until the third leaf (sig. a4r) does the reader encounter Aeneas, fleeing Troy with his father and son. The writer makes no mention of the Wooden Horse, Aeneas's dream of Hector, Pyrrhus's murder of Priam, or the appearance of Venus. Rather than specifying any events of the siege, his narrative describes the general scale of the devastation, the piteous state of the Trojans, and their abrupt fall from prosperity. Perhaps the compiler had already acquired the other components of his *Aeneid*, and composed this section quickly to serve as an introduction.

Approximately a third of this Troy account (sig. a3r-v) is devoted to the murder of Priam's fourteenth son, Polydorus.[17] When Agamemnon laid siege to the city, Priam sent Polydorus to stay with Polymestor,[18] King of Thrace, so as to keep him safe from harm. After the city's fall, Polymestor murdered the young prince, and seized his gold. This story sets the foundations for the second section of the *Livre des Eneydes*, in which Aeneas sails to Thrace, discovers the tomb of Polydorus, and conducts his funeral.[19] This episode, which covers eight pages (sigs a5r-b1r), is translated from *Aeneid* III.1-68. It is the only episode of Book III to be included in the *Livre des Eneydes*, which omits to mention Helenus, the harpies, and Scylla and Charybdis. If indeed this translation originated as an independent work, the compiler probably included it for its moral potential. The translator makes long amplifications condemning Polymestor's 'mauldicte et faulce

---

[16] In the *Livre des Eneydes*, this first section extends from 'POur ouir et ouurir et declarier la matiere...' to '...maleureuses destinees' (sigs a2v-a5r). In Caxton's *Eneydos*, see 'FOr to here / opene / and declare the matere.... maleurouse and vnhappy destynees' (Chs 1-2, sigs B1r-B3v).

[17] The Polydorus story extends from 'PRiame doncques voulant...' to '...peu de dommaige luy en pouuoit venir ne encourir' (sig. a3r-v). In Caxton's *Eneydos*, see 'PRyame thenne...lityl damage and hurte myght come to hym:' (Ch. 1, sigs B1v-B2v).

[18] The *Livre des Eneydes* and *Eneydos* both refer to 'Polymestor' as 'Plasmator'.

[19] The second section is 'CEste noble compaignie troyenne...per plusieurs iours' (sigs a5r-b1r). In Caxton's *Eneydos*, see 'THis noble companye troian...longe and many dayes' (Chs 2-5, sigs B3v-B7r).

decepuable auarice' (sig. a7v).[20] This moral interpretation is found among Virgilian allegorists, and derives from Virgil's description of Thrace as 'litus auarum' (*Aeneid* III.44).[21] In contrast with the fall of Troy section, therefore, the *Aeneid* III episode directly translates from Virgil's text, and draws on medieval exegetic traditions. This learned content looks forward to the forthcoming translations of *De Casibus* and *Aeneid* IV.[22]

Once the Trojan fleet departs that avaricious shore, the text breaks abruptly from Aeneas's narrative:

> LAutrier en passant temps lisoie le cas des nobles dont iehan boccasse a bien parle *et* mis en brief les aduentures de fortune...
>
> (*Livre des Eneydes*, sig. b1r)[23]

As Monfrin has suggested, this passage might once have marked the beginning of an independent text. Over the next two pages, the Dido-translator introduces two contradictory accounts of Dido's death (sig. b1r-v), the first from Boccaccio's *De Casibus*, and the other being Virgil's *Aeneid* IV. Considering that Boccaccio's story does not mention Aeneas at all, he resolves to recount both versions of events.[24] First of all (sigs b1v-8v), he translates the relevant chapters of *De Casibus*: Book II, Chapters 10 ('De Didone') and 11 ('In laudem Didonis').[25] Boccaccio recounts that Dido's brother, Pygmalion, killed her first husband, Sycheus, for his gold. Boccaccio includes heavy condemnation of Pygmalion's avaricious conduct, resonating with the earlier murder of Polydorus. After her brother's betrayal, Dido fled from her home city of Tyre, sailed for Africa, and founded Carthage. When

---

[20] For the equivalent passage in Caxton's *Eneydos*, see Ch. 4, sig. B5v.

[21] For example, *The Commentary on the First Six Books of the 'Aeneid' Commonly Attributed to Bernard Silvestris*, ed. Jones and Jones, p. 17.

[22] On the tragic aspects of the narrative, see Singerman, *Under Clouds of Poesy*, pp. 204–5.

[23] Caxton: 'That other daye in passyng tyme I redde the fall of noblys / of whom Ihon bochace hath spoken & in brief ye aduentures of fortune' (*Eneydos*, Ch. 6, sig. B7r).

[24] The introduction to the two Dido narratives begins at 'Si lesseros a parler de enee et retournerons a parler de dydo...' and ends '...lopinion iehan boccase qui dit ainsi' (sig. b1r-v). In Caxton's *Eneydos*, see 'Soo thenne we shall leue to speke of Eneas...here after shall ensiewe ad folowe' (Chs 5–6, sigs B7r-v).

[25] This section begins with an interpolation on the art of writing. In the French, 'CE aulcunement foy doit estre adioustee aux escriptures...la tainctare de rouge couleur', sigs b1v-2r. In the *Eneydos*, 'YF In ony maner fayth...the tayntare of reed coloure:' (Ch. 6, sigs b1v-2r). The translation of Boccaccio's text is 'Le nom doncques et royaulme de fenice...' to '...et en honneur parcreue' (sigs b2r-8v). In the *Eneydos*, 'THe name thenne and Royalme of Fenyce...growe in honour' (Chs 6–9, sigs B8r-C6v). For the Latin text, see *De casibus virorum illustrium*, ed. Pier Giorgio Ricci and Vittorio Zaccaria, in *Tutte le Opere di Giovanni Boccaccio*, ed. Vittore Branca, 10 vols in 11 (Milan: A. Mondadori, 1964–98), IX (1983), pp. 134–45.

she eventually kills herself, her motive is not the love of Aeneas, but to escape marriage to Iarbas, one of the kings of Africa. Soon after the founding of Carthage, Iarbas demanded that Dido marry him, threatening war. While appearing to consent, Dido prepared a ceremony to release herself from her first marriage, and had a pyre built for these rites. Dido then stabbed herself on the pyre, so as to avoid betraying her marriage vows, and to spare her people from Iarbas' dominion.

For Boccaccio and his contemporaries, this narrative was considered the historical version of Dido's suicide, and Virgil was thought to have invented her whole affair with Aeneas.[26] Rather than the lovesick queen of Virgil's *Aeneid*, this tradition emphasizes Dido's status as a political leader. She shows great resourcefulness in founding the city of Carthage, and is not the victim of a ruinous passion. As Marilynn Desmond puts it, 'Dido is a heroic figure; her suicide is an act of defiance which testifies to the nobility of her nature'.[27] In *De Casibus*, Boccaccio underscores both Dido's chastity and her civic service.[28] Soon before her death, she speaks eloquently on the value of sacrificing oneself 'pour le salut de pais', and censures those who neglect 'le bien publique' (*Livre des Eneydes*, sig. b6v).[29]

Having provided Boccaccio's Dido narrative, the *Livre des Eneydes* recounts the Virgilian version of events. First, the Dido-translator summarizes the main points of *Aeneid* I (sigs b8v-c2v): Juno's ire, the storm sequence, and Aeneas's arrival in Carthage.[30] Immediately afterwards, he launches into his prose translation of *Aeneid* IV (sigs c2v-h8r).[31] Much like the translation of *Aeneid* III, the Dido-translator heavily amplifies Latin, more than doubling the length of Virgil's text. As this chapter will discuss in detail, he made copious use of Virgil glosses, certainly using a glossed manuscript of Virgil if not a full copy of Servius's commentary. In juxtaposing these different legends of Dido's suicide, the Dido-translator specifically contrasts Boccaccio's chaste and heroic leader with Virgil's passionate

---

[26] On the historical tradition and its ancient sources, see Desmond, *Reading Dido*, pp. 24–33, 55–73.
[27] Desmond, *Reading Dido*, p. 24.
[28] For an overview of Boccaccio's treatments of the Dido myth, see Desmond, *Reading Dido*, pp. 58–73.
[29] For the passage in Boccaccio, see *Tutte le Opere di Giovanni Boccaccio*, IX, p. 140.
[30] This summary is 'LEquel cas... et deuisoyt auec luy moult volentiers' (sigs b8v-c2v). Caxton: 'THe whiche caas... and deuysed wyth him moche gladely' (Chs 9–10, sigs C6v-C8r).
[31] The translation of *Aeneid* IV extends from 'donc sensuiuit quelle griefuement naufuree du dart damours...' to '...dont le regne iamays ne fine (sigs c2v-h8r). Caxton: 'wherof followed that she was greuously hurte wyth the darte of loue... wherof the regne shalle neuer fynyshe' (Chs 10–29, sigs C8r-H5r).

lover.[32] In the first story, Dido shuns her suitor Iarbas, and sacrifices herself for the safety of her people; in the second, she falls in love with her Trojan suitor, kills herself in passion, and causes the ruin of Carthage. Many of the Dido-translator's additions to *Aeneid* IV (discussed later in the chapter) are designed to enhance this moralistic contrast, drawing attention to Dido's sins, and to the consequent suffering of her people. In Boccaccio, the reader witnesses the merits of civic service and chastity; in Virgil, the ruinous consequence of love.

After this moral diptych, the *Livre des Eneydes* recounts Aeneas's voyage to Italy and wars against Turnus (sigs h8v-m5v).[33] This text is a near-verbatim transcription from the *Histoire ancienne jusqu'à César*, a thirteenth-century prose history spanning from Genesis through to the Siege of Troy and the Roman Empire. One of the most popular histories of the Middle Ages, the *Histoire* was still circulating widely in the late fifteenth century, so it is not surprising that the compiler of the *Livre des Eneydes* had access to a copy.[34] The Aeneas section of the *Histoire* is an abridged version of Virgil's *Aeneid*, closely based on Virgil's Latin.[35] Since the *Livre des Eneydes* had already covered Aeneas's escape from Troy and affair with Dido, the compiler begins his transcription at the chapter 'Que Eneas revint en Sesile', which starts at approximately *Aeneid* V.35.[36] No less than the Dido-translator, the original thirteenth-century writer of the

---

[32] Virgil, also writing in the context of the historical tradition, might have expected his own readers to do the same. On Virgil and the historical Dido, see Desmond, *Reading Dido*, pp. 27-33.

[33] This final section is 'IE diray ie plus de la royne dydo...' (sigs h8v-m5v). In the *Eneydos*, see 'What shall I more saye...' (Chs 30-65, sigs H5r-L7r).

[34] The first complete edition is *Histoire ancienne jusqu'à César. A digital edition*, BnF, f. fr. 20125 and BL, Royal MS 20 D I. Semi-diplomatic edition, ed. Hannah Morcos with the collaboration of Simon Gaunt, Simone Ventura, Maria Teresa Rachetta and Henry Ravenhall; with technical support from Paul Caton, Ginestra Ferraro, Marcus Husar and Geoffroy Noël (London: King's College London), accessible at the addresses <http://www.tvof.ac.uk/textviewer/?p1=Fr20125> and <http://www.tvof.ac.uk/textviewer/?p1=Royal> (Accessed 18 March 2019). For analysis of the Aeneas section, see Leube, *Fortuna in Karthago*, pp. 30-40; Monfrin, 'Translations Vernaculaires de Virgile', pp. 200-11; Singerman, *Under Clouds of Poesy*, pp. 152-79; Desmond, 'Reading Dido', pp. 119-27.

[35] The *Values of French* edition (cited in the above footnote) transcribes both of the extant redactions of the *Histoire*, using BnF, MS f. fr. 20125 and BL, MS, Royal 20 D I. The Aeneas section is at Chapters 588-644 in the first redaction, Chapters 525-59 in the second. The 'Que Eneas revint en Sesile' chapter is numbered 606 in the first, 535 in the second.

[36] Monfrin, in 'Translations Vernaculaires de Virgile', pp. 211-7, criticizes the transcription for omitting passages. At least some of the alleged omissions, however, were because the compiler was using the second redaction of the *Histoire*. Whereas Monfrin compares the *Livre des Eneydes* to BnF, MS, f. fr. 20125 (first redaction), the text is more similar (but not identical to) that in BL, MS, Royal 20 D I (second redaction).

Histoire worked closely with Virgil's Latin text and its commentaries. Although he abridged rather than amplified the Latin, his mode of working was no less studious. Like the Dido-translator, he too was using a glossed Virgil manuscript, and incorporated explanatory material from Servius.[37] The *Histoire*, however, is written in a concise, direct prose style, avoiding overt moralization and rhetorical elaboration.[38] Compared with the preceding section of the *Livre des Eneydes*, the prose is a striking break from the Dido-translator's effusive eloquence.

When the *Histoire* writer modifies Virgil's narrative, it often reflects his intention to write a rationalized history of Aeneas's adventures. In contrast with the Dido-translator, he excised all Virgil's references to the supernatural.[39] The pagan gods (as discussed briefly in Chapter 1) were regarded as the fictions of poets, and sometimes interpreted as allegories for the elements or the motions of planets. Because these poetic licences had no place in a history, the *Histoire* writer prominently omitted Aeneas's descent to the underworld in *Aeneid* VI, writing:[40]

> ... et celle le meneroit en enfer pour veoir lame anchises son pere et les ames de toutes ses meignees qui estoient trespassees. mais ce fut mensonge et qui la vouldra trouuer si la quiere ou romant de eneas ou en virgille.
>
> (*Livre des Eneydes*, sigs i3r-v)[41]

Through an implicit comparison with Virgil and the *Roman d'Eneas*, the *Histoire* writer distinguishes his aims from those of poets. Treating Virgil's epic poetry as an historical source, the *Histoire* writer mined the *Aeneid* for the factual details of Aeneas's adventures, but ignored its fabulous and poetic embellishments. After narrating Turnus's death, the *Histoire* goes on to recount historical events which are not included in the *Aeneid*. Later chapters briefly note Aeneas's marriage to Lavinia, his kingship in Italy, and the

---

[37] As noted in Monfrin, 'Translations Vernaculaires de Virgile', pp. 207-8.
[38] On the *Histoire*'s prose, see Catherine Croizy-Naquet, Ecrire l'histoire romaine au début du XIIIe siècle: L'Histoire Ancienne jusqu'à César et les Faits des Romains (Paris: Champion, 1999), pp. 264-81.
[39] Singerman, *Under Clouds of Poesy*, pp. 176-9.
[40] On anti-poetic aspects of the *Histoire*, see Singerman, *Under Clouds of Poesy*, pp. 152-79.
[41] Caxton: '[she] shulde haue brought eneas in to helle for to see the sowle of Anchises his fadre / and the sowles of alle his meynee that were decessed / but this mater I leue for it is fayned and not to be byleuyd / who that will knowe how eneas wente to helle late hym rede virgyle claudyan or the pistelles of Ouyde. and there he shall fynde more than trouthe. For whiche cause I leue it and wryte not of it' (*Eneydos*, Ch. 33, sig. H8v). He changes 'ou romant de eneas ou en virgille' to 'virgyle claudyan or the pistelles of Ouyde'.

reigns of his descendants. This historical continuation bridges the gap between the *Aeneid* and the next section of the *Histoire*, the founding of Rome. The account of Aeneas's successors also forms the conclusion of the *Livre des Eneydes*.

Although Caxton probably did not recognize the array of different sources, the *Livre des Eneydes* is a dissonant compilation of original composition, translation and abridgement. The translated sections, likely by the same translator, comprise the Polydorus episode of *Aeneid* III, Boccaccio's legend of Dido in *De Casibus*, and Virgil's Dido narrative in *Aeneid* IV. Written in ornate, amplified style, the Dido-translator foregrounds the moral contrast between Dido's noble sacrifice in *De Casibus* and her self-destructive passion in the *Aeneid*. By contrast, the later sections of the *Livre des Eneydes* avoid moralization, poetic embellishments and supernatural references. Their source, the *Histoire Ancienne*, specifically defines its historical authenticity in contrast with the fantasies of poets. Whereas the Dido-translator amplified Virgil's poetry, the writer of the *Histoire* heavily abridged the *Aeneid* into a 'factual', historical narrative.[42] Through this juxtaposition of expansion and abridgement, the legends of Dido take greater prominence in the *Livre des Eneydes* than in the *Aeneid* itself. Aeneas's glorious conquests, by contrast, are narrated in a succinct, abbreviated style. While the compiler's prologue advertises the 'valereux faictz darmes', the centrepiece of the *Livre des Eneydes* is in fact a diptych of elaborate Dido narratives rather than Aeneas's clipped displays of martial prowess.

The Dido-Translator and Contemporary Translation Practice

The Dido-translator's rendering of *Aeneid* IV accounts for approximately half the *Livre des Eneydes*. By far the longest of his three translations, it exemplifies his treatment of the source, his ornate prose style, and his moral agenda. Whereas scholarly accounts typically call it a 'paraphrase' of Virgil,[43] this term understates the Dido-translator's close dependence on the *Aeneid* text, and obscures his precise translation practices. His approach shares typical features of fifteenth- and early sixteenth-century translations

[42] On this dissonance of style and genre, see Singerman, *Under Clouds of Poesy*, pp. 214–6.
[43] Monfrin, 'Translations Vernaculaires de Virgile', p. 216; Leube, *Fortuna in Karthago*, p. 67.

of classical Latin texts, both in French and English. These observations (as later chapters will show) are also present in Gavin Douglas's work and (to a lesser extent) the Earl of Surrey.

Characteristic of contemporary translators, the Dido-translator amplifies Virgil's Latin. Virgilian glosses supplied some of his amplifications, while others were his own invention. In part, he intended his additions to explain and clarify Virgil's meaning, but his principal aims were rhetorical. Through his additions, he reworked the Latin text into a copious, amplified prose style, the 'eloquence' so admired by Caxton. According to fifteenth-century fashions of vernacular prose, the Dido-translator and his contemporaries favoured complex, hypotactic sentences, dilated with explanatory clauses, intensifying adjectives, circumlocutions, and tautologies.[44] As well as amplifying his choice of expression, he also expanded on the content of the text, extending orations and descriptive passages with original material. Although the Dido-translator amplifies to an unusual degree, sometimes up to a hundred words at a time, the practice of expanding a source-text is frequent in fifteenth-century translations. Treating their sources flexibly, translators sought to enrich the rhetorical effects of the original, and to foreground its moral import. Throughout the *Aeneid* IV translation, for example, these additions cumulatively advance a negative, moralistic view of Dido's passion. Far from producing a nebulous 'adaptation' or 'paraphrase', therefore, the Dido-translator approaches Virgil's text with specific, definable intentions. Drawing upon contemporary classical exegesis and common translation practices, he reworks Virgil for the stylistic tastes and moral profit of the fifteenth-century French reader.[45]

After briefly summarizing Aeneas's arrival in Carthage from *Aeneid* I (sigs b8v-c2v), the Dido-translator seamlessly begins his translation of Book IV. The opening lines, though relatively close to the Latin, exemplify his many amplifications, and his pervasive reworking of syntax. His main additions are underlined:

---

[44] On French prose style, see Jens Rasmussen, *La prose narrative française du XVe siècle: étude esthétique et stylistique* (Copenhagen: Aarhuus Stiftsbogtrykkerie, 1958), pp. 32–38, 39–54. On similar trends in English style, see below p. 126, references at fn. 83.
[45] On the ethnocentrism of medieval translation, see Frédéric Duval, 'Quels passés pour quel Moyen Âge?', in *Translations médiévales: cinq siècles de traductions en français au Moyen Âge (XIe-XVe siècles): étude et répertoire*, ed. Claudio Galderisi and Vladimir Agrigoroaei, 2 vols in 3 (Turnhout: Brepols, 2011), I, pp. 47–92 (pp. 72–91).

At regina gravi iamdudum saucia cura	...donc sensuivit quelle griefuement nafuree du dart damours
But the queen, wounded for a long time with heavy care,	...so it followed that she was grievously wounded by the dart of love
vulnus alit venis et caeco carpitur igni	Et nourrit par lo*n*gtemps celle playe embrasee d*e* la doulce femble inuicible en son estomac
nourishes the wound in her veins, and is consumed with blind love.	And [she] nourished this wound for a long time, enflamed with the sweet, invisible fire in her heart,
multa viri virtus animo multusque recursat | gentis honos...	considerant les grans vertus dont sa perso*n*ne estoit decoree sa noblesse *et* honneur de la gent troyenne
The great virtue of the man runs again and again through her mind, and the great honour of his people.	considering the great virtues with which his person was decorated, his nobility and the honour of the Trojan people,
...haerent infixi pectore vultus | verbaque nec placidam membris dat cura quietem	sa grant beaulte et doulx langaige quelle imprima tellement en sa memoire que ses membres reffusoy-ent le doulx repos de dormer
His words and his looks stay fixed in her heart, nor does the care give her limbs peaceful rest.	his great beauty and sweet language, which she imprints so much in her memory that her limbs refuse the sweet rest of sleeping.

(*Aeneid* IV.1–5; *Livre des Eneydes*, sig. c2r)[46]

In many cases, these additions add little to the meaning of the Latin, and are purely stylistic. For example, when Virgil commends Aeneas's 'virtus' and the 'honos' of the Trojan people, the translator adds the near-synonym 'noblesse', listing 'les grans vertus...sa noblesse *et* honneur de la gent troyenne'. To fifteenth-century rhetoricians and prose-writers, synonymy

---

[46] Caxton: 'wherof folowed that she was greuously hurte wyth the darte of loue / And the wounde nourysshed by longe tyme enbraced wyth the swete assemble inuyncible in hyr stomacke . considerynge the grete vertues of whiche his persone was decorate / his noblenes *and* honour of the peple of Troye / his grete beaulte *and* swete langage / whiche she e*n*prynted in her remembrau*n*ce / that her membres refuseden the swete reste of slepe /' (*Eneydos*, sig. C8r, Ch. 10). Caxton's 'enbraced' anglicizes the French 'embrasee', meaning 'set on fire'. With 'inuyncible', he misreads the French 'inuicible' i.e. 'invisible'.

was a basic means of amplification, showing copiousness of expression.[47] Also characteristic of this effusive, amplified style, the translator commonly embellishes his prose with intensifying adjectives, turning Aeneas's 'vultus' and 'verba' into 'sa grant beaulte et doulx langaige'.[48] Although these amplifications might seem nugatory, their cumulative effect throughout the translation is to make the language more diffuse, more heightened.

Like many translators of the classics, the Dido-translator often sourced these amplifications from glosses. Possibly he used Servius's commentary directly, but more likely he had a glossed Virgil manuscript with a mix of Servian and non-Servian interpretations (such as those described in Chapter 1). Whereas the translator incorporates these glosses in a literary work, they were originally written for an exegetic function, explaining Virgil's literal sense and clarifying ambiguities of diction. From a stylistic perspective, the use of glosses makes the French translation more diffuse than Virgil's Latin, and the language more explicit and concrete. In the first line of *Aeneid* IV, for example, the Dido-translator replaces 'cura' with an explicit reference to 'du dart damours'. Whereas Virgil's term has a wide semantic range, the French indicates that 'cura' refers specifically to Dido's love of Aeneas. Moreover, the reference to Cupid's dart clearly shows why Dido is described as 'saucia' ('wounded'). Following Servius's commentary, *Aeneid* manuscripts often gloss 'cura' as 'amore', and note that Virgil 'bene adludit ad Cupidinis tela'.[49] By combining text with gloss, the translator produces a more explicit rendering of Virgil's mythological allusion. The translator's expansive, expository style is characteristic of contemporary translation practice. Even when no commentary source has been identified, translators of Latin typically approached their texts like glossators, giving an expanded and specific rendering of the author's meaning.[50]

Since the Dido-translator almost certainly worked from a glossed Virgil manuscript, it is likely that he drew his additions specifically from the manuscript's interlinear glosses. Rather than circulating Servius's full commentary, marginal and interlinear glosses were the more common means of presenting exegesis in the Virgilian manuscript tradition, as seen in Chapter 1. The translator's additions in this passage, such as 'amore' and

---

[47] On synonymy as a means of amplification, see Rasmussen, *La prose narrative*, pp. 49–51.
[48] Rasmussen, *La prose narrative*, pp. 51–4.
[49] For example, see TCC, MS R.I.40, fol. 54r.
[50] On this style, see Andrea Valentini, 'Entre traduction et commentaire érudit: Simon de Hesdin translateur de Valère Maxime', in *La Traduction vers le Moyen Français*, ed. Claudio Galderisi and Cinzia Pignatelli (Turnhout: Brepols, 2007), pp. 353–65 (esp. p. 356).

'Cupidinis tela', are short, lexical explanations. Virgil scribes typically presented this material in the interlinear gloss, while more detailed expositions were sequestered in the margins.[51] Brief in length, the translator could easily transpose these interlinear glosses into his translation, merging the Latin text and Latin glosses to produce his vernacular rendering. In the above passage, further examples include the addition of 'la gent troyenne' to clarify the identity of 'gentis', and the expansion of 'placidam quietem' into 'le doulx repos de dormer'. In manuscripts, 'gentis' is usually glossed 'Troianis', 'quietem' as 'dormicionem'.[52] Although neither reading appears in Servius's commentary, they were common in Virgil manuscripts. Because glosses varied from manuscript to manuscript, it is difficult to gauge exactly how many of the translator's additions derived from this source. In any case, his translation reads like a synthesis of source-text and interlinear glossing.

Although written for an exegetic function, interlinear glosses not only provided material for explanatory additions, but also for stylistic embellishment. While some translators incorporated portions of exegesis simply to elucidate obscure passages, such as the implied reference to the 'dart d'amours', expository practices were also germane to the Dido-translator's stylistic virtues: periphrasis and tautology. Interlinear glosses expounded the Latin text primarily by supplying synonyms. Since synonymy was a common means of amplification, glossators inadvertently provided translators with a vast stockpile of potential additions. In 'le doulx repos de dormer', for example, the translator was probably combining Virgil's 'placidam quietem' with a synonym gloss from his manuscript, such as 'dormicionem'. Although he could have substituted 'dormicionem' for 'quietem', he instead chose to translate both the gloss and the text, resulting in a periphrasis. Glossing might also have assisted him in cultivating a Latinate, polysyllabic lexis.[53] While he sometimes uses loan-words from Virgil's text, the translator more often chooses terms which are more precise or elaborate than the original Latin, for example when he renders 'caeco' as 'inuicible'. As Servius explains, 'caeco' sometimes means 'blind' ('quod non cernat'), but here it is 'unseen' ('quod non cernatur'). Manuscripts often clarified this ambiguity with a synonym gloss, such as 'invisibili'. While the glossator would have

---

[51] See also Raymond J. Cormier, 'An Example of Twelfth Century *Adaptatio*: The *Roman d'Eneas* Author's Use of Glossed *Aeneid* Manuscripts', *Revue d'Histoire des Textes* 19 (1989), 277–89.
[52] Both glosses are from TCC, MS R.I.40, fol. 54r.
[53] On Latinity and prose style, see Rasmussen, *La Prose Narrative*, pp. 24–32.

used the term for exegetic specificity, it provided the translator with a stylistic ornament.[54] While Virgil glosses assisted these lexical embellishments, the translator reworked Virgil's syntax into a more elaborate, hypotactic arrangement.[55] The opening lines of *Aeneid* IV are structured in five coordinate clauses ('At regina...vulnus alit venis', 'caeco carpitur igni', 'multa...recursat gentis honos, 'haerent...verbaque', 'nec...dat cura quietem'), but the translator makes them subordinate. In place of '[regina] caeco carpitur igni' and 'animo...recursat', the translator gives two participial constructions, 'embrasee de la doulce semble inuicible' and 'considerant'. The next clause, 'vultus verbaque haerent infixi pectore', is divided in two. While its objects 'vultus verbaque' are transferred to 'considerant', 'haerent infixi pectore' is turned into a relative clause, 'quelle imprima tellement en sa memoire'. In a further layer of subordination, the translator introduces 'nec placidam membris dat cura quietem' as a causal construction, 'que ses membres reffusoyent le doulx repos de dormer'. While the co-ordinate structure of *Aeneid* IV.4-5 ('haerent infixi pectore vultus / verbaque' and 'nec placidam membris dat cura quietem') merely implies that Dido's sleeplessness resulted from her persistent thoughts of Aeneas, the translator's causal construction ('tellement...que...') makes this connection explicit. Extensive hypotactic constructions, with interlocking layers of subordination, were the mark of an elaborate prose style. Consistently applied throughout *Aeneid* IV, these wide-reading syntactic changes transform the paratactic syntax of Virgil's epic into an equivalent register of fifteenth-century prose.[56]

The translator shows his craft especially in his use of rhyme. As Monfrin has discussed, he introduces passages of sustained rhyme in speeches and other points of high drama.[57] Possibly due to the difficulties of finding rhymes, these poetic sections are usually accommodated with extra additions to the Latin text. For example, when the lovelorn Dido appears to have

---

[54] Wakelin, in *Humanism, Reading, and English Literature*, pp. 46-8, has noted similar excess of Latinate vocabulary in the fifteenth-century English translation of Palladius's *De Re Rustica*.
[55] On syntax of fifteenth-century prose, see Rasmussen, *La Prose Narrative*, pp. 42-6.
[56] As Duval discusses in 'Quels passés pour quel Moyen Âge?', pp. 73-6, stylistic reworking of the source-text was common in fifteenth-century translations.
[57] Monfrin, at 'L'Histoire de Didon et Enée au XVe siécle', pp. 177-81 (and footnotes), lists several examples, not including the one quoted below.

a hallucinatory vision of Aeneas (*Aeneid* IV.82-3), he expands two lines of Latin into:[58]

> ...la dame qui se mect seulle en sa chamber triste et pensiue laissant les repos de son lit assise sur vng tapis ou aultre part
> toute solitaire et desolee
> comme vne chose habandonnee
> desirant la presence denee
> par ymaginacion imprimee
>
> en la fantasme de son entendement luy semble quelle le voit illec present et actent ses paroles en deuisant auec luy
>
> The lady, who alone enters her chamber, sad and pensive, leaving the repose of her bed, sits on her tapestry or at another place,
> all solitary and desolate,
> like an abandoned thing,
> desiring the presence of Aeneas
> imprinted through her imagination
>
> on the phantasm of her understanding. It seems to her that she sees him present and listening to his words in conversing with him.
>
> (*Livre des Eneydes*, sig. c5v)[59]

Through his expansions, the translator crafts four (loosely) octosyllabic rhyming lines (lineation is my own). In the original Latin, this emotional moment is marked with the famous line 'illum absens absentem auditque videtque.' Although he does not translate the exact semantic meaning, the Dido-translator possibly introduced the rhyming lines to reflect Virgil's 'absens absentem' juxtaposition, seeking to recreate an equivalent rhetorical effect in the vernacular. Other features of elaborate style, namely the prolix phrasing and use of interlocking subordinate clauses, are abundant throughout the passage. Although modern Latinists might lament the distortion of Virgil's concise, tightly-wrought verses, the translator likely considered his

---

[58] Latin: 'sola domo maeret vacua stratisque relictis | incubat. illum absens absentem auditque videtque.' My translation: 'Alone she grieves in the empty house and sleeps in empty sheets. She, absent, hears and sees him, absent.'
[59] Caxton: 'The lady that alone entreth to her chaumbre / tryste and pencyfulle. leuynge her bedde reste syttynge vpon tapysserye werke / or other parte alle solitarye and desolate. as a thynge habandouned / Desirynge the presence of Eneas by Imagynacyon impraynted wyth in the fauntasme of her entendemente. Her semeth that she seeth hym there presente heringe after his wordes playsaunte / And deuysynge wyth hym /' (*Eneydos*, sig. D4r, Ch. 13).

many stylistic changes necessary for reproducing Virgil's epic register in French, just as the Earl of Surrey would later use blank verse in English. If the translator had not effected this stylistic transformation, would Virgil have seemed too plain and terse to fifteenth-century tastes? The *Aeneid* might have lost all semblance of epic without such heavy rewriting.

Not only does the Dido-translator rework the style, but he also uses his amplifications for rhetorical purposes. In orations, he expands Virgil's text to enhance the speaker's rhetorical argument. When introducing Anna's first speech to Dido, for example, his translation begins by specifying her intention as a speaker. He replaces Virgil's curt 'Anna refert' (*Aeneid* IV.31) with following *incipit*:

> A Donc anne sa seur benigne ayant pitie de sa doleur considerant la voye salutaire a conuertir tost son dueil en liesse luy dist en ceste maniere.
>
> (*Livre des Eneydes*, sig. c3r)[60]

Where Virgil's reader is left to surmise Anna's intention from the content of the oration, the Dido-translator makes it explicit: Anna sought to console her sister. In his translation of the *oratio consolatoria*, he invents extra material to support Anna's perceived argument. His many additions are underlined:

O luce magis dilecta sorori	O seur de moy plus amee que lumi-ere enluminee de grant resplendis
O [you who are] more beloved to your sister than light,	O my sister more loved than light illumined with great brightness!
solane perpetua maerens carpere iuuenta	seur comment as tu determine viure seulete en consumant ta ieunesse en perpetuelle tristesse
Will you consume your perpetual youth lonely and grieving?	Sister, how have you determined to live alone, consuming your youth in perpetual sadness?
nec dulcis natos Veneris nec prae-mia noris	ramembre toy des doulx esbatemens les grans soulas et ioyeuses plai-sances. dont les effans esiouissent leurs meres lex doulx baisiers et le

---

[60] Caxton: 'Than Anne her benygne suster / hauynge pyte of her sorowe. consideringe the waye salutary to reuerte soone her sorrow in to gladnesse / sayd to hir in this manere' (*Eneydos*, sig. D1r, Ch. 12).

	bel passe temps quelles y prenne*nt* ainsi les ioyes *et* consolatio*ns* que font les homes a leurs doulces espouses
Will you not know sweet children nor the gifts of Venus?	Do you remember the sweet enjoyments, the great comforts and joyful pleasures, by which children make their mothers happy, the sweet kisses and the fair amusement which they take in it, and moreover the joys and consolations which men do to their sweet wives.
[No Latin]	oste ce dueil ces lamentacio*ns* ces grans souprirs et douloureuses larmes reprens couraige raferme despera*n*ce
[No Latin]	Put away this sorrow, these lamentations, these great sighs, and sorrowful tears. Take back your courage. Refortify your hope.
id cinerem aut manis credis curare sepultos	cest il aduis que les os de sichee ou son tombel lombre d*e* son ame soyent en payne de garder tes amours
Do you think that ashes and buried ghosts care for this?	Do you think that the bones of Sicheus or his tomb, the shadow of his soul, take pain to keep your love?

(*Aeneid* IV.31–4; *Livre des Eneydes*, sig. c3r)[61]

---

[61] Caxton: 'O suster more loued of me. than the lyghte illumyned wyth grete bryghtnes / How haste thou determyned to lyue alone consumyng thyn yongthe in perpetuall heuynesse. Remembre the of the swete dysportynges. the grete consolacions and Ioyfull playsures wherby the children reioyissen their moders / the swete kysshynges and the fayre pase tyme that they take therat / Also the ioye and consolacyon that the men do on to theyr swete spouses. putte away this sorowe / thees lamentacyons. these grete sighynges and sorufull teeres take ayen corage and make thy selfe ferme wyth hope / Troweste thou that the bones of Sycheus or his tombe / the shadowe of his soule. take peyne or care to kepe thy loue /' (*Eneydos*, sig. D1r-v, Ch. 12).

Although some of the expansions are explanatory and stylistic,[62] the volume of added material suggests a more overt rhetorical purpose. The translator sought to enhance Anna's consolatory arguments with a medley of supporting facts and imagery. Most prominently, the phrase 'dulcis natos' receives five separate renderings in French, organized in a triplet ('des doulx esbatemens les grans soulas et ioyeuses plaisances') and a doublet ('lex doulx baisiers et le bel passe temps'). Amid this mass of tautologies, the translator specifies why children might be considered 'dulcis', because they 'esiouissent leurs meres', and visualizes the children's filial love in their 'doulx baisiers'. Whereas Virgil only briefly mentions the 'dulcis natos', the translation imagines mothers playing with their children. As if putting himself in Anna's place, the translator designed this visual, concrete description to appeal to Dido's emotions, and thus to enhance the speech's primary argument. In his second major amplification, the translator adds a sentence between *Aeneid* IV.33-4, 'oste ce dueil...reprens couraige raferme desperance'. In this trio of imperatives, the translator directly states the clear implication of Anna's speech: that Dido should act on her love, rather than persist in grief.

These amplifications, at their most conspicuous, can extend for hundreds of words. For example, after translating the line 'id cinerem aut manis credis curare sepultos?' (*Aeneid* IV.34), the French writer adds a further 190 words to support its point ('pense que non ne plus que la flameche...et conuerty en pouldre', sigs c3r-v).[63] Just as the translator's rendering of 'dulcis natos' extends ideas present in Virgil text, this lengthy amplification of *Aeneid* IV.34 likewise repeats and rephrases the content of its parent line. Anna affirms that Sycheus's soul is very much separate from his body, that all his worldly works and desires are of no consequence, and that no-one can return the dead to life. Speaking of his soul, she urges her sister:

---

[62] In expository additions, the translator clarifies the addressee ('O seur'), the allusion to Dido's dead husband ('de sichee'), and the referent of 'id' ('tes amours'). He also replaces the metonymy 'Veneris' with the more concrete 'que font les homes a leurs doulces espouses'. This reading of 'Veneris' likely derived from a gloss, such as 'matrimonii' (TCC, MS R.I.40, fol. 54v). Among his stylistic changes, the translator expands 'praemia' into the doublet 'ioyes et consolations'.

[63] Caxton: 'thynke it nomore than the sperkell...*and* conuerted in to poulder' (sig. D1v, Ch. 12).

...pense que non ne plus que la flameche yssant du feu auec la fume tost se berist et reduist en neant sans plus auoir vigeur ne aultre puissance sans faire feu flamboyant ne lumiere pareillement

(*Livre des Eneydes*, sig. c3r)[64]

Likely inspired by Virgil's 'cinerem', the translator conveys Sycheus's deadness through an extended comparison with a dead flame. As this example suggests, he treated *Aeneid* IV.34 not just as an object of translation, but also as a basis from which to invent copious additional material. Amplifications of this kind characterize the remainder of Anna's speech, which alternates between translation of Virgil and supporting passages of the translator's own invention.

Although his additions are by no means unprecedented, the volume of added material sets the Dido-translator apart from most of his contemporaries. While expanding the source was a common practice in fifteenth-century translations of the classics, the extent varied from translator to translator, ranging from the short additions of glosses to the invention of entire new passages. In length and frequency, the Dido-translator represents an extreme degree of amplification. While particularly evident in speeches, such additions are a pervasive feature of his ordinary practice. For example, he extends Virgil's description of the tempest with copious extra details. Two lines of Latin (*Aeneid* IV.160-1), which mention only a 'magno misceri murmure' and 'commixta grandine nimbus', are inflated into 275 words of French. As in Anna's speech, the translator not only expands on Virgil's text, but also invents material not present in the original. In his version of events, the weather took the hunters by surprise, a strong wind swept over them, and lightning illumined the earth (sigs c8v-d1r).[65] Although the Dido-translator represents every line of the Latin in his French translation, he treated his Virgilian source as a starting-point rather than a confine. His intention was not merely to render Virgil's

---

[64] Caxton: 'thynke it nomore than the sperkell yssuyng oute of the fyre wyth the smoke / whiche is soone reduced and broughte to noughte wythout to haue ony vygoure more ne other puyssaunte to make fyre lyghte nor flamme' (*Eneydos*, sig. D1v, Ch. 12).

[65] The description is: 'pendant le temps de laquelle chase...comme sil fust nuyt' (sigs c8v-d1r). In Caxton, see 'Durynge the tyme of the whiche chasse...as thoughe it had be nyghte' (*Eneydos*, Ch. 15, sigs D7v-8r).

grammatical meaning in idiomatic French, but to flaunt his own faculties of rhetorical invention.[66] In particular, the Dido-translator uses his amplifications to promote a negative portrayal of Dido's passion. Building on ideas already present in the Latin, he advances a moral contrast with her heroism in Boccaccio's *De Casibus*. As Dido burns with desire, for example, Virgil spends four lines describing the decline of Carthage (*Aeneid* IV.86-9). The construction work all ceases, the city's youths no longer train for battle, and the defences lie open to attack. In the *Livre des Eneydes*, the equivalent passage is expanded to 195 words (sigs c5v-c6r).[67] From the very beginning, the Dido-translator explicitly states the cause of the city's decay. Virgil precedes his Carthage description with an account of Dido's lovelorn thoughts (*Aeneid* IV.68-85), and the Dido-translator makes an explicit connection between the two:

> A Cause de laquelle occupacion ou continuelle pencee en ce rauie et transportee inexplicablement toutes les aultres affaires de dydo sont demoures en lestat dimperfection   (*Livre des Eneydes*, sig. c5v)[68]

Whereas Virgil leaves this connection implicit, the French translation directly states that Dido's passions are the cause of her people's woes. Thereafter, the Dido-translator amplifies the description of Carthage with extra details of the city's dilapidation. For example, he states that the stones in the city walls are 'rechinees toutes bossues cortes et contrefaictes'. Whereas Virgil's Carthage merely ceases to be constructed, the *Livre des Eneydes* describes a city in ruins: 'mossues et brisees toutes raoulles et plaines de laidure' (sig. c6r).[69] The perceptive reader might remember that Boccaccio's Dido, by contrast, ordered the fortifications to be strengthened

---

[66] The other long additions are four digressions explaining references to the Caucasus, Cadmus, Orestes and Laomedon. These digressions are at: *Aeneid* IV.366-7, 469, 471, 542; *Livre des Eneydes*, sigs e3r, f3r-v, f3v, g2r; *Eneydos*, Chs 19, 22, 22, 25 and sigs E8r, F5v, F5v-6r, G1v-2r. For discussion, see Leube, in *Fortuna in Karthago*, p. 71.

[67] See 'A Cause de laquelle occupacion...' to '...a cause de sa grant fureur' (sigs c5v-c6r). Caxton: 'And for by cause of the whiche forsayd occupacyon... by cause of her grete furoure' (*Eneydos*, Ch. 13, sig. D4v).

[68] Caxton: 'And for by cause of the whiche forsayd occupacyon or contynuelle thoughte wherinne she is Inexplycable occupied as transported and rauysshed Alle the werkes and doynges of Dydo are taryed and lefte in the astate of Inperfection' (*Eneydos*, Ch. 13, sig. D4v).

[69] The stones are 'alle awry sette. croked bowed and counterfette... spredde wyth mosse all to tourne / rusty and full of lothlinesse' (*Eneydos*, Ch. 13, sig. D4v).

prior to her death.[70] To conclude the description, the translator restates Dido's guilt: '*et* brief tout d*e*chiet en ruyne a cause d*e* sa gra*n*t fureur' (sig. c6v).[71] Through these lengthy additions, he draws a clear moral lesson from Virgil's text. Not only does he amplify the city's plight, but he also gives explicit statements of the blame.

In his amplification of Dido's speeches, the translator expands the more vindictive passages. Her threats against Aeneas and his people receive copious gory detail. When Dido foretells that a mighty warrior, Hannibal, will wreak vengeance on the Romans, the translator specifically amplifies the line ('face Dardanios ferroque sequare colonos') 'harass the Trojan settlers with fire and sword', *Aeneid* IV.626). Not only will Hannibal 'les brulera tout en feu *et* en flambe', but also 'les occira en diuerses manieres' (sig. h1v). With a page of further description, the translator leaves no manner of death to the imagination, listing that some will be hanged ('les aultres pendre'), others flayed ('et aultres escorchier'), others sold like beasts ('vendus seront comme bestes sauuaiges'), and so on.[72] While Dido relishes the gory destruction of the Romans, the translator also introduces explicit references to hell. In Virgil's text, Dido's dabbling in witchcraft and imprecations of Aeneas are riddled with chthonic invocations of Hecate, the Furies and Pluto. The translator, throughout these invocations, adds epithets such as 'infernal' and 'le grant dieu de*n*fer'.[73] At *Aeneid* IV.638, for example, he (incorrectly) glosses the river Styx as a lake of fire, sulphur and pitch (sig. h2v).[74] To the Christian reader, Dido's pagan rituals are given overtones of diabolic worship. Along with her murderous words, her hellish religion puts her on the path to damnation.

This religious language is most prominent in Anna's response to Dido's suicide (*Aeneid* IV.675-85). Whereas Virgil's Anna cries 'hoc illud, germana, fuit? me fraude petebas?' (*Aeneid* IV.675), her French counterpart adds 'par

---

[70] 'Et ce pendant comme le presuppose si aulcune deffence estoit en la cite qui ne fust en conuenable fortificatio*n* emparee' (*Livre des Eneydes*, sig. b7r). Cf. *Tutte le Opere di Giovanni Boccaccio*, XI, p. 140 and *Eneydos*, Ch. 8, sig. C5r.

[71] Caxton: 'And shortely alle falleth in to ruyne. by cause of her grete furoure' (*Eneydos*, Ch. 13, sig. D4v).

[72] The full amplification of IV.626 extends from 'les occira en diuerses manieres...' to '...tant que ciel *et* terre durera' (sigs h1v-2r). Caxton: '*and* shall slee *and* distroie them in diuerse manere... as long as heuyn *and* erthe shall last' (*Eneydos*, Ch. 27, sigs G6v-7r).

[73] See *Aeneid* IV.509-10, 610, 638; *Livre des Eneydes* sigs f6v, g6v, h2v; *Eneydos*, Ch. 24, sig. F8r, and Ch. 27, sigs G5r, G7r.

[74] Perhaps more fitting for the Phlegethon, the French description reads: 'fleuue du stige qui est vng lac de feu ardant decourant tout parmy enfer compose de souffre et de poix' (sig. h2v). Caxton calls it a river of 'fyre', 'brymston' and 'pitche' (*Eneydos*, Ch. 26, sig. G7v).

quelle maniere et raison te as tu voulu mectre a eternelle perdicion du tout en tout' (sig. h4v).[75] Over the remainder of the speech, the translator makes targeted amplifications whenever Anna implies that Dido has committed a wrongdoing. For example, when she laments 'quid primum deserta querar?' (*Aeneid* IV.677), the French translator also has Anna recount that she has served and loved Dido her all her life. The addition further implies that Dido's suicide is a selfish and ungrateful act.[76] Five lines later, he extends Anna's lament 'exstinxti te meque, soror, populumque patresque' (*Aeneid* IV.682).[77] To quote just the end of the amplified section:

> ...se ma seur se fust maintenue sans desespoir dont tout lespoir tant a eulx comme a moy nous fault par elle qui nous a estaint et a couppe tout nostre atainte maintenant sommes sans pasteur comme brebis habandonnee
> (*Livre des Eneydes*, sig. h5r)[78]

Through Anna's grief, the translator emphasizes that Dido's actions have brought infamy and ruin upon her sister and her people. This passage echoes Virgil's earlier warnings about the ruinous consequences of love, such as the heavily-amplified description of the city's dilapidation. In concluding with the resonant biblical image 'comme brebis habandoneee' ('like abandoned sheep'), the French translator poignantly contrasts the sinful suicide of Virgil's Dido with the self-sacrifice of Boccaccio's Dido, who never once abandoned her flocks, and willingly died for their protection.

The translator's Christianizing approach and heavy amplification culminate with the book's closing lines. Juno sees Dido's soul struggling to leave her body, and sends Iris to assist her (*Aeneid* IV.693–705). Inspired by Virgil's brief reference to Proserpina (IV.698-9), the translator turns the thirteen-line episode into a six-page contest over the fate of Dido's soul (sigs h5v-8v). Since she is wife of the infernal Pluto, the translator

---

[75] Fairclough: 'Was this your purpose, sister? Did you aim your fraud at me?' Caxton: 'and by what maner *and* rayson hast *thou* broughte thi selfe thus to eternall perdycyon' (*Eneydos*, Ch. 28, sig. H1v).

[76] The whole addition is: 'toute ma vie tay volu honnourer... *que* de toy mesmes' (*Livre des Eneydes*, sig. h5r), corresponding to *Eneydos*, Ch. 28, sig. H1v.

[77] Fairclough: 'You have destroyed yourself and me together, sister'. The amplification of IV.682-3 begins roughly at 'O quelle douleur...' and ends '...comme brebis habandoneee' (sig. h5r). Cf. *Eneydos*, Ch. 28, sig. H2r.

[78] Caxton: 'yf my suster had mayntened and kept herself wythout dysperacyon / Wherof alle hope / aswell to theym as to me failleth by her y*at* hath extyncted oure goode renommee *ad* brought vs in a grete blame *and* nowe be we without pastoure. as the sheep that is habaundou*n*ed' (*Eneydos*, Ch. 28, sig. H2r).

introduces Proserpina as queen of Hell, describing at length her evil influence on humans. Proserpina claims Dido's soul on account of her suicide and sinful despair:

> Quelle se estoit occise par desespoir comme a cause de furie et de raige qui est chose inhumaine dependans des operacions et dernieres infernalles... et si a voulu subiuguer a seruir et soubzmectre parquoi de raison elle luy doict demourer (*Livre des Eneydes*, sig. h6v)[79]

To oppose Proserpina's diabolic claims, the translator makes Juno the representative of the heavens, mapping Christian theology onto the pagan pantheon. While Virgil characterizes Juno as a malicious foil to Jupiter, opposing Aeneas's divine mission to Italy, she now takes the role of the Christian God himself. In one of Dido's earlier prayers, the translator added a reference to Juno's 'diuine prouide*n*ce', possibly intending to foreshadow this concluding passage.[80] Iris, who argues the case against Proserpina, claims that Juno created Dido, brought her into the world, and nourished her from birth. On these grounds, Juno must be the lawful owner of her soul.[81]

As in Virgil's text, the matter is resolved when Iris offers to give Proserpina Dido's hair, and Proserpina agrees in exchange to renounce her unjust claim. Through divine grace of Iris and Juno, the translation thus concludes with the liberation of Dido's soul:

> Et puis [Iris] se print a deslier les membres auecques lesperit de vie... et la liureret franc et quicte au lieu selon sa demerite qui a toutes gens ainsi comme il est ordonne par la prouidence diuine dont le regne iamays ne fine. (*Livre des Eneydes*, sig. h8r)[82]

---

[79] Caxton: 'she hadde slayn herself by dysperacion as for cause of furye and of rage whiche is a thinge Inhumayne dependynge of the operacyons and wodnesses of helle...wherunto she hathe subdued and submytted herself. wherfor by reson she oughte to abyde vnder her' (*Eneydos*, Ch. 29, sig. H3v).
[80] *Livre des Eneydes*, sig. g6r; *Eneydos*, Ch. 27, sig. G5v. Cf. *Aeneid* IV.608.
[81] *Livre des Eneydes*, sig. h7r; *Eneydos*, Ch. 29, sig. H4r.
[82] Caxton: 'And thenne she [Iris] toke vp on her selfe for to vnbynde the membres from the spyrite of lyffe... and delyuered her free and quytte to that place after her demeryte that to alle folke is propyce as it is ordeynded by the prouydence deuyne wherof the regne shalle neuer fynyshe' (*Eneydos*, Ch. 29, sig. H5r).

Caxton and Style

The Dido-translator thus presents *Aeneid* IV as a morality tale of Dido's sinful passion and the power of divine grace. Although his Christianizing approach only surfaces in the closing pages, it embodies his overall treatment of Virgil's text, frequently amplifying for stylistic and rhetorical purposes. Even as he translates every line of the Latin, he treats the *Aeneid* merely as a starting-point for his own faculties of invention. Through his amplifications, he sought to recast Virgil's epic register according to fifteenth-century ideas of elevated style. To create an elaborate French prose, he embellished the original *Aeneid* with hypotactic constructions, rhyme, periphrastic diction, and Latinate lexis. As witnessed in many translations of the time, these stylistic additions were often sourced from Virgilian glosses. Moreover, he expanded Virgil's text with extra rhetorical content, sometimes adding hundreds of words at a time. By this means, he foregrounded the moral utility of Virgil's Dido legend, and contrasted it with Boccaccio's story of nobility and self-sacrifice. While the Dido-translator is an extreme example, this practice of amplification typifies fifteenth- and early sixteenth-century translations of the classics. Rather than a stringent reproduction of the original Latin, the Dido-translator and his contemporaries reworked their sources for contemporary stylistic tastes, rhetorical flair, and moral edification.

Caxton was not insensible to the Dido-translator's literary craft. According to his prologue, it was the 'eloquence' of the *Livre des Eneydes* that first inspired him to translate it:

> ...In whiche booke I had grete playsyr. by cause of the fayr and honest termes *and* wordes in frenshe / Whyche I neuer sawe to fore lyke. ne none so playsaunt ne so wel ordred. whiche booke as me semed sholde be moche requysyte to noble men to see as wel for the eloquence as the historyes /
> (*Eneydos*, sig. A1r)

If Caxton's 'grete playsyr' was genuine, he was surely referring to the Dido-translator's elaborate, amplified style in his renderings of *De Casibus* and *Aeneid* IV. The other sections of the *Livre des Eneydes*, lifted from the *Histoire Ancienne*, would have seemed concise and unadorned by comparison. While both halves were more or less the same length, the *Histoire* section covers a far greater proportion of the *Aeneid*, and is written in a more compressed prose style. When Caxton translated the French *Livre des*

Eneydes into English, he treated these amplified and compressed styles in a different manner. He probably did not know that the two halves had been written by separate authors, but was sensitive to their stylistic disparities. In the lengthy translations of *Aeneid* IV and *De Casibus*, he preserved the Dido-translator's elaborate lexis and syntax, while eliminating the more egregious circumlocutions. In the compressed *Histoire*, however, he added several amplifications, making the terse historical narrative more suspenseful and dramatic. Although not a consistent programme, Caxton thus reacted to the distinct, contrasting styles in his French source.

Studies of Caxton's translation practice rarely credit him with such flexibility.[83] His translations, for the most part, are close, literal reproductions of their source-texts. Caxton stringently reproduces the French syntax and phrasing, calques French idioms, and anglicizes French words. Samuel Workman has termed this method a 'stencil translation' on account of its extreme literalism.[84] During his later career, Caxton's language became more idiomatic, but rarely elicits literary praise.[85] Although he makes minor additions to his source-texts, his 'overwhelming' motive (as one recent study puts it) was to clarify ambiguities in the French, and only rarely did he embellish.[86] In this regard, his practice resembles an editor as much as a translator. Throughout the *Livre des Eneydes*, for example, he extensively revised the punctuation. Whereas the French source punctuated only at major text breaks, such as the beginnings of sentences and occasionally at main clauses, Caxton used frequent virgules or *punctus* to distinguish every clause of the translation. Particularly in the Dido-translator's sections, Caxton's unobtrusive additions would have helped readers to make sense of the long, hypotactic sentences. Scholars have observed similar interventions in Caxton's printing of English literature. For example, he often added punctuation and short explanatory additions when revising his copy-texts

---

[83] On Caxton's translation practice, see Blake, *Caxton and his World*, pp. 125–50; Joanne M. Despres, 'Translation Techniques in the Romances of William Caxton' (Unpublished Ph.D. Dissertation, University of Pennsylvania, 1991). On Caxton and fifteenth-century English translators of French in general, see Samuel K. Workman, *Fifteenth Century Translation as an Influence on English Prose* (Princeton: Princeton University Press, 1940).

[84] Workman, *Fifteenth Century Translation*, pp. 1–32 (esp. p. 8). Baswell, in *Virgil in Medieval England*, p. 272, describes Caxton's *Eneydos* as 'almost a transliteration' of its French source.

[85] Despres, in 'Translation Techniques', pp. 234–7, argues that Caxton improves as a translator, but adds that 'His improvements are on the whole not dramatic'.

[86] See Despres's conclusion in 'Translation Techniques', pp. 235–6.

for publication.[87] Whether he was editing a Middle English work or translating the *Livre des Eneydes*, Caxton aimed to prepare an intelligible text for the English market.

Although so often disparaged,[88] his literalistic method nonetheless had a stylistic purpose. During the fifteenth-century, English prose style was pervasively influenced by French models, which promoted prolixity and hypotaxis. Caxton used his 'stencil' translations to preserve these fashionable stylistic features from his French source-texts.[89] When he translated the *Livre des Eneydes*, Caxton stopped short of reproducing the Dido-translator's artful rhymes, but retained all the elaborate, hypotactic syntax and interlocking subordinate clauses. As he wrote in his prologue, the Dido-translator's 'eloquence' is 'moche requysyte to noble men to see', and his translation essentially transposed the French word-by-word into English. Because he aimed to replicate rather than modify, modern studies have noted that his independent stylistic input was relatively limited.[90] Although Despres has noted minor rhetorical embellishments, she often judges them to be 'awkward' and 'crude'. His later works are more lucid, but only because they are 'relatively error-free' and have 'virtually no confusing or awkward passages'.[91] As N.F. Blake puts it, '[Caxton] was not primarily a literary man.'[92]

Despite these pronouncements, Caxton's prologues are often cited for their comments on style. In the *Eneydos* prologue, for example, he famously discusses his treatment of Latinate loan-words, so called 'curyous termes'.[93] It is no accident that the *Eneydos* translation elicited this famous discussion, because Latinate lexis figures prominently in the Dido-translator's ornate

---

[87] For examples of Caxton's editorial practice, see Daniel Wakelin, 'Caxton's exemplar for The Chronicles of England?', *Journal of the Early Book Society* 14 (2011), 75–113 (90–4).
[88] Despres, in 'Translation Techniques', pp.14–20, surveys critical evaluations of Caxton's translation practice.
[89] Workman, *Fifteenth Century Translation*, pp. 5–13; Despres, 'Translation Techniques', pp. 11–4, 21–2.
[90] Despres, 'Translation Techniques', p. 235.
[91] For the critical comments, see Despres, 'Translation Techniques', pp. 32, 36 (on *Recuyell*). For the more positive comments, see pp. 235, 190 (on the later *Blanchardin and Eglantine*).
[92] Blake, *Caxton and his World*, p. 126.
[93] On this passage and Caxton's translation practice, see Samuel K. Workman, 'Versions by Skelton, Caxton and Berners of a Prologue by Diodorus Siculus', *Modern Language Notes* 56 (1941), 252–8; Despres, 'Translation Techniques', pp. 7–11, 22–3. On its broader literary and historical contexts, see Seth Lerer, *Chaucer and his Readers: Imagining the Author in Late-Medieval England* (Princeton: Princeton University Press, 1993), pp. 168–75; Wakelin, *Humanism, Reading, and English Literature*, pp. 147–9.

prose style. Although Caxton wanted to preserve these 'fayr *and* straunge termes' in his English translation, he anticipates criticism:

> And whan I sawe the fayr *and* straunge termes therin / I doubted that it sholde not please some gentylmen whiche late blamed me sayeng *that* in my translacyons I had ouer curyous termes whiche coude not be vnderstande of comyn peple /   (*Eneydos*, sig. A1r)

In this passage, Caxton weighs the drawbacks of stylistic embellishment and the needs of intelligibility. His resolution is to translate the *Livre des Eneydes* in a middle style:

> And for as moche as this present booke is not for a rude vplondyssh man to laboure therin / ne rede it / but onely for a clerke *and* a noble gentylman that feleth and vnderstondeth in faytes of armes in loue *and* in noble chyualrye / Therfor in a meane bytwene bothe I haue reduced *and* translated this sayd booke in to our englysshe not ouer rude ne curyous but in suche termes as shall be vnderstanden by goddys grace accordynge to my copye.   (*Eneydos*, sig. A2r)

Although evidently foregrounding a stylistic problem, Caxton's discussion of 'curyous termes' serves a commercial purpose and cannot be taken as a reliable indication of his practice. In saying that the *Eneydos* is 'not for a rude vplondyssh man...but onely for a clerke *and* a noble gentylman', Caxton presents his work as high-brow literature for intellectually aspirational readers. As Despres has convincingly suggested, he intended the passage merely as an apology for the Latinity of his translation.[94] Admiring the Dido-translator's elaborate prose style, Caxton incorporated many of its 'fayr *and* straunge termes' into his English *Eneydos*.

Because French and English shared this stylistic preference for Latinate loan-words, the *Eneydos* retains traces of Virgil's lexis even after two stages of translation. For example, when Dido invokes 'nocturnisque Hecate triviis ululata per urbes' (*Aeneid* IV.609), the Dido-translator renders Hecate's epithet 'tressouue*nt* inuoq*ue* en voix vlutatiue' (*Livre des Eneydes*, sig. g6v). Just as Virgil's participle 'ululata' became 'voix vlutatiue', Caxton's English translation reads 'voyces vlulatyue' (*Eneydos*, Ch. 27, sig. G5v).

---

[94] Despres, 'Translation Techniques', pp. 22–3. Cf. Workman, 'Versions', who argues that Caxton indeed took a middle way.

Because the Dido-translator and Caxton sought to embellish their style in the same manner, the same term passed from Virgil to the *Livre des Eneydes* and finally to the *Eneydos*. As well as the *Aeneid*, similar examples appear in the Dido-translator's rendering of *De Casibus*, for example when Boccaccio praises Dido 'O mulieris virile robur'. Whereas Laurent de Premierfait's popular 1409 translation renders the line as 'O force de homme en corps de femme',[95] the Dido-translator in the *Livre des Eneydes* opts for 'Des femmes fortitude virile' (sig. b8r). He directly imports Boccaccio's 'virile', and translates 'robur' with the Latinate 'fortitude'. Typical of the Dido-translator's practice, this latter term has a more elevated register than Boccaccio's original. Preserving both Latinate words, Caxton renders the line 'O the fortytude viryle of wymmen' (*Eneydos*, Ch. 9, sig. C6r). For the fifteenth-century reader, therefore, the *Eneydos* was replete with lexical ornaments, derived from and sometimes even exceeding the original Latin sources.

These examples ('viryle', 'vlulatyue') might have presented difficulties for Caxton's readers, since the *Eneydos* marks their first attested uses in English. Even if they were not completely new, they would likely have been regarded as rare and 'curyous' terms, intelligible 'onely for a clerke *and* a noble gentylman'.[96] Given the difficulties of comprehending such vocabulary, fifteenth-century authors would often introduce doublets, pairing Latinate loan-words with readily-intelligible synonyms. Caxton scholars have long noted his pervasive use of this technique, and he added heavily to the doublets in his French sources.[97] For example, when he came across the terms 'vaticinant' (*Livre des Eneydes*, sig. b4r) and 'alimentee' (*Livre des Eneydes*, sig. h7r), he amplified them with an extra synonym, creating the doublets 'vaticynaunte or prophecyeng' (*Eneydos*, Ch. 6, sig. C2v) and 'alymented and noryshed' (*Eneydos*, Ch. 29, sig. H4r). Similarly, when the French refers to Dido's 'douleur intrinseque' (*Livre des Eneydes*, sig. e3r), Caxton uses a short amplification to clarify the use of the Latinate adjective: 'sorow intrysinque wythin her hert' (Ch. 19, sig. E7v).[98] Not only were these amplifications a vehicle for fashionable Latinisms, but they also sustain and enhance the diffuse style of the French. Just as the Dido-translator amplified Virgil, so too did Caxton

---

[95] For the Latin, see *Tutte le Opere di Giovanni Boccaccio*, Ch. 11, p. 142. For De Premierfait's French, see *De casibus virorum illustrium*, tr. Laurent de Premierfait (Lyon: Mathias Huss and Johannes Schabeler, 1483; *ISTC* ib00712000), sig. f7v.
[96] They are the first attested uses at *OED*, 'ululative', adj.; 'virile', adj., 1a.
[97] On Caxton's doublets, see Despres, 'Translation Techniques', pp. 81–93, 144–153, 210–18.
[98] In *OED*, Caxton's *Eneydos* is the first attested of 'vaticinant', adj., 1; 'aliment', v., 1a; 'intrinsic', adj., A, 1a.

amplify the *Livre des Eneydes* with added synonyms and tautologies. From this perspective, Caxton's doublets build upon the Dido-translator's overall stylistic project. By embellishing the French prose, Caxton further accommodated the *Aeneid* to fifteenth-century conventions of ornate writing.

Much as Caxton admired, preserved and enhanced the Dido-translator's elaborate prose style, he also exercised restraint. Throughout the *Livre des Eneydes*, Caxton makes slight abbreviations to his source, usually to eliminate redundant phrases. This practice is seen throughout Caxton's translations,[99] but the *Eneydos* examples cluster especially in the *Aeneid* IV section. Given his expansive style, the Dido-translator gave Caxton more occasions for abbreviation than any other part of the *Livre des Eneydes*. As he translated, Caxton sought to curb the Dido-translator's most obvious pleonasms. For example, Virgil's description of Fame begins:

Fama, malum qua non aliud velocius ullum.

(*Aeneid* IV.174)

dont sourdet vne mauluaise deesse appellee fame ou renommee qui est celle ainsi que lon dit. fame est vne malle meschine dont il nest chose plus legiere

(*Livre des Eneydes*, sig. d1r)[100]

wherby arose one euylle goddesse callyd fame or renommee whiche is more lighte than ony other thynge /

(*Eneydos*, Ch. 15, sig. D8v)

In trimming the French text, Caxton happens upon a closer translation of Virgil's Latin than does his source. He eliminates 'qui est celle ainsi que lon dit', a redundant addition by the Dido-translator, and 'est vne malle meschine', since 'vne mauluaise deesse' already establishes Fame's wickedness. While it is rare for Caxton's English and Virgil's Latin to correspond so closely, this example nonetheless reflects a broader project to edit and cut the *Livre des Eneydes*. Passage-by-passage, he judged what to preserve, what to remove. The cumulative effect of these deletions is to show Caxton's reservations about the Dido-translator's unchecked amplification.

Whereas Caxton trimmed the Dido-translator's excesses, the sparse style of the *Histoire* elicited the opposite treatment. Throughout his career as a

---

[99] Despres, 'Translation Techniques', pp. 40–1, 45–6, 114–5, 174–6, 181–3, 123–5.
[100] My translations: 'Fame, than whom no other evil [is] more swift'; 'And so an evil goddess arose called fame or renown which is that which is said. Fame is a wicked servant than which there is no thing more swift'.

translator, Caxton often added small amplifications to his sources, making descriptions more vivid and events more dramatic.[101] The *Histoire*, with its compressed and unadorned prose, gave him particular cause for such additions. So as to give the impression of historical authenticity, the thirteenth-century writer of the *Histoire* had deliberately avoided any rhetorical embellishment, instead giving a direct, factual narration of events. Although Caxton probably did not know this authorial intention, he registered the discrepancy between the 'historical' prose-style of the *Histoire* and his readers' expectations of a vernacular *Aeneid*. In specific passages, he attempted to make the sparse narration of historical events into a more engaging literary narrative. For this reason, most of Caxton's amplifications in the *Eneydos* appear in the *Histoire* section, showing a concerted attempt to embellish its clipped style. The Dido-translator, by contrast, received only couple of additions from Caxton, since his prose was already elaborate and expansive. While Caxton's changes are only slight, they cumulatively reduce the stylistic disparities between the components of the *Livre des Eneydes*.

As with the deletion of the Dido-translator's pleonasms, Caxton did not have an overall plan for his amplifications, but worked spontaneously passage-by-passage. For this reason, the distribution of Caxton's additions does not necessarily reflect the narrative importance of any given section. For example, one of the longer amplifications appears during an excursus about Theseus and Ariadne (*Livre des Eneydes* sigs i1v-3r; *Eneydos* Ch. 31-2, sigs H6v-8r).[102] Upon arriving in Italy, Aeneas famously visits Daedalus's temple at Cumae, and sees his engravings of Minos, the labyrinth and the death of his son (*Aeneid* VI.14-33). Although tangential to Aeneas's story, the *Histoire* author narrates these events at greater length, following Servius's commentary on the passage. In his English translation, Caxton embellished the *Histoire*'s digression yet further, inventing extra psychological details. When Ariadne falls in love with Theseus, Caxton elaborates:

quant elle [i.e. Ariadne] vit theseus si bel et si auenable ella layma moult *et* luy dist

(*Livre des Eneydes*, sig. i2r)[103]

---

[101] Blake, *Caxton and his World*, pp. 128-37; Despres, 'Translation Techniques', pp. 33-6, 42-5, 111-2, 120-1, 168-71, 177-8.
[102] On digressions in the *Historie* section, see Monfrin, 'Translations Vernaculaires de Virgile', p. 208.
[103] My translation: 'When she saw Theseus so handsome and so agreeable, she greatly loved him, and said to him'.

whan she saw Theseus <u>that was</u> so fayre and so amyable <u>and that was come for to be in thraldom vnder her fader</u> / she hadde pyte of hym / and for hys honneste behauoure / Began to be taken with his loue / And vnto hym <u>vpon a daye</u> she sayde /

(*Eneydos*, Ch. 31, sig. h7r-v)

Whereas brief *Histoire* narrates only that Ariadne saw the fair Theseus and fell in love, Caxton expands on the cause of her passion, namely his honest conduct and her pity for his adverse circumstances. In dilating the clause 'elle layma moult', Caxton's inceptive and passive construction 'began to be taken with his loue' suggests Ariadne's gradual, spontaneous increase of affection. Where the *Histoire* directly states 'et luy dist', the temporal marker 'vpon a daye' softens the abrupt narration of factual events. By these means, Caxton elaborates the clipped prose with psychological and circumstantial detail, despite the fact that Ariadne and Theseus were only an expository excursus.

Since chapters from the *Histoire* cover Aeneas's wars in Italy, most of Caxton's amplifications fall in battle-scenes. Through adding a word or short phrase, he amplifies the *Histoire*'s displays of prowess and pathos. For example, Aeneas fights not just in the 'bataile', but the 'thyckest presse of the bataylle'. His 'folke' are not just slain ('detranchier'), but 'slayne afore his eyen' (both examples from *Livre des Eneydes*, sig. k8r; *Eneydos*, Ch. 50, sig. K3r). Caxton's longer additions sometimes extend for several clauses, and substantially change the course of battle. For example, when the French version describes how the Trojans routed Turnus's forces, Caxton expands on the abrupt 'que force leur fut de retourner arriere' (sig. l5r). Before revealing the outcome, his translation builds the suspense:[104]

And the Latynes bare theym selfe full well a while that by force of armes they made the troyens to retoure bak / But atte the last the troyens that were neuer wery of batayylles / made there merueylles of armes so that the latynes might susteyne noo lenger the weight of theyre swerdes / but were ageyne putte abak   (*Eneydos*, Ch. 55, sigs K7v-8r)

Caxton by no means equals the Dido-translator's hundred-word additions to Virgil, but he shows similar willingness to engage in original composition. Instead of directly stating Aeneas's victory, he delays the event by several

---

[104] The French is a result clause meaning 'that they were forced to go back'.

clauses, and the Latins initially have the upper hand. Caxton goes on to embellish the Trojans' prowess, for they were 'neuer wery of bataylles' and made many 'merueylles of armes'. Whereas the historian is satisfied to report only the battle's outcome, Caxton sought to create suspense and drama for his English readers.

Caxton, therefore, adjusted his translation practice according to local shifts in subject-matter and style. Although generally characterized as a rigid 'stencil' approach, the *Eneydos* reveals a more flexible practice. Caxton freely invented extra material to amplify abrupt phrases or terse descriptions, while editing out the more overt pleonasms. These amplifications and deletions were not implemented with any overarching plan, but on a passage-by-passage basis. Because the *Histoire* is so succinct, most of the amplifications fall in this section of the translation. Meanwhile, the diffuse Dido-translator receives most of the omissions. The cumulative effect of Caxton's changes is to reduce (if only slightly) the stylistic rifts between the components of the *Livre des Eneydes*. Caxton's *Eneydos*, at least in terms of style, is a more unified text than its source.

Conclusion

Caxton's *Eneydos* and his French source, the *Livre des Eneydes*, therefore, were not straightforward 'adaptations' of the *Aeneid*. Whereas the *Roman d'Eneas* or the *Ovide Moralisé* were adapted by a single author, the *Livre des Eneydes* was an unusual compilation of original writing, translation and abridgement. Probably a hasty production in a printing house, this compilatory approach was a shortcut for the French printer, Guillaume le Roy, to make a vernacular *Aeneid*. Caxton almost certainly did not know of its complex construction, but he discerned and edited the stylistic differences between its components. For several decades, the *Livre des Eneydes* and *Eneydos* were the only French and English *Aeneid* translations to have been printed. In France, the publication of Octavien de Saint Gelais's *Aeneid* did not mark a sudden influx of translations, seeing that only two editions (1509, 1514) were printed prior to 1529. In England, moreover, there were no printed translations of the *Aeneid* until the edition of Gavin Douglas's *Eneados* in 1553.[105] Copies of Caxton's *Eneydos*, meanwhile, bear evidence

[105] St-Gelais: *USTC* 26178, 72685. Douglas: *STC* 24797.

of use throughout the sixteenth century, including annotations and bindings in *Sammelbände*. Even as more faithful *Aeneid* translations began to circulate, Caxton's *Eneydos* continued to find readers.[106]

Whereas the overall compilation was an unusual patchwork of sources, the individual components of the *Livre des Eneydes* show close dependence on the Latin text, notably the Dido-translator's rendering of *Aeneid* IV. His work exemplifies common features of fifteenth- and early sixteenth-century translations of classical Latin texts. Characteristic of the period, he amplifies his source-text, and frequently incorporates material from glosses. Through these additions, the Dido-translator reworked Virgil's style and syntax, recreating his epic verse with an equivalent register of fifteenth-century prose. He differs from most contemporary translators in the volume of his amplifications, sometimes exceeding a hundred words at a time. Even as he translates every word of the *Aeneid*, he invents extra material to expand its rhetorical effects, and to foreground a moral interpretation of Dido's passion. Although translations of the classical authors all display a degree of amplification, the Dido-translator represents a particularly expansive approach, which ultimately did not persist into later generations. Sixteenth-century translators, as the next chapter will show, continued to amplify their sources, but tended to limit their additions to a clause or a line. If humanism had an effect on translating classical texts, it was to moderate the extremes of amplification, and to narrow the range of typical practice. The Dido-translator became a relic of an earlier, more inclusive era of translation.

---

[106] For provenances of several surviving copies, see Y.-C. Wang, 'Caxton's Romances and their Early Tudor Readers', *Huntington Library Quarterly* 67 (2004), 173–88 (182, 185, 186–7).

5
Douglas's *Eneados*

In 1513, the Scottish clergyman and poet Gavin Douglas (*c.* 1476–1522) completed the *Eneados*, the first full translation of Virgil's *Aeneid* in the Scots language and indeed any language related to English.[1] To accompany his vernacular epic, Douglas also translated the *Supplementum* of Maffeo Vegio, provided verse prologues to each of the thirteen books, and began writing a set of vernacular glosses to *Aeneid* I. Translating a major classical poet in full for the first time, the *Eneados* has often been described as a work of 'vernacular humanism'.[2] A few classical *auctores* had previously been translated into English, but translators had tended to choose practical or philosophical texts in prose rather than works of poetry. Portraying himself as Virgil's 'scolar' and 'traste interpreter', Douglas translated from Badius Ascensius's 1501 edition of Virgil's *Opera*, extensively consulting Ascensius's recent commentary, as well as the major Late Antique commentaries by Servius and Tiberius Claudius Donatus.[3] Although Douglas's interest in classical poetry reflects a humanist influence, his overall practice is consistent with earlier translating traditions. Rather than inaugurating a new, humanist approach, early sixteenth-century translators of the classics tended to use similar techniques to their fifteenth-century forebears. Like previous translators of other classical works, Douglas resolved interpretative difficulties predominantly by amplifying the original text, synthesising the *Aeneid* with extra material from glosses. Sometimes these amplifications were meant to clarify Virgil's *sentence*, sometimes to embellish his style. Douglas was groundbreaking in translating a major work of classical poetry,

---

[1] References to Douglas are from *Virgil's Aeneid Translated into Scottish Verse by Gavin Douglas*, ed. D.F.C. Coldwell, 4 vols, Scottish Text Society, 3rd ser., 25, 27–8, 30 (Edinburgh: W. Blackwood & Sons Ltd, 1957–64). Coldwell's edition is based on TCC, MS O.3.12, copied by Matthew Geddes, Douglas's secretary.

[2] Most notably, Priscilla Bawcutt, *Gavin Douglas: A Critical Study* (Edinburgh: Edinburgh University Press, 1976), p. 36.

[3] Quotations of Virgil's text and commentaries are from Ascensius's 1501 edition, abbreviated as '*Opera* (1500-1)'. On Douglas's use of the edition, see Bawcutt, 'Gavin Douglas and the Text of Virgil', *Edinburgh Bibliographical Society Transactions*, 4 (1973), 211–31; *Gavin Douglas*, pp. 95–102. On his use of commentaries, the authoritative study remains Bawcutt, *Gavin Douglas*, pp. 110–27.

but humanist influences did not cause him to break decisively from earlier translation practices.

Definitions of Douglas's humanism are prone to understate his consistencies with fifteenth-century literary traditions.[4] They rarely contextualize Douglas in the broader history of translating the classics, but compare the *Eneados* almost exclusively with Caxton's *Eneydos* and other Virgil translations.[5] Douglas famously initiated these comparisons in his prologue to *Aeneid* I, where he supposedly 'articulates most clearly his position as translator and thus as humanist interpreter'.[6] During the prologue, he condemns the many discrepancies between Caxton's *Eneydos* and the *Aeneid* (I.Prol.137–282), and declares his intention to translate Virgil's text more closely ('Virgillis versys to follow *and* no thing feyn', I.Prol.266). This comparison is said to establish his novel, textual approach to translation. Caxton's *Eneydos* is taken to represent a medieval practice of adapting classical works, while Douglas's *Eneados* stands for the new 'humanist view of genuine translation.[7] 'His concern with the interpretation of Virgil's *sentence*', it is argued, 'fits with humanist intentions to return to the text'.[8] This dichotomy, characterizing the Middle Ages as an era of adaptation, the Renaissance as the dawn of translation, ignores Douglas's precedents in fourteenth- and fifteenth-century translations of the *auctores*. Douglas was indeed novel 'to translate the *Aeneid*, rather than to rewrite or rework its material', but only insofar as he applied this closer, textual approach to a major classical poet such as Virgil.[9]

---

[4] On Douglas's humanism, see Nicola Royan, 'The Humanist Identity of Gavin Douglas', *Medievalia et Humanistica* 41 (2015), 119–36; A.E.C. Canitz, 'From *Aeneid* to *Eneados*: Theory and Practice of Gavin Douglas's Translation', *Medievalia et Humanistica* 17 (1991), 81–99; Bawcutt, *Gavin Douglas*, pp. 31–6. Lois Ebin, meanwhile, emphasizes Douglas's 'faithfulness' to the Latin, but does not explicitly connect it with humanism. See *Illuminator, Makar, Vates: Visions of Poetry in the Fifteenth Century* (Lincoln, NE: University of Nebraska Press, 1988), p. 112.

[5] For brief comparison with Octavien de St Gelais's *Aeneid* translation, see William Calin, *The Lily and the Thistle: The French Tradition and the Older Literature of Scotland: Essays in Criticism* (Toronto: University of Toronto Press, 2014), pp. 38–9. For comparisons with Surrey, see Chapter 6, pp. 168–9. Bawcutt suggests that Douglas 'probably knew earlier translations, such as Nicholas Oresme's *Aristotle* or Chaucer's *Boethius*' (*Gavin Douglas*, p. 111), but does not directly address the conventionality of Douglas's technique.

[6] Royan, 'The Humanist Identity of Gavin Douglas', 121.

[7] The quotation is from Canitz, 'From *Aeneid* to *Eneados*', 81. For similar comparisons with Caxton's *Eneydos*, see Royan, 'The Humanist Identity of Gavin Douglas', 123–4; Bawcutt, *Gavin Douglas*, pp. 79–81.

[8] Royan, 'The Humanist Identity of Gavin Douglas', 133; see also Bawcutt, *Gavin Douglas*, p. 31 on Douglas's 'need to return *ad fontes*'.

[9] Quotation from Royan, 'The Humanist Identity of Gavin Douglas', 120.

Because the *Eneados* tends to be studied in isolation from wider translation-history, the conventionality of Douglas's translation practice often goes unrecognized. Studies of the *Eneados*, in the act of describing Douglas's technique, inadvertently observe common traits of fifteenth- and early sixteenth-century translations of the *auctores* (which have been outlined in Chapter 4). Priscilla Bawcutt, Lois Ebin, and A.E.C. Canitz, for example, all comment on Douglas's frequent amplification of the original, his explicitness of diction, and his use of commentaries. Where Virgil is concise, Douglas 'explains', 'expands', 'glosses', 'expounds', and 'clarifies'. If Virgil is allusive or ambiguous, Douglas is more 'explicit', turning 'hints or ambiguities into definite statements'.[10] Douglas's rhetorical additions, meanwhile, make the descriptions more vivid, the action more dramatic, the pathos more affective.[11] His declarations of textual fidelity manifest primarily in restraining the length of individual amplifications, since he rarely adds more than a line at a time. Although not shared by all fifteenth-century translators, Douglas's more moderate approach has ample precedents, including Chaucer's *Boece*, the Middle English translation of Palladius's *De Re Rustica* as well as a translation of Cicero's *De Amicitia* attributed to John Tiptoft.[12] This moderate practice of amplification still allowed translators to make interpretative and rhetorical interventions, but limited their deviations from the source-text.

Caxton's Eneydos and Douglas's Eneados

Douglas's prologue to *Aeneid* I, already discussed above, is often seen as a humanist rebuke to Caxton's *Eneydos* and medieval adaptations of Virgil's *Aeneid*, yet such comparisons over-simplify Caxton's French source, the

---

[10] On his translation practice, the definitive study remains Bawcutt, *Gavin Douglas*, pp. 110–27 (quotations from p. 115). For similar comments, see Douglas Gray, 'Gavin Douglas', in *A Companion to Medieval Scottish Poetry*, ed. Priscilla Bawcutt and Janet Hadley Williams (Cambridge: Brewer, 2006), pp. 149–64 (pp. 160–4); Canitz, 'From *Aeneid* to *Eneados*', 85–97; Ebin, *Illuminator, Makar, Vates*, pp. 112–5.

[11] As described in Bawcutt, *Gavin Douglas*, pp. 137–43, 158–63; Canitz, 'From *Aeneid* to *Eneados*', 93–7; Ebin, *Illuminator, Makar, Vates*, pp. 113–4.

[12] On the Palladius and its closeness to the Latin, see Daniel Wakelin, *Humanism, Reading, and English Literature, 1430–1530* (Oxford: OUP, 2007), p. 43. On Chaucer's closeness in *Boece*, see Tim William Machan, *Techniques of Translation: Chaucer's Boece* (Norman: Pilgrim Books, 1985), p. 126. On the Cicero, see Douglas Gray, 'Some Pre-Elizabethan Examples of an Elizabethan Art', in *England and the Continental Renaissance: Essays in Honour of J.B. Trapp*, ed. Edward Chaney and Peter Mack (Woodbridge: Boydell, 1990), pp. 24–36.

Livre des Eneydes.[13] Although taken to represent a tradition of adapting the *Aeneid*, the production of the *Livre des Eneydes* and *Eneydos* was an unconventional, extreme case. As summarized in Chapter 4, it does not resemble any other extant vernacular version of a classical text, whether adaptation or translation. Rather than the work of a single author, it was stitched together from a patchwork of several earlier texts, including an abridgment of *Aeneid* I–III, direct translations of *Aeneid* III.1–68 and *Aeneid* IV, and sections from the thirteenth-century *Histoire ancienne jusqu'à César*. Probably a hasty production in a Lyon printing-house, this compilational approach was the printer's short-cut to produce a vernacular *Aeneid* for the print market. The printer titled the compilation as if it were 'translate de latin', but in fact there were book-length omissions from and evident distortions of Virgil's narrative. Caxton, who probably did not know the Latin *Aeneid*, repeated the same dubious claim in his prologue to the *Eneydos*, saying that it was 'translated oute of latyn'. The *Livre des Eneydes* and *Eneydos*, in this light, are not a benchmark for fifteenth-century attitudes to translation.

Douglas's criticisms of Caxton's *Eneydos* largely pertain to the French compiler's unusual patchwork mode of production rather than broader conventions of translating classical authors. He only knew the *Livre des Eneydes* through Caxton's translation, and was not aware of the text's compilational origins. The portions of direct *Aeneid* translation, by contrast, have much in common with Douglas's own practice. The anonymous French translator of *Aeneid* IV (the Dido-translator) draws on the same body of fifteenth-century translation techniques. He and Douglas differ principally in the length of their amplifications rather than their overall approach. While the Dido-translator sometimes adds up to a hundred words at a time, representing an extreme of fifteenth-century practice, Douglas restricts his additions to a line or less. Because Douglas and the Dido-translator differ in degree more than in kind, the English renderings of *Aeneid* IV in Caxton's *Eneydos* and Douglas's *Eneados* bear telling lexical and syntactic resemblances. As we shall see, these similarities attest to shared use of commentaries, similar procedures of amplification, and stylistic preferences for hypotaxis and Latinate diction. Douglas's prologue indeed vituperates Caxton's *Eneydos*, but his criticisms do not target these common translation practices.

---

[13] For the standard discussions of this prologue, see Bawcutt, *Gavin Douglas*, pp. 80–1; Canitz, 'From *Aeneid* to *Eneados*', 81–5; Royan, 'The Humanist Identity of Gavin Douglas', 121–5.

Moreover, when criticizing previous vernacular versions of the *Aeneid*, Douglas is more concerned with their mishandling of specific plot-points rather than their treatment of the text. This thematic, rather than textual, emphasis shows why Douglas commented on Chaucer's 'Legend of Dido' (I.Prol.339-46, 405-449) as well as Caxton. Whereas Caxton's *Eneydos* was styled 'translated oute of latyn', Chaucer did not claim to produce a fulllength translation or even adaptation of the *Aeneid*, but retold Virgil's Didonarrative as part of a longer poem. Even so, Douglas criticized Chaucer for misrepresenting the relationship of Aeneas and Dido. While claiming to 'folwe' the *Aeneid* story, Chaucer 'offendit' Virgil in suggesting that Aeneas and Dido were married. Rather than a service to the gods and the Trojan people, he presents Aeneas's departure from Carthage as a betrayal of a marital oath.[14] Virgil's Aeneas was typically understood as a model of *pietas*, but Chaucer propagates a derogatory counter-tradition, that Aeneas was a deceitful lover.[15] Douglas, believing it a wrongful interpretation of Virgil, frames his *Aeneid* translation as a corrective. He exhorts his reader 'Reid *the* ferd buke', for '*Th*ar sal 3e fynd Ene maid nevir aith, | Promyt nor band with hir fortill abyde' (I.Prol. 437-9). Douglas's prologue, tellingly, makes no claims to novelty in translation practice, but emphasizes the proper representation of plot and character. Rather than 'new' and 'old', Douglas speaks of following and feigning, of truth and falsehood. Instead of rebuking specific practices of translating or even adapting a text, the prologue is concerned with the misrepresentation of Aeneas's character and the wider *Aeneid* narrative.

As with Chaucer, Douglas's criticisms of Caxton's *Eneydos* focus on these large-scale distortions. Because of the unusual, patchwork production, the *Livre des Eneydes* and Caxton's *Eneydos* have long, book-length omissions from Virgil. Although Douglas did not know the French, he could easily see the differences between Caxton's English and the Virgilian narrative. Working book-by-book, Douglas's prologue enumerates the more egregious omissions, for example:

---

[14] In 'Legend of Dido', the offending lines are: 'Glorye and honour, Virgil Mantoan, | Be to thy name! and I shal, as I can, | Folwe thy lanterne, as thow gost byforn, | How Eneas to Dido was forsworn.' (*The Legend of Good Women*, ll. 923-6). *The Riverside Chaucer*, ed. Larry D. Benson (1987; Oxford: OUP, 1988).

[15] On Chaucer's narrative, the best account is Baswell, *Virgil in Medieval England*, pp. 249-69. On positive and negative presentations of Aeneas, see surveys in Bawcutt, *Gavin Douglas*, pp. 83-5; Wilson-Okamura, *Virgil in the Renaissance*, pp. 196-203, 208-12.

> The thre first buki*s* he hass ourhippyt quyte
> Salfand a litill twychyng Polidorus
> And *the* tempest furth sent by Eolus,
>
> (*Eneados* I.Prol.154–6)

The *Livre des Eneydes* and *Eneydos* (as described in the previous chapter) began with a brief summary of Troy's fall. It bore virtually no resemblance to Virgil's account in *Aeneid* II, and omitted most of *Aeneid* I and III. The 'litill twychyng Polidorus' refers to an embedded translation of *Aeneid* III.1-68, and Douglas might have mentioned it specifically because he recognised its Virgilian source. The 'tempest furth sent by Eolus', meanwhile, is briefly summarized before the Dido-translator's rendering of *Aeneid* IV. These abbreviations, as noted in Chapter 4, likely reflect the limited texts available to the French compiler. Although he had portions of direct Virgil translation, he had to improvise to make the rest of the *Aeneid* narrative. Probably working in haste, he did not have the time or inclination to fill the gaps between each component. Douglas blamed these omissions on Caxton's translation practice, but they in fact stemmed from the unusual production-history of the *Livre des Eneydes*.

Douglas identifies further abbreviations in the second half of the Aeneas story. For the events of *Aeneid* V onwards, the compiler transcribed verbatim from the thirteenth-century *Histoire ancienne jusqu'à César*, which heavily abridged Virgil's text. Seeking to produce a history of Aeneas rather than an *Aeneid* translation, the writer of the *Histoire* used Virgil's text to ascertain the 'historical' facts of Aeneas's adventures, but ignored its poetic embellishments and supernatural content. This generic difference, between factual history and epic poetry, underpins Douglas's main criticisms of these sections. In particular, he criticizes the omission of *Aeneid* VI and Aeneas's fantastical journey to the underworld:

> The saxt buke eyk, he granti*s*, *th*at wanti*s* hail,
> And, for *th*arof he vnd*er*stude noc*h*t *th*e tail,
> He callis it fenʒeit and noc*h*t forto belief;
>
> (I.Prol.177–9)

For thirty lines (I.Prol. 177–206), Douglas discusses the moral and allegorical significance of the book's 'fenʒeit' story. Virgil, he says, shows himself to be a 'hie philosophour', concealing many 'suythfast materi*s*' beneath '*th*e clowdi*s* of dyrk poecy'. Perhaps Douglas might have excused the omission in a work of history, but it could not be tolerated in a translation of Virgil's poetic design. Among his other complaints, Douglas reprehends 'Caxton' for removing the 'lusty gamys' of Book V (I.Prol.173-6), for abridging the 'strang batalis *and* werys' in *Aeneid* VII-XII (I.Prol.249-52), and for ignoring the elaborate description of Aeneas's armour in *Aeneid* VIII (I.Prol.253-9). Although some fifteenth-century translators omitted and abridged their sources, this scale of abbreviation was an extreme case, not least because the *Histoire* was never intended as a translation. This extreme level of abridgement reflects the original purpose of the *Histoire* and the compilation practices of the *Livre des Eneydes* more than typical fifteenth-century approaches to translating or even adapting classical texts.

The Dido-translator's rendering of *Aeneid* IV is the one part of the volume to be translated from Virgil's original Latin. Although Douglas could not have known it to be an independent work, he identifies that it makes prolific amplifications of the text (as Chapter 4 noted). Douglas's criticisms are worth quoting at length:

> He ry*n*nys sa fer from Virgill in mony place,
> On sa prolixt and tedyus fasson,
> So *th*at *th*e ferd buke of Eneadon,
> Twichand *th*e lufe and ded of Dido queyn,
> *Th*e twa part of his volume doith conteyn
> *Th*at in *th*e text of Virgill, trast*is* me,
> *Th*e twelt part scars co*n*tenys, as 3e may se.
>
> (*Eneados* I.Prol.163-72)

Douglas possibly identified the Dido-translator's work as a translation, commenting that it 'ry*n*nys sa fer' from Virgil. His rendering of *Aeneid* IV is 'prolixt' and 'tedyus', dilating the original with long amplifications. Because the other eleven books are given only in abridged versions, the result of the elongated *Aeneid* IV is to misshape the proportions of Virgil's narrative, considerably increasing the prominence of Dido's story to comprise the 'twa part' of the volume. Douglas's objections, once again, relate to the sheer extent of the changes. They not only arise from Dido-translator's unusually high degree of additions, but also from the compiler's unorthodox decision to juxtapose his work with abridgements of the other books. These processes, neither of which reflects widespread practices of the period, are the root cause of Douglas's criticisms, since they introduce evident distortions between the *Livre des Eneydes* and its professed Virgilian source.

Douglas and the Dido-Translator

While objecting to the Dido-translator's extreme additions, Douglas suggests that limited expansion of the *Aeneid* text is the obligation of any 'traste interpreter' (I.Prol.401). When he describes his translation practice, he does not attempt to carve a new, humanist technique, but invokes a series of translator's commonplaces to justify traditional fifteenth-century practices of amplifying the source. For almost seventy lines (I.Prol.339–408), Douglas explains that a translator should not translate 'word eftir word', but must follow the 'sentence', alluding to the famous dictum of Horace and St Gregory (I.Prol.395–402).[16] In practice, as we shall see, this justification licenses Douglas to perform the same kinds of amplifications as the Dido-translator. Although more restrained in length, amplification is Douglas's standard technique of elucidating ambiguous phrases, keeping his metre and rhyme, and indeed for introducing the rhetorical embellishments so common among fifteenth-century translators.

At least according to the prologues, however, his main reason for these expansions is to produce a full rendering of Virgil's *sentence*. He insists that every word of the *Aeneid* is significant, claiming that Virgil 'sa wisely wrocht never a word invane' (I.Prol.30). This praise of semantic plenitude is more commonly associated with Scripture than pagan texts, and it informs Douglas's scrupulous attempts to render every shade of meaning.[17] Scarcely any of Virgil's 'precyus wordys deir' (I.Prol.23) are omitted from the *Eneados*, and Douglas uses multiple translations to unravel their multiple senses and connotations. As he foregrounds in the prologue, his pursuit of semantic completeness necessarily involves expanding the original text:[18]

> Sum tyme *the* text mon haue ane expositioun,
> Sum tyme *the* collour will causs a litill additioun,
> And sum tyme of a word I mon mak thre,
> In witnes of *th*is term "oppetere."
>
> (I.Prol.347–50)

---

[16] Copeland, in *Rhetoric, Hermeneutics, and Translation*, pp. 21–35, 42–55, has noted that this sentiment is often used to justify expansion of a source.

[17] Kantik Ghosh, '"The Fift Quheill"; Gavin Douglas's Maffeo Vegio', *Scottish Literary Journal* 22 (1995), 5–21 (15–6 and fn. 50).

[18] For praise of Douglas's 'fowth of language', see Priscilla Bawcutt, 'Douglas and Surrey: Translators of Virgil', *Essays and Studies* 27 (1974), 52–67 (60). By contrast, Chapter 6 will discuss Surrey's consistent omissions of words from the Latin.

In accordance with his actual practice, Douglas indicates that he expands on obscure and specifically figurative passages ('*the* collo*ur*'). Even using the term 'expositioun', he alludes to the common practice of incorporating portions of commentary into the translation, widely seen in the Dido-translator. Douglas's example, 'oppetere', literally means 'go to meet' or 'encounter', but figuratively 'meet death' or 'die'. When the term appears at *Aeneid* I.96, Servius gives a (specious) etymology for this euphemism: 'Oppetere: ore terram petere. i. mori'. In the *Eneados* prologue, Douglas details Servius's exposition in a marginal gloss:

> Oppetere is alsmekil to say as 'ore terram petere', lyke as Seruius exponys the sammyn term, quhilk to translate in our tung is 'with mowth to seik or byte the erd'. (I.Prol.350n)[19]

When Douglas translates this line of the *Aeneid*, he works Servius's (specious, but widely-repeated) interpretation into the Scots text, rendering 'oppetere' as 'Deit in *th*ar fader*is* syght, bytand *th*e erd!' (I.iii.6).[20] Had he only rendered the general meaning ('deit'), his translation would not have represented the perceived connotations of Virgil's word-choice. In this example, Douglas shows his reader how vernacular amplifications help to transmit 'eu*er*y deill' ('Direction', l. 45) of *sentence* in the original Latin. In line with his predecessors, such as the Dido-translator, this technique is a standard feature of Douglas's practice.

While he makes no secret of his additions, Douglas does not describe his approach transparently. So as to establish his credentials as Virgil's 'traste interpreter', he understates his rhetorical motivations for amplifying the source. Rather than a creative choice, his amplifications are presented as a necessity, frequently using metaphors of binding and constraint. In contrast with the licences of the Dido-translator, he describes himself 'to Virgillis text ybund' (I.Prol.299), as if he made no creative interventions and embellishments. He expanded, so he claims, only when the rendering of Virgil's *sentence* forced him to do so:

> And *th*us I am co*n*strenyt als near I may
> To hald hys verss and go nane other way,
> Less sum history, subtell word or *th*e ryme
> Causith me mak digressioun sum tyme.
>
> (I.Prol.303–6)

---

[19] I have added the inverted commas to mark the Virgilian quotation and Douglas's translation.
[20] As well as in I.Prol, Douglas provides a further marginal gloss to 'oppetere' at I.iii.6.

Douglas is 'co*n*strenyt' to follow Virgil's verses, except when the difficulties of rendering Virgil's meaning forced him to 'mak digressioun'. By 'history' and 'subtell word', Douglas refers to Virgil's obscure cultural references, polyvalent vocabulary and figurative language, which receive expansive translations throughout the *Eneados*. By 'ryme', meanwhile, he acknowledges that formal constraints prompted many minor additions, filling out his decasyllabic metre and couplet rhymes. Whereas the Dido-translator often expanded for purely rhetorical purposes, Douglas claims that his expansions of the source are all demanded by the explanation of his Latin source-text and the restrictions of his target verse-form. At least according to his prologue, his departures from Virgil's exact words are each necessary for conveying Virgil's full meaning in Scots poetry. Through downplaying his interventions as a poet, he portrays himself as a reliable translator of Virgil's *sentence*.

Douglas's actual practice, however, is more like the Dido-translator than the prologue suggests. While he presents himself as a scrupulous interpreter of Virgil's *sentence*, his typical treatment of the *Aeneid* text is more flexible and creative. Even in a passage of relatively close translation, his expansions cannot all be reduced to the necessities of *sentence* and verse-form. Much like the Dido-translator, he amplifies for a range of explanatory, metrical and rhetorical concerns, as seen in the opening lines of *Aeneid* IV:

At regina graui veneris iamdudum saucia cura
Vulnus alit venis: & cæco carpitur igni.

(*Aeneid* IV.1-2)[21]

Be *th*is *th*e queyn, throw hevy thoch*t*i*s* onsound,
In every vayn nurysys *th*e greyn wound,
Smytyn so deip wit*h* *th*e blynd fyre of lufe

(*Eneados* IV.i.1-3)

'[...] she was greuously hurte wyth the darte of loue / And the wounde nourysshed by longe tyme enbraced wyth the swete assemble inuicible in hyr stomacke.

(*Eneydos*, sig. C8r, Ch. 10)[22]

---

[21] *Opera* (1500-1), II, fol. 115r. My translation: 'But the queen, wounded for a long time with heavy care, nourishes the wound in her veins, and is consumed with blind fire.'

[22] The Dido-translator is quoted from Caxton's English *Eneydos* rather than the French *Livre des Eneydes*, since Douglas only knew the work in Caxton's English. I have corrected Caxton's 'inuyncible' to the Dido-translator's 'inuicible' [i.e. invisible], which closely renders the Latin 'caeco'. For further analysis of this passage, see Chapter 4, pp. 111-5.

Setting aside Douglas's several syntactic changes,[23] the underlining indicates three additions which have no basis in the Latin text: 'every', 'so deip' and 'of lufe'. Only one of the additions, 'of lufe', relates directly to the explanation of Virgil's *sensus*, clarifying the metaphorical meaning of 'igni'. Just as the Dido-translator replaces 'cura' with 'darte of loue', Douglas likewise explains his author's figurative frame of reference, following the common glosses 'cura. i. amore' and 'igni. i. amoris'.[24] Douglas's two remaining additions, meanwhile, have no equivalents in Virgil or the commentaries. Adding an intensifying adjective and adverb, he turns the Latin 'venis' into 'every vayn', and renders 'carpitur' as 'smytyn so deip'. As they were in the Dido-translation, these intensifiers are commonplace across the *Eneados*, and several studies of Douglas are devoted to these manifold additions.[25] Although the demands of metre almost certainly influenced their exact placement, they cumulatively suggest a broader design, heightening the descriptions of Dido's passion and demise. As far as Douglas's practice indicates, the faithful transmission of the *sentence* could sustain minor rhetorical amplifications of its verbal vessel.

Throughout the *Eneados*, this principle manifests itself in Douglas's extended translations of given words and lines. As with the Dido-translator, his diffuseness reflects not only explanatory but also rhetorical concerns. For example, when Virgil describes Dido's insistent thoughts of Aeneas, Douglas expands for several lines:

Multa viri virtus animo: multusque recursat
Gentis honos:

(*Aeneid* IV.3–4)[26]

---

[23] Although syntax will receive further discussion below, Douglas's changes are as follows. First, both translators give a participial translation of 'carpitur igni', Douglas producing 'Smytyn [with the fire of love]', the Dido-translator 'enbraced'. In this syntactic change, Douglas probably sought to explain that the fire was the origin of Dido's 'greyn wound'. Second, they both treat 'iamdudum' with 'Vulnus alit' rather than 'saucia'. Possibly compelled by metre, Douglas writes 'greyn wound', while the Dido-translator has 'nourysshed by longe tyme'. Regarding 'greyn' ('fresh' or 'recent', see *DOST*, 'grene', 5.1–3), Douglas was probably thinking of Servius's glosses 'Iamdudum: aut nimium...aut iamdudum a quo tempore vidit ęneam' (*Opera* (1500–1), II, fol. 114v).

[24] The quoted glosses of 'igni' and 'cura' derive from Ascensius's commentary, but Servius's commentary is similar. See *Opera* (1500–1), II, fols 114v–5r.

[25] Gordon Kendal lists many other examples in *Translation as Creative Retelling: Constituents, Patterning and Shift in Gavin Douglas' Eneados* (unpublished Ph.D. Thesis, University of St Andrews, 2008). On Douglas's many formulaic additions, see also Bawcutt, *Gavin Douglas*, pp. 137–63.

[26] My translation: 'The great virtue of the man runs again and again through her mind, and the great honour of his people'.

Hir trublyt mynd gan fra all rest remufe.
Compasing the gret prowes o Ene,
The large wirschip feill syss remembris sche
Of his lynnage and folkis;

(Eneados IV.i.4–7)

Because of Douglas's three additions, the description of Dido's distress receives greater narrative space in the *Eneados* than the *Aeneid*. In two cases, the additions have both explanatory and rhetorical functions. The 'lynnage and folkis', although a stylistic doublet in its own right, elucidates two possible meanings of 'gentis', which could refer to Aeneas's direct ancestors or to his people in general.[27] Likewise, Douglas gives two renderings of 'animo...recursat', a phrase which receives particular comment in Servius and Ascensius. While 'compasing' approximates the literal meaning of the verb, conveying the turbulent movement of Dido's thoughts, 'feill syss remembris sche' shows the frequentative aspect, and clarifies the figurative reference to Dido's cognition.[28] The third addition, by contrast, has no exact equivalent in Virgil's Latin, no object of explanation. The added line 'Hir trublyt mynd gan fra all rest remufe' does not translate any specific word, but restates the general subject-matter of the passage, Dido's restlessness. Much like the examples of the Dido-translator's practice in Chapter 4, Douglas buttresses Virgil's description with extra supporting detail. Collectively, these additions demonstrate Douglas's fluid conception of *sentence* as opposed to text. Because Douglas does not seek a word-for-word translation, his practice sanctions brief, rhetorical additions to the original Latin, as long as they support Virgil's overall meaning.[29]

Douglas, as expositor and rhetorician, shows similar fluidity in the treatment of syntax.[30] As observed in the previous chapter, the Dido-translator frequently introduces subordinate constructions, partly for the needs of

---

[27] Servius: 'dardani a numinibus aut veneris'. *Opera* (1500–1), II, fol. 114v.

[28] Servius: 'Recursat: bene frequentatiuo vsus est verbo in frequenti amantis cogitatione.' Ascensius: 'recursat. i. frequenter reuoluitur animo mire dixit recursat quasi ipse cogitationes vi se ingerant & libere recurrant'. *Opera* (1500–1), II, fols 114v–5r. My translations: '**Recursat**: Rightly he has used a frequentative verb for the frequent thought of a lover'; '**Recursat**: i.e. "frequently is turned over in her mind". Rightly he said **recursat** as if the thoughts multiply themselves in force and repeat of their own accord'.

[29] As Bawcutt notes, 'Sometimes Douglas inserts lines which have no strict equivalent in Virgil but are appropriate in the context...' *Gavin Douglas*, p. 126.

[30] On Douglas's syntax, see Bawcutt, *Gavin Douglas*, pp. 161–2.

sentence, partly for rhetorical effect. Douglas's adaptations are strikingly similar:

Multa viri virtus animo: multusque recursat
Gentis honos: hęrent infixi pectore vultus:
Verbaque: nec placidam membris dat cura quietem.

(*Aeneid* IV.3–5)[31]

Compasing *the* gret prowes o Ene,
The large wirschip feill syss reme*m*bri*s* sche
Of his ly*n*nage and folk*is*; for ay present
Deip in hir breist so was hys figur prent,
And all hys word*is* fixt, *th*at, for bissy tho*ch*t,
Noyn eys hir me*m*bris nor quyet suffir mocht.

(*Eneados* IV.i.6–10)

The passage has four main syntactic changes, each of which has been underlined.[32] To select one example, Douglas uses the conjunction 'for' to subordinate 'hęrent infixi pectore vultus' to 'multusque recursat | Gentis honos'. In its explanatory functions, this syntactic change was probably influenced by Ascensius's gloss: 'sed quomodo recursant: quia vultus sc*ilicet* veri here*n*t infixi pectore'.[33] Much like Ascensius's 'quia', Douglas's 'for' elucidates an implied causal connection between two of Virgil's verses. For Douglas as much as the Dido-translator, syntactic manipulation was the means of conveying these implications in the vernacular. From a rhetorical perspective, meanwhile, these concatenations of subordinate clauses conform to contemporary stylistic trends, a marked concern of the Dido-translator. They might also show Douglas attempting to sustain momentum in his verse, particularly when these structures extend over ten or fifteen lines.[34] While preserving Virgil's overall *sentence*, Douglas thus develops a

---

[31] My translation: 'The great virtue of the man runs again and again through her mind, and the great honour of his people. His words and his looks stay fixed in her heart, nor does the care give her limbs peaceful rest.'

[32] The other syntactic changes are: 1) the double translation of 'animo... recursat' (discussed above); 2) the conjunction '*that*' subordinates the two concluding clauses; 3) Douglas makes 'cura' ('for bissy tho*ch*t') the indirect object rather than subject of 'dat' ('suffir').

[33] *Opera* (1500–1), II, fol. 115r. My translation: 'But how do **they run again and again**: because **his looks** actually **stay fixed in her heart**.'

[34] On hypotaxis and verse momentum, see Bawcutt, *Gavin Douglas*, pp. 136–7.

different syntactic vessel so as to clarify passage-specific details and cultivate local rhetorical effects. There is no definite evidence that Douglas borrowed phrasing from the *Eneydos*, but there are several lexical and syntactic similarities. These coincidental resemblances reflect the shared techniques of Douglas and the Dido-translator. For example, both translators include the same purpose clause between 'hęrent infixi pectore vultus | Verbaque:' and 'nec placidam membris dat cura quietem'. As quoted in Chapter 4, the Dido-translator's version reads:

> ... considerynge the grete vertues of whiche his persone was decorate / his noblenes *and* honour of the peple of Troye / his grete beaulte *and* swete langage / whiche she enprynted in her remembraunce / that her membres refuseden the swete reste of slepe /' (*Eneydos*, sig. C8r, Ch. 10)

While the two translations introduce the same syntactic change, Douglas could easily have devised his version independently of the *Eneydos*. His most likely influence was Ascensius, who likewise indicates a connection between the two clauses. As Ascensius writes, '[cura] dat ergo quietem... sed non placidam: quia cura recursat animo' ('her care therefore gives rest, but not peaceful rest, because the care runs repeatedly in her mind').[35] To communicate this connection in Scots, Douglas inadvertently adopted the same technique as the Dido-translator, introducing the subordinate construction 'that her membres refuseden the swete reste of slepe'. Over the opening lines of *Aeneid* IV, there are several other syntactic resemblances between the two translations, namely the participial translations of 'carpitur' (Douglas's 'enbraced', Caxton's 'smytyn') and 'recursat' (Douglas's 'compasing', Caxton's 'considerynge'). Such close similarities are only scattered through the translation, but they pointedly attest Douglas's and the Dido-translator's similar treatment of Virgil's Latin. Had Douglas looked more closely at that 'buke of Inglys gross', he would have found the Dido-translator's practice germane to his own aims.

As well as syntax, the shared technique of Douglas and the Dido-translator manifests itself in lexical resemblances throughout *Aeneid* IV. Both translators, as already discussed, referred frequently to commentaries or glossed manuscripts, and these shared exegetic sources account for

---

[35] *Opera* (1500–1), II, fol. 115r.

their similarities of expression. For example, when Dido makes offerings to the gods, Virgil says that she sacrifices 'to Juno before all' ('Iunoni ante omnes', *Aeneid* IV.59). In place of 'ante omnes', the Dido-translator and Douglas both substitute an adverbial construction, the former having 'specyally vnto Iuno' (*Eneydos*, sig. D3r, Ch. 13), while Douglas writes 'principaly onto *the* queyn Iuno' (*Eneados* IV.ii.14). Although Douglas could have copied it from the *Eneydos*, his source was more likely Ascensius, who glosses 'ante omnes id est pręcipue Iunoni'.[36] It is not hard to imagine that the Dido-translator had a similar gloss in his Virgil manuscript, and that the two translators independently decided to incorporate this phrasing. Concerned with clarity of explanation, both translators might have considered 'specyally' and 'principaly' to be a clearer of rendering of Virgil's meaning than 'before all'. At a stylistic level, the French and Scots translators alike might have considered the adverbial translation an opportunity to introduce Latinate diction, a common stylistic trait of the two translations. Common use of commentaries, desire for explicitness, and use of lexical ornament informed a similar adaptation of Virgil's words.

Whereas Douglas normally constrains his additions to a line, he occasionally amplifies Virgil's text to the same extent as the Dido-translator. In these rare passages, he gives more freedom to his faculties of rhetorical invention, using Virgil's lines as a basis for his own composition. Douglas's *Eneados* is often admired for the artistry of its descriptive passages, and they frequently result from the embellishment of the source.[37] For example, at the wrestling match in Book V, Douglas amplifies one line into seven:

Immisce*nt*q*ue* manus manibus: pugna*m*q*ue* lacessunt:

(*Aeneid* V.429)[38]

Now, hand to hand, *the* dynt lycht*is* w*ith* a swak;
Now bend*is* he vp hys burdon with a mynt,
On syde he brad*is* fortil eschew *the* dynt;
He etlys ʒondir hys avantage to tak,

---

[36] For Virgil and Ascensius quotes, see *Opera* (1500–1), II, fol. 17r–v.
[37] On such embellished passages, see particularly Douglas Gray's, '"As quha the mater held tofor thar e": Douglas's treatment of Vergil's Imagery', in *A Palace in the Wild: Essays on Vernacular Culture and Humanism in Late-Medieval and Renaissance Scotland*, ed. L.A.J.R. Houwen, A.A. MacDonald and Sally Mapstone (Leuven: Peeters, 2000), pp. 95–123; 'Gavin Douglas', pp. 161–4.
[38] *Opera* (1500–1), II, fol. 165r. Fairclough translates: '... they spar, hand with hand, and provoke the fray'.

He met*is* hym *th*ar, *and* charr*is* hym wi*th* a chak;
He wat*is* to spy, *and* smyt*is* in al hys my*ch*t,
The to*ther* keppys hymon hys burdon wycht;

(*Eneados* V.viii.10–6)

Where Virgil provides only a general comment, Douglas amplifies the fight by describing specific feints and punches.[39] Aside from 'hand to hand', his work bears no resemblance to the semantic or syntactic content of Virgil's text. As did the Dido-translator on numerous occasions, he treats the source-text merely a starting-point for his own composition. While he still describes a wrestling-match, he disregards Virgil's choice of expression, and invents his own, more visceral material.[40]

Original composition at such length is common for the Dido-translator, but rare for Douglas. While both writers amplify to explain Virgil's *sentence* and heighten its rhetorical effect, Douglas's interventions rarely exceed a line. Compared with the Dido-translator, who represents an extreme of fifteenth-century practice, Douglas's claims of textual fidelity manifest themselves in controlling the length of these expansions. He ensures that his additions closely reflect the content of the original passage, often grounding them in commentaries. This approach probably reflects Douglas's aim to represent the correct proportions of the *Aeneid* text. As seen in his prologue to Book I, he repudiates long omissions from and distortions of the plot, such as the varying lengths of the *Aeneid* books in Caxton's *Eneydos*. By restricting his additions, Douglas ensures that no book or episode of the *Aeneid* receives disproportionate prominence over others. While humanist influences might have induced Douglas to adopt such an approach, it does not represent an innovation in itself. Douglas's policy of amplification is consistent with other fifteenth-century translations of the classics, whereas it is the Dido-translator and generally Caxton's *Eneydos* which show a more unusual degree of textual reworking.

Use of Commentaries

Printed Virgil commentaries, particularly those of Servius and Ascensius, supplied Douglas with material for his amplifications. His main edition of

---

[39] This well-known example is quoted in Bawcutt, *Gavin Douglas*, p. 136; Canitz, 'From *Aeneid* to *Eneados*', 95–6.

[40] Douglas's translation became more expansive in later books, especially Vegio's Book XIII. On Douglas's Christianizing amplifications to Vegio, see Ghosh, '"The Fift Quheill"', 10–14.

Virgil, edited by Ascensius in 1501, had both commentaries printed alongside the Latin text. Just as the Dido-translator used interlinear glosses from a manuscript, Douglas incorporates portions of the two commentaries in his translation, normally words and short phrases. Servius and Ascensius were so useful because the principal method of grammatical exposition, namely the provision of synonyms, was likewise a principal method of rhetorical amplification. In grammatical exegesis, commentators explained the literal sense of the Latin by providing synonymous words and phrases. For ambiguous, figurative and polyvalent terms, they gave several synonyms, teasing out multiple interpretations or different shades of meaning. Through this method of exegesis, they inadvertently provided Douglas with a copious source of amplifications. Line by line, he translated their synonym glosses alongside or instead of Virgil's original Latin. Whereas Servius and Ascensius produced their glosses for pedagogic and scholarly exegesis, Douglas the translator repurposed them for rhetorical and stylistic invention.

Although the influence of Servius and Ascensius is well-known, Douglas's use of these commentaries is typically seen as a means to elucidate rather than embellish the *Aeneid* text. According to Bawcutt, it reflects merely his intention to convey Virgil's *sentence*, a sign of scholarly, humanist diligence. Such an argument assumes that Douglas's aims in using the commentaries are exegetical rather than rhetorical. Bawcutt segregates her discussion of commentaries from that of style into separate chapters.[41] Because the majority of Virgilian commentaries were produced to expound the literal meaning of the text, she assumes that Douglas used them for the same purpose. This logic, Bawcutt asserts, explains why the majority of Douglas's borrowings derive from Ascensius rather than Servius. 'Ascensius's aims as an editor,' she writes, 'were in harmony with Douglas's aims as a translator: to bring out the "sentence" of his author and make it "braid and plane" (I.Prol.110) to not very learned readers'.[42] Ascensius (as discussed in Chapter 3) designed his familiar commentaries to popularize classical texts among elementary Latinists. Because Ascensius explained the difficult Latin so thoroughly, his commentary supposedly helped Douglas to translate

---

[41] Bawcutt, in *Gavin Douglas*, discusses his use of commentaries in the chapter on *sentence* (pp. 92–127), and his poetic style in the chapter on *eloquence* (pp. 128–63). Royan, in 'The Humanist Identity of Gavin Douglas', 120, suggests that Douglas's use of commentaries is a sign of his humanism.
[42] Bawcutt, *Gavin Douglas*, p. 111.

Virgil's obscure *sentence* clearly and intelligibly for a wider Scottish readership.

Even as she separates commentaries from rhetorical concerns, Bawcutt suggests that such a distinction is too stringent. Douglas's commentaries, she writes, not only provided 'explanations' of *sentence* but occasionally 'poetic additions'. When Douglas read Ascensius's interpretations, he found concrete and vivid details with which to amplify descriptive passages, such as the chariot race in Book V. Ascensius's commentary, Bawcutt explains, supplied a short rhetorical amplification (underlined):[43]

Non sic immissis aurigę vndantia lora
Concussere iugis: pronique in verbera pendent.

(*Aeneid* V.146-7)[44]

Nor nevir sa thyk, with mony lasch *and* dusch,
The cartar*is* smate *th*ar horss*is* fast in teyn,
With ren3eys slakkyt, <u>and swete repand bedeyn</u>;

(*Eneados* V.82-4)

The detail 'swete repand bedeyn' ('sweat dripping continuously') derives from Ascensius's double interpretation of 'lora vndantia'. Although Ascensius rightly prefers 'effusa' and 'laxa' (i.e. 'ren3eys slakkyt'), he also gives an alternative reading 'spumis abundantia'.[45] To incorporate this gloss, Bawcutt suggests, is not simply an explanatory device. As much as Douglas explains the two possible senses of 'undantia', his 'swete repand bedeyn' also augments the description of speed and strain. Although she presents commentaries as scholarly aids, Bawcutt's analysis of this passage opens the possibility that Douglas conceived Ascensius as more than a mere summary of Virgil's *sentence*. The commentaries underpinned not only Douglas's project to convey the meaning of the *Aeneid*, but also assisted his attempts to heighten and embellish its verbal expression.

Although Bawcutt presents it as an afterthought, this rhetorical purpose was in fact the more pervasive motive for Douglas's use of commentaries.

---

[43] Bawcutt, *Gavin Douglas*, p. 159.
[44] *Opera* (1500-1), II, fol. 146v. Fairclough: 'Not so wildly over the dashing steeds do the charioteers shake the waving reins, bending forward to the lash'.
[45] The full gloss reads: 'lora vndantia. i. valde effusa: aut spumis abundantia: sed meli*us* effusa. i. laxa & colla flue*n*tia'. *Opera* (1500-1), II, fol. 147r. My translation: '**Lora vndantia:** i.e. "very much slackened", or "flowing with foam". But "slackened" is better, i.e. "loose" and "flowing at the necks"'.

Moreover, it underpins why Douglas used Ascensius more than any other commentary source. Contrary to Bawcutt's argument, Douglas's preference for Ascensius was not based only on a shared 'popularizing' aim, but the commentary's utility for rhetorical amplification. Ascensius's specific genre of commentary, the familiar commentary, provided a particularly rich source of potential additions, such as 'vndantia lora'. Written for elementary learners, familiar commentaries construe Virgil line-by-line, providing synonym glosses for almost every word of the text. In this regard, Ascensius is more thorough (some might say laborious) than any other Virgil commentary and most extant sets of interlinear glosses. Although Servius also includes such lexical material, only familiar commentaries were so comprehensive. Through this pedagogic procedure, Ascensius inadvertently provided Douglas with hundreds of glosses to work into the *Eneados*. This genre of pedagogic commentary thus complemented the common rhetorical practices of fifteenth- and sixteenth-century translators. Whereas Ascensius had written for a pedagogic, expository purpose, Douglas repurposed this vast mass of synonyms to expand the *copia* of his writing.

Ascensius's glosses, albeit compiled for elementary learners, nonetheless constitute a varied source of style and diction. Contrary to Bawcutt's estimation, not every gloss makes Virgil's *sentence* 'braid and plane'. Like all interlinear glossing and familiar commentaries, Ascensius compresses multiple types of gloss into a deceptively single stream of interpretation. For example, Dido complains of Aeneas ruthlessness:

Cur mea dicta negat duras demittere in aures?

(*Aeneid* IV.428)[46]

...**cur negat.** i. renuit **demittere mea dicta.** i. preces meas **in aures:** s*cilicet* suas **duras.** i. inexorabiles:

(Ascensius on *Aeneid* IV.428)[47]

Arguably, the glosses 'dicta. i. preces' and 'duras. i. inexorabiles' make the Latin more difficult. Ascensius's readers, one speculates, would likely understand the relatively basic vocabulary 'dicta' and 'duras', especially given the French cognates 'dicts' and 'dur'. In both cases, he substitutes a specific term

---

[46] *Opera* (1500–1), II, fol. 130v. Fairclough: 'Why does he refuse to admit my words to his stubborn ears?'

[47] *Opera* (1500–1), II, fol. 131v. My translation: '**Why does he refuse** i.e. he rejects **to admit my words** i.e. my prayers **in ears**, namely his **hard ears** i.e. his stubborn ears'.

for Virgil's general language. His aim is to define the exact meanings of 'dicta' and 'duras' in the given context, thus demonstrating these specific usages to his readers. 'Dicta' refers to Dido's entreaties to Aeneas, while 'duras' indicates that he cannot be entreated. Deriving from the verb 'orare' (to entreat, to pray), the adjective 'inexorabilis' explicates this meaning precisely, yet might have been unfamiliar to a readership of learners. In choosing such a complex synonym, Ascensius perhaps sought to enlarge his student readers' *copia* of vocabulary. As this example demonstrates, the demands of expository precision and grammatical pedagogy often caused glosses to be more varied than the original Latin.

So as to expand his variety of expression, Douglas mined Ascensius for this choice vocabulary. Much like the Dido-translator and other fifteenth-century writers, so too did Douglas regard copiousness of expression as a stylistic virtue, often incorporating synonyms in doublets. Douglas adopts both 'preces' and 'inexorabilis' for his translation:

Quhy doith he reffuss my word*is* and prayer*is*
To lat entir in his dul ontretabill er*is*?

(*Eneados* IV.viii.39–40)

In amplifying 'dicta' and 'duras', Douglas translates both Virgil's general term and Ascensius's specific gloss. As in the commentary, 'prayer*is*' does not have a straightforward explanatory function, but was probably included to rhyme with 'er*is*'. Ascensius's synonyms, moreover, helped Douglas to cultivate a learned, Latinate lexis, translating 'inexorabilis' literally as 'ontretabill' (i.e. un-entreat-able). Whereas Aeneas's hardness is evident in 'dul', 'ontretabill' serves to embellish Douglas's style, and to amplify Dido's pejorative description of her lover. Rather than a mere adjunct to Virgil's *sentence*, Douglas treats the commentary as a hoard of stylistic and rhetorical material. In this example, he deploys Ascensius's glosses to fulfil his verse-form, to embellish his Latinate diction, and to intensify Dido's invective of Aeneas. Douglas's *copia* of words, at least in this case, derives from the *copia* of pedagogic glossing.

Through Ascensius's influence, Douglas's diction often appears more elevated than does Virgil's. Bawcutt frames this quality in a negative light, observing that Douglas translates 'comparatively simple words' in 'a way which seems unnecessarily formal'.[48] To cite a few of Bawcutt's examples,

---

[48] For these examples, see Bawcutt, *Gavin Douglas*, pp. 119–20. For Ascensius's glosses, see *Opera* (1500–1), II, fols 38v, 233r.

'iura dabat' ('gives judgements'), glossed 'pronunciabat' in Ascensius's commentary, becomes 'The domys and law pronuncis sche to thame then' (*Aeneid* I.507, *Eneados* I.viii.24). Likewise, 'in bella feram' ('I bring [the cities] to war'), which has the gloss 'inducam', is translated as 'induce' to war (VII.549, VII.ix.21). As with 'duras' and 'dicta', both 'dabat' and 'feram' are common Latin terms with wide semantic range. Just as Ascensius attempts to specify their meanings in context, Douglas incorporates Ascensius's terms to elaborate his lexis. Throughout the *Eneados*, these Latinate, polysyllabic words commonly derive from Ascensius's exegetic specificity, particularly terms with the suffixes '-ive' or '-ible'.[49] When describing the gates of war, for example, Virgil's 'ęternaque ferri | Robora' ('eternal strength of iron') is glossed 'inconsumptibilia' ('that cannot be destroyed', VII.609, VII.x.23). Whereas Ascensius uses the term in relation to rusting, Douglas detaches it from this context, making the doublet 'eternal and inconsumptive'.[50] These lexical differences expose Douglas's and Virgil's different means of cultivating an elevated register. Whereas Virgil's epic diction often relies on common terms in secondary or metaphorical senses, Douglas concentrates on the copiousness and variety of his discourse, ranging from Scots dialectal terms to the overtly Latinate 'inconsumptibilia'. Ascensius supported Douglas's linguistic inventiveness, and assisted the Latinate ornamentation.

Although produced for needs of exposition and teaching, Ascensius's glosses often constitute amplifications in their own right. In seeking specificity of interpretation, he expands on Virgil's Latin, intensifies his choice of expression, and elevates his register. From a literary perspective, Ascensius's commentary might be considered a copious, amplified Latin prose retelling of the *Aeneid*, and these stylistic qualities are evidently germane to Douglas's *Eneados*. For example, when Anna beseeches Aeneas to remain in Carthage, Ascensius and Douglas expand on his emotional reaction. While Virgil's text reads '& magno persentit pectore curas' ('and he deeply feels sorrows in his great heart', *Aeneid* IV.448),[51] they specifically expand on his pity and love:

---

[49] For this observation and the 'inconsumptibilia' example, see Bawcutt, *Gavin Douglas*, pp. 118–19.

[50] Ascensius's choice of term, at *Opera* (1500–1), II, fol. 235r, links back to his previous gloss on 'Centum vectes ærei': 'obstacula ex ęre ne rubigine consumantur facta' ('A hundred bolts of bronze', 'bars made from bronze so that it is not consumed by rust').

[51] *Opera* (1500–1), II, fol. 131v. My translation.

And in his stout breast, ful of thocht*is* het,
Of reuth and amo*uris* felt *the* perturbance

(Eneados, IV.viii.84-5)

& persentit. i. perfecte sentit: **magno**. i. magnanimo & constanti **pectore: curas**. i. sollicitudines amoris & miserationis.

(Ascensius on *Aeneid* IV.448)[52]

Rather than translating 'curas', Douglas instead renders Ascensius's expansive gloss, 'sollicitudines amoris & miserationis', to specify the nature of Aeneas's cares, '*the* perturbance of reuth and amo*uris*'.[53] Considering that Douglas also adds 'ful of thocht*is* het', the resulting translation amplifies the single word 'curas' across one and a half lines. Whereas Virgil writes broadly of Aeneas's 'cares', Douglas's 'perturbance' intensifies his state of distress. Possibly he sought to encourage sympathy for Aeneas, sacrificing his love of Dido for his divine destiny. Ascensius's amplification of 'curas', then, forms the basis of Douglas's additional interventions.

Besides these direct lexical borrowings, details in the commentaries inspired Douglas to devise amplifications of his own. In book IV's hunt sequence, for example, Douglas's additions are as follows:

Ecce ferę saxi deiectę vertice capræ
decurrere iugis:

(Aeneid IV.152-3)[54]

The ry*n*nyng hund*is* of cuppillys sone *th*ai kest [i.e. soon cast from their leashes]
And our *the* clewys and *the* holtis, belyve, [ravines]
The wild beist*is* doun to *the* dail *th*ai dryve.
Lo! *th*ar *the* rays, ry*n*nyng swyft as fyre, [roe-deer]
Drevyn from *the* hyght*is*, brekk*is* out at *the* swyre [a high pass]

(Eneados IV.46-50)[55]

---

[52] *Opera* (1500-1), II, fol. 132r. My translation: '**And he feels deeply** i.e. he feels completely **in his great** i.e. in his great-hearted and constant heart **cares** i.e. anxieties of love and pity'.

[53] This example appears in Bawcutt, *Gavin Douglas*, p. 115. She uses it to show Douglas's 'explicitness' in conveying Virgil's *sensus*, seeing as he specifies the nature of Aeneas's 'curas'.

[54] For text and commentaries, see *Opera* (1500-1), II, fol. 121v. My translation: 'Look the wild deer driven off the summit of rock run down the ridges'.

[55] See *DOST*, 'Cuppill', n., 3; 'Cleuch', n.; 'Ra, Ray', n.; 'Swire', n., 2.

ecce quasi ex improuiso: **caprę ferę**. i. siluestres capreę: **deiectę**. i. deorsum co*m*pulsę a canibus: **vertice saxi** idest rupis in qua diuersantur: **decurrere**. i. deorsum cucurrere: **iugis**. i. per iuga mo*n*tium quę sub verticibus sunt: (Ascensius on *Aeneid* IV.152–3)[56]

While Virgil mentions the preparation of the hounds (*Aeneid* IV.132), they are absent from the hunt itself. Only Ascensius mentions them: 'deiectę. i. deorsum co*m*pulsę a canibus'. Douglas, reading this short gloss, makes the hounds the centrepiece of the hunt. He provides them with two additional lines, makes them the subject of the following clauses, and even furnishes them with leashes. Moreover, he gives his dogs new landscapes to roam. Whereas Virgil mentions only the mountain peak ('saxi…vertice') and ridges ('iugis'), Douglas also has 'clewys' (i.e. cleuchs, ravines), 'holtis', a 'dail' and a 'swyre', exploiting his full range of Older Scots topographical vocabulary.[57] Furthermore, Douglas expands 'ferę capræ deiectę' into two clauses, probably thinking it more dramatic to render 'ferę' ('wild beist*is*') as a noun rather than a description of 'capræ' ('wild deer'). Stock similes, such as 'swyft as fyre', are typical of Douglas's amplifications, although this instance was probably inspired by Servius's comment 'Decurrere: præterito vsus est ad exprimenda*m* celeritatem'.[58] Through these many additions, Douglas embellishes the hunt with new topographic and procedural detail, visualizing the hounds running through the wild. One word from Ascensius, and Douglas reimagines the whole scene.

While verbal details and direct borrowings are easiest to trace, there is some evidence that discursive passages of commentary also prompted Douglas to amplification. Where commentators, for example, discuss rhetorical intention in orations, Douglas sometimes sought to embellish the speaker's rhetorical strategy. Several examples appear in Iarbas's prayer to Jupiter (*Aeneid* IV.206ff), in which he complains that Dido has spurned him for Aeneas. The major commentators all discuss how Iarbas's choice of words

---

[56] My translation: 'Look as if from something unexpected **the wild deer** i.e. woodland-dwelling roe deer **driven down** i.e. chased downwards by dogs **from the summit of rock** i.e. of the cliff in which they dwelled **run down** i.e. ran downwards **from the ridges** i.e. through the ridges of mountains which are below the summits.' Ascensius glosses 'capra' (female goat) as 'caprea' (roe-deer). For this meaning, see *DMLBS*, 'Capra', n., 1.c.

[57] Douglas's 'swyre' captures Ascensius's gloss of 'iugis', meaning 'a pass near the top of a valley between two summits'. See *DOST*, 'Swire, Swyr(e, n.'. It might also be significant that Caxton has 'dales' (see *Eneydos*, Ch. xv, sig. D7v).

[58] On Douglas's stock similes, see Bawcutt, *Gavin Douglas*, p. 141. The Servius quote means 'he has used the perfect infinitive to express speed'.

reflects his disdain for Carthage and its queen. Douglas's amplifications further this purpose:

Fœmina quę nostris errans in finibus vrbem
Exiguam precio posuit: cui littus arandum:
Cuiq*ue* loci leges dedimus: connubia nostra
Reppulit:

(*Aeneid* IV.211–4)[59]

3one woma*n*, lait exile and vagabond
Com to our bound*is*, that by pryce bocht *the* grund
A litil village to byg, and quha*m*to we
For to manuyr gave *the* strand of *the* see,
Quha*m*to our lawis and statut*is* we gart mak,
Our marriage gan lychtly and forsaik,

(*Eneados* IV.v.69–75)

In his first line, Douglas amplifies the contemptuous reference to Dido, 'Fœmina quę...errans'. According to Servius, Ascensius and Donatus, it is significant that Iarbas 'non dicit regina: sed in diminutione*m* dignitatis ei*us* fœmina'.[60] Not content merely with 'woma*n*' and 'exile', Douglas adds the demonstrative pronoun '3one' and 'vagabond', both of which have derogatory force.[61] Continuing this tone of contempt, he and the commentators next turn to 'exiguam vrbem'. Given that Carthage was no small city, Servius draws attention to Iarbas's use of hyperbole ('exaggeratio'). Douglas evidently relished this device, turning the 'exiguam vrbem' into a 'litil village'.[62] While Iarbas's contempt is evident in both languages, Douglas readily reworks and embellishes the original wording of this sentiment. In this speech at least, the commentators' analyses guide Douglas to potential sites of amplification, where he then devised appropriate material.

---

[59] *Opera* (1500–1), II, fol. 123r. Fairclough: 'This woman who, straying in our bounds, set up a tiny city at a price, to whom we gave coastland to plough and terms of tenure, has spurned my offers of marriage.'

[60] This quotation comes from Ascensius, meaning 'He does not say "queen", but says "woman" to diminish her dignity'. Servius has 'Fœmina: inuidia a sexu', while Donatus has 'quasi abiecti sexus: vnde magis dolendu*m*'. See *Opera* (1500–1), II, fol. 123r-v.

[61] In translating 'errans' as 'exile', Douglas was probably thinking of Ascensius's gloss 'pr*o*fuga'. On the derogatory force of '3one', see *DOST*, '3on', demonstr. adj., A.1.a.

[62] For this gloss, Douglas would have had to refer to a full copy of Servius's commentary rather than the abridged version in Ascensius edition.

Douglas likely expected his readers to recognize these moments of elaboration. Although his prologues profess that he translates for 'eue*ry* churlych wight' ('Exclamation', l. 37), the manuscripts of the *Eneados* in fact circulated among university-educated individuals.[63] Like Douglas himself, they had probably studied the *Aeneid* in school, and might well have been familiar with passages of Servius and other major commentaries. Such readers might have appreciated, for example, how Douglas exceeded the hyperbole in Iarbas's speech, or embellished Dido's hunting with extra holts and hounds. While Douglas kept his amplifications concise, his consistent expansions of and deviations from the original Latin are the setting for an independent rhetorical performance. The *Eneados* was not intended to be a grammatically correct rendering of Virgil's original Latin, but a work of literature in its own right. *Aeneid* commentaries, albeit produced as pedagogic expositions, provided Douglas with the material for these amplifications. Consistent with previous translators' use of commentaries, he read Ascensius and Servius for their copious diction as much as their intellectual content, using the glosses to enhance his variety of expression.

Vernacular Glossing

This close reading of commentaries influenced Douglas beyond the bounds of his translation, as he sought to emulate their academic style in his vernacular glosses. After completing the main translation, Douglas composed glosses to the prologue and first half of *Aeneid* I, which survive in the margins of a single *Eneados* manuscript. He probably left the glosses unfinished, because they peter out in the middle of chapter vi (*Eneados* I.vi.151, *Aeneid* I.394).[64] In the 'Direction', a dedication poem at the end of the translation, Douglas explicitly refers to his glossing project and its purpose:

> I haue alsso a schort comment compilyt
> To expon strange histouris and termys wild
> ('Direction', ll. 141–2)

---

[63] Bawcutt, *Gavin Douglas*, pp. 192–3; Emily Wingfield, 'The Ruthven Manuscript of Gavin Douglas's *Eneados* and a New Manuscript Witness of Julius Caesar Scaliger's *Epidorpides*', *Renaissance Studies* 30 (2016), 430–42.

[64] TCC, MS O.3.12. On their date, see Bawcutt, *Gavin Douglas*, p. 108.

As suggested by 'strange histouris' and 'termys wild', most of Douglas's glosses explain names of places, mythological characters, and references to ancient customs. Their content resembles that of manuscript and print exegeses of the *Aeneid*, except that they do not (of course) expound grammar and rhetoric. Unlike Servius or Ascensius, Douglas did not produce the glosses to teach Latin language, but to accompany a work of vernacular translation. Virgil's mythological, historical and geographic references, however, still required explanations to explain their significance. Marginal glossing allowed Douglas to provide his readers with these more detailed discussions, freed from the constraints of textual fidelity, metre and rhyme.

From a literary perspective, Douglas's glosses have typically been seen either as an imitation or a subversion of their Latin commentary sources. According to Bawcutt, for example, Douglas primarily intended to emulate the content of the Latin commentary editions. He sought to provide his vernacular readership not only with Virgil's text, but also with its learned apparatus, reproducing the experience of reading the original Latin. The content of Douglas's glosses, Bawcutt rightly notes, almost exclusively comprises excerpts and paraphrases of Servius, Ascensius and the other commentators in his 1501 *Opera* edition.[65] Jane Griffiths and Daniel Pinti, by contrast, have argued that Douglas's glosses subvert the conventions of Latin commentary. Through his more inventive glosses, Douglas is said to intimate that no literary work has a single, authoritative interpretation, and that interpretative power lies with individual readers.[66] Neither of these arguments, however, reflects the eclectic mix of subjects in Douglas's 'Comment'. Whereas Bawcutt conflates his aims with those of Servius and Ascensius, Pinti and Griffiths too readily read the glosses as artful and insincere. Douglas's 'Comment' synthesizes exegetic traditions rather than simply imitating or subverting them. Not only does Douglas use the 1501 edition and its commentaries, but he also copies material from Cristoforo Landino's widely-printed 1487 commentary, as well as Giovanni Boccaccio's *De Genealogia Deorum Gentilium*. Whereas Latin exegetes wrote for pedagogic contexts, Douglas in the vernacular had the freedom to select the content of his glosses without the constraints of a prescribed academic purpose.

[65] Bawcutt, *Gavin Douglas*, pp. 86–7, 102, 107–10, 116.
[66] Daniel J. Pinti, 'The Vernacular Gloss(ed.) in Gavin Douglas's *Eneados*', *Exemplaria* 7 (1995), 443–64; Griffiths, *Diverting Authorities*, pp. 81–102.

Although the Ascensius edition provided the raw material of Douglas's glosses, his selective technique of compilation recalls the work of Virgilian annotators in manuscripts and print editions, who (as described in Chapters 1–2) usually compiled their glosses by excerpting passages of longer variorum commentaries. Like Douglas, they excerpted, they paraphrased, and added only minimal material of their own. Rather than copying the full commentaries, they selected their information according to their particular needs or interests. It would not be surprising if Douglas glossed books in this manner, perhaps even a manuscript of Virgil. Douglas's vernacular glosses, likewise, arise from this selective, compilatory practice. He did not seek to cover Virgil's text as densely as Servius, nor reproduce Ascensius's exhaustive familiar commentary. In this light, Douglas's comment is best described as a sequence of glosses rather than a commentary of Virgil. While Servius and Ascensius were Douglas's sources, his approach reflected longstanding traditions of selection, excerption and annotation.

These selections were guided not only by the needs of explaining difficult passages, but also by generic concerns. To recreate the experience of reading a copy of the Latin *Aeneid*, Douglas sought to provide the core types of glosses which one would expect in any Virgil manuscript or commentary. A prominent example of these glosses occurs at I.i.62n (*Aeneid* I.34), when Juno catches sight of the Trojan ships off the coast of Sicily. In the gloss, Douglas explains that the *Aeneid* begins *in medias res*, and summarizes the structure of the opening of Book I. The gloss begins:

> First abuf the poete proponis his entent, sayand, "The batellis and the man, &c."; nyxt makis he inoucation, calland on his muse to tech him thar, "O thou my Muse &c." ... Now heir thridly proceidis he furth on his narration and history, and beginnys at the sevint ʒeir of Eneas departyng of Troy...
>
> (I.i.62n)

Douglas first refers to Virgil's 'Arma virumque cano' (*Eneados* I.i.1, *Aeneid* I.1), next to 'Musa mihi causas memora' (*Eneados* I.i.12, *Aeneid* I.8), and finally to the glossed line 'Vix e conspectu...' (I.i.62, *Aeneid* I.34). These comments follow Servius's remark that all Latin poets begin their epics with the same tripartite structure: 'proponunt', 'inuocant', 'narrant'.[67] It is common among glossed manuscripts of the *Aeneid* that lines 1, 8, and 34 of

---

[67] *Opera* (1500–1), II, fol. 4v.

Book I are marked 'propositio', 'invocatio', 'narratio'.[68] Besides, Douglas could have found the same terminology repeated in printed commentaries on many classical texts.[69] This structural gloss, therefore, is more than just a helpful guide to navigating the poem. It shows Douglas emulating the conventions of his scholarly genre in Older Scots, giving his readers the core features of a Virgilian exposition.

While the structural gloss on the opening lines was widely disseminated throughout the fifteenth and sixteenth centuries, some of Douglas's exegetic techniques reflect specifically the influence of earlier manuscript glosses rather than commentaries in print. When explaining difficult geographical or historical references, for example, he makes comparisons between places in the ancient world and sixteenth-century equivalents:[70]

> And thir schald bankis of sand heir nammyt bein the twa dangeris of the sey Affrican, callit Syrtis, the mair and the leß; mar perellus than 3airmuth sandis or Holland cost. (I.iii.29n)

This comparison has an expository function to describe the Syrtes, invoking two shallow, sandy coastlines more familiar to Scottish readers. While the major commentators Ascensius and Landino do not use this technique, similar notes have been found in English manuscripts of the *Aeneid*. Douglas's own schoolteacher, during lessons on the classical authors, might have introduced aspects of ancient geography and history in the same manner.[71] Another of these teaching devices was to convey information in mnemonic verses, also attested in *Aeneid* manuscripts. Douglas writes one Older Scots example:[72]

---

[68] For a fifteenth-century English example, see TCC, MS R.1.40, fol. 2r-v.

[69] For example, see Raphael Regius's commentary in Ovid, *Metamorphoses* (Venice: Bonetus Locatellus, for Octavianus Scotus, 4-5 June 1493; ISTC: io00188000), sig. A1r. Douglas possibly used this commentary when writing his *Palice of Honour*. See Sandra Cairns, 'The *Palice of Honour* of Gavin Douglas, Ovid, and Raffaello Regio's commentary on Ovid's *Metamorphoses*', *Res Publica Litterarum* 7 (1984) 17-38.

[70] In addition to the example below, there are three other glosses of this kind. In one case, Douglas states that Libya is now called 'the land or cost of Barbary' (I.i.37n). Likewise, in two glosses about Augustus, Douglas refers to Christ's birth in the Gospel of Luke (I.v.102n, I.v.113n). Given the prominent mention of Augustus at the beginning of Luke 2, the biblical references help Douglas's readers to place Virgil's imperial patron in their Christian knowledge of history.

[71] On this use of contemporary geography and biblical history, see Baswell, *Virgil in Medieval England*, pp. 66, 143-4.

[72] For example, BodL, MS Ashmole 54, fol. 119v, in which the scribe copies four lines from *Graecismus* on the judges of the underworld.

DOUGLAS'S *ENEADOS* 163

Attrides beyn in Latyn clepit thus
Thir nevois reput of Kyng Attryus,
That in our langage are the broder tway,
Kyng Agamenon and Duke Menelay.

(I.vii.70n)

In composing these verses, Douglas sought to adorn his vernacular *Aeneid* with the same range of glosses as the Latin manuscripts. These pedagogic features not only served a practical function to elucidate obscure references, but also reproduced familiar procedures of *Aeneid* exegesis. Even if such techniques were not common in print, Douglas's readers, recalling their manuscripts of the *Aeneid* or expositions from their school-days, would have recognized the conventions of Latin exposition.

While the majority of glosses are excerpted from Servius and Ascensius, Douglas supplements them with additional allegorical interpretations.[73] Compared with most *Aeneid* commentaries and glossed manuscripts, his Comment has a greater proportion of glosses allegorizing Virgil's references to pagan deities. Some are euhemeristic interpretations, others moral allegories, while others interpret the gods as natural forces or planetary bodies. As well as copying the allegorical passages in Servius and Ascensius, he draws material from outside the *Aeneid* commentary tradition.[74] The chief sources are Boccaccio's *De Genealogia Deorum Gentilium* and Augustine's *De Civitate Dei*. Whereas Servius and Ascensius had produced their commentaries for grammatical instruction, Boccaccio wrote *De Genealogia* specifically to unveil the hidden meanings of pagan myths.[75] Not only did he supply Douglas with general euhemeristic and allegorical interpretations of the gods, but he also expounded specific lines of the *Aeneid*, such as Virgil's description of Aeolus.[76] Augustine's critique of pagan religion,

---

[73] On the allegorical glosses, see Bawcutt, *Gavin Douglas*, pp. 72–8; Griffiths, *Diverting Authorities*, pp. 87–9.
[74] The following six glosses could have come from Servius and Ascensius: I.i.82n (Servius on *Aeneid* I.47); I.ii.44n (Servius on *Aeneid* I.78, more likely Boccaccio (see footnote below)); I.v.2n (Servius on I.223 supplies the astrological allegory); I.v.122n (Servius on I.223 supplies the astrological allegory); I.vi.1n (astrological allegory from Servius on I.223, the rest from Ascensius on I.305 (see *Opera* (1500–1), II, fol. 27r)); I.vi.15n (Servius on I.312). There is also one Christianizing allegory of Jupiter's eagle at I.vi.151, source unknown.
[75] Boccaccio's proems in *De Genealogia* frequently discuss reading pagan myths *sub cortice* and *sub velamento*. For instance, see *Tutte le Opere di Giovanni Boccaccio*, VII, p. 50 (in proem to book I).
[76] Seven allegorical and euhemeristic glosses have material from Boccaccio: I.i.82n (Juno) from *De Genealogia* IX.i; I.ii.3n (Aeolus) from XIII.xx and IV.liv; I.ii.12n and I.ii.44n (Aeolus) from XIII.xx; I.iii.54n and I.iii.75n (Neptune) from X.i; and I.v.2n (Jupiter) from XI.i, V.i and II.

meanwhile, provided extra euhemeristic explanations for the origins of pagan deities.[77] One of Douglas's allegorical glosses also derives from Cristoforo Landino's 1487 commentary on the *Aeneid*. Landino incorporated Platonizing allegorical interpretations in his otherwise grammatical and rhetorical exposition (as noted in Chapter 1).[78] In supplementing Servius and Ascensius with these additional sources, Douglas thus uses his Comment to demonstrate the depth of meaning in the *Aeneid* and neutralize dangerously pagan content.

Douglas's allegorical glosses on the pagan gods, together with remarks in his prologues, make a broader case for the moral value of reading the *Aeneid*. As already discussed, his prologue to Book I admiringly alludes to the 'suythfast mater*is*' hidden in Virgil's '*th*e clowd*is* of dyrk poecy' (I.Prol.191–7), defending the *Aeneid* from charges of pagan falsehood. Praising Virgil as a 'hie theolog sentencys' and 'maste p*ro*found philosoph*our*' (VI.Prol.75–6), his later prologues IV and VI provide a moralistic interpretation of Dido's tragedy (esp. IV.Prol.250–6), and a Christianizing allegorization of the pagan underworld (VI.Prol.137–52). He also alludes to a common interpretation that Books I–VI allegorize the stages of human life, culminating in life after death (VI.Prol.33–40).[79] In his dedication at the end of the *Eneados*, Douglas explicitly invokes Boccaccio's famous defence of poetry in *De Genealogia* XIV–XV, exhorting his readers 'Go reid Bochas in *th*e Genolygy of Godd*is*' and specifically 'Hys twa last buk*is*' ('Direction', ll. 68–9).[80] In tandem with his prologues and dedication, Douglas possibly intended his allegorical glosses to have an argumentative force. By

---

ii. Boccaccio supplies non-allegorical material for two glosses: I.iii.85 (Cymothoe and Triton) from VII.vii; I.v.81n (Romulus) from IX.xl–xli. Douglas cites these specific chapters in his glosses, and Coldwell lists them (with a few corrections) in the notes to his edition.

[77] Two glosses have material from Augustine: I.v.2n (Jupiter) from *De Civitate Dei* IV.xi–xii and VII.ix; I.v.81n (Romulus) from *De Civitate Dei* III.xv. There is also a reference to Augustine's sermons at I.v.85n, but this is translated from Ascensius's commentary on I.279 (see *Opera* (1500–1), II, fol. 24v). For other citations copied from Ascensius, see Bawcutt, *Gavin Douglas*, pp. 108–9.

[78] I.iii.100n is closely translated from Landino's commentary on *Aeneid* I.125. See *Opera* (1487/8), sig. b1r. On this gloss, see Griffiths, *Diverting Authorities*, pp. 87–8; Bawcutt, *Gavin Douglas*, pp. 75–6. Douglas names Landino as a source in two other glosses, but these are on historical rather than allegorical topics. I.v.28n is based on Landino's commentary on *Aeneid* I.242, and I.iv.49n from his commentary on *Aeneid* I.184 (*Opera* (1487/8), sigs. b6v, b4r). Douglas might have copied the latter from Ascensius, who quotes Landino's explanation in full (*Opera* (1500–1), II, fol. 18r).

[79] On the allegories in prologue VI, see Bawcutt, *Gavin Douglas*, pp. 75, 77–8.

[80] On Douglas and Boccaccio's defence of poetry, see Bawcutt, *Gavin Douglas*, pp. 72–4; Ebin, *Illuminator, Makar, Vates*, pp. 106–11.

explaining allegorical meanings, they simultaneously proved the presence of hidden lore in Virgil's fantastical narrative.

This inclusion of supplementary allegorical material also reflects the freedom afforded by writing commentary in the vernacular. Whereas Latin commentaries and glosses were typically written for linguistic study of the *Aeneid* text, the vernacular glosses to an *Aeneid* translation were not bound to a disciplinary, pedagogic framework. Rather than providing grammatical instruction, he chose instead to demonstrate the moral *utilitas* of the text. Even as he sought to reproduce the style and authority of Latin exegesis, he was free to adapt and supplement exegetic conventions to his chosen purposes.[81] Notably, two other vernacular commentaries of the *Aeneid*, the one by Ciampolo di Meo (*c*. 1313-5), the other by Enrique de Villena (1427-8), similarly expand on the allegorical material.[82] Freed from the generic constraints of the grammatical commentary, they too chose to use their commentaries to elucidate Virgil's hidden depths. They perhaps feared that Virgil's pagan deities might provoke misunderstanding among readers, and were keen to demonstrate the underlying moral value of their venerable author.[83]

Conclusion

To praise Douglas's *Eneados* for its 'novelty' and 'humanism', therefore, is to impose an anachronistic significance on the project. Although it was indeed the first complete translation of Virgil, it was steeped in longstanding

---

[81] On such freedom, see A.J. Minnis, *Magister Amoris: The Roman de la Rose and Vernacular Hermeneutics* (Oxford: OUP, 2001), pp. 301-2.

[82] For editions, see *L'Eneide di Virgilio volgarizzata nel buon secolo della lingua da Ciampolo di Meo degli Ugurgeri senese*, ed. Aurelio Gotti (Florence: Le Monnier, 1858); Enrique de Villena, *Obras completas*, ed. Pedro M. Cátedra, 3 vols (Madrid: Turner, 1994-2000), II-III. In his glosses to *Aeneid* I, for example, Ciampolo extends Servius's allegories on *Aeneid* I.47 and I.78 (both on Juno, equivalent to Douglas's glosses on *Eneados* I.i.82n and I.ii.44n). In the above edition of Ciampolo's translation, the first gloss is printed on p. 435, and the second spans much of pp. 435-6. Villena, likewise, expands Servius's allegories on these lines, this time across four glosses. In the above edition, see vol. II, pp. 69, 70 (x2 glosses), 81-2. Moreover, Villena makes significant independent additions, for example his introductions to each of the Olympian gods (pp. 86-9), his moral allegory of the storm (p. 102), and his allegories of Jupiter and Venus (pp. 113-4).

[83] The correct interpretation of the pagan gods might be a feature of vernacular glossing more generally. Daniel Wakelin, for example, has discussed mythological notes in Chaucerian and Lydgatean anthologies, including euhemeristic and symbolic interpretations of deities. See *Humanism, Reading, and English Literature*, pp. 65-6.

traditions of translation and exegesis. Douglas would not have recognized twentieth- and twenty-first-century distinctions between 'humanist' and 'medieval' translation-practice. In criticizing Caxton's *Eneydos*, he did not seek to develop a new, 'humanist' standard for translation, but to rebuke an aberration according to standards of the time. His treatment of the *Aeneid* text, as we have seen, is in line with common fifteenth-century procedures for translating classical authors. For example, Douglas amplifies the Latin to elucidate ambiguities, to maintain his verse-form, and to intensify Virgil's perceived rhetorical intentions. Although he restricted the length of his additions, he did not aim for rigorous philological precision at the expense of rhetorical flair. His use of commentaries, moreover, does not show a specific interest in 'humanist' scholarship, but instead provided him with a source of amplifications and embellishments. When he came to produce his vernacular glosses, he synthesized a range of exegetic traditions, new and old. His sources combined recently-printed commentaries, longstanding traditions of glossing manuscripts, and extra allegorical and euhemeristic material from Boccaccio's *De Genealogia*. With its high proportion of allegorical glosses, his resulting 'Comment' has precedents in two vernacular *Aeneid* commentaries produced centuries before.

Such observations do not reflect an out-dated 'medievalism', but broader continuities of practice across the fifteenth and early sixteenth centuries. Douglas's policy of restrained amplification, for instance, is in keeping with near-contemporary works, such as the first complete English translation of Terence's *Andria* (1520). In the epilogue, the Terence-translator explicitly discusses his restraint, boasting that 'the englysh almost as short as the latten is'. The 'almost' is significant, because his translation still includes short amplifications like those in Douglas's *Eneados*. This restraint, he goes on, distinguishes the role of a translator from that of an exegete. Had he added a 'long expocysyon' to 'make the sentence opynly to appere', his work would have been 'a co*mm*ent *and* no translacion'.[84] The Terence-translator, much like Douglas, does not decry amplification in itself, but amplifications of excessive length. Even as mid and later sixteenth-century translators began new experiments in verse-form, these techniques of expanding the source and integrating glosses persisted throughout the century. The influence of such longstanding methods, as the next chapter will show, is seen even in a supposed paragon of 'humanist' translation: Surrey's *Aeneid*.

---

[84] *Terens in englysh*, tr. anon ([Paris: P. le Noir?, ca. 1520]; *STC* 23894), sig. D5v.

6
Surrey's *Aeneid*

Henry Howard, the Earl of Surrey (1516/7–1547), in his famous translations of *Aeneid* II and IV (*c.* 1543), is the earliest known English poet to write in decasyllabic blank verse.[1] The title of the earliest print edition (1554) explicitly draws attention to his 'straunge metre'.[2] Whereas Gavin Douglas used decasyllabic rhyming couplets, adopting the familiar form of Chaucerian narrative poetry, Surrey's innovation shows a more concerted project to imitate the formal effects of unrhymed Latin verse. In the mid-century, he was the first of three *Aeneid* translators to attempt such formal experiments. Thomas Phaer used rhyming fourteeners to reflect the length of the hexameter (1558), while Richard Stanyhurst applied Virgil's quantitative metre directly to English (1582).[3] Surrey's *Aeneid* is widely considered the most successful translation, earning him the epithet 'England's first classical poet'. He purportedly achieved a close, 'humanist' rendering of Virgil's text, while reproducing the essence of the hexameter form. As James Simpson puts it, Surrey exemplifies the 'humanist understanding of the act of translating'.[4] Widespread as it is, this view represents only a modern ideal of English humanism, unrepresentative of wider sixteenth-century translation practice. Although popular among Elizabethan dramatists, blank verse decasyllables

---

[1] On Surrey, the main biography is W.A. Sessions, *Henry Howard, the Poet Earl of Surrey: A Life* (Oxford: OUP, 1999). The date of the *Aeneid* translations is disputed, but Sessions at pp. 266–8 suggests *c.* 1543.

[2] Surrey's *Aeneid* translations survive in John Day's 1554 edition of *Aeneid* IV (*STC* 24810a.5) and Richard Tottel's 1557 edition of *Aeneid* II and IV (*STC* 24798). BL, MS Hargrave 205 has a transcription of *Aeneid* IV, dating probably from the 1560s and independent of the print editions. In the present chapter, Surrey's translation is quoted from *The Aeneid of Henry Howard, Earl of Surrey*, ed. Florence H. Ridley (Berkeley: University of California Press, 1963). At pp. 5–13, Ridley surveys the three primary sources and their textual differences.

[3] For Phaer and Stanyhurst, see Sheldon Brammall, *The English Aeneid: Translations of Virgil, 1555–1646* (Edinburgh: Edinburgh University Press, 2015), pp. 19–54.

[4] Simpson, 'The *Aeneid* Translations of Henry Howard', p. 601. For other major discussions of Surrey's 'humanist' translation practice, see D.A. Richardson, 'Humanistic Intent in Surrey's *Aeneid*', *English Literary Renaissance*, 6 (1976), 204–19; O.B. Hardison, *Prosody and Purpose in the English Renaissance* (Baltimore: John Hopkins University Press, 1989), pp. 127–47; W. A. Sessions, *Henry Howard, Earl of Surrey* (Boston: Twayne, 1986), pp. 134–52; Sessions, *Henry Howard: A Life*, pp. 260–87; Arturo Cattaneo, *L'ideale umanistico: Henry Howard, Earl of Surrey*, Biblioteca di Studi Inglesi, 53 (Bari: Adriatica Editrice, 1991), pp. 251–367.

were rarely used for translating the classical authors in the sixteenth century. Phaer's experiments in rhyming fourteeners became the dominant verse-form, whereas Surrey found only one sixteenth-century imitator, Christopher Marlowe in his *Pharsalia*. In the history of sixteenth-century translation, Surrey was an outlying, experimental figure, whose 'straunge metre' was eclipsed by a competing tradition.[5]

Idealized assumptions of Surrey's humanism have shaped scholarly accounts of his models and influences. As is widely known, Surrey pervasively borrowed words and short phrases from Douglas's *Eneados* and from sixteenth-century Italian translations of the *Aeneid*.[6] Although the borrowings from both sources are equally numerous, the influence of Italy, the centre of humanism, is often said to be more significant than that of Scottish Douglas. Douglas, according to this argument, merely supplied particular lexical choices and turns of phrase, whereas the Italians influenced more generally Surrey's form and technique, especially his experiments in blank verse.[7] In the early sixteenth century, Italian poets began translating single books of the *Aeneid* into unrhymed hendecasyllables, known as *versi sciolti*. Surrey knew at least two of these Italian blank verse translations, Cardinal Ippolito de'Medici's *Aeneid* II and Niccolò Liburnio's *Aeneid* IV.[8] Not only did Surrey adopt their chosen verse-form, but Ippolito and Liburnio are also said to be the models of his humanist translation practice. According to

---

[5] On the rarity of blank verse translation, see O.B. Hardison, 'Blank Verse Before Milton', *Studies in Philology* 81 (1984), 253–74 (254–5); *Prosody and Purpose*, p. 146.

[6] For a list of borrowings from Douglas, see Florence H. Ridley, 'Surrey's Debt to Gawin Douglas', *PMLA* 76 (1961), 25–33. For a broader comparison of Surrey and Douglas, see Bawcutt, 'Douglas and Surrey: Translators of Virgil', 52–67. On Surrey's use of Italian translations, the best studies are Arturo Cattaneo, 'The Italian Sources of Surrey's *Aeneid*', in *Italy and the English Renaissance*, ed. S. Rossi and D. Savoia (Milan: Edizioni Unicopli, 1989), pp. 89–106; *L'ideale umanistico*, pp. 317–43. Unlike English studies of Surrey, Cattaneo is sensitive to differences of technique between the various *verso sciolto* translations of the *Aeneid*.

[7] Ridley, for example, writes 'The Italians not only suggested a form to Surrey; they also set a dual standard for him of conciseness and of literal accuracy in translation. In these respects Surrey again seems more like Vergil than does Douglas.' See her 'Introduction', in *The Aeneid of Henry Howard, Earl of Surrey*, pp. 1–46 (p. 36). For similar comments, see Simpson, 'The *Aeneid* Translations', pp. 612–14; Sessions, *Henry Howard, Earl of Surrey*, pp. 134–5, 137, 139; Sessions, *Henry Howard: A Life*, pp. 278–80. For a critique of this prevailing view, see S.M. Foley, 'Not-Blank-Verse: Surrey's *Aeneid* Translations and the Prehistory of a Form', in *Poets and Critics Read Vergil*, ed. S. Spence (New Haven: Yale University Press, 2001), pp. 149–71 (esp. pp. 153–7, arguing for a syntactic debt to Douglas).

[8] Ippolito's *Aeneid* II is included in a 1540 collection of *verso sciolto* translations, *I sei primi libri dell'Eneide di Vergilio*, trans. various (Venice: Niccolò Zoppino, 1540; USTC 862762). Liburnio's *Aeneid* IV, not included in the collection, was printed in parallel text with the Latin (Giovanni Antonio Nicolini da Sabbio, 1534; USTC 862712). All quotations from the Italian translations are from these editions.

Arturo Cattaneo, for example, they show a classicizing 'sensibility' absent in Douglas.[9] Their *verso sciolto* provided a model for imitating Virgil's hexameter form, while their concision guided Surrey in producing a fluent, yet philologically accurate translation of the Latin text.[10] Through these Italianate models, Surrey supposedly succeeded in capturing the ineffable essence of Virgil's poetic style, which Simpson has recently called 'the Virgilian effect'. As Bawcutt writes, 'at his best Surrey mirrors in his own work the polished surface of Virgil'.[11] With humanist finesse, he supposedly unites philological accuracy with a replica of Virgil's form.

Surrey's translation practice, however, is less polished and less consistent than such analyses suggest. He shifts his approach from passage to passage, sometimes concise, sometimes more expansive.[12] Rather than scrupulously following the original, his treatment of the *Aeneid*'s text ranges from compression to amplification. Considerable portions of the translation, as several studies have noted, are copied almost verbatim from Douglas's *Eneados*. Surrey reorganizes the Older Scots text to eliminate the rhymes, but otherwise preserves Douglas's expansions of the *Aeneid*, his reworking of the syntax, and his pervasive rhetorical embellishments. As frequently as he follows Douglas, however, Surrey breaks from this amplified approach, and several passages of the translation are abbreviations of Virgil's original. At his most extreme, Surrey strives to render each hexameter in a single pentameter, rigorously abridging the Latin *Aeneid* for the sake of this line-for-line parity. Although the Italian translators occasionally omit words from the Latin, Surrey applies this compressed approach to sustained (often famous) passages. Much like the amplifications, Surrey's routine omissions advance rhetorical and formal objectives at the expense of preserving Virgil's original semantics and syntax. Rather than making a 'mirror' of the *Aeneid*, Surrey, much like Douglas and the Dido-translator before him, decided to trade textual fidelity to cultivate particular literary effects.

---

[9] Cattaneo, 'The Italian Sources of Surrey's *Aeneid*', p. 106. Cf. Simpson, 'The *Aeneid* Translations', pp. 608–14.
[10] Cf. Bawcutt, 'Douglas and Surrey', p. 57. She argues that Surrey devised his blank verse independently of the Italians, but still considers it an innovation with humanist influence.
[11] Simpson, 'The *Aeneid* Translations', p. 611; Bawcutt, 'Douglas and Surrey', p. 67. For similar comments, see also Hardison, *Prosody and Purpose*, p. 129.
[12] Cf. Hardison, *Prosody and Purpose*, p. 135–6. 'It neither expands nor contracts. Instead, it is extraordinarily faithful to the literal sense of the original and to its artistry'.

Amplification and Omission

From Hardison and Bawcutt to Cattaneo and Simpson, scholarly accounts of Surrey's translation practice routinely commend his concision.[13] They identify this brevity as a quality of Virgil's poetic style, and Surrey is said to have produced an effective imitation. Whereas Douglas is branded 'diffuse' and 'expansive', Surrey supposedly avoids amplifying or reworking Virgil's text. True to modern conceptions of a textual, philological humanism, he is meant to have remained scrupulously close to the original Latin. This quality is often connected with Italian influence, but Surrey's concision surpasses even these precedents. As several studies point out, Surrey translates Virgil in fewer lines than both Ippolito's Book II and Liburnio's Book IV (Table 6.1).

Table 6.1. Comparison of numbers of lines in *Aeneid* translations

	II	IV
Virgil	804	705
Douglas	1,442	1,374
Ippolito/Liburnio	1,217	1,141
Surrey	1,070	943

Whereas Ippolito and Liburnio were somewhat more concise than Douglas, Surrey evidently 'goes beyond' these Italian precedents.[14] Cattaneo, for example, has compared Surrey's 'compressed', 'epigrammatic' quality with the slightly more expansive Ippolito. Hardison and Richardson, counting syllables between Virgil's hexameters and Surrey's pentameters, has noted some passages of equal (and indeed fewer) syllable numbers.[15] Although Ippolito and Liburnio likely inspired the compressed style, Surrey produces a distinctive, more rigorous manifestation of their concision.

This concision is all the more surprising because Surrey frequently models passages of his translation on Douglas's *Eneados*. Whereas the similarities of Douglas and Caxton derived (via the Dido-translator) merely from a shared body of translation-techniques, the resemblances of Surrey and Douglas are the product of direct influence and verbatim borrowing.

---

[13] Hardison, *Prosody and Purpose*, p. 135–6; Sessions, *Henry Howard: A Life*, p. 279; Bawcutt, 'Douglas and Surrey', pp. 55–8; Simpson, 'The *Aeneid* Translations', pp. 611–12.

[14] The data in Table 6.1 and the quotation are from Ridley, 'Introduction', p. 36.

[15] Cattaneo, 'The Italian Sources of Surrey's *Aeneid*', p. 102; Richardson, 'Humanistic Intent', pp. 210–2; Hardison, *Prosody and Purpose*, p. 135.

There is no definite evidence that Douglas made sustained use of Caxton's *Eneydos*, but Surrey consistently borrowed from the Scots translation, routinely incorporating Douglas's amplifications of the Latin. For example, at the beginning of *Aeneid* II:

fracti bello fatisque repulsi
ductores Danaum tot iam labentibus annis
instar montis equum divina Palladis arte
aedificant, sectaque intexunt abiete costas;
(*Aeneid* II.13–6)

The Grek*is* chiftanys, irkit of *the* weir	The Grekes chieftains <u>all</u> irked with the war,
Bypast or *th*an samony <u>langsum</u> ȝeir,	Wherein they wasted had so many yeres,
And <u>oft</u> rebutyt by <u>fatale</u> destany,	And <u>oft</u> repulst by <u>fatal</u> destinie,
Ane <u>huge</u> horss, lyke ane <u>gret</u> hil, <u>in hy</u>	A <u>huge</u> hors made, <u>hye</u> <u>raised</u> like a hill,
Craftely *th*ai wroc*h*t in wirschip of Pallas	By the diuine science of Minerua:
(Of sawyn beche *the* ribbis forgyt was)	Of clouen fir compacted were his ribbs:
	(Douglas II.i.1–6; Surrey II.18–23)[16]

Line for line, Surrey's translation (on the right) closely copies Douglas's lexis, syntax, and lineation. Douglas, following his common practice, amplifies the Latin with intensifying adjectives to fill out his decasyllabic lines. Surrey, modeling his work on Douglas, incorporates the same amplifications in his later translation. For instance, when Douglas translates 'fatis repulsi' as a full line, he adds 'oft' and 'fatale' to fill up the syllable-count, both included in Surrey's version. The next line, which translates 'instar montis equum', likewise has the intensifiers 'huge', 'gret' and 'in hy'. Douglas clearly chose this last addition to rhyme with 'destany'. Given his use of blank verse, Surrey transposes 'hy' to the third foot, using it only for the syllable-count. Moreover, he independently adds 'raised' and 'all', both of them serving the same metrical purpose. In both Douglas and Surrey, three and a half lines of Latin become six in English.

Surrey's translation, in this passage, reads like a blank verse re-editing of Douglas's *Eneados*. While retaining the overall structure of Douglas's

---

[16] As in previous chapters, underlining indicates translators' additions to the Latin.

original, he makes the passage slightly closer to the Latin, slightly more idiomatic in English. For example, his treatment of the ablative absolute ('labentibus annis') uses a relative construction ('Wherein they wasted had') rather than a simple participle ('Bypast...'). Noting these technical differences throughout Surrey's work, Cattaneo has suggested that he drew inspiration from *verso sciolto* translations, particularly Ippolito de Medici's varied and more fluent handling of ablative absolute constructions.[17] Likewise, Surrey makes targeted grammatical changes to lessen deviations from the Latin. When Douglas renders 'divina Palladis arte' as 'Craftily...in worship o Pallas', he makes the noun 'arte' an adverb 'craftely', and the adjective 'divina' becomes the noun 'in worship'. Surrey's rendering, 'By the diuine science of Minerva', returns to Virgil's grammar. While he keeps Douglas's lineation, he restores 'arte' ('science') and 'divina' to the original parts of speech. He fills out the line by replacing 'of Pallas' with the longer name of the goddess, 'of Minerva'. Surrey, in this case, works more like an editor or corrector of Douglas than an independent translator of Virgil. While making slight idiomatic and grammatical changes, he retains Douglas's overall syntax and lineation, and thereby his amplified style.[18]

Even when Surrey works independently from Douglas's model, he nonetheless shows the same tendency to amplify. Although this expansiveness is more commonly associated with Douglas, the supposedly concise Surrey routinely adds words and short phrases. Not merely for metrical concerns, some of his amplifications have an expository function. Like Douglas, for example, he uses double translations to show multiple shades of meaning, recalling academic practices of double-glossing. When Dido does away with 'monimenta' of Aeneas, Surrey unfolds this term in two clauses:

> abolere nefandi
> cuncta viri monimenta iuvat monstratque sacerdos.
>
> (*Aeneid* IV.497–8)[19]

> ...for so the Nunne commaundes;
> To do away, what did to him belong,
> Of that false wight that might remembraunce bring.
>
> (Surrey IV.663–5)

---

[17] Cattaneo, 'The Italian Sources of Surrey's *Aeneid*', pp. 99–100.
[18] Additionally, see Hardison, *Prosody and Purpose*, pp. 132–45, for prosodic differences between Surrey and Douglas.
[19] 'Fairclough: I want to destroy all memorials of that abhorred wretch, and the priestess so directs'.

In this instance, the supposedly pithy Surrey translates 'monimenta' twice over. His first translation 'what did to him belong' clarifies that 'monimenta' refers literally to Aeneas's possessions. Virgil's specific Latin term, moreover, also implies why Dido wants these items gone, as the word derives etymologically from 'monere' (warn, advise; remind). Surrey's second translation, 'Of that false wight that might remembraunce bring', represents this implied meaning. It derives from Douglas's 'Quhilk may 30n wareit man to memor bring' (Douglas IV.ix.54), and the original source is Ascensius's commentary, 'monumenta idest quæ memoriam faciant'.[20] Surrey's translation, explaining this one term at length, thus recalls the combination of translation and explanatory gloss so common in Douglas's *Eneados*.

Some of the amplifications, moreover, accentuate specific interpretations of the Latin. Douglas (as seen in Chapter 5) is well-known for the 'explicitness' of his translation, making Virgil's ambiguities 'braid and plain'. This tendency to articulate Virgil's perceived implications is also present in Surrey's translation, often in regard to significant plot-points. More so than Virgil, Surrey explicitly indicates that Dido was wrong to call herself Aeneas's wife:

coniugium vocat, hoc praetexit nomine culpam.

(*Aeneid* IV.172)[21]

Wedlock she cals it: vnder the pretence
Of which fayre name she cloketh now her faut.

(Surrey IV.221–2)

Surrey's longest amplification, 'vnder the pretence', leaves no doubt as to Dido's marital state. In making this point explicit, Surrey promotes the Augustan interpretation of the events, accepted as standard throughout the fifteenth and sixteenth centuries. Aeneas, he indicates, had no marital obligations to Dido, and his departure is consequently blameless. Such interpretative interventions in the text are more commonly associated with Douglas, who fervently defends Aeneas's character from moral detractors.[22] Surrey's 'fayre name', sourced from Douglas (*Eneados* IV.iv.89), instead suggests that Dido is in the wrong for abusing the institution of marriage. Similar to his Older Scots model, Surrey's translation advances a pejorative presentation of Dido in this particular passage and uses minor amplifications to further Virgil's supposed moral intention.

---

[20] *Opera* (1500–1), II, fol. 133v.
[21] Fairclough: 'She calls it marriage, and with that name veils her sin'.
[22] On Douglas's attitude to Aeneas's character, see Bawcutt, *Gavin Douglas*, pp. 82–5.

Some of the expansions, again similar to the *Eneados*, embellish the rhetoric of the *Aeneid*. For instance, when Iarbas demeans Dido's city in *Aeneid* IV, Surrey adds several short phrases to make the speech more disdainful. In the opening lines:

femina, quae nostris errans in finibus urbem
exiguam pretio posuit...

(*Aeneid* IV.211–2)[23]

A woman that wandring in our coastes <u>hath bought</u>
A <u>plot</u> for price: <u>where she a</u> citie set:

(Surrey IV.271–2)

Aeneid commentators (as seen in Chapter 5) analysed this speech for its *vituperatio* of Dido, and *exaggeratio* of her poverty. Just as Douglas substituted 'village' for 'urbem', Surrey's Iarbas refers to a mere 'plot' of land. Whereas Virgil's main verb ('posuit') refers to the founding of the city, Surrey relegates it to a subordinate clause ('where she a citie set'). Rather than the illustrious beginnings of Carthage, his rendering of the speech foregrounds Dido's purchase of territory, inserting 'hath bought'. More strongly than Virgil's original, Surrey's mercenary allusion evokes the myth of the bull's hide, in which Dido tricked Iarbas into selling her greater territory than he intended. *Aeneid* commentators frequently discuss the story at this point of Book IV, and Surrey's readers might have recalled it from schoolroom expositions.[24] Through these few amplifications, Iarbas's speech becomes ever more hateful of Dido, disdaining her 'plot' of land and the cunning by which she purchased it.

Additions, as well as enhancing a rhetorical argument, also facilitate the introduction of rhetorical figures. For example, when Aeneas informs Dido of his forthcoming departure, he declares of Italy:

hic amor, haec patria est...

(Virgil, IV.347)[25]

That is <u>my</u> loue, <u>my</u> country, <u>and my</u> land.

(Surrey, IV.452)

---

[23] Fairclough: 'This woman who, straying in our bounds, set up a tiny city at a price...'.
[24] At IV.212, Servius writes '[Iarbas] defraudatus sit per coriam', Ascensius 'Mercatique solum: facti nomine byrsam Taurino quantum possent circumdare tergo'. See *Opera* (1500–1), II, fol. 123v.
[25] Fairclough: 'There is my love, there my country!'

Whereas this phrase fills only the first half of the hexameter, Surrey recasts Aeneas's maxim into a full pentameter line. He inserts a third noun ('land') to form a tricolon, and his triple repetition of 'my' reflects the Latin 'hic... haec...'. This range of amplifications, from the metrical to the expository and rhetorical, reflects the common practice of Douglas. Far from breaking with his predecessor, Surrey too amplifies with the same frequency and literary intentions. With added words and short phrases, he embellishes Virgil's rhetoric, explicates his presumed meaning, and fills out the decasyllabic metre. In copying from and imitating Douglas's *Eneados*, Surrey's *Aeneid* inherits earlier translation practices stretching back to the fourteenth and fifteenth centuries.

Surrey achieves his greater concision because he omits words as often as he adds them. Whereas Douglas (as described in Chapter 5) believed that Virgil 'wrocht never a word invane', Surrey has no such scruples. In marked contrast to his predecessor, he does not consistently attempt to translate every word of the original Latin. Sometimes Surrey fills his lines with amplifications, but he is equally ready to abbreviate for the sake of metre. While Douglas tended only to amplify, Surrey forms his decasyllabic lines through a constant exchange of minor amplifications and omissions. When he needed to omit syllables, he targeted terms which could be perceived as redundant, particularly pairs of synonyms. For example:

sed si tantus amor casus cognoscere nostros
et breviter Troiae supremum audire laborem,

(*Aeneid* II.10–11)[26]

Bot sen *th*ou hast sic <u>plesour and</u> delyte
To knaw our <u>chanc*is* and</u> fal of Troy <u>in weyr</u>,
And schortly *th*e last end <u>*th*arof</u> wald heir

(Douglas I.xii.18–20)

But sins so great is thy delight to here
Of our mishaps, and Troyes last decay:

(Surrey II.14–5)

Whereas Douglas translates the Latin in three lines, Surrey omits 'cognoscere' and 'breviter' to produce a more concise two-line translation.

---

[26] My translation: 'But if [you have] such a desire to know our mishaps, and briefly to hear Troy's last labour...'.

Considering that 'audire' and 'cognoscere' are synonymous in this context, he probably judged that he could omit one of terms without altering the overall meaning. Douglas's attempt to preserve both synonyms, by contrast, forced him to add further synonymous doublets. To maintain his decasyllabic metre, he had to amplify the original text into three lines, turning 'amor' into 'plesour and delyte', and 'casus' into 'chancis and fal'. Douglas's method succeeds in maintaining every 'precyus' word of Virgil, whereas Surrey's omissions avoid an excess of extra synonyms. In these lines at least, Surrey prioritized a stylistic concern for concision over the semantic completeness of his translation. Alternating his method from passage to passage, he treated omission and amplification as equally viable techniques of crafting his decasyllabic lines.

Because Surrey so often modelled his work on Douglas's *Eneados*, many sections read like abridgements of the earlier translation. He adopted Douglas's syntax and lexis, but then truncated the text into a more concise lineation. Given Douglas's habitual tendency to amplify the original, there were frequent opportunities for Surrey to make cuts. For example, when Pyrrhus murders Priam in Book II, Douglas inflates two hexameters in three pentameters:

**qualis ubi in lucem coluber mala gramina pastus,
frigida sub terra tumidum quem bruma tegebat,**

(*Aeneid* II.471–2)[27]

Lyke to the edder, with schrewit herbis fed,
Cummyn furth to lycht and on the grond lyis spred,
Quham wynter lang hid vnder the cald erd,

(Douglas II.viii.57–9)

The second line of Douglas's translation consists predominantly of amplifications. Only a few terms in the line have a basis in Virgil's Latin, 'to lycht' translating 'in lucem', 'lyis spred' for 'tumidum'. 'Cummyn furth', which has no equivalent in the original, was probably added to introduce 'to lycht' more idiomatically. 'Terra' is translated twice as 'on the grond' and 'vnder the cald erd'. Surrey, though retaining much of Douglas's lexis, clips these additions:

---

[27] Fairclough: 'As when into the light comes a snake, fed on poisonous herbs, whom cold winter kept swollen underground [...]'.

Like to the adder with venimous herbes fed,
Whom cold winter all bolne hid vnder ground,

(Surrey II.609–10)

Surrey's translation maintains both Douglas's first and third lines but omits the pleonastic second. The removal of this line, however, also necessitated that Surrey omit a phrase from Virgil, 'in lucem'. Having removed 'cummyn furth', perhaps he could not find a pithy, idiomatic means to preserve 'to lycht' in his new lineation. Surrey thus formed his new translation by selectively editing that of his predecessor. While retaining the earlier translation's overall lexis and syntax, he concisely truncated Douglas's three decasyllables into two. His rendering, as a result, matches the same number of lines as Virgil's original.

Although Surrey produces the more abridged translation, Douglas's choices of expression occasionally helped Surrey to find means of abbreviation. From Latin to English, Surrey often sought to avoid adding extra pronouns and prepositions. Such additions were grammatically necessary for translating an inflected to an uninflected language, but they encumbered his stylistic aims of concision. Because Douglas pervasively reworked the syntax of the Latin, some of his constructions were more amenable to abridgement than Virgil's. When Dido states her intent never again to marry, Douglas and Surrey translate:

si mihi non animo fixum immotumque sederet

(*Aeneid* IV.15)[28]

Now cert*is*, war it not determyt with me
And fixit in my mynd onmovabilly

(*Eneados* IV.i.33)

But that my mind is fixt vnmoueably,

(Surrey IV.21)

Translating with the *Eneados* to hand, Surrey borrowed Douglas's phrase 'fixt vnmoueably'. Douglas made Virgil's participle 'fixum' a passive verb with 'sederet', translating 'war it not determyt [...] And fixit'. So as to rhyme with 'me', he turned the adjective 'immotum' into the adverb 'onmovabilly'. Whereas Douglas represented every word of the Latin, expanding

---

[28] My translation: 'If it did not sit fixed and unmoving in my mind'.

Virgil's hexameter into a decasyllabic couplet, Surrey exploited Douglas's reworked phrasing to halve the length of the English translation. With 'fixt' as a verb and 'immotum' an adverb, Douglas's phrasing rendered Virgil's main verb 'sederet' redundant, as well the conjunction 'que'. Because Douglas made the whole phrase passive, Surrey turned the indirect object 'animo' into the subject 'my mind', thus eliminating the need for a subject pronoun ('it') and for an ablative preposition ('in'). He likewise omitted the dative 'mihi', partially represented in the possessive 'my mind'. In streamlining the grammar, he found a means to remove redundant phrases, extra pronouns, and prepositions. Whereas Douglas used 'fixt vnmoueably' to fill his rhymes, Surrey repurposed the phrase to produce a concise pentameter line.

While Surrey tended to prioritize concise lineation over lexis and syntax, this valuation did not always detract from the rhetorical effect of the translation. Adding as well as omitting, he often used a combination of these approaches to introduce rhetorical effects. For example, when Sinon describes the despair in the Greek army, Surrey omits several words to make space for *repetitio*:

ex illo fluere ac retro sublapsa referri
spes Danaum, fractae vires, aversa deae mens.

(*Aeneid* II.169–70)[29]

Sith that, their hope gan faile, their hope to fall
Their powr appeir, their Goddesse grace withdraw,

(Surrey II.216–7)

Whereas Virgil has 'spes' only once, Surrey repeats 'their hope' twice for rhetorical effect. Evidently seeking to preserve a 1:1 ratio of hexameters and pentameters, he concurrently omits 'Danaum', 'referri', 'ac' and 'retro'. 'Danaum' is represented in the repeated prefix 'their', whereas 'referri' is synonymous with 'sublapsa'. 'Ac' and 'retro', meanwhile, represent Surrey's common habit of omitting Virgil's conjunctions and adverbs. Just as these short, semantically void terms were popular amplifications, Surrey could also omit them without impairing Virgil's meaning. To remove a syllable, he often targets Latin terms such as 'nunc', 'et', 'tum', 'vero'. To add a syllable,

---

[29] My translation: 'From then on, the hope of the Greeks flowed back, fell, and receded, their strength broken, the mind of the goddess [Pallas] averse'.

meanwhile, 'eke', 'yet' and 'now' are common fillers. Through this range of modifications, Surrey facilitated the addition of a rhetorical figure, while achieving a concise translation of hexameter to pentameter. The function of this omission, at its most rigorous, is to produce extended passages of line-for-line correspondence between the Latin and vernacular. Since pentameters have fewer syllables than hexameters, this approach places considerable restraint on the translator, necessitating radical abbreviation or at least reworking of the original text. Surrey could have found precedents in one of his Italian sources, Ippolito's *Aeneid* II. In his description of the Trojan horse, for example, Ippolito translated each of Virgil's hexameters into a single Italian hendecasyllabic line:

huc delecta virum sortiti corpora furtim
includunt caeco lateri penitusque cavernas
ingentis uterumque armato milite complent.

(*Aeneid* II.18–20)[30]

Huomini scelti ascosamente quiui
Cihudon nel cieco albergo, e le cauerne
El uentre empiendo di soldati, e d'arme.

(Ippolito)[31]

As well as keeping the same number of lines, Ippolito's hendecasyllables also preserve the enjambments and syntax of their respective hexameters. To sustain these three lines of linear equivalence, Ippolito omits four Latin terms, all of which could be considered redundant to Virgil's meaning. Foreshadowing Surrey's methods, 'delecta virum sortiti corpora' becomes simply 'Huomini scelti', since 'sortiti' and 'corpora' are broadly synonymous with 'delecta' and 'virum'. In the description of the horse's interior, meanwhile, Ippolito omits 'Penitus' and 'ingentis', since the metaphorical 'cavernas' ('le cauerne') conveys this sense of size and depth. When handling 'cavernas... uterumque', he removes the conjunction 'que', rendering the phrase 'the caverns of the stomach' rather than 'the caverns and the stomach'. In the last line, 'armato milite' is expanded with a hendiadys, 'di soldati, e d'arme', thus filling up the rest of the last hendecasyllable. In translating

---

[30] My translation: 'Here, they stealthily enclose the bodies of men, chosen by lot, in the dark flank and deep in the huge caverns, and they fill the belly with armed soldiery'.

[31] *USTC* 862762 (1540), sig. a2v. My translation: 'There, they enclose chosen men secretly in the dark interior, and filling the caverns and the stomach with soldiers and with arms'.

Virgil line-for-line, Ippolito radically truncates Virgil's lexis for stringent parity of linear form.

Only isolated passages of Ippolito show this line-for-line approach, but Surrey applies it more frequently and for sustained periods. In *Aeneid* II, he maintains a 1:1 ratio for thirty-three passages of three or more consecutive lines, including four passages of seven lines and three passages of eight lines.[32] In *Aeneid* IV, this line-for-line correspondence appears in twenty-six passages of three or more lines, the longest numbering eleven and twelve lines.[33] Not only did Surrey use his blank verse pentameters to imitate the general sound of unrhymed Latin poetry, but he also made these clear, sustained experiments to keep the same number of lines as Virgil's hexameters. The description of the Trojan horse is one of his shorter instances:

In the dark bulk they closde bodies of men
Chosen by lot, and did enstuff by stealth
The hollow womb with armed soldiars.

(Surrey II.26–8)

Though his syntax is looser than in Ippolito, Surrey still produces a 1:1 ratio of Latin to vernacular lines. To begin, he shortens the first clause by omitting 'huc', while transposing 'furtim' to the next line. As for the second clause, he omits 'penitus', and compresses 'cavernas | ingentis uterumque' into 'The hollow womb'. Through these modifications, Surrey 'enstuffs' Virgil's

---

[32] The 33 passages of 3+ consecutive lines are listed as follows (all line numberings are inclusive). In *Aeneid* II, there are 12 passages of 3 lines: Surrey 61–3 (Virgil 45–8), 94–6 (73–5), 216–18 (169–71), 264–6 (209–11), 440–2 (344–6), 469–71 (364–6), 480–2 (373–5), 584–5 (451–2), 766–8 (582–4), 897–9 (679–81), 1025–7 (771–3), 1030–2 (775–7). 6 passages have 4 lines: 240–3 (189–92), 250–3 (197–200), 288–91 (228–31), 295–8 (234–7), 387–90 (302–5), 790–3 (600–3). 7 passages of 5 lines: 101–5 (81–5), 174–8 (137–41), 183–7 (145–9), 233–7 (183–7), 426–30 (332–6), 496–500 (386–90), 505–9 (394–8). 1 passage of 6 lines: 26–31 (18–23). 4 passages of 7 lines: 67–73 (50–6), 517–23 (403–9), 607–13 (469–75), 1055–61 (792–8). 3 passages of 8 lines: 48–55 (34–41), 82–9 (63–70), 822–9 (624–31). As well as these more sustained passages of 3+ lines, there are a further 46 single lines, and 23 pairs of lines, but these could be coincidental.

[33] In *Aeneid* IV, there are 6 passages of 3 consecutive lines: Surrey 40–2 (Virgil 32–4), 240–2 (185–7), 252–4 (195–7), 368–70 (285–7), 528–30 (401–3), 744–6 (553–5). 7 passages have 4 lines: Surrey 94–7 (Virgil 74–7), 154–7 (120, 122–4), 208–11 (162–5), 276–9 (215–18), 321–4 (248–51), 424–7 (327–30) 536–9 (408–11). 3 passages of 5 lines: 67–71 (52–6), 223–7 (173–7), 844–8 (630–4). 3 passages of 6 lines: 31–6 (24–9), 114–19 (90–5), 606–11 (459–64). 2 passages of 7 lines: 21–7 (15–21), 778–84 (582–8). 2 passages of 8 lines: 263–70 (203–10), 832–9 (620–7). 1 passage of 10 lines: 868–77 (648–58, 1 line of Latin is untranslated). 1 passage of 11 lines: 750–60 (558–68). 1 passage of 12 lines: 396–407 (305–16). In addition, there are 28 single lines, and 19 pairs of lines.

forty-three syllables into a mere thirty. In this passage, his method of translating each hexameter line is to truncate its content until it fits the requisite ten syllables. As with Ippolito, Surrey achieves this stringent formal imperative by sacrificing semantic for lineal equivalence. When pursuing this line-for-line parity, Surrey frequently uses monosyllabic vocabulary. Compared with Latin and Italian, he exploits an asset of the uninflected English vernacular. While this technique minimizes his direct omissions of words, the effect is often to simplify Virgil's choice of expression, trading semantic richness for formal concision. For example, Iarbas entreats his father:

Iuppiter omnipotens, cui nunc Maurusia pictis
gens epulata toris Lenaeum libat honorem

(Virgil, IV.206-7)[34]

Almighty God whom the Moores nacion
Fed at rich tables presenteth with wine

(Surrey, IV.266-7)

While omitting 'nunc', Surrey opts to translate several Latin terms in monosyllables. He has 'God' for 'Iuppiter', 'Moores' for 'Maurusia', 'fed' for 'epulata', and 'rich' for 'pictis'. Particularly in 'fed' and 'rich', Surrey loses the particularity of the original language, making no reference to the luxury of the eating or the embroidery of the tables. Unlike Douglas's 'hie fest' and 'brusyt beddis' (*Eneados* IV.v.62), it seems as if one were reading the most elementary lexical glosses. Conspicuously, Surrey compresses the periphrasis 'Lenaeum honorem' into mere 'wine'. As a point of contrast, Douglas and even Liburnio choose to retain something of the original diction, and they both turn Virgil's two hexameters into four lines of vernacular translation. Although they do not use the obscure epithet 'Lenaeus', Liburnio has the lengthy 'di generoso Bacco dolce honore',[35] and Douglas 'the honour of Bachus' (*Eneados* IV.v.64). As Bawcutt has pertinently commented, Surrey might attain Virgil's brevity, but Douglas is more 'responsive' to the richness of Virgil's language.[36] When Surrey so rigorously pursues a correspondence of hexameters and pentameters, his

---

[34] Fairclough: 'Almighty Jupiter, to whom now the Moorish race, feasting on embroidered couches, pour a Lenaean offering...'.
[35] *USTC* 862712 (1534), sig. D4r.   [36] Bawcutt, 'Douglas and Surrey', p. 67.

chosen metre does not afford him the space for inventive, polysyllabic vocabulary.

As well as exploiting monosyllabic lexis, Surrey also uses syntactic subordination, usually with participial constructions. By reworking the grammar in this way, he obviates the need for adding conjunctions, auxiliary verbs and extra pronouns, which would otherwise be necessary in English. Whereas Douglas's hypotaxis served a stylistic need, Surrey's reworking of Virgil's syntax here relates to his formal concern. For example, Virgil's description of Atlas comprises four co-ordinate clauses (numbered as follows):

[1] Atlantis, cinctum adsidue cui nubibus atris
piniferum caput et vento pulsatur et imbri,
[2] nix umeros infusa tegit, [3] tum flumina mento
praecipitant senis, [4] et glacie riget horrida barba.

(*Aeneid* IV.248–51)[37]

[1] Whose head forgrowen, with pine, circled alway,
With misty cloudes, beaten, with wind and storme:
[2] His shoulders spred with snow, [3] and from his chin
The springes descend: [4] his beard frosen with yse.

(Surrey IV.321–4)

Besides several omissions of words,[38] Surrey increases his concision by subordinating three of the four co-ordinate clauses. In the first ('caput... pulsatur'), he makes 'pulsatur' a participle 'beaten', eliding the auxiliary verb 'is beaten'. For the second clause ('nix umeros infusa tegit'), Surrey makes a passive participial phrase 'His shoulders spred with snow'. 'Umeros' becomes the subject, 'nix' the indirect object, 'tegit' the participle, and 'infusa' is omitted. While the third clause remains intact, the fourth clause likewise becomes participial. Instead of 'and his beard is frozen with ice', Surrey's participial phrase again allows him to omit 'and' and 'is'. In this instance, then, Surrey was prepared to compromise on sustaining the original syntax for his formal concision.

---

[37] Fairclough: '[1] Atlas, whose pine-wreathed head is ever girt with black clouds, and beaten with wind and rain [2] fallen snow mantles his shoulders [3] while rivers plunge down the aged chin [4] and his rough beard is stiff with ice'.
[38] The omitted terms are: 'Atlantis', 'tegit', 'senis', 'et', 'horrida'.

At his most rigorous, however, Surrey aims to retain the same relationship of syntax to lineation. Whereas Ippolito does not attempt to sustain linear parity for more three lines, Surrey's *Aeneid* tightly reproduces the form of the Latin over sustained passages. When Dido swears to keep her chastity, for example, Surrey applies this approach to six lines of her speech, transposing each Latin hexameter into one blank verse pentameter:

sed mihi vel tellus optem prius ima dehiscat
But first I wish, the earth me swalow down:
vel pater omnipotens adigat me fulmine ad umbras,
Or with thunder the mighty Lord me send
pallentis umbras Erebo noctemque profundam,
To the pale gostes of hel, and darknes deepe:
ante, pudor, quam te violo aut tua iura resolvo.
Ere I thee staine, shamefastnes, or thy lawes
ille meos, primus qui me sibi iunxit, amores
He that with me first coppled, tooke away
abstulit; ille habeat secum servetque sepulcro.
My loue with him enioy it in his graue.
(*Aeneid* IV.24-9; Surrey IV.31–6)[39]

Each pentameter replicates the syntax and content of its equivalent hexameter. In the third line, Surrey mirrors the chiastic word-order of the Latin. The last two lines, meanwhile, retain the enjambment of 'amores | abstulit' in 'tooke away | My loue'. To accomplish this mirroring, Surrey selects three terms for omission, likely considering them all redundant to Virgil's meaning. First, he removes Virgil's *repetitio* of 'umbras', since the figure of speech is dispensable to the semantic meaning of the line. Second, he omits verbs from the Latin doublets 'violo aut...resolvo' ('staine') and 'habeat...servetque' ('enioy'). Monosyllabic translations abound, notably 'Hel' for 'Erebo', 'graue' for 'sepulcro' and 'deepe' for 'profundam'. By simplifying the lexis, omitting words, and removing rhetorical figures, Surrey truncates the hexameters one-by-one into pentameters. The result is one of Surrey's closest replicas of Virgil's lineation.

---

[39] My translation: 'But first I would wish, may the earth swallow me down deep, or may the almighty father send me with his thunderbolt to the ghosts, to the pale ghosts of Erebus and profound darkness, before, Shame, I violate you or break your laws. He who first married me stole my love; may he keep it with him and watch over it in his grave'.

Surrey often selected speeches and other famous passages for this exacting, line-by-line treatment. In Dido's speech above (*Aeneid* IV.9–29; Surrey IV.12–36), the full 21 hexameters become only 24.5 lines in Surrey's translation. Later in *Aeneid* IV, when Mercury urges Aeneas to depart, his ten lines of Latin are translated into eleven lines of English (*Aeneid* IV.560-9, Surrey IV.752–62). Surrey breaks his line-pattern only in the closing line:

heia age, rumpe moras. varium et mutabile semper femina.

(*Aeneid* IV.569–70)

<u>Come of, haue done,</u> set all delay aside.
For full of change these women be alway,

(Surrey IV.761-2)

Whereas the rest of the speech carefully sustains the exact relation of syntax to lineation, Surrey adjusts Mercury's ending so that his famous, misogynist maxim has a line of its own. These periods of line-for-line equivalence often start and end abruptly, as if Surrey considered them to be set-pieces in the translation. After Mercury finishes speaking, the translation abruptly abandons the 1:1 ratio of hexameters and pentameters, and he resumes reworking the syntax and lineation. Another example occurs a hundred lines later, when Virgil applies the line-for-line method to one of Dido's laments before her suicide (*Aeneid* IV.648–58; Surrey IV.868–77, 1 line of Latin is not translated). Orations, such as those of Mercury and Dido, received particular attention in Virgilian schooling. Commentaries produced extensive rhetorical analysis, and they were possibly learned by heart by students (as noted in Chapter 1). As such, the speeches of the *Aeneid* would have been particularly recognizable to Surrey's readership, who could have appreciated the close rendering of the hexameters.

In isolated lines, Surrey even experiments in replicating the effect of Virgil's *ordo artificialis*. Through the use of hyperbaton, Latin poetry often delays critical information to the ends of clauses and lines. Only on certain occasions does Surrey attempt to capture how the Latin word-order controls the revelation of meaning. Since English is an uninflected language, he achieves this effect by introducing a syntactic ambiguity, and then clarifying it only at the end of the given line. For example, when Aeneas famously encounters the ghost of Creusa:

ter conatus ibi collo dare bracchia circum;
ter frustra comprensa manus effugit imago,
par levibus ventis volucrique simillima somno.
sic demum socios consumpta nocte reviso.
(Aeneid II.792–5)[40]

Thrise raught I with mine armes taccoll her neck:
Thrise did my handes vaine hold thimage escape:
Like nimble windes, and like the flieng dreame.
So night spent out, returne I to my feers:
(Surrey II.1055–8)

Surrey's grammar in the second line has been called a 'confusing ambiguity'.[41] Although possibly a product of his extreme concision, the close reproduction of Virgil's word-order suggests that Surrey had more deliberate design. As does Virgil's 'effugit imago', Surrey delays subject and main verb to the very end of the clause, 'thimage escape'. Only with 'escape' does the actual syntax become clear, 'Thrise did thimage escape my hands' vaine hold'. The grammatical structure unfolds with the word-order, replicating the experience of reading the Latin verse. It seems no accident that Surrey would introduce this device in this particular line. Both ghost and syntax slip from readers' grasp.

Rather than closeness to Virgil, then, Surrey's concision is the effect of an unconventional practice of omission. Whereas translators such as Douglas frequently amplified the Latin, Surrey omits words as often as he adds them. Possibly inspired by Italian precedents in Ippolito, he used his omissions to complete his decasyllabic verses, trimming excess syllables. Certain passages, what is more, evince a clear, sustained objective to translate each of Virgil's hexameters into a single pentameter. Surrey, where he follows this approach, trades semantic fidelity to pursue this stringent formal end, mirroring the rhetorical and even syntactic effects of the original Latin. These extended passages of line-for-line parity, while scattered throughout the translation and at most twelve lines in duration, are often targeted in famous passages of the text, including Dido's and Mercury's orations in *Aeneid* IV, the death of Priam in *Aeneid* II, and Aeneas's final encounter with Creusa's ghost. They

---

[40] Fairclough: 'Thrice there I strove to throw my arms about her neck; thrice the form, vainly clasped, fled from my hands, even as light winds, and most like a winged dream. Thus at last, when night is spent, I revisit my companions'.
[41] Bawcutt, 'Douglas and Surrey', pp. 57–8.

were likely designed for a close-knit group of educated, courtly readers, who would have recognized the attempts to mirror the original Latin.

Humanism and the Line

These scattered passages of Surrey's *Aeneid* are an early example of a wider mid- and late sixteenth-century trend. Experiments in line-for-line translation became increasingly fashionable in the decades after Surrey's death. Beginning with Thomas Phaer in 1558, English translators of classical poetry in hexameters increasingly regarded the line as the basic unit of translation, transposing one line of Latin into one line of English. This more rigorous brand of classical imitation, attempting to recreate Virgil's epic line-by-line, has been widely observed in translations after 1550, but its significance is rarely contextualized with the earlier works of Douglas and Surrey.[42] The growing emphasis on the line, as opposed more generally to poetic form, is the most distinctive change in sixteenth-century translation practice. Although Surrey is often taken to exemplify English 'humanist' translation, he bears only an oblique relation to this wider development. He applied the line-for-line approach only to select passages, and his blank verse decasyllabic metre did not find imitators. Only in the broadest sense does his work resemble the consistent, meticulous line-for-line translation which became so popular (and so widely admired) in the latter half of the century. Modern scholars might regard Surrey as the paragon of English 'humanist' translation, but sixteenth-century translators did not aspire to follow his model.

Although the sixteenth century witnessed a new emphasis on the poetic line, it does not mean that prior translators had no aspirations to imitate aspects of the hexameter verse-form. Surrey experiments in blank verse were foreshadowed a hundred years earlier in the first English translation of an ancient poem in hexameters, namely the anonymous 1445 translation of Claudian's *De Consulatu Stilichonis*.[43] Similar to Surrey's decasyllables, the translator uses blank verse lines to imitate the effects of the unrhymed Latin verse, and probably contrived the form independently for this purpose. Although the translation survives only in one manuscript and was almost

---

[42] See Hardison's chapter 'Heroic Experiments', in *Prosody and Purpose*, pp. 196–225.
[43] On this translation, see A.S.G. Edwards, 'The Middle English Translation of Claudian's *De Consulatu Stilichonis*', in *Middle English Poetry: Texts and Traditions: Essays in Honour of Derek Pearsall*, ed. A.J. Minnis (York: York Medieval Press, 2001), pp. 267–78; Wakelin, *Humanism and Reading*, pp. 70–80.

certainly unknown to Surrey, the similarity of their verse-forms reveals a shared formal purpose. Douglas's *Eneados*, seven decades later, was only the second English translation of classical poem in hexameters. His use of the decasyllabic couplet was also a deliberate choice of form. Middle English literature had used a range of forms for classicizing narrative poetry. Chaucer, for example, had written his *Troilus and Criseyde* in rhyme royal, Lydgate his *Troy Book* in octosyllabic couplets akin to the *romans antiques*. Compared with these alternative options, Douglas might have chosen the decasyllabic couplet for its more expansive syllable-count, reflecting the capacious length of the hexameter. He typically, but not exclusively, translates at a ratio of one Latin line to one Scots couplet.[44] The task of translating hexameters, therefore, prompted even the earliest translators of classical poetry to find an equivalent verse-form in English, and line-for-line translation was only one particular manifestation of this general practice.

Thomas Phaer, two decades after Surrey, was the principal initiator of this more rigorous emphasis on the line. His *Aeneid* became the paradigm for translating classical epic in the later sixteenth century. Eclipsing Douglas's and Surrey's respective metres, he popularized the fourteener as the standard English equivalent of the hexameter line.[45] Whereas Surrey applied the line-for-line practice only to specific passages, Phaer more consistently sought a 1:1 parity of lines across the whole epic.[46] His translation of *Aeneid* II, for example, made 804 hexameters into 812 fourteeners, adding just eight lines to Virgil's count. Using the span of the fourteener, Phaer sought to approximate even the word-order of certain hexameters, thus making 'an almost absolute mirror of the Latin'.[47] Longer than Surrey's pentameter, the fourteener enabled Phaer to achieve consistent line-for-line translations with fewer omissions. Even while seeking linear equivalence, the fourteener relaxed the pressure to omit words and use monosyllabic lexis, hence allowing a more complete rendering of Virgil's Latin. The hexameters, moreover, had between thirteen and seventeen syllables, so the fourteener was approximately the same length.[48] Perhaps because the fourteener

[44] Canitz, 'From *Aeneid* to *Eneados*', 85.
[45] On Phaer's fourteeners, see Hardison, *Prosody and Purpose*, pp. 197–203; Brammall, *The English Aeneid*, pp. 19–31. For the first edition of Phaer's translation, see STC 24799 (London: John Kingston, for Richard Jugge, 28 May 1558), containing *Aeneid* I–VII.
[46] Brammall, *The English Aeneid*, pp. 24–6, discusses Phaer's parity of lines, but does not draw a connection with the similar approach in Surrey.
[47] Brammall, *The English Aeneid*, p. 25.
[48] On the 'capaciousness' of the fourteener, see Hardison, *Prosody and Purpose*, p. 198.

avoided a trade of semantics and form, Elizabethan translators widely adopted it for translating hexameters with this line-for-line approach. Arthur Golding used the fourteener for the first English *Metamorphoses*, Abraham Fleming for the first English *Bucolics*.[49] One might question whether the fourteener had the same rhetorical impact as the pithier pentameter, but sixteenth-century responses are overwhelmingly positive. To Elizabethan ears, the fourteener was the 'lofty' English equivalent to Virgil's sublime verse.[50]

This pursuit of lineal equivalence manifests itself yet more rigorously in Christopher Marlowe's translation of *Pharsalia* I. Marlowe, as already mentioned, was the only other sixteenth-century translator of the classics to adopt Surrey's pentameter line. Perhaps his background as a dramatist encouraged his choice of verse-form, since he was used to writing pentameter poetry for the stage. As did Phaer, Marlowe seeks 1:1 parity in virtually every line, translating Lucan's 695 hexameters into 694 pentameters.[51] Quite appropriately, the 1600 edition was titled *Lucans First Booke Translated Line for Line*. For example, in a passage close to the beginning:[52]

Quis furor, o cives, quae tanta licentia ferri?
Romans, what madnes, what huge lust of warre
Gentibus invisis Latium praebere cruorem,
Hath made *Barbarians* drunke with *Latin* bloud?
Cumque superba foret Babylon spolianda tropaeis
Now Babilon, (proud through our spoile) should stoop,
Ausoniis umbraque erraret Crassus inulta,

---

[49] For the first editions, see STC 18956 (London: William Seres, 1567) and 24,816 (London: John Charlewood for Thomas Woodcocke, 1575). A decade later, Fleming also wrote translations of *Bucolics* and *Georgics* in blank verse fourteeners. Probably he chose this verse-form to combine the merits both of Phaer and Surrey, emulate the length of the hexameter *and* its lack of rhyme. These understudied translations of *Bucolics* and *Georgics* were published together in see STC 24817 (London: Thomas Orwin, for Thomas Woodcocke, 1589).

[50] Brammall, *The English Aeneid*, pp. 20–1, records admiring contemporary responses to Phaer (as opposed to Surrey).

[51] Latin and English are cited from: Lucan, *The Civil War*, ed. and trans. J.D. Duff (Cambridge, MA: Harvard University Press, 1928); *The Works of Christopher Marlowe*, ed. C. F. Tucker Brooke (Oxford: Clarendon, 1910), with one line not translated. For brief comments on Marlowe's line-for-line approach, see for example Dan Hooley, 'Raising the Dead: Marlowe's Lucan', in *Translation and the Classic: Identity as Change in the History of Culture*, ed. Alexandra Lianeri and Vanda Zajko (Oxford: OUP, 2008), pp. 243–60 (p. 251).

[52] STC 16883.5 (London: P. Short, 1600).

While slaughtred *Crassus* ghost walks vnreueng'd,
Bella geri placuit nullos habitura triumphos?
Will ye wadge war, for which you shall not triumph?
(*Pharsalia* I.8-12)[53]

Transposing each hexameter into a pentameter, Marlowe demonstrates the same techniques of abbreviation as does Surrey. For example, he omits 'ausoniis' (adjective with 'tropaeis'), and contracts the six-syllable 'gentibus invisis' to four-syllable 'barbarians'. He adopts monosyllabic translations of 'should stoop' for 'foret...spolianda' and 'spoile' for tropaeis'. Perhaps Marlowe had identified these passages of abbreviation in Surrey's *Aeneid*, and then decided to apply the technique to every line. Whereas Surrey's practice shifts between amplification and compression, Marlowe fixes consistently on the latter approach.

This trend of line-for-line translation, linking Surrey, Phaer, and Marlowe, also underpins contemporary experiments in syllabic metres, notably Richard Stanyhurst's 1582 translation of *Aeneid* I-IV.[54] Not only did Stanyhurst write his English translation in the hexameter metre, but he too sought to translate Latin to English hexameters at a 1:1 ratio. Just as Surrey, Phaer, and Marlowe with done for the fourteener and blank-verse pentameter, Stanyhurst treated his English hexameter line as a directly equivalent unit of form to the Latin hexameter.[55] The difficulties of writing syllabics in English prevented Stanyhurst from equalling Phaer's or Marlowe's consistency, but his formal aspiration remains evident throughout. Although these poets used diverse verse-forms, the principle of lineal parity animates their application of these verse-forms to the translation of hexameters, Surrey in specific passages, Phaer, Marlowe, and Stanyhurst throughout their entire works. Earlier translators such as Douglas still had formal interests, but they did not extend to these fastidious line-for-line ratios.

Conclusion

Surrey's *Aeneid*, then, does not straightforwardly exemplify or initiate a 'humanist' approach to translation. His approach shifts from passage-to-

---

[53] Quotations are from the Lucan and Marlowe editions cited above at p. 188, fn. 51.
[54] The two editions of the translation are: STC 24806 (Leiden: John Pates, 1582) and 24,807 (London: Henry Bynneman, 1583). On Stanyhurst's translation practice, see Brammall, *The English Aeneid*, pp. 37-48; Derek Attridge, *Well-Weighed Syllables: Elizabethan Verse in Classical Metres* (Cambridge: CUP, 1974), pp. 165-72.
[55] Brammall, *The English Aeneid*, pp. 42-3.

passage, ranging from extreme line-for-line concision to short amplifications. He likely adopted his blank verse-form from Italian models, but his treatment of the *Aeneid* text reflects Douglas's influence as much as theirs. Through imitating Douglas's practice and copying parts of his text, Surrey echoes longer traditions of translating the classics, steeped in explanatory glossing and rhetorical amplification. In certain passages, however, Surrey's imitation of the hexameter line is more rigorous than any of these precedents. Transposing hexameters to pentameters at a 1:1 ratio, he replicates the formal, rhetorical, and sometimes even syntactic effects of the original Latin, albeit at the cost of being unable to render the full semantic meaning. Possibly inspired by passages of Ippolito, he achieves this formal aim by omitting words from the Latin, truncating each hexameter line into ten syllables. While much of Surrey's practice is consistent with earlier tradition, this pursuit of line-for-line translation looks forward to the more rigorous formal projects of mid- and later sixteenth-century translators. The same principle underpins Phaer's use of the fourteener, Stanyhurst's of syllabic metres, and later Marlowe's of blank verse. Surrey, then, is deeply rooted in Douglas's past model, but fleetingly foreshadows this future line-for-line trend.

Surrey's modern reputation for philological accuracy and expert classicism reflect modern ideals of humanism rather than the actual influences on sixteenth-century translation practice. After the Claudian translator and Gavin Douglas, Surrey was still one of the first Englishman to translate a major classical poem from the Latin. In this light, his use of earlier models is only to be expected, as are his experiments with multiple translation strategies. Up to 1550, English translators made only a few isolated forays into the field of classical Latin poetry, trying and testing different approaches to style and verse-form. Only in the second half of the century, when the number of translations rose more steeply, did translators start to coalesce around particular methods. Phaer, rather than Surrey, set the later sixteenth-century conventions for translating classical epic, namely the consistent line-for-line technique and the fourteener. Translators largely did not adopt Surrey's blank verse decasyllables, nor did they imitate Douglas's overt addition of expository material from commentaries and glosses. Whereas Surrey and Douglas are nowadays lauded for humanism, sixteenth-century readers came to prefer Phaer's more consistent, line-for-line replicas of Virgil's hexameters.

Conclusion

As this monograph has argued, Virgil's reception in fifteenth and early sixteenth centuries was as much a narrative of continuity as of change. For English readers in this period, the humanist reception of classical poets was characterized by a combination of canonical change and methodological traditionalism. Even as the humanists promoted the wider reading of the classical poets, emphasized their moral and literary value and thereby elevated their canonical status, their methods of exegesis and translation were inherited from earlier, well-established traditions of grammatical and rhetorical study. For the majority of readers, therefore, the humanist reception of the classical poets was a variation on traditional themes, reflecting the very gradual pace of humanist development and the continuous influence of medieval learning on the *studia humanitatis*. While the humanists sought to return to classical texts *ad fontes* and significantly elevated the prestige of these ancient works, their reception of the classics was shaped, at a fundamental level, by the exegetic and translation practices of their 'medieval' forbears. In this respect, the humanists looked back at classical antiquity through the lens of preceding centuries.

The impact of humanism, for the readers discussed in this monograph, was primarily a canonical rather than methodological development. Although Virgil had been studied throughout the preceding centuries for his linguistic artistry, profound learning and moral import, the humanists promoted his works to a yet wider readership, first in Latin and later in the vernacular. In the fifteenth century, the development of the *studia humanitatis* in Italy sparked a new interest in Virgil among educated Englishmen, such as the 'early English humanists' discussed in Chapter 1. Because the humanists emphasized the classical authors as models of Latin style, Virgil became increasingly central to school, and later university, curricula. Meanwhile, the rising readership of the Latin classics inspired the first vernacular French and English translations of Virgil. In the last quarter of the fifteenth century, Caxton's decision to print and translate the *Livre des Eneydes* suggests an incipient commercial market for translations of Virgil.

As the widespread printing of Phaer's *Aeneid* shows, this market only increased in the next hundred years.

However, the humanists' project of canonizing classical poetry was not accompanied by corresponding innovations in exegetic methods. As it had been for hundreds of years, the reading of the poets in the fifteenth and sixteenth centuries was founded on well-established traditions of grammatical and rhetorical study. Throughout the period, the glosses of readers at all levels of study reflect the traditional procedures of the *enarratio poetarum*. 'Humanist' reading of Virgil, in this respect, followed similar procedures to 'medieval' reading. Although the glossing of Virgil's poetry is particularly consistent due to the pervasive influence of Servius, such consistency is witnessed across other major classical poets, as indicated in Chapter 1. While there are differences between individual annotators, these differences do not reflect wider chronological trends. To over-emphasize individual variations masks the broader consistency of glossing practices from the Middle Ages to the Renaissance, from manuscript to print, from schoolroom to adulthood. Although humanism placed greater emphasis on learning a classical Latin style, this development was achieved primarily through the canonical change in literary models rather than a methodological change in poetic exegesis. To pursue the *studia humanitatis*, therefore, was to study a particular canon of texts rather than adopt a particularly novel approach to reading and glossing. To distinguish too rigidly between 'medieval' and 'humanist' studies of the poets, therefore, is to overlook the fundamental continuity of the *enarratio poetarum*.

Meanwhile, developments in humanist philology and textual scholarship had only a gradual influence on the wider reading of classical poets. Among the glosses analysed in this monograph, only a handful of exegetic activities are distinctively 'humanist'. For instance, some readers show an interest in textual emendation, comparing multiple versions of Virgil's texts and making conjectural emendations on their own initiative. This practice, however, was the preserve of a few highly-educated individuals, for example the Oxford fellow John Haster. For most readers discussed in this volume, humanist textual scholarship only impacted them insofar as printers incrementally adopted humanist emendations and orthography in printed Virgil texts, slowly improving the quality of editions available. In addition to the incipient influence of humanist textual scholarship, the fruits of humanist philology and lexicography increasingly filtered into dictionaries, commentaries and readers' glosses. Even so, traditional works of reference such as the *Catholicon* and *Doctrinale* were still widely used in the early sixteenth century alongside the works of humanists. While English readers were evidently engaging with humanist philological and textual innovations, their influence remained supplementary to well-established 'medieval' grammarians and the traditional procedures of grammatical and rhetorical study. The insights of humanist scholarship supplemented, but did not revolutionize, the fifteenth- and sixteenth-century reading of the poets.

Just as in the reading of Virgil's Latin, an analogous situation emerges in English translation. While humanism dramatically increased the number of Virgil translations, the methods of English translators were structured by prior convention. Although 'medieval translators' and 'humanist translators' are frequently periodized on the grounds of style and textual fidelity, the impact of humanist learning, at least in the early sixteenth century, did not bring about a sudden overhaul in these areas. As seen in Caxton, Douglas and even the Earl of Surrey, the early English translators of Virgil adopted common stylistic techniques of fourteenth- and fifteenth-century translation, for example in the use of loan-words, amplification, the reworking of syntax and the influence of glossing and exegesis. Although English humanist translation practice has typically been associated with textual and philological rigour, sixteenth-century translators, moreover, continued to amplify their source-text much like their fourteenth- and fifteenth-century precursors. Steeped in humanist commentaries, Douglas habitually amplifies the Latin *Aeneid* to clarify Virgil's presumed meaning and to achieve certain literary effects. Surrey, meanwhile, deploys a combination of amplification and abbreviation for his experiments in imitating classical poetic form. Their reworking of Virgil's text, moreover, is not particular to English translation. As we have seen, amplification was just as, if not more, pervasive among Italian blank verse translations and French translators of Virgil including the Dido-translator and Octavien de St-Gelais. Just as the reading of Virgil was highly consistent throughout the Middle Ages and Renaissance, continuities in translation practices suggest that the periodization of 'medieval' and 'humanist' translation is too rigid.

If humanism indeed inspired a new method of translating classical epic, its emphasis was formal rather than textual. In the mid and later sixteenth century, translators of Virgil increasingly sought to represent the formal effects of the Latin hexameter in their native vernaculars. In Italy, this formal interest inspired a tradition of vernacular blank verse translation throughout the century. Although Surrey skilfully imitated these Italian models in his own translations, no equivalent tradition of blank verse translation emerged in England, apart from isolated experiments. Rather, English readers and translators preferred the template of Thomas Phaer, who promoted the English fourteener as an equivalent to the Latin hexameter line. With his novel use of the fourteener and his rigorous emphasis on line-for-line translation, his *Aeneid* became the model for many subsequent English translations of classical epic up to 1600. In the history of translating the classics, this new emphasis on translating classical poetry, and especially on classical poetic form, distinguishes the translations of the later 1500s from the translations of predominantly prose classical texts in preceding centuries.

Virgilian reception in the fifteenth and sixteenth centuries, therefore, was marked by continuity and piecemeal evolution. As the bibliographic evidence in this monograph has shown, English study and translation of Virgil is marked by widespread methodological consistency from the Middle Ages to the Renaissance. While the humanists promoted reading a specific canon of texts, their engagement with these texts was structured by the aims, methods and conventions of earlier scholarly and literary traditions, particularly the processes of the *enarratio poetarum*. Although humanist innovations and attitudes often inflected individual readings and translations of classical texts, the degree and nature of these inflections varied considerably depending on the interests of the individual reader or translator.

APPENDIX A

List of Manuscripts

This appendix lists the 25 extant manuscripts of *Bucolics, Georgics* and *Aeneid* with evidence of English or Scottish ownership or use *c.* 1400–1550.
    Christopher Baswell, in *Virgil in Medieval England*, pp. 285–308, has an appendix giving detailed descriptions of 37 'Manuscripts of Virgil written or owned in England during the Middle Ages'. The list below follows the information in Baswell's descriptions, and additionally includes Oxford, Balliol College, MS 140.

A) Manuscripts Produced Before 1400 with Evidence of English or Scottish Ownership or Use *c.* 1400–1550

Cambridge, Jesus College, MS 33
Cambridge, Pembroke College, MS 260
TCC, MS R.3.50
NLS, Adv. MS 18.5.12
BL, MS Add. 16,166
BL, MS Add. 32319A
BL, MS Harley 4967
BL, MS Royal 15.B.VI
LPL, MS 471
Oxford, All Souls College, MS 82
Vatican City, Biblioteca Apostolica Vaticana, MS Ottob. Lat. 1410

B) Manuscripts Produced in England During the Fifteenth Century

Cambridge, Queens' College K.17.5 (pastedown fragments)
Cambridge, Peterhouse, MS 159
TCC, MS R.1.40
BL, MS Add. 11,959
BL, MS Burney 277
London, Society of Antiquaries, MS 44
BodL, MS Ashmole 54
BodL, MS Auct. F.2.7
Shrewsbury, Shrewsbury School, MS IV

C) Manuscripts Produced Abroad During the Fifteenth Century with English or Scottish Owners c. 1400-1550

SJC, MS C.4
SJC, MS H.2
Edinburgh, University Library, MS 195
Oxford, Balliol College, MS 140
Oxford, New College, MS 271

APPENDIX B

List of Printed Copies

This appendix lists 48 copies of Virgil with an English provenance before 1550. The sample was compiled from copies of Virgil in Oxford libraries, Cambridge libraries, Princeton University Library, and the Huntington Library.

A) Imported Copies

Opera ([Strasbourg: Johann Mentelin, about 1470]; *ISTC* iv00151000).

- O.1470: Oxford, New College, BT1.39.1.

Opera, comm. Servius, *Supplementum, Opuscula*] (Venice: Jacobus Rubeus, Jan. 14 [75/76]; *ISTC* iv00166000).

- O.1475: Cambridge, University Library, Inc.2.B.3.15[1409].

Opera, comm. Servius (Venice: Antonio di Bartolommeo Miscomini, Oct. '1486' [i.e. 1476]; *ISTC* iv00167000).

- O.1476.1: Oxford, All Souls College, a.1.9.
- O.1476.2: Cambridge, University Library, Inc.2.B.3.21[1445].
- O.1476.3: Cambridge, University Library, Inc.2.B.3.21[1446].
- O.1476.4: Cambridge, Jesus College, F.1.12.

Opera, comm. Servius (Venice: Petrus de Plasiis, Cremonensis, Bartholomaeus de Blavis de Alexandria, and Andreas Torresanus de Asula, 1 Aug. 1480; *ISTC* iv00169000).

- O.1480: BodL, Auct. P inf. 2.3.

Opera, comm. Servius (Venice: Baptista de Tortis, 23 May 1487; *ISTC* iv00178000).

- O.1487: Oxford, Brasenose College Library, Latham Room: UB/S I 40.

Opera, ed. Philippus Beroaldus, rev. Paulus Malleolus Andelocensis ([Paris: Georg Wolf], 20 Nov. 1489; *ISTC* iv00164800).

- O.1489: BodL, Auct. O 1.17.

Opera, comm. Servius, Donatus, Landinus and Calderinus (Venice: Lazarus de Suardis, de Saviliano, 1491/92; *ISTC* iv00187000).

- O.1491: Oxford, Exeter College, Strong Room: 9I 1491.

Opera, comm. Servius, Donatus, Landinus and Calderinus (Lyons: Antonius Lambillon, for Franciscus Girardengus, 5 Nov. 1492; *ISTC* iv00187500).

- O.1492.1: BodL, Auct. O 1.18a.

Opera, comm. Servius, Donatus, Landinus and Calderinus (Nuremberg: Anton Koberger, 1492; *ISTC* iv00188000).

- O.1492.2: Oxford, All Souls College, b.5.6.
- O.1492.3: BodL, Auct. O 1.15.
- O.1492.4: CUL, Inc.3.A.7.2[887].
- O.1492.5: HEHL, 493771.

Bucolica (cum commento) (Paris: Félix Baligault, [about 1492-94]; *ISTC* iv00208800).

- B.1492: CUL, Inc.5.D.1.26[2568].

Georgica (cum commento familiari) (Paris: Antoine Caillaut, 7 June 1492; *ISTC* iv00225000).

- G.1492: PUL, VRG 2945.325.004.

Opera, comm. Servius, Donatus, Landinus, Mancinellus and Calderinus (Venice: Bartholomaeus de Zanis, for Octavianus Scotus and Lucantonio Giunta, 31 July 1493; *ISTC* iv00189000).

- O.1493: Oxford, All Souls College, b.4.4.

Bucolica (cum commento) (Paris: Félix Baligault, [c. 1493-94]; *ISTC* iv00208850).

- B.1493: CUL, Peterborough.Sp.61.

Opera, ed. Philippus Beroaldus, rev. Paulus Malleolus Andelocensis (Paris: Ulrich Gering and Berthold Rembolt, 12 Sept. 1494; *ISTC* iv00165000).

- O.1494: CUL, Inc.5.D.1.38[2623].

Bucolica (cum commento) (Paris: Wolfgang Hopyl, 1 Feb. 1494; *ISTC* iv00209000).

- B.1494: PUL, VRG 2945.325.004.

Bucolica (cum commento) (Deventer: Jacobus de Breda, 6 Nov. 1495; *ISTC* iv00211000).

- B.1495: CCC, Phi.C.1.9(4).

Georgica, comm. Hermannus Torrentinus (Deventer: Richardus Pafraet, 26 Aug. 1496; *ISTC* iv00229000).

- G.1496: CCC, Phi.C.1.9(5).

Bucolica (cum commento) (Paris: Andre Bocard, about 1497; *ISTC* iv00212450).

- B.1497: PUL, VRG 2945.325.006.2

APPENDIX B: LIST OF PRINTED COPIES 199

Georgica (cum commento familiari) ([Paris]: Philippe Pigouchet, [about 1498]; *ISTC* iv00228500).

- **G.1498.1:** CUL, Inc.5.D.1.26[2568].
- **G.1498.2:** CUL, Inc.5.D.1.29[2587].

Opera, ed. Badius Ascensius, comm. Servius, Donatus, Ascensius, Beroaldus and Calderinus, 3 vols (Paris: Thielman Kerver, for Jean Petit and Johannes de Coblenz, 1500–1; *ISTC* iv00196000).

- **O.1500.1:** CUL, Inc.3.D.1.48[4305]
- **O.1500.2:** PUL, (Ex) PA6804.A21.B32.1500q

Opera, ed. Sebastian Brant, comm. Servius, Donatus, Landinus, Mancinellus and Calderinus (Strasbourg: Johann Grüninger, 28 Aug. 1502; *USTC* 688629).

- **O.1502:** BodL, Douce V subt. 21.

Opera, ed. Badius Ascensius, comm. Servius, Donatus, Ascensius, Mancinellus, Beroaldus and Calderinus, 2 vols (Paris: Badius Ascensius, for Jean Petit, 1 Jun. and 8 Nov. 1507; *USTC* 143282).

- **O.1507.1:** Oxford, Bodleian Library, M 2.21,22 Art.
- **O.1507.2:** Oxford, Bodleian Library, Antiq.c.F.1507.1

Opuscula (cum familiari expositione) (Strasbourg: Johann Knobloch, 28 Apr. 1509; *USTC* 687444).

- **Op.1509:** CUL, 5000.d.122.

Opera, comm. Servius, Donatus, ps-Probus, Ascensius, Mancinellus, Datus, Beroaldus and Calderinus, 2 vols (Paris: Jean Barbier and Francis Regnault, 21 June 1515 and 17 July 1515; *USTC* 183592).

- **O.1515.1:** PUL, VRG 2945.1515.

Opera, comm. Servius, Donatus, ps-Probus, Ascensius, Mancinellus, Datus, Beroaldus and Calderinus (Lyon: Jacques Sacon and Cyriaque Hochperg, 1517; *USTC* 144785).

- **O.1517:** BodL, Lawn c.100

Opera (Strasbourg: Johann Knobloch and Paul Götz, 1520; *USTC* 700667).

- **O.1520.1:** BodL, 8° K 86 Linc.

Opera, ed. Pierre Baquelier (Paris: Jacques Le Messier, 6 July 1520; *USTC* 184099).

- **O.1520.2:** BodL, (OC) 90 c.58
- **O.1520.3:** PUL, VRG 2945.1520.2

Opera, comm. Servius, Donatus, ps-Probus, Ascensius, Mancinellus, Datus, Beroaldus and Calderinus (Venice: Lucantonio Giunta, for Gregorio de Gregori, 1522: *USTC* 862711).

- **O.1522:** CUL, X.7.34.

Opera comm. Servius, Donatus, ps-Probus, Ascensius, Valerianus, Mancinellus, Datus, Beroaldus, Calderinus and excerpts of Landinus (Lyon: Jacques Mareschal, 29 Aug. 1527; *USTC* 155738).

- **O.1527:** CUL, O*.8.15(B).

B) Copies Printed in England

Bucolica (cum commento) (London: Wynkyn de Worde, 1514; *STC* 24814).

- **B.1514:** BodL, 4°E 6(3) Art.Seld.

Opera (London: Richard Pynson, c. 1515; *STC* 24787).

- **O.1515.2:** Oxford, Exeter College, Strong Room: 9M 24,787.
- **O.1515.3:** JRL, 12272.
- **O.1515.4:** PUL, VRG 2945.1501.3.

Bucolica (cum commento) (London: Wynkyn de Worde, 22 Aug.1522; *STC* 24814.5).

- **B.1522.1:** BodL, 4° Rawl. 206 (1).
- **B.1522.2:** BodL, Douce V 173.
- **B.1522.3:** PUL, VRG 2945.325.022.

Bucolica (cum commento) (London: Wynkyn de Worde, 12 Mar. 1529; *STC* 24815).

- **B.1529:** VRG 2945.325.029.

Bibliography

1. Primary Works

A) Manuscripts

Manuscripts of Virgil's Bucolics, Georgics and Aeneid
Cambridge, Jesus College, MS 33
Cambridge, Pembroke College, MS 260
Cambridge, Peterhouse, MS 158
Cambridge, Peterhouse, MS 159
SJC, MS C.4
SJC, MS H.2
TCC, MS R.1.40
TCC, MS R.3.50
NLS, Adv. MS 18.5.12
Edinburgh, Edinburgh University Library, MS 195
BL, MS Add. 16166
BL, MS Add. 11959
BL, MS Add. 27304
BL, MS Add. 32319A
BL, MS Harley 4967
BL, MS Royal 15.B.VI
LPL, MS 471
London, Society of Antiquaries, MS 44
Oxford, All Souls College, MS 82
Oxford, Balliol College, MS 140
BodL, MS Ashmole 54
BodL, MS Auct. F.2.7
Oxford, New College, MS 271
Shrewsbury, Shrewsbury School, MS IV

Other Manuscripts
TCC, MS O.3.12
Edinburgh, Edinburgh University Library, MS 136
BL, MS Add. 10089
BL, MS Add. 16380
BL, MS Egerton 646
BL, MS Harley 2693
BodL, MS Bodley 487
BodL, MS Bodley 587

202 BIBLIOGRAPHY

BodL, MS Digby 100

Oxford, Lincoln College, MS 91

B) Early Printed Editions Cited in Specific Copies

Editions of Virgil

Opera ([Strasbourg: Johann Mentelin, about 1470]; *ISTC* iv00151000). Oxford, New College, BT1.39.1.

Opera, comm. Servius (Venice: Jacobus Rubeus, Jan. 14[75/76]; *ISTC* iv00166000). CUL, Inc.2.B.3.15[1409].

Opera, comm. Servius (Venice: Antonio di Bartolommeo Miscomini, Oct. '1486' [i.e. 1476]; *ISTC* iv00167000). Cambridge, Jesus College, F.1.12. CUL, Inc.2.B.3.21 [1445]. CUL, Inc.2.B.3.21[1446]. Oxford, All Souls College, a.1.9.

Opera, comm. Servius (Venice: Petrus de Plasiis, Cremonensis, Bartholomaeus de Blavis de Alexandria, and Andreas Torresanus de Asula, 1 Aug. 1480; *ISTC* iv00169000). BodL, Auct. P inf. 2.3.

Opera, comm. Servius (Venice: Baptista de Tortis, 23 May 1487; *ISTC* iv00178000). Oxford, Brasenose College Library, Latham Room: UB/S I 40.

Opera, ed. Philippus Beroaldus, rev. Paulus Malleolus Andelocensis ([Paris: Georg Wolf], 20 Nov. 1489; *ISTC* iv00164800). BodL, Auct. O 1.17.

Opera, comm. Servius, Donatus, Landinus and Calderinus (Venice: Lazarus de Suardis, de Saviliano, 1491/92; *ISTC* iv00187000). Oxford, Exeter College, Strong Room: 9I 1491.

Opera, comm. Servius, Donatus, Landinus and Calderinus (Lyons: Antonius Lambillon, for Franciscus Girardengus, 5 Nov. 1492; *ISTC* iv00187500). BodL, Auct. O 1.18a.

Opera, comm. Servius, Donatus, Landinus and Calderinus (Nuremberg: Anton Koberger, 1492; *ISTC* iv00188000). CUL, Inc.3.A.7.2[887]. HEHL, 493771. Oxford, All Souls College, b.5.6. BodL, Auct. O 1.15.

Georgica (cum commento familiari) (Paris: Antoine Caillaut, 7 June 1492; *ISTC* iv00225000). PUL, VRG 2945.325.004.

Bucolica (cum commento) (Paris: Félix Baligault, [about 1492–94]; *ISTC* iv00208800). CUL, Inc.5.D.1.26[2568].

Opera, comm. Servius, Donatus, Landinus, Mancinellus and Calderinus (Venice: Bartholomaeus de Zanis, for Octavianus Scotus and Lucantonio Giunta, 31 July 1493; *ISTC* iv00189000). Oxford, All Souls College, b.4.4.

Bucolica (cum commento) (Paris: Félix Baligault, [c. 1493–94]; *ISTC* iv00208850). CUL, Peterborough.Sp.61.

Opera, ed. Philippus Beroaldus, rev. Paulus Malleolus Andelocensis (Paris: Ulrich Gering and Berthold Rembolt, 12 Sept. 1494; *ISTC* iv00165000). CUL, Inc.5.D.1.38 [2623].

Bucolica (cum commento) (Paris: Wolfgang Hopyl, 1 Feb. 1494; *ISTC* iv00209000). PUL, VRG 2945.325.004.

Bucolica (cum commento) (Deventer: Jacobus de Breda, 6 Nov. 1495; *ISTC* iv00211000). CCC, Phi.C.1.9(4).

BIBLIOGRAPHY 203

Georgica, comm. Hermannus Torrentinus (Deventer: Richardus Pafraet, 26 Aug. 1496; *ISTC* iv00229000). CCC, Phi.C.1.9(5).

Bucolica (cum commento) (Paris: Andre Bocard, about 1497; *ISTC* iv00212450). PUL, VRG 2945.325.006.2

Georgica (cum commento familiari) ([Paris]: Philippe Pigouchet, [about 1498]; *ISTC* iv00228500). CUL, Inc.5.D.1.26[2568]. CUL, Inc.5.D.1.29[2587].

Opera, ed. Badius Ascensius, comm. Servius, Donatus, Ascensius, Beroaldus and Calderinus, 3 vols (Paris: Thielman Kerver, for Jean Petit and Johannes de Coblenz, 1500–1; *ISTC* iv00196000). CUL, Inc.3.D.1.48[4305] PUL, (Ex) PA6804.A21.B32.1500q

Opera, ed. Philippus Beroaldus, rev. Augustinus Caminadus (Paris: Johann Philippi de Cruzenach, 19 Mar. 1501; Not in *ISTC* or *USTC*). PUL, VRG 2945.1501.2.

Opera, ed. Sebastian Brant, comm. Servius, Donatus, Landinus, Mancinellus and Calderinus (Strasbourg: Johann Grüninger, 28 Aug. 1502; *USTC* 688629) BodL, Douce V subt. 21.

Opera, ed. Badius Ascensius, comm. Servius, Donatus, Ascensius, Mancinellus, Beroaldus and Calderinus, 2 vols (Paris: Badius Ascensius, for Jean Petit, 1 Jun. and 8 Nov. 1507; *USTC* 143282). BodL, M 2.21,22 Art. BodL, Antiq.c.F.1507.1

Opuscula (cum familiari expositione) (Strasbourg: Johann Knobloch, 28 Apr. 1509; *USTC* 687444). CUL, 5000.d.122.

Bucolica (cum commento) (London: Wynkyn de Worde, 1514; *STC* 24814). BodL, 4°E 6(3) Art.Seld.

Opera (London: Richard Pynson, *c.* 1515; *STC* 24787). JRL, 12272. Oxford, Exeter College, Strong Room: 9M 24787. PUL, VRG 2945.1501.3.

Opera, comm. Servius, Donatus, ps-Probus, Ascensius, Mancinellus, Datus, Beroaldus and Calderinus, 2 vols (Paris: Jean Barbier and Francis Regnault, 21 June 1515 and 17 July 1515; *USTC* 183592). PUL, VRG 2945.1515.

Opera, comm. Servius, Donatus, ps-Probus, Ascensius, Mancinellus, Datus, Beroaldus and Calderinus (Lyon: Jacques Sacon and Cyriaque Hochperg, 1517; *USTC* 144785). BodL, Lawn c.100

Opera (Strasbourg: Johann Knobloch and Paul Götz, 1520; *USTC* 700667). BodL, 8° K 86 Linc.

Opera, ed. Pierre Baquelier (Paris: Jacques Le Messier, 6 July 1520; *USTC* 184099). BodL, (OC) 90 c.58 PUL, VRG 2945.1520.2

Opera, comm. Servius, Donatus, ps-Probus, Ascensius, Mancinellus, Datus, Beroaldus and Calderinus (Venice: Lucantonio Giunta, for Gregorio de Gregori, 1522: *USTC* 862711). CUL, X.7.34.

Bucolica (cum commento) (London: Wynkyn de Worde, 22 Aug.1522; *STC* 24814.5). BodL, 4° Rawl. 206 (1). BodL, Douce V 173. PUL, VRG 2945.325.022.

Opera comm. Servius, Donatus, ps-Probus, Ascensius, Valerianus, Mancinellus, Datus, Beroaldus, Calderinus and excerpts of Landinus (Lyon: Jacques Mareschal, 29 Aug. 1527; *USTC* 155738). CUL, O*.8.15(B).

Bucolica (cum commento) (London: Wynkyn de Worde, 12 Mar. 1529; *STC* 24815). PUL, VRG 2945.325.029.

Other

Cicero, *Epistolae ad familiares*, comm. Hubertinus clericus (Venice: Baptista de Tortis, 24 May 1485; *ISTC* ic00525000). Oxford, Magdalen College, Arch.B. III.1.13.

Ovid, *Fasti*, ed. and comm. Paulus Marsus (Venice: Antonius Battibovis, 27 Aug. 1485; *ISTC* io00172000) CCC, phi.C.3.3(2).

C) Early Printed Editions Not Cited in Specific Copies

Boccaccio, Giovanni, *De casibus virorum illustrium*, trans. Laurent de Premierfait (Lyon: Mathias Huss and Johannes Schabeler, 1483; *ISTC* ib00712000).

Cato, *Disticha*, *Disticha*, ed. and comm. Erasmus ([London: Wynkyn de Worde, c. 1525?]; *STC* 4841.5).

——, *Disticha*, ed. and comm. Erasmus ([London: Southwark, Peter Treveris, 1531?]; *STC* 4841.7).

——, *Disticha*, ed. and comm. Erasmus (London: Wynkyn de Worde, 1532; *STC* 4842).

Expositio hymnorum secundum usum Sarum, ed. Badius Ascensius (Paris: Andre Bocard, for John Baldwin in London, 1502; *STC* 16116).

Lefèvre, Raoul, *Recuyell of the Historyes of Troye*, trans. William Caxton ([Ghent?: David Aubert?, for William Caxton, c. 1473–74]; *ISTC* il00117000).

——, *The Historie of Jason*, trans. William Caxton ([Westminster: William Caxton, 1477]; *ISTC* il00112000).

——, *Le Recueil des histoires de Troyes* (Lyons: Jacques Maillet, 16 Apr. 1494/95; *ISTC* il00114500).

Lucan, *Pharsalia I*, trans. Christopher Marlowe (London: P. Short, 1600; *STC* 16883.5).

Mantuanus, Baptista, *Bucolica*, comm. Badius Ascensius (London: Wynkyn de Worde, May 1523; *STC* 22978).

——, *Bucolica*, comm. Badius Ascensius (London: Wynkyn de Worde, November 1526; *STC* 22979).

Ovid, *Metamorphoses*, comm. Raphael Regius (Venice: Bonetus Locatellus, for Octavianus Scotus, 4–5 June 1493; *ISTC* io00188000).

——, *Metamorphoses*, trans. Colard Mansion (Bruges: Colard Mansion, May 1484; *ISTC* io00184000).

——, *Metamorphoses*, trans. Colard Mansion [styled 'La bible des Poetes'] (Paris: Antoine Vérard, 1 Mar. 1493/4; *ISTC* io00184200).

Papias, *Vocabularium*, ed. Boninus Mombritius (Venice: Andreas de Bonetis, 30 June 1485; *ISTC* ip00078000).

Persius, *Satyrae*, comm. Joannes Britannicus, ed. and comm. Badius Ascensius (Lyons: Nicolaus Wolf, 27 Jan? 1499; *ISTC* ip00359000).

Servius, *Vocabula* ([Milan: Uldericus Scinzenzeler, about 1480]; *ISTC* is00485000).

Terence, *Comoediae*, comm. Aelius Donatus and Guido Juvenalis, ed. and comm. Badius Ascensius (Strasbourg: Johann Grüninger, 1 Nov. 1496; *ISTC* it00094000).

——, *Comoediae*, comm. Aelius Donatus and Guido Juvenalis, ed. and comm. Badius Ascensius (Strasbourg: Johann Grüninger, 11 Feb. 1499; *ISTC* it00101000).

——, *Andria* [titled *Terens in englysh*], trans. anon ([Paris: P. le Noir?, ca. 1520]; *STC* 23894).

Theodulus, *Ecloga*, comm. Odo Picardus (London: Wynkyn De Worde, 10 Mar. 1515; *STC* 23943).

Tortelli, Giovanni, *Orthographia* (Venice: Nicolaus Jenson, 1471; *ISTC* it00395000).

Valeriano, Piero, *Castigationes et varietates Virgilianae lectionis* (Rome: Antonio Blado, 1521; *USTC* 861710).

Virgil, *Aeneis (cum familiari expositione)*, ed. Johann Schott (Strasbourg: Johann Knobloch, 28 Mar. 1509; *USTC* 682141).

——, *Bucolica (cum commento)* (Deventer: Jacobus de Breda, 31 Oct. 1492; *ISTC* iv00208700).

——, *Bucolica (cum commento)* (Paris: Wolfgang Hopyl, 1 Feb. 1494; *ISTC* iv00209000).

——, *Bucolica (cum commento)* (Cologne: Heinrich Quentell, 6 Apr. 1495; *ISTC* iv00210000).

——, *Bucolica (cum commento)* (London: Wynkyn de Worde, 1512; *STC* 24813).

——, *Bucolica*, comm. Hermannus Torrentinus (Cologne: Heinrich Quentell, 1506; *USTC* 617336).

——, *Bucolica*, comm. Petrus Ramus (Paris: André Wechel, 1558; *USTC* 152391).

——, *Opera*, comm. Servius, Donatus and Landinus (Florence: [Printer of Vergilius (C 6061)], 18 Mar. 1487/88; *ISTC* iv00183000).

——, *Bucolica et Georgica (cum commento familiari)* (Seville: Compañeros alemanes (Johann Pegnitzer, Magnus Herbst and Thomas Glockner), for Johannes Laurentius, 3 Oct. 1498; *ISTC* iv00220000).

——, *Opera*, ed. Philippus Beroaldus, rev. Augustinus Caminadus (Paris: Jean Petit and François Regnault, [1510?]; *USTC* 143738).

——, *Opera*, ed. Philip Melanchthon (Haguenau: Johann Setzer, Mar. 1530; *USTC* 701364).

——, *Opera*, comm. Servius and Valeriano, 2 vols (Paris: Robert Estienne, 16 Jul. 1532 and 24 Nov. 1529; *USTC* 146074, 203367).

——, *Opera*, ed. Paulo Manuzio ([London]: Henry Bynneman, 1570; *STC* 24788).

——, *Livre des Eneydes*, trans. unknown (Lyons: Guillaume Le Roy, 30 Sept. 1483; *ISTC* iv00200000).

——, *Eneydos*, trans. William Caxton ([Westminster]: William Caxton, [after 22 June 1490]); *ISTC* iv00199000, *STC* 24796).

——, *Aeneid IV*, trans. Niccolò Liburnio (Giovanni Antonio Nicolini da Sabbio, 1534; *USTC* 862712).

——, *I sei primi libri dell'Eneide di Vergilio*, trans. various (Venice: Niccolò Zoppino, 1540; *USTC* 862762).

D) Modern Editions

Tutte le Opere di Giovanni Boccaccio, ed. Vittore Branca et al., 10 vols in 11 (Milan: A. Mondadori, 1964–98).

BIBLIOGRAPHY

The Middle English Text of Caxton's Ovid, Book I, ed. Diana Rumrich (Heidelberg: Winter, 2011).

The Middle English Text of Caxton's Ovid, Books II–III, ed. Wolfgang Mager (Heidelberg: Winter, 2016).

Caxton's Eneydos, 1490: Englisht from the French Liure des Eneydes, 1483, ed. W.T. Culley and F.J. Furnivall, Early English Text Society, Extra Series 57 (1890; London: OUP, 1962).

The Riverside Chaucer, ed. Larry D. Benson (1987; Oxford: OUP, 1988).

Tiberi Claudi Donati ad Tiberium Claudium Maximum Donatianum filium suum Interpretationes Virgilianae: Primum ad vetustissimorum codicum fidem recognitas, ed. H. Georges, 2 vols (Leipzig: Teubner, 1905–6).

Virgil's Aeneid Translated into Scottish Verse by Gavin Douglas, ed. D.F.C. Coldwell, 4 vols, Scottish Text Society, 3rd ser., 25, 27–8, 30 (Edinburgh: W. Blackwood & Sons Ltd, 1957–64).

Erasmus, *The Correspondence of Erasmus*, trans. various, 17 vols (Toronto: University of Toronto Press, 1974–Present).

——, *Poems*, ed. Clarence H. Miller and Harry Vredeveld, 2 vols (Toronto: University of Toronto Press, 1993).

Fox, Richard, *The Foundation Statutes of Bishop Fox for Corpus Christi College, in the University of Oxford, A.D. 1517: Now First Translated into English, With a Life of the Founder*, trans. G.R.M. Ward (London: Longman, Brown, Green, and Longmans, 1843).

The Aeneid of Henry Howard, Earl of Surrey, ed. Florence H. Ridley (Berkeley: University of California Press, 1963).

Lucan, *The Civil War*, ed. and trans. J.D. Duff (Cambridge, MA: Harvard University Press, 1928).

L'Eneide di Virgilio volgarizzata nel buon secolo della lingua da Ciampolo di Meo degli Ugurgeri senese, ed. Aurelio Gotti (Florence: Le Monnier, 1858).

Servii grammatici qui feruntur in Vergilii carmina commentarii, ed. G. Thilo and H. Hagen, 3 vols (Lepizig: Teubner, 1878–1902).

The Commentary on the First Six Books of the 'Aeneid' Commonly Attributed to Bernard Silvestris, ed. J.W. Jones and E.F. Jones (Lincoln, Nebr.: University of Nebraska Press, 1977).

Lavrentii Vallensis De Linguae Latinae Elegantia: Ad Ioannem Tortellium Aretinum: Per me M. Nicolaum Ienson Venetiis Opus Feliciter Impressum Est. M.CCCC.LXXI, ed. Santiago López Moreda, 2 vols (Cáceres: Universidad de Extremadura, 1999).

The Works of Christopher Marlowe, ed. C. F. Tucker Brooke (Oxford: Clarendon, 1910).

de Villena, Enrique, *Obras completas*, ed. Pedro M. Cátedra, 3 vols (Madrid: Turner, 1994–2000).

Virgil, ed. and trans. H.R. Fairclough, rev. G.P. Goold, 2 vols (London; Cambridge, MA: Harvard University Press, 1999, repr. 2006).

Acta Facultatis Artium Universitatis Sanctiandree, 1413–1588, ed. Annie I. Dunlop, 2 vols (Edinburgh: T. & A. Constable, Printers to the University of Edinburgh, for the Scottish History Society, 1964).

Histoire ancienne jusqu'à César. A digital edition, BnF, f. fr. 20125 and BL, Royal MS 20 D I. Semi-diplomatic edition, ed. Hannah Morcos, with the collaboration of Simon Gaunt, Simone Ventura, Maria Teresa Rachetta and Henry Ravenhall; with technical support from Paul Caton, Ginestra Ferraro, Marcus Husar and Geoffroy Noël (London: King's College London), online at <http://www.tvof.ac.uk/textviewer/?p1=Fr20125> and <http://www.tvof.ac.uk/textviewer/?p1=Royal> (Accessed 18 March 2019).

Records and Reminiscenses of Aberdeen Grammar School, ed. H.F.M. Simpson (Aberdeen: D. Wyllie and Son, 1906).

Register of Congregations, 1505–1517, ed. W.T. Mitchell, 2 vols (Oxford: Oxford Historical Society, 1998).

University of Oxford, *Statuta Antiqua Universitatis Oxoniensis*, ed. Strickland Gibson (Oxford: Clarendon Press, 1931).

University of Cambridge, *Statuta academiæ Cantabrigiensis* (Cambridge: J. Archdeacon, 1785).

2. Secondary Works

A) Online Catalogues and Reference Works

Craigie, W.A., A.J. Aiken, J.A.C. Stevenson and M.G. Dareau, eds, *A Dictionary of the Older Scottish Tongue from the Twelfth Century to the End of the Seventeenth*, 12 vols (Chicago: University of Chicago Press; London: Humphrey Milford; Oxford: OUP, 1937–2002), online at <https://dsl.ac.uk> (Accessed 9 Feb. 2019).

British Library and Consortium of European Research Libraries, *Incunabula Short Title Catalogue* (London: British Library and Consortium of European Research Libraries, 2016), online at <https://data.cerl.org/istc/> (Accessed 9 Feb. 2019).

Pettegree, Andrew, and Graeme Kemp, *Universal Short Title Catalogue* (St Andrews: University of St Andrews, 2017), online at <https://www.ustc.ac.uk> (Accessed 4 Feb. 2019).

Sharpe, Richard, and James Willoughby, eds, *Medieval Libraries of Great Britain*, (Oxford: Bodleian Libraries, 2015), online at <http://mlgb3.bodleian.ox.ac.uk> (Accessed 29 June 2019).

Simpson, John et al., eds, *The Oxford English Dictionary* (Oxford: OUP, 2019), online at <http://www.oed.com/> (Accessed 1 Feb. 2019).

B) Printed Catalogues and Reference Works

Coates, Alan, *A Catalogue of Books Printed in the Fifteenth Century Now in the Bodleian Library, Oxford*, 6 vols (Oxford: Oxford University Press, 2005).

Hunt, R.W. and A.G. Watson, *Bodleian Library Quarto Catalogues IX: Digby Manuscripts*, Reproduction of 1883 Catalogue by W.D. Macray (Oxford: Bodleian Library, 1999).

Kallendorf, Craig, *A Catalogue of the Junius Spencer Morgan Collection of Virgil in the Princeton University Library* (New Castle: Oak Knoll Press, 2009).

——, *A Bibliography of the Early Printed Editions of Virgil, 1469–1850* (New Castle, Delaware: Oak Knoll Press, 2012).
Latham, R.E., D.R. Howlett, and R.K. Ashdowne, eds, *Dictionary of Medieval Latin from British Sources*, 3 vols (Oxford: OUP, 2018).
Mynors, R.A.B., *Catalogue of the Manuscripts of Balliol College Oxford* (Oxford: Clarendon Press, 1963).
Pollard, Alfred W. and G.R. Redgrave, *A Short-Title Catalogue of Books Printed in England, Scotland, & Ireland and of English Books Printed Abroad 1473–1640*, 2nd edn, rev. William A. Jackson, F.S. Ferguson and Katharine F. Pantzer, 3 vols (London: Bibliographical Society, 1976–91).

C) Other Secondary Works

Attridge, Derek, *Well-Weighed Syllables: Elizabethan Verse in Classical Metres* (Cambridge: CUP, 1974).
Baker, Patrick, *Italian Renaissance Humanism in the Mirror* (Cambridge: CUP, 2015).
Baldwin, T.W., *William Shakespere's Small Latine & Lesse Greeke*, 2 vols (Urbana: University of Illinois Press, 1944).
Baswell, Christopher, *Virgil in Medieval England: Figuring the Aeneid from the Twelfth Century to Chaucer* (Cambridge: CUP, 1995).
——, 'Master Anselm', in *The Virgilian Tradition: the First Fifteen Hundred Years*, ed. Jan M. Ziolkowski and Michael C.J. Putnam (New Haven: Yale University Press, 2008), pp. 717–21.
Bawcutt, Priscilla, 'Gavin Douglas and the Text of Virgil', *Edinburgh Bibliographical Society Transactions*, 4 (1973), 211–31.
——, 'Douglas and Surrey: Translators of Virgil', *Essays and Studies* 27 (1974), 52–67.
——, *Gavin Douglas: A Critical Study* (Edinburgh: Edinburgh University Press, 1976).
——, '"My bright buke": Women and their Books in Medieval and Renaissance Scotland', *Medieval Women: Texts and Contexts in Late Medieval Britain: Essays for Felicity Riddy*, ed. Jocelyn Wogan-Browne (Turnhout: Brepols, 2000), pp. 17–34.
Bierlaire, Franz, 'Érasme et Augustin Vincent Caminade', *Bibliothèque d'Humanisme et Renaissance* 30 (1968), 357–362.
——, 'Augustinus Vincentius Caminadus', in *Contemporaries of Erasmus: A Biographical Register of the Renaissance and Reformation*, ed. Peter G Bietenholz and homas Brian Deutscher, 3 vols (Toronto: University of Toronto Press, 1985–1987), I, pp. 250–1.
Black, Robert, *Humanism and Education in Medieval and Renaissance Italy: Tradition and Innovation in Latin Schools from the Twelfth to the Fifteenth Century* (Cambridge: CUP, 2001).
Blair, Ann, 'Errata Lists and the Reader as Corrector', in *Agent of Change: Print Culture Studies after Elizabeth L. Einstein*, ed. Sabrina Alcorn Baron, Eric N. Lindquist and Eleanor F. Shevlin (Amherst, MA: University of Massachusetts Press, 2007).

Blake, N.F., *Caxton and his World* (London: Deutsch, 1969).

——, 'Wynkyn de Worde: The Later Years', *Gutenberg Jahrbuch* 47 (1972), 128–38.

Brammall, Sheldon, *The English Aeneid: Translations of Virgil, 1555–1646* (Edinburgh: Edinburgh University Press, 2015).

Botley, Paul, *Latin Translation in the Renaissance: The Theory and Practice of Leonardo Bruni, Giannozzo Manetti, and Desiderius Erasmus* (Cambridge: CUP, 2004).

Burrow, Colin, 'Virgil in English Translation', *The Cambridge Companion to Virgil*, ed. Charles Martindale (Cambridge: CUP, 1997), pp. 21–37.

Bursill-Hall, G.L., 'Johannes de Garlandia—Forgotten Grammarian and the Manuscript Tradition', *Historiographia Linguistica* 3 (1976), 155–77.

Cairns, Sandra, 'The *Palice of Honour* of Gavin Douglas, Ovid, and Raffaello Regio's commentary on Ovid's *Metamorphoses*', *Res Publica Litterarum* 7 (1984) 17–38.

Calin, William, *The Lily and the Thistle: The French Tradition and the Older Literature of Scotland: Essays in Criticism* (Toronto: University of Toronto Press, 2014).

Camargo, Martin, 'Medieval Rhetoric Delivers: or, Where Chaucer Learned how to Act', *New Medieval Literatures* 9 (2008, for 2007), 41–62.

——, 'Rhetoricians in Black: Benedictine Monks and Rhetorical Revival in Medieval Oxford', in *New Chapters in the History of Rhetoric*, ed. L. Pernot (Leiden: Brill, 2009), pp. 375–84.

——, 'The Late-Fourteenth-Century Renaissance of Anglo-Latin Rhetoric', *Philosophy and Rhetoric* 45 (2012), 107–33.

Canitz, A.E.C., 'From *Aeneid* to *Eneados*: Theory and Practice of Gavin Douglas's Translation', *Medievalia et Humanistica* 17 (1991), 81–99.

Cannon, Christopher, *From Literacy to Literature: England, 1300–1400* (Oxford: OUP, 2016).

Carley, James P. and Ágnes Juhász-Ormsby, 'Survey of Henrician Humanism', in *The Oxford History of Classical Reception in English Literature: Volume I: 800–1558*, ed. Rita Copeland (Oxford: OUP, 2016), pp. 515–40.

Carlisle, Nicholas, *A Concise Description of the Endowed Grammar Schools in England and Wales*, 6 vols (London: Baldwin, Craddock and Joy, 1818).

Carter, Harry, *A View of Early Typography up to about 1600* (Oxford: Clarendon Press, 1969).

Cattaneo, Arturo, 'The Italian Sources of Surrey's *Aeneid*', in *Italy and the English Renaissance*, ed. S. Rossi and D. Savoia (Milan: Edizioni Unicopli, 1989), pp. 89–106.

——, *L'ideale umanistico: Henry Howard, Earl of Surrey*, Biblioteca di Studi Inglesi, 53 (Bari: Adriatica Editrice, 1991).

Christianson, C.P., 'The Rise of London's Book Trade', in *The Cambridge History of the Book in Britain: Volume III: 1400–1557*, ed. Lotte Hellinga and J.B. Trapp (Cambridge: CUP, 1998), pp. 128–47.

Clark, James, *A Monastic Renaissance at St. Albans: Thomas Walsingham and his Circle, c. 1350–1440* (Oxford: Clarendon, 2004).

——, 'Humanism and Reform in Pre-Reformation English Monasteries', *Transactions of the Royal Historical Society* 19 (2009), pp. 57–93.

——, 'Ovid in the Monasteries', in *Ovid in the Middle Ages*, ed. J.G. Clark, F.T. Coulson, K.L. McKinley (Cambridge: CUP, 2011), pp. 177–96.

Coates, Alan, 'The Latin Trade in England and Abroad', *A Companion to the Early Printed Book in Britain, 1476–1558*, ed. Vincent Gillespie and Susan Powell (Cambridge: D.S. Brewer, 2014), pp. 45–58.

Comparetti, Domenico, *Vergil in the Middle Ages*, trans. E.F.M. Benecke, with introduction by Jan M. Ziolkowski (Princeton: Princeton University Press, 1997).

Considine, John, 'Neo-Latin Lexicography in the Shadow of the *Catholicon*', in *Acta Conventus Neo-Latini Vindobonensis. Proceedings of the Sixteenth International Congress of Neo-Latin Studies (Vienna 2015)*, ed. Astrid Steiner-Weber and Franz Römer (Leiden: Brill, 2018), pp. 206–15.

——, '"Si hoc saeculo natus fuisset": Refurbishing the Catholicon for the 16th Century', *Historiographia Linguistica* 44 (2018), 412–29.

Cooper, Helen, *Pastoral: Mediaeval into Renaissance* (Cambridge: D.S. Brewer, 1977).

Copeland, Rita, *Rhetoric, Hermeneutics and Translation in the Middle Ages: Academic Traditions and Vernacular Texts* (Cambridge: Cambridge University Press, 1991).

Copeland, Rita and Ineke Sluiter, eds, *Medieval Grammar and Rhetoric: Language Arts and Literary Theory, AD 300–1475* (Oxford: OUP, 2010).

Cormier, Raymond J., 'An Example of Twelfth Century *Adaptatio*: The *Roman d'Eneas* Author's Use of Glossed *Aeneid* Manuscripts', *Revue d'Histoire des Textes* 19 (1989), 277–89.

Crab, Marijke and Jeroen De Keyser, 'Il commento di Guarino Guarini a Valerio Massimo', *Aevum* 87 (2013), 667–84.

Crane, Mark, '"Virtual Classroom"': Josse Bade's Commentaries for the Pious Reader', *The Unfolding of Words: Commentary in the Age of Erasmus*, ed. Judith Rice Henderson (Toronto: University of Toronto Press, 2012), pp. 101–17.

Croizy-Naquet, Catherine, *Ecrire l'histoire romaine au début du XIIIe siècle: L'Histoire Ancienne jusqu'à César et les Faits des Romains* (Paris: Champion, 1999).

de Hamel, Christopher, *A History of Illuminated Manuscripts*, 2nd edn (London: Phaidon Press, 1994).

de la Mare, A.C. and R. Hunt, *Duke Humfrey and English Humanism in the Fifteenth Century* (Oxford: Bodleian Library, 1970).

Desmond, Marilynn, *Reading Dido: Gender, Textuality, and the Medieval Aeneid* (Minneapolis: University of Minnesota Press, 1994).

Despres, Joanne M., 'Translation Techniques in the Romances of William Caxton' (Unpublished PhD Dissertation, University of Pennsylvania, 1991).

Durkan, John, 'Education in the Century of the Reformation', *Innes Review* 10 (1959), 67–90.

——, *Scottish Schools and Schoolmasters, 1560–1633*, ed. and rev. J. Reid-Baxter, Scottish Historical Society (Woodbridge: Boydell, 2013).

BIBLIOGRAPHY 211

Duval, Frédéric, 'Quels passés pour quel Moyen Âge?', in *Translations médiévales: cinq siècles de traductions en français au Moyen Âge (XIe-XVe siècles): étude et répertoire*, ed. Claudio Galderisi and Vladimir Agrigoroaei, 2 vols in 3 (Turnhout: Brepols, 2011), I, pp. 47-92.

Ebin, Lois, *Illuminator, Makar, Vates: Visions of Poetry in the Fifteenth Century* (Lincoln, NE: University of Nebraska Press, 1988).

Edwards, A.S.G., 'The Middle English Translation of Claudian's *De Consulatu Stilichonis*', in *Middle English Poetry: Texts and Traditions: Essays in Honour of Derek Pearsall*, ed. A.J. Minnis (York: York Medieval Press, 2001), pp. 267-78.

Eisenstein, Elizabeth, *The Printing Press as an Agent of Change: Communications and Cultural Transformations in Early Modern Europe*, 2 vols (Cambridge: CUP, 1979).

Emden, A.B., *A Biographical Register of the University of Oxford to A.D. 1500*, 3 vols (Oxford: Clarendon Press, 1957-9).

——, *A Biographical Register of the University of Cambridge to A.D. 1500*, 2 vols (Cambridge: Cambridge University Press, 1963).

——, *A Biographical Register of the University of Oxford, A.D. 1500-1540* (Oxford: Clarendon Press, 1974).

Finlayson, Charles P.: 'A Glamis Virgil?', *Scottish Historical Review* 32 (1953), 99-100.

——, 'Florius Infortunatus', *Scriptorium* 16.2 (1962), 378-80.

——, 'Florius Infortunatus, Scribe and Author', *Scriptorium* 19 (1965), 108-9.

Fletcher, J.M., 'Developments in the Faculty of Arts 1370-1520', in *The History of the University of Oxford: Volume II: Late Medieval Oxford*, ed. J.I. Catto and T.A.R. Evans (Oxford: OUP, 1992), pp. 315-45.

Foley, S.M., 'Not-Blank-Verse: Surrey's *Aeneid* Translations and the Prehistory of a Form', in *Poets and Critics Read Vergil*, ed. S. Spence (New Haven: Yale University Press, 2001), pp. 149-71.

Ford, M. Lane, 'Importation of Printed Books into England and Scotland', in *The Cambridge History of the Book in Britain: Volume III: 1400-1557*, ed. Lotte Hellinga and J.B. Trapp (Cambridge: CUP, 1998), pp. 179-201.

Ford, Philip, 'Alexandre de Villedieu's *Doctrinale puerorum*: A Medieval Bestseller and Its Fortune in the Renaissance', in *Forms of the 'Medieval' in the 'Renaissance': A Multidisciplinary Exploration of a Cultural Continuum*, ed. George Hugo Tucker (Charlottesville, VA: Rookwood Press, 2000), pp. 155-71.

Ghosh, Kantik, '"The Fift Quheill"; Gavin Douglas's Maffeo Vegio', *Scottish Literary Journal* 22 (1995), 5-21.

Gillespie, Vincent, 'The Study of Classical Authors from the Twelfth Century to c. 1450', in *Cambridge History of Literary Criticism, Volume 2, The Middle Ages*, ed. A.J. Minnis and I. Johnson (Cambridge: CUP, 2005), pp. 145-235.

Goodman, Jennifer R., 'Caxton's Continent', in *Caxton's Trace: Studies in the History of English Printing*, ed. William Kuskin (Notre Dame: University of Notre Dame Press, 2006), pp. 101-23.

Grafton, Anthony, and Lisa Jardine, *From Humanism to the Humanities: Education and the Liberal Arts in Fifteenth- and Sixteenth-Century Europe* (Cambridge, MA: Harvard University Press, 1986).

Gray, Douglas, 'Some Pre-Elizabethan Examples of an Elizabethan Art', in *England and the Continental Renaissance: Essays in Honour of J.B. Trapp*, ed. Edward Chaney and Peter Mack (Woodbridge: Boydell, 1990), pp. 24–36.

——, '"As quha the mater held tofor thar e": Douglas's treatment of Vergil's Imagery', in *A Palace in the Wild: Essays on Vernacular Culture and Humanism in Late-Medieval and Renaissance Scotland*, ed. L.A.J.R Houwen, A.A. MacDonald and Sally Mapstone (Leuven: Peeters, 2000), pp. 95–123.

——, 'Gavin Douglas', in *A Companion to Medieval Scottish Poetry*, ed. Priscilla Bawcutt and Janet Hadley Williams (Cambridge: Brewer, 2006), pp. 149–64.

Greene, Thomas, *The Light in Troy: Imitation and Discovery in Renaissance Poetry* (New Haven: Yale University Press, 1982).

Griffiths, Jane, *Diverting Authorities: Experimental Glossing Practices in Manuscript and Print* (Oxford: OUP, 2014).

Hall, Louis Brewer, 'Caxton's "Eneydos" and the Redactions of Virgil', *Mediaeval Studies* 22 (1960), 136–47.

Hankins, James, *Virtue Politics: Soulcraft and Statecraft in Renaissance Italy* (Cambridge, MA: Harvard University Press, 2019).

Hardison, O.B., 'Blank Verse Before Milton', *Studies in Philology* 81 (1984), 253–74.

——, *Prosody and Purpose in the English Renaissance* (Baltimore: John Hopkins University Press, 1989).

Hexter, R.J., *Ovid and Medieval Schooling: Studies in Medieval School Commentaries on Ovid's Ars Amatoria, Epistulae ex Ponto, and Epistulae Heroidum* (München: Arbeo-Gesellschaft, 1986).

Hiatt, Alfred, 'The Reference Work in the Fifteenth Century: John Whethamstede's Granarium', in *Makers and Users of Medieval Books: Essays in Honour of A.S.G. Edwards*, ed. C.M. Meale and D. Pearsall (Cambridge: D.S. Brewer, 2014), pp. 13–33.

Hooley, Dan, 'Raising the Dead: Marlowe's Lucan', in *Translation and the Classic: Identity as Change in the History of Culture*, ed. Alexandra Lianeri and Vanda Zajko (Oxford: OUP, 2008), pp. 243–60.

Houghton, L.B.T. and Marco Sgarbi, eds, *Virgil and Renaissance Culture* (Turnhout: Brepols, 2018).

Hunt, Tony, *Teaching and Learning Latin in 13th-Century England*, 3 vols (Cambridge: D.S. Brewer, 1991).

Isaac, Frank, *English and Scottish Printing Types 1501–35, 1508–41* (Oxford: Printed for the Bibliographical Society at the Oxford University Press, 1930).

Jones, Howard, *Printing the Classical Text* (Utrecht: Hes & de Graaf Publishers BV, 2004).

Jones, J.W. Jr, 'Allegorical Interpretation in Servius', *The Classical Journal* 56 (1961), 217–26.

Kallendorf, Craig, 'Cristoforo Landino's *Aeneid* and the Humanist Critical Tradition', *Renaissance Quarterly* 36 (1983), 519–546.

——, *In Praise of Aeneas: Virgil and Epideictic Rhetoric in the Early Italian Renaissance* (Hanover: University Press of New England, 1989).

——, *Virgil and the Myth of Venice: Books and Readers in the Italian Renaissance* (Oxford: Clarendon, 1999).

——, 'Virgil in the Renaissance Classroom: From Toscanella's *Osservationi... sopra l'opere di Virgilio* to the *Exercitationes rhetoricae*', in *The Classics in the Medieval and Renaissance Classroom: The Role of Ancient Texts in the Arts Curriculum as Revealed by Surviving Manuscripts and Early Printed Books*, ed. J.F. Ruys, J. Ward, and M. Heyworth (Turnhout: Brepols, 2013), pp. 309–28.

——, *The Protean Virgil: Material Form and the Reception of the Classics* (Oxford: OUP, 2015).

——, *Printing Virgil: The Transformation of the Classics in the Renaissance* (Leiden: Brill, 2019).

Kendal, Gordon, *Translation as Creative Retelling: Constituents, Patterning and Shift in Gavin Douglas' Eneados* (unpublished Ph.D. Thesis, University of St Andrews, 2008).

King, Andrew and Matthew Woodcock, eds, *Medieval into Renaissance: Essays for Helen Cooper* (Rochester: D.S. Brewer, 2016).

Kraebel, Andrew, 'Biblical Exegesis and the Twelfth-Century Expansion of Servius', in *Classical Commentary: Explorations in a Scholarly Genre*, ed. Christina Kraus and Christopher Stray (Oxford: OUP, 2016), pp. 419–34.

Kristeller, Paul Oskar, *Renaissance Thought and Its Sources*, ed. Michael Mooney (New York: Columbia University Press, 1979).

——, *Renaissance Thought and the Arts: Collected Essays* (Princeton: Princeton University Press, 1981).

Kuskin, William, *Symbolic Caxton: Literary Culture and Print Capitalism* (Notre Dame, IN: University of Notre Dame Press, 2008).

Lazarus, Micha, 'Greek Literacy in Sixteenth-Century England', *Renaissance Studies* 29 (2015), 433–58.

Lerer, Seth, *Chaucer and his Readers: Imagining the Author in Late-Medieval England* (Princeton: Princeton University Press, 1993).

Leube, Eberhard, *Fortuna in Karthago: Die Aeneas-Dido-Mythe Vergils in den romantischen Literaturen vom 14. bis 16. Jahrhundert* (Heidelberg: Carl Winter, 1969).

Lowry, Martin, *The World of Aldus Manutius: Business and Scholarship in Renaissance Venice* (Ithaca, NY: Cornell University Press, 1979).

——, 'The arrival and use of continental printed books in Yorkist England', in *Le Livre dans L'Europe de la Renaissance*, ed. P. Aquilon & H.-J. Martin (Paris: Promodis-Ed. du Cercle de la Librairie, 1988), pp. 449–59.

Machan, Tim William, *Techniques of Translation: Chaucer's Boece* (Norman: Pilgrim Books, 1985).

Mack, Peter, 'Ramus Reading: The Commentaries on Cicero's *Consular Orations* and Vergil's *Eclogues* and *Georgics*', *Journal of the Warburg and Courtauld Institutes* 61 (1998), 111–41.

―, 'Melanchthon's Commentaries on Latin Literature', in *Melanchthon und Europa*, ed. Günter Frank, Treu Martin, and Kees Meerhoff, 2 vols (Stuttgart: Jan Thorbecke, 2001–2), II, pp. 29–52.

―, *Elizabethan Rhetoric: Theory and Practice* (Cambridge: CUP, 2002).

Marshall, Peter K., 'Tiberius Claudius Donatus in the Fifteenth Century', in *Tria Lustra: Essays and Notes Presented to John Pinsent, Founder and Editor of Liverpool Classical Monthly by Some of its Contributors on the Occasion of the 150th Issue*, ed. H.D. Jocelyn and Helena Hunt (Liverpool: Liverpool Classical Monthly, 1993), pp. 325–9.

McDonnell, Michael, *The Annals of St. Paul's School* (Cambridge: Privately printed for the Governors, 1959).

McKitterick, David, *Print, Manuscript and the Search for Order* (Cambridge: CUP, 2003).

Minnis, *Magister Amoris: The Roman de la Rose and Vernacular Hermeneutics* (Oxford: OUP, 2001).

Monfasani, John, 'Toward the Genesis of the Kristeller Thesis of Renaissance Humanism: Four Bibliographical Notes', *Renaissance Quarterly* 53 (2000), 1156–73.

Monfrin, Jacques, 'Humanisme et traductions au moyen âge', *Journal des savants* 148 (1963), 161–90.

―, 'Les *translations* vernaculaires de Virgile au Moyen Âge', in *Lectures Médiévales de Virgile: Actes du Colloque Organisé par l'École Française de Rome: Rome, 25–28 Octobre 1982*, ed. Jean-Yves Tilliette (Rome: École de Française de Rome, 1985), pp. 189–249.

―, 'L'Histoire de Didon et Enée au XVe siécle', *Études littéraires sur le XVe siècle, Actes du Ve colloque international sur le moyen français, Milan 6-8 mai 1985*, ed. Sergio Cigada (Milan: Vita e Pensiero, 1986), pp. 161–197.

Munk Olsen, Birger, *L'Étude des Auteurs Classiques Latins aux XIe et XIIe Siècles*, 3 vols (Paris: Éditions du CNRS, 1982–9).

―, 'Virgile et la renaissance du XIIe siècle', in *Lectures Médiévales de Virgile: Actes du Colloque Organisé par l'École Française de Rome: Rome, 25–28 Octobre 1982*, ed. Jean-Yves Tilliette (Rome: École de Française de Rome, 1985), pp. 31–48.

Orme, Nicholas, *English Schools in the Middle Ages* (London: Methuen, 1973).

―, 'Schools and School-books', in *The Cambridge History of the Book in Britain: Volume III: 1400–1557*, ed. Lotte Hellinga and J.B. Trapp (Cambridge: CUP, 1998), pp. 449–69.

―, *English School Exercises, 1420–1530* (Toronto: Pontifical Institute of Mediaeval Studies, 2013).

Pellegrini, A.L., ed., *The Early Renaissance: Virgil and the Classical Tradition* (Binghamton: State University of New York at Binghamton, The Center for Medieval and Early Renaissance Studies, 1984).

Percival, W. Keith, 'Renaissance Grammar', in *Renaissance Humanism: Foundations, Forms, and Legacy*, ed. Albert Rabil, 3 vols (Philadelphia: University of Pennsylvania Press, 1988), III, pp. 67–84.

Pinti, Daniel J., 'The Vernacular Gloss(ed.) in Gavin Douglas's *Eneados*', *Exemplaria* 7 (1995), 443–64.

Purcell, Mark, 'Master Petypher's Virgil: The Anatomy of a Tudor School Book', *The Book Collector* 50 (2001), 471–92.

Ramires, Giuseppe, 'Servio e l'Umanesimo inglese: Robert Flemmyng, allievo di Guarino Veronese', in *Servius et sa réception de l'Antiquité à la Renaissance*, ed. Bruno Méniel, Monique Bouquet and Guiseppe Ramires (Rennes: Presses universitaires de Rennes, 2011), pp. 539–554.

Rasmussen, Jens, *La prose narrative française du XVe siècle: étude esthétique et stylistique* (Copenhagen: Aarhuus Stiftsbogtrykkerie, 1958).

Renouard, Philippe, *Bibliographie des impressions et des œuvres de Josse Badius Ascensius: imprimeur et humaniste, 1462–1535*, 3 vols (Paris: E. Paul et fils et Guillemin, 1908).

——, *Imprimeurs et Libraires Parisiens du XVIe siècle: Ouvrage publié d'après les manuscrits de Philippe Renouard*, 5 vols (Paris: Service des travaux historiques de la Ville de Paris, 1964-Present).

Reynolds, Suzanne, *Medieval Reading: Grammar, Rhetoric and the Classical Text* (Cambridge: Cambridge University Press, 1996).

Richardson, D.A., 'Humanistic Intent in Surrey's *Aeneid*', *English Literary Renaissance*, 6 (1976), 204–19.

Ridley, Florence H., 'Surrey's Debt to Gawin Douglas', *PMLA* 76 (1961), 25–33.

Robinson, Pamela, 'Materials: Paper and Type', in *A Companion to the Early Printed Book in Britain, 1476–1558*, ed. Vincent Gillespie and Susan Powell (Cambridge: D.S. Brewer, 2014), pp. 61–74.

Royan, Nicola, 'The Humanist Identity of Gavin Douglas', *Medievalia et Humanistica* 41 (2015), 119–36.

Rundle, David, 'Of Republics and Tyrants: Aspects of Quattrocento Humanist Writings and Their Reception in England, *c.* 1400–*c.* 1460' (unpublished D.Phil. thesis, University of Oxford, 1997).

——, 'Humanist Eloquence among the Barbarians in fifteenth-century England', in *Britannia Latina: Latin in the Culture of Great Britain from the Middle Ages to the Twentieth Century*, ed. Charles Burnett and Nicholas Mann (London: Warburg Institute, 2005), pp. 68–85.

——, 'The Scribe Thomas Candour and the Making of Poggio Bracciolini's English Reputation', *English Manuscript Studies* 12 (2005), 1–25.

——, *The Renaissance Reform of the Book and Britain: The English Quattrocento* (Cambridge: CUP, 2019).

Rutledge, Thomas, 'Humanism in Late-Fifteenth-Century Scotland', in *Humanism in Fifteenth-Century Europe*, ed. David Rundle (Oxford: Society for the Study of Medieval Languages and Literature, 2012), pp. 237–63.

Ruysschaert, J., *Miniaturistes 'Romaines' Sous Pie II* (Siena: Accademia Senese degli Intronati, 1968).

Sessions, W.A., *Henry Howard, Earl of Surrey* (Boston: Twayne, 1986).

——, *Henry Howard, the Poet Earl of Surrey: A Life* (Oxford: OUP, 1999).

Simpson, James, *Reform and Cultural Revolution: The Oxford English Literary History: Volume 2: 1350-1547* (Oxford: OUP, 2002).

——, 'The Aeneid Translations of Henry Howard, Earl of Surrey: The Exiled Reader's Presence', in *The Oxford History of Classical Reception in English Literature: Volume 1: 800-1558*, ed. Rita Copeland (Oxford: OUP, 2016), pp. 601-23.

Simpson, James and Brian Cummings, eds, *Cultural Reformations: Medieval and Renaissance in Literary History* (Oxford: OUP, 2010).

Singerman, Jerome E., *Under Clouds of Poesy: Poetry and Truth in French and English Reworkings of the 'Aeneid', 1160-1513* (New York: Garland, 1986).

Smith, Lesley, *The Glossa Ordinaria: The Making of a Medieval Bible Commentary* (Leiden: Brill, 2009).

Summit, Jennifer and David Wallace, eds, *Medieval/Renaissance: After Periodization*, Special Issue, *Journal of Medieval and Early Modern Studies* 37 (2007).

Tilliette, Jean-Yves, ed., *Lectures Médiévales de Virgile: Actes du Colloque Organisé par l'École Française de Rome: Rome, 25-28 Octobre 1982* (Rome: École de Française de Rome, 1985).

Tudeau-Clayton, Margaret, *Jonson, Shakespeare and the Early-Modern Virgil* (Cambridge: CUP, 1998).

Valentini, Andrea, 'Entre traduction et commentaire érudit: Simon de Hesdin translateur de Valère Maxime', in *La Traduction vers le Moyen Français*, ed. Claudio Galderisi and Cinzia Pignatelli (Turnhout: Brepols, 2007), pp. 353-65.

Venier, Matteo, *Per una storia del testo di Virgilio nella prima età del libro a stampa (1469-1519)* (Udine: Forum, 2001).

Wakelin, Daniel, *Humanism, Reading, and English Literature, 1430-1530* (Oxford: OUP, 2007).

——, 'Possibilities for Reading: Classical Translations in Parallel Texts ca. 1520-1558', *Studies in Philology* 105 (2008), 463-86.

——, 'Caxton's exemplar for The Chronicles of England?', *Journal of the Early Book Society* 14 (2011), 75-113.

——, 'England: Humanism Beyond Weiss', in *Humanism in Fifteenth-Century Europe*, ed. David Rundle (Oxford: Society for the Study of Medieval Languages and Literature, 2012), pp. 265-306.

——, 'Classical and Humanist Translations', in *A Companion to Fifteenth-Century English Poetry*, ed. Julia Boffey and A.S.G. Edwards (Woodbridge: D.S. Brewer, 2013), pp. 171-85.

——, 'Early Humanism in England', in *The Oxford History of Classical Reception in English Literature: Volume 1: 800-1558*, ed. Rita Copeland (Oxford: OUP, 2016), pp. 487-513.

Wallace, Andrew, *Virgil's Schoolboys: The Poetics of Pedagogy in Renaissance England* (Oxford: OUP, 2010).

Ward, John O., 'The Lectures of Guarino da Verona on the *Rhetorica ad Herennium*: A Preliminary Discussion', in *Rhetoric and Pedagogy: Its History, Philosophy, and Practice: Essays in Honor of James J. Murphy*, ed. Winifred Bryan Horner, Michael Leff, et al. (Hillsdale, NJ: Erlbaum, 1995), pp. 97-127.

——, 'Rhetoric in the Faculty of Arts at the Universities of Paris and Oxford in the Middle Ages: A Summary of the Evidence', *Archivum Latinitatis Medii Aevi* (Union Académique Internationale: Bulletin Du Cange) 54 (1996), 159–231.

——, 'The Medieval and Early Renaissance Study of Cicero's *de Inventione* and the *Rhetorica ad Herennium*: Commentaries and Contexts', in *The Rhetoric of Cicero in its Medieval and Early Renaissance Commentary Tradition*, ed. Virginia Cox and John O. Ward (Leiden: Brill, 2006), pp. 1–75.

Weiss, Roberto, *Humanism in England During the Fifteenth Century*, 3rd edn (1941; Oxford: Blackwell, 1967), consulted in 4th edn, ed. David Rundle and Anthony John Lappin (Oxford, 2010), accessible online at <https://aevum.space/OS4>.

White, Paul, *Jodocus Badius Ascensius: Commentary, Commerce and Print in the Renaissance* (Oxford: OUP, 2013).

Wilson-Okamura, David Scott, *Virgil in the Renaissance* (Cambridge: CUP, 2010).

Wingfield, Emily, 'The Ruthven Manuscript of Gavin Douglas's *Eneados* and a New Manuscript Witness of Julius Caesar Scaliger's *Epidorpides*', *Renaissance Studies* 30 (2016), 430–442.

Ronald G. Witt, *'In the Footsteps of the Ancients': The Origins of Humanism from Lovato to Bruni* (Leiden: Brill, 2000).

——, *The Two Latin Cultures and the Foundation of Renaissance Humanism in Medieval Italy* (Cambridge: CUP, 2012).

Woods, Marjorie Curry, 'Rhetoric, Gender, and the Literary Arts: Classical Speeches in the Schoolroom', *New Medieval Literatures* 11 (2009), 113–32.

——, 'What are the Real Differences between Medieval and Renaissance Commentaries?', in *The Classics in the Medieval and Renaissance Classroom: The Role of Ancient Texts in the Arts Curriculum as Revealed by Surviving Manuscripts and Early Printed Books*, ed. Juanita Feros Ruys, John O. Ward, and Melanie Heywood (Turnhout: Brepols, 2013), pp. 329–341.

——, 'Performing Dido', in *Public Declamations: Essays on Medieval Rhetoric, Education, and Letters in Honour of Martin Camargo*, ed. Georgiana Donavin and Denise Stodola (Turnhout: Brepols, 2015), pp. 253–65.

Workman, Samuel K., *Fifteenth Century Translation as an Influence on English Prose* (Princeton: Princeton University Press, 1940).

——, 'Versions by Skelton, Caxton and Berners of a Prologue by Diodorus Siculus', *Modern Language Notes* 56 (1941), 252–58.

Wang, Y.-C., 'Caxton's Romances and their Early Tudor Readers', *Huntington Library Quarterly* 67 (2004), 173–88.

Zabughin, Vladimiro, *Vergilio nel Rinascimento Italiano da Dante a Torquato Tasso*, 2 vols (Bologna: N. Zanichelli, 1921–1923).

Ziolkowski, Jan M., 'Virgil', in *The Oxford History of Classical Reception in English Literature: Volume 1: 800–1558*, ed. Rita Copeland (Oxford: OUP, 2016), pp. 165–85.

——, and Michael C.J. Putnam, eds, *The Virgilian Tradition: The First Fifteen Hundred Years* (New Haven: Yale University Press, 2008).

Index

Aeneid
  exegesis of the *Aeneid*, *see* exegesis;
    annotation; commentary
  copies of the *Aeneid*, *see* manuscripts;
    printing
  translations of the *Aeneid*, *see* Caxton,
    William; Douglas, Gavin; Surrey, Earl of
Aesop 25, 27–8, 50n. 22, 75n. 22, 84–5, 89, 91
Alan of Lille 18, 25, 75, 85, 88
allegory
  of the *Aeneid* 6, 38–9
  of the *Eclogues* 39–40, 75
  in Douglas's *Eneados* 140–1, 163–5
amplification
  in Caxton's *Eneydos* 102, 107–8, 111–24,
    130–3
  in Douglas's *Eneados* 137, 142–59, 165–6
  in Surrey's *Aeneid* 172–5
annotation, of Virgil
  interlinear annotation 16, 18, 20–1, 30,
    32–4, 36–7, 50–5
  marginal annotation 20–1, 32–4, 35–42,
    55–61
  influence of annotations on
    translations 107, 109, 111–15
  annotations in manuscripts 16, 18, 20–1,
    30, 31–43
  annotations in printed books 50–61
  on grammatical issues 16, 18, 20–1, 30,
    32–8, 50–61
  on lexicography 35–7, 57–61
  on syntax 21n. 30, 32, 37–8, 52n. 33, 53
  finding aids 55–7
  textual corrections 18, 54–15
  on rhetorical figures 16, 21, 30, 40–1, 51
  rhetorical analysis of speeches 41–2
  on metrical issues 51
  on moral issues 21, 56
  on allegory 38–40
Anselm of Laon 32n. 80, 38
Anwykyll, John 26

Appendix Virgiliana
  manuscripts of the *Appendix* 25, 88
  printing of the *Appendix* 46, 48, 63, 80, 81
  commentaries 81
  in English schools 25, 88
Aristotle 29
Ascensius, Jodocus Badius
  as an author of familiar
    commentaries 71–2, 73–4, 81, 82–4, 93
  as a source of Gavin Douglas 144–9,
    150–9, 160–1, 163–4
Auctores Octo 25, 75–6, 84–5, 86–90, 98–9
Augustine, St. 48, 163–4

Balbus, Johannes 48, 54n. 40, 59, 60, 69, 79,
  80n. 34, 192–3
Benedictines 17–19
Beroaldo, Filippo
  Annotationes contra Servium 81
  as editor of Virgil 62
Bernardus Silvestris 6, 39
Boccaccio, Giovanni
  De Genealogia Deorum 160, 163–5, 166
  De Casibus Virorum Illustrium 103–4,
    106–8, 121–3, 129
Bucolics 40
Boethius 11, 71
blank verse, *see* Surrey, Earl of
Brant, Sebastian 55n. 44
Brygon, William 20
Bucolics, of Virgil, see *Eclogues*
Bynneman, Henry 67–8

Caillaut, Antoine 71, 72, 76, 80; *see also*
  familiar commentary
Calderini, Domizio 81
Cambridge, University of
  copies of Virgil 30
  lectures on classical authors 29n. 67
Caminade, Augustine 63–8
Candour, Thomas 20

Catholicon, see Balbus, Johannes
Cato, see *Distichs of Cato*
Caxton, William
 sources of the *Eneydos* 100–24
 translation technique 102–3, 125–34
 comparison of Caxton's *Eneydos* with Douglas's *Eneados* 10–12, 136–50
 Metamorphose 101–2
 Recuyell of the Historyes of Troye 101–2
 Historie of Jason 101–2
Chaucer, Geoffrey
 Boece 137
 House of Fame 5, 10n. 34, 139
 Legend of Good Women 5, 10n. 34, 139
 verse form 167, 187
Christianising interpretations of Virgil
 of the *Aeneid* 38
 of the *Eclogues* 39–40
 of *Aeneid* IV in the *Livre des Eneydes* 122–5
 by Gavin Douglas 150n. 40, 163n. 74, 164
Cicero, Marcus Tullius 9, 26, 28–9, 41–2, 45, 53n. 37, 64, 91, 137
Claudian 11, 48, 186–7
Claymond, John 57n. 54
Colet, John 28
commentary, to Virgil
 manuscript circulation of commentaries 31–42, 45–50
 print circulation of commentaries 45–50, 62–8, 70–86
 influence of commentaries on translations 111–15, 135–7, 143, 144–9, 150–9, 159–66
 vernacular commentaries 92–3, 159–65
 see also exegesis; Servius; Donatus, Tiberius Claudius; familiar commentary; Anselm of Laon; Landino, Cristoforo
correction, textual 9–10, 18, 54–5, 94–8, 192–3

Dido
 portrayal in Caxton's *Eneydos* 106–8, 121–5
differentiae verborum 35–6, 57, 58
Distichs of Cato 25, 84, 85, 89, 90, 91, 94
Doctrinale, see Villa Dei, Alexander de
Donatus, Tiberius Claudius 50, 66, 81
 as a source of Gavin Douglas 136, 158
Donatus, Aelius
 life of Virgil 46, 62

Douglas, Gavin
 humanism 10–12, 135–6, 165–6
 education 27
 use of commentaries 135, 142–50, 150–9, 159–66
 translation technique 135–50, 150–9, 165–6
 vernacular glossing to the *Eneados* 159–65
 comparison of Douglas's *Eneados* with Caxton's *Eneydos* 10–12, 136, 137–50
 comparison of Douglas's *Eneados* with Surrey's *Aeneid* 10–12, 168–9, 170–8, 181, 182, 189–90

Eclogues
 use in schools 25, 27, 28, 70–3, 82–91
 printing of the *Eclogues* 8, 62, 70–3, 82–91, 92–9
 commentary to the *Eclogues* 18, 43n. 116, 70–86
 allegory 39–40, 75
 translation 188
education, *see* schooling; universities
Eleanor of Scotland 21–2
emendation, textual, *see* correction
Eneados, see Douglas, Gavin
Eneydos, see Caxton, William
Erasmus, Desiderius 42, 59n. 66, 63, 90
 edition of Cato's *Distichs* 85n. 50, 91, 94, 98
euhemerism 163–4, 165n. 83
Évrard of Béthune, *Graecismus* 59, 60, 79, 80n. 34, 162n. 72
exegesis, of Virgil
 'pedagogic' exegesis of Virgil 5–7, 14–15, 16, 20–1, 30, 32–44, 50–61, 64–9, 73–82
 medieval vs humanist exegesis 5–10, 14–15, 43–4, 58–61, 63–8, 69, 77–80, 191–3
 on grammatical issues 16, 18, 20–1, 30, 32–8, 50–61, 64–6, 73–80
 on lexicography 35–7, 57–61
 on syntax 21n. 30, 32, 37–8, 52n. 33, 53, 73–7
 on rhetorical issues 16, 21, 30, 40–3, 51, 65–7
 on metrical issues 51, 65–6, 78–9
 on moral issues 21, 56
 on allegory 38–40, 75, 140–1, 163–5
 see also annotation; commentary; familiar commentary; Servius; humanism; allegory
Expositio hymnorum 72, 83–4, 88, 93

Facetus 86–7
familiar commentary
 to Virgil's works 70–82
 to hymns 83–4
 to the *Auctores Octo* 84–5
 to grammatical texts 85–6
 manuscript antecedents 75–6
 see also Ascensius, Jodocus Badius;
  Torrentinus, Hermannus; *Expositio hymnorum*
Flemmyng, Robert 22–3, 30, 49n. 17, 58
Free, John 23–4, 30n. 72
Fulgentius 39

Georgics
 commentaries 18, 23n. 42, 68n. 103, 71, 76, 77, 80
 translation 188
Gloss, *see* annotation; commentary
Grammar
 as a discipline 3–4, 5, 8–10, 14–15, 42–4, 191–3
 in the exegesis of Virgil's works 16, 18, 20–1, 30, 32–8, 50–61, 64–6, 73–80
 in the schoolroom 3–4, 26–8
 see also exegesis; pedagogy
Greek 24–5
Grey, William 22–3, 30
Guarino da Verona 22–5, 58

Haster, John 49, 52–4, 56n. 49, 57
Hermogenes 29
Histoire ancienne jusqu'à César 103–4, 108–10, 125–6, 130–3, 141
Horace 23, 28, 68, 79n. 33, 89, 142
Howard, Henry, *see* Surrey, Earl of
Hugutio of Pisa 59, 60
humanism
 development of humanism 3–5
 diffusion to England 4–5, 19–25
 humanism and the exegesis of Virgil 5–7, 8–10, 14–15, 23–5, 42–3, 63–7, 69, 191–3
 humanism and allegorical exegesis 6, 39–40
 lexicography 58–61, 69
 humanist pedagogy 3–5, 14–15, 23–5, 42–3, 63–8
 humanist pedagogy in England 26–8, 82–91, 98–9

humanism and printing 92–8
humanism and translation practice 10–12, 135–50, 165–6, 186–90, 193–4
hymns 28, 72, 83–4, 88, 89, 93

imitation
 in the study of rhetoric 4, 42, 63–5
 translators' imitation of Virgil's style 167–9, 170, 181–2
 translators' imitation of classical verse form 167–9, 170, 179–86, 186–90
interlinear glossing, *see* annotation

John of Garland 36–7, 59, 75n. 22, 85–7, 88
John of Salisbury 48
Jouenneaux, Guy (Guido Juvenalis) 50n. 22, 72, 73n. 15, 82
Juvenal 30, 71

Landino, Cristoforo 39, 50, 160, 164
Lefèvre, Raoul 101–2
le Roy, Guillaume 100–1, 103–5, 133
Liburnio, Niccolò 168–9, 170, 181
Lily, Willam 89–91
Livre des Eneydes
 Content 100–2, 103–10
 use of Virgil glosses 111–15
 translation practice 110–24, 133–4, 137–50
 see also Caxton, William

Magdalen College School, Oxford 26–7, 53n. 37
Mancinelli, Antonio 64n. 83, 76–7
Mantuan (Johannes Baptista Spagnolo) 90–1, 94, 98
manuscripts, of Virgil
 owned in monasteries 17–18
 owned by early English humanists 19–25
 used in schooling 25–6, 75–6, 87–9
 owned in English universities 29–30
 owned by clerics 19–25, 31
 produced outside England 19–23
 see also scribes; annotation
Manuzio, Aldo 61–2
Manuzio, Paolo 67–8
marginalia
 printed marginalia in Virgil editions 63–7
 see also annotation; commentary
Marlowe, Christopher 168, 188–90

222 INDEX

Medici, Ippolito de 168-9, 172, 179-80
Melanchthon, Philip 42, 67
Meo, Ciampolo di 165
Miscomini, Antonio 48-50
monasteries 17-19

octavo, *see* printing
Opuscula, of Virgil, see *Appendix Virgiliana*
Ovid
  poetry 17, 48, 57n. 54, 68, 79, 102
  argumenta of the *Aeneid* 18, 46
Oxford, University of
  study of Virgil at Oxford 17, 28-30
  copies of Virgil at Oxford 30

Palladius, Middle English translation of *De Re Rustica* 115n. 54, 137
Papias 59, 60, 61, 69, 80n. 34
pedagogy, *see* schooling; universities; exegesis; commentary
Persius 30, 71, 73, 88
Petrarch 40
Perotti, Niccolò 26, 59n. 64
Phaer, Thomas 167-8, 186, 187-90, 192, 194
Philippi de Cruzenach, Johann 62-3
Picardus, Odo 75, 80n. 34, 84n. 48, 87
Premierfait, Laurent de 129
printing, of Virgil
  of Virgil's complete works (*Opera*) 45-7, 49-50, 61-9
  of Virgil's *Eclogues* and *Georgics* 70-3, 80-6, 92-9
  of the *Appendix Virgiliana* 46, 48, 63, 80, 81
  with commentary 45-50, 62-8, 70-86
  in England 8, 62-8, 70-3, 82-6, 92-9
  in octavo format 61-8
  see also commentary; familiar commentary; Worde, Wynkyn de; Pynson, Richard; Manuzio, Aldo
Priscian 59n. 66
Proba 28, 88
Prudentius 28
Pynson, Richard
  1515 edition of Virgil's works 8, 46-7, 61-7
  printing of schoolbooks 83-6, 89-90, 93

Quintilian 29

Raynoldes, John 31-2
Ramus, Petrus 42, 43n. 116, 62
reading, of Virgil
  in monasteries 17-18
  by early English humanists 19-25
  in English schools 25-6, 86-91
  in English universities 29-30
  by adult readers in comparison with schoolboys 14-15, 47-8, 52-4
  see also annotation; commentary; exegesis; manuscripts; printing; schools
rhetoric
  as a discipline 3-5, 8-10, 14-15, 42-4, 191-3
  study of rhetoric in schools 3-5, 7, 17, 28, 40-3, 65-7, 91
  study of rhetoric in universities 28-9
  in Virgilian exegesis 16, 21, 30, 40-3, 51, 65-7
  see also amplification
romance 5, 101, 104
Roman d'Eneas 5, 104-5, 109, 133
Russell, John 20-1, 30, 34, 45, 52-3

Saint Gelais, Octavien de 11n. 39, 133
Sammelbände 30, 86-9, 90-1, 134
scholia, *see* annotation, commentary
schools
  curricula in English schools 25-8, 82-91
  schoolbooks 25-8, 53, 82-91, 98-9
  exegesis of Virgil in schools 14-15, 23-5, 31-43, 53, 62-8, 73-82, 162
  see also familiar commentary
scribes, of Virgil 16, 20, 30, 31-43
Sedulius 28
Servius, commentary to Virgil
  circulation in manuscripts and printed editions of Virgil 45-7, 49-50, 68
  use by annotators 23, 30, 31-8, 40-1, 47-8, 50-61, 192
  as a source of later commentaries 18, 65-6, 76, 78-9, 81
  as a source of the *Livre des Eneydes* 107, 109, 113-15, 131
  as a source of Gavin Douglas 135, 143, 146, 150-1, 157-9, 160-1, 163
  allegory in Servius's commentary 38-40, 163
Seward, John 25
Sherborne, Robert 20
Shirwood, John 55n. 43

INDEX 223

Stanbridge, John 26, 53n. 37, 89
Stanyhurst, Richard 167, 189, 190
Statius 42
St Paul's School 28
style
 of Latin composition 3–5, 40–4, 63–5
 of Virgil translators 107–10, 111–16,
   125–33, 144–9, 154–6, 170–85
 see also imitation
Sulpizio, Giovanni 89
Surrey, Earl of
 humanism 10–12, 167–9, 186–90
 Italian models 168–9, 170, 172,
   179–81
 translation practice 167–86
 blank verse 11, 167–9, 179–90
 concision 167–86
 comparison of Surrey's Aeneid with
   Douglas's Eneados 10–12, 168–9,
   170–8, 181, 182, 189–90
syntax, of Virgil
 in annotations 21n. 30, 32, 37–8,
   52n. 33, 53
 in commentaries 73–7
 in translations 115, 126–7, 146–8, 159,
   182–5

Terence 26, 28–9, 50n. 22, 64, 68, 72,
 73n. 15, 91
 1520 English translation of Andria 166

Theodulus 25, 75, 80n. 34, 84–5, 87, 89,
 93n. 70
Tiptoft, John 137
Torrentinus, Hermannus 78n. 31, 80–1, 82,
 87, 92
Tortelli, Giovanni 48, 59
translation, of Virgil
 humanism and Virgil translation 10–12,
   135–50, 165–6, 186–90, 193–4
 see also Douglas, Gavin; Caxton, William;
   Surrey, Earl of

universities 28–30

Valla, Lorenzo 26, 48, 59, 60
Vegetius 11
Vegius, Mapheus 20–1, 46, 48, 81, 135,
 150n. 40
Villa Dei, Alexander de 78–9, 81, 85, 86
Villena, Enrique de 165
Virgil
 see Eclogues, Georgics, Aeneid, Appendix
   Virgiliana

Walsingham, Thomas 18–19
Whethamstede, John 18–19
Whittinton, Robert 89, 90, 94
Worde, Wynkyn de
 editions of Virgil's Eclogues 8, 70–82, 92–9
 printing of schoolbooks 83–6, 89–91